The Works of Peter Handke

International Perspectives

Studies in Austrian Literature, Culture and Thought

General Editors:

Jorun B. Johns
Richard H. Lawson

The Works of Peter Handke
International Perspectives

Edited by David N. Coury
and Frank Pilipp

ARIADNE PRESS
Riverside, California

Ariadne Press would like to express its appreciation to the Bundesministerium für Bildung, Wissenschaft und Kultur, Vienna for assistance in publishing this book.

Library of Congress Cataloging-in-Publication Data

The works of Peter Handke : international perspectives / edited by David N. Coury and Frank Pilipp
       p.   cm. -- (Studies in Austrian literature, culture and thought)
    Includes bibliographical references and index.
    Contents: Handke's early fiction / Thomas F. Barry – Place, autonomy and the individual: Short letter, Long farewell and A sorrow beyond dreams / Robert Halsall – The quest of authenticity, a trilogy: The goalie's anxiety at the penalty kick, A moment of true feeling, Left-handed woman / Frank Pilipp – The Slow homecoming tetralogy / Karl Wagner – Storytelling in imagery: Across, Repetition, and Afternoon of a writer / Maria Luisa Roli – Handke's trilogy of Try-outs / David N. Coury – Handke's theater / Franz Wefelmeyer – Handke's poetry / Christiane Weller – Handke as Filmmaker / John E. Davidson – Handke's non-fiction / Thomas F. Barry – Language, life, and art: Handke and/on Nietzsche / Andrea Gogröf-Vorhees – Land and landscape in Handke's texts / Mireille Tabah – Reflections of a travel companion: Handke and Yugoslavia / Scott Abbott.
    ISBN 1-57241-139-2
    1. Handke, Peter–Criticism and interpretation. I. Coury, David N. II. Pilipp, Frank, 1961- III. Series

    PT2668.A5Z97 2005
    838'.91409--dc22

                                    2005041146

Cover Design:
Art Director, Designer: George McGinnis
Photo: Courtesy Lillian Birnbaum

Contents

Preface

IN THE SUMMER OF 2004, the *Süddeutsche Zeitung* began publishing a special series of books which they termed the "50 Great Novels of the 20th Century." Selected by the editors of the feuilleton section of the paper, the series included masterpieces by the likes of F. Scott Fitzgerald, William Faulkner and James Joyce as well as canonical works by German-speaking writers, such as the Nobel laureates Günter Grass and Hermann Hesse. Number 13 on the list, though, was an early novel by the Austrian-born writer Peter Handke, *Die Angst des Tormanns beim Elfmeter* (1970; *The Goalie's Anxiety at the Penalty Kick*, 1972). For a German-speaking audience, this choice would come as little surprise (particularly from the *Süddeutsche Zeitung*, which has long been a supporter of Handke's works), but for an Anglo-American audience, it might be a bit more unusual.

In academic circles, Handke is consistently one of the most canonized of contemporary German writers. A glance at the scholarship on his works reveals hundreds of studies, articles and monographs devoted to his writings. However, upon closer analysis, one finds that the majority of these scholarly studies is in German and most often published by German presses.[1] In part, this has to do with the fact that Handke is considered a difficult writer as well as one who is linguistically playful yet serious, and whose use of the German language and neologisms is rarely surpassed. His works demand analysis not just on a thematic but also a linguistic level; consequently, most studies of his texts tend to be in his native language, although his works are consistently translated into English and are quite well received when reviewed.

Handke's status as one of the great writers in the German language was perhaps best evidenced when, on December 6, 2002,

---

[1] There are only few English-language books that focus exclusively on Handke, the most recent ones being Richard Firda's *Peter Handke* in the Twayne World Author Series, which appeared in 1993, Christopher Parry's *Peter Handke's Landscapes of Discourse: An Exploration of Narrative and Cultural Space* (2004), and, though not with singular focus on Handke, David N. Coury's *The Return of Storytelling in Contemporary German Literature and Film – Peter Handke and Wim Wenders* (2004).

he turned sixty years old. The occasion was marked with tributes in all of the major German-language newspapers as well as the premiere of a television documentary on his life and writings directed by a long-time friend, Peter Hamm. Once the *enfant terrible* of the German literary and cultural scene, Handke has over the years ironically become part of the establishment as witnessed by the front page retrospective essays in the feuilleton section of such papers as the *Frankfurter Allgemeine* and the *Neue Zürcher Zeitung*. While Handke has in his later years continued to be a source of controversy, he is nonetheless almost universally considered one of the most important German-speaking writers active today.

Since his now famous appearance on the literary stage in 1966, Handke, a novelist, playwright, poet, essayist and filmmaker, has remained on the forefront of the literary vanguard, having earned the praise and recognition of critics in Europe and North America alike. In fact, a recent review of his works in the *New York Review of Books* called him "the premier prose stylist in the German language, and one of postwar Europe's most recognizable literary figures."[2] While his earliest works, termed *Sprechstücke* (speakins), were theatrical explorations into the relationship between words and meaning, Handke soon moved to prose producing two early novels in the tradition of the French *nouveau roman*. Gradually his narratives moved away from this influence and became noted for their intense subjectivity, a style that heralded a wave of literary works in the 1970s known as the New Subjectivity. He has since gone on to publish over two dozen works of prose fiction.

Handke has not limited himself, however, to prose. He regularly publishes collections of poetry which, while having received critical praise, have more often than not been overshadowed by his other writings. His dramatic works, on the other hand, have stood their own and have been performed throughout Europe to critical acclaim as well. In addition, Handke has published several diaries and essay collections which shed light not only on his aesthetics but his influences and the literary process itself. Earlier in his career, Handke showed, like many of his generation, an affinity for American arts and popular culture, whereas in the last ten to fifteen years, one

---

[2]J. S. Marcus, "Apocalypse Now," *New York Review of Books* 47.14 (21 Sept. 2000) 80.

recognizes decidedly European influences and referential frameworks.

While Handke has always been on the forefront of European literature (he has won many of the major European literary awards), his detractors fault him for being an opportunist whose works follow the most recent philosophical and theoretical trends. This same tendency though has led most scholars and critics to view him as a trendsetter who has a unique sensibility to produce works in tune with the most recent currents in Western writing. In the late 1990s, however, Handke was criticized severely by scholars and intellectuals for his unorthodox and highly unpopular essays in defense of Serbia during the civil war in Yugoslavia. His writings and statements do reveal a partisan position, but on another level reflect his deep-seated attachment to the Balkans and his ethnic Slovenian heritage. Moreover, the essays are also a sharp departure from his previous apolitical stance in that they represent a clear socio-political critique, in which he attacks the Western media for its failure to analyze the complexity of the conflict. His defenders argue that Handke is once again setting out uncompromisingly in a direction which reinvigorates the political discourse in the literary sphere, whereas his detractors, both in the United States and abroad, see him as a neo-Romantic who seeks to mythologize history. Whatever the end result may be, there is no doubt that Handke has once again, as in so many cases before, placed himself in the middle of a controversy both in the academy and in the feuilleton. Yet despite the criticism of his politics, Handke's more recent writing still receives praise from scholars and critics alike.

Despite the fact that almost all of his works have been translated and published in both the United States and Great Britain, Handke has not achieved the same status in the English-speaking world as in Europe. A collection of essays on Handke in English, addressing that disparity, is long overdue. Although a long-time resident of France – he splits his time between the outskirts of Paris and Salzburg for many years now – Handke continues to write in his native German. Yet Handke sets his stories not only in Germany and Austria, but also France, Spain, the U.S., the Balkans, and particularly in his ancestral homeland of Slovenia. As such, he is considered by European critics and scholars alike as one of the more international – and above all European – writers, as the themes he addresses and the controversies he often becomes embroiled in are debated by European intellectuals and politicians. As the European Union becomes progressively more consolidated, while at the same time its identity is called into question by the forces of globalization, a study of this most European of writers is especially opportune.

An international array of literary scholars and Handke experts from eight countries on four continents has contributed original essays discussing the various aspects of Handke's expansive and multifaceted œuvre. As the first comprehensive volume entirely in English, these essays bring Handke's major texts into view, thus providing various access routes to his work, particularly to a readership not necessarily familiar with German. At the same time this book should be of equal interest to the Handke scholar in that the essays assembled here aim to advance literary scholarship on this author. Since many of Handke's books have been translated into English – though unfortunately not all are readily available at this time – the contributors have worked exclusively with the English texts and have provided translations of those not (yet) available in English. The individual chapters investigate the various phases of Handke's epic output as well as the different genres of his wide-ranging work: the dramas, the poetry, the non-fiction, and, for the first time, Handke's style as filmmaker. Several contributions take a broader approach to Handke's œuvre but with a more specific thematic focus, as in the case of the comparative analysis of Handke and Nietzsche or the discussion of Handke's landscapes.

In the chapter on Handke's early narrative fiction, Thomas F. Barry stresses the themes of psychotherapeutic self-exploration and the dismantling of the conventions of fictional realities in these largely experimental texts. Robert Halsall examines the relationship between the narrating subject and place through the utopia exemplified by America in *Der kurze Brief zum langen Abschied* (1972; *Short Letter, Long Farewell*, 1977) and the dystopia represented by the narrator's Austrian homeland in *Wunschloses Unglück* (1971; *A Sorrow Beyond Dreams*, 1976), thus illustrating important elements of the relationship between autonomy, development of the self, and the process of writing in Handke's work. By means of a close reading of three of Handke's novels of the 1970s, *The Goalie's Anxiety at the Penalty Kick*, *Die Stunde der wahren Empfindung* (1975; *A*

Moment of True Feeling, 1977), and *Die linkshändige Frau* (1976; *The Left-Handed Woman*, 1977), Frank Pilipp points up Handke's critique of automatized systems of perception and interaction. The thematic nexus of these texts consists in that each seeks to expose existing parameters of human existence, leading to the protagonist's quest for a more authentic form of existence.

Karl Wagner demonstrates how the four texts that make up the *Slow Homecoming* cycle (1979-1981; trans. 1985; 1996) reflect Handke's revision of his writing approach from a more meaning-centered style of the seventies to an ostentatious and often over-stated aestheticism. Handke's forced aestheticism that is carried by a sermonic rhetoric of proclamation marks both the success and the shortcomings of these texts. In her discussion of three of Handke's works of the eighties, Maria Luisa Roli highlights the visual and spatial dimension as constitutive narrative elements in *Nachmittag eines Schriftstellers* (1987; *The Afternoon of a Writer*, 1989) and *Der Chinese des Schmerzes* (1983; *Across*, 1986), and illustrates the construction of a personal mythology in *Die Wiederholung* (1986; *Repetition*, 1988).

From 1989 through 1991, Handke published a series of essays which he titled *Versuche* (*The Jukebox and Other Essays on Story-telling*, 1994), recalling at once the European essayistic tradition and an "attempt" at writing such an essay. David N. Coury considers these essays as meta-narratives about the act of writing, symptomatic of Handke's narratological turn in the late 1980s whereby he embraced the story as a trope best able to convey a sense of wholeness within the subjective reality that was the topic of many of his texts. In the chapter on Handke's theater, Fritz Wefelmeyer shows that already with his early speech-plays Handke laid down the basis for a non-illusionist, non-representational theater that would, despite various changes and innovations, become the mainstay for all his later plays. The study concludes with an analysis of the later plays, which Wefelmeyer terms theater of narrative.

In the chapter on Handke's poetry, Christiane Weller examines the poetic trajectory of the object in reference to the subject. She reconstructs the development of Handke's conception of the inanimate object in which the subject is threatened by the indifference or even violence of the object-world as reflected in the collections *Die Innenwelt der Außenwelt der Innenwelt* (1969; *The Innerworld of the Outerworld of the Innerworld*, 1974), *Als das Wünschen noch geholfen hat* (1974; When Wishing Still Helped) and *Das Ende des Flanierens* (1976; The End of Idling)[3] through to the transcendent object in which the subject seeks refuge (*Gedicht an die Dauer*, 1986; Ode to Permanence).

Peter Handke's cinema has most often been seen in terms borrowed from the study of his literary works. Handke himself feels that film allows him to tell stories in a manner that is no longer possible in written language. John E. Davidson explores Handke's film *Die Abwesenheit* (1992; *The Absence*) to see if tensions arise from creating or approaching Handke's work through these literary lenses by asking the question whether Handke's use of the filmic medium to liberate oral storytelling takes place because or at the expense of cinematic power.

Thomas F. Barry's contribution on Handke's early non-fictional writings examines the author's theoretical formulations of his existential and aesthetic program and discusses the experimental project of Handke's journals, especially *Das Gewicht der Welt* (1977; *The Weight of the World*, 1984). In the chapter on Handke and Nietzsche, Andrea Gogröf-Voorhees highlights specific temperamental, intellectual, and aesthetic affinities between the two authors and argues that the writing of both authors is characterized by a will to avoid theory and classification and to affirm and to translate for the reader the immediacy of living as experienced during the process of writing. By examining the depiction of landscapes in Handke's prose works of the 1980s and 1990s, Mireille Tabah demonstrates how Handke deconstructs the archaic myth of inherent and coherent meaning of the world expressed in his landscape depictions by juxtaposing the cruelty of history and the protagonists' fears and aggression. In the end, the landscapes mirror the unfulfillable desire of postmodernity for universal harmony.

During the wars in Yugoslavia, Scott Abbott translated Handke's *Eine winterliche Reise zu den Flüssen Donau, Save, Morawa und Drina oder Gerechtigkeit für Serbien* (1996) into what became *A Journey to the Rivers: Justice for Serbia* (1997). In 1998, Abbott

---

[3]The title piece of this volume, "The End of Idling," has been translated by Michael Roloff and is included in *Nonsense and Happiness*, a bilingual collection of four long poems by Handke.

drove and hiked along the Drina River in central Yugoslavia with Handke, his Serbo-Croatian translator Žarko Radaković, his Salzburg friend Zlatko Bokokić, and Thomas Deichmann, editor of *Novo* magazine, looking for signs of recovery after the war in Bosnia. Together they struggled to comprehend those signs and to translate them into a language which could make sense of what they saw. This questioning, translating and struggling to understand form the basis of what would become five essays on Yugoslavia (and two plays) that Handke was to write in the 1990s. Handke encountered the sharpest criticism of his career in reaction to these essays, prompting writers and literary critics from Jürgen Habermas and Günter Grass to Susan Sontag and Salman Rushdie to condemn him and summarily reject not only the essays, but much of his writing as a whole. Handke also had his supporters, including Nobel laureate Elfriede Jelinek and a score of Yugoslav writers and intellectuals. In particular, Handke's media critique and his condemnation of Europe's leading newspapers for their reporting of the war led not only to lengthy debates but at times personal attacks. So much has already been written and debated about these works that it is nearly impossible to find a neutral account of the essays. In surveying them, then, Abbott attempts first to contextualize the pieces by presenting a broader understanding of Handke's conception of Yugoslavia and, second, to offer an understanding of Handke's methodology, based on personal encounters and travels with the writer in the Balkans. As a result, Abbott views the works as "models of dialectical rhetoric" and representative of what he sees as a "narrative, non-systematic philosophy." By mixing first-hand accounts with textual analysis, he argues that Handke's main concern is both raising questions as well as offering a counterargument to every question raised.

The thirteen chapters provide a critical and comprehensive overview of one of the most scintillating, individualistic, and controversial writers of our time. The essays are preceded by a list of abbreviations used for parenthetical documentation throughout this book and followed by a bibliography of Handke's works in German and English translation.

The editors
2005

Abbreviations of Handke's Works

The Translations:

Ab – Absence
Ac – Across
AW – The Afternoon of a Writer
CS – Child Story
DN – On a Dark Night I Left My Silent House
GA – The Goalie's Anxiety at the Penalty Kick
IO – The Innerworld of the Outerworld of the Innerworld
J – The Jukebox and Other Essays on Storytelling
JR – A Journey to the Rivers: Justice for Serbia
K – Kaspar and Other Plays
LSV – The Lesson of Mont Sainte-Victoire
LW – The Left-Handed Woman
LWA – The Long Way Around
M – A Moment of True Feeling
MY – My Year in the No-Man's-Bay
NH – Nonsense and Happiness
Th – Once Again for Thucydides
P – Plays 1
R – Repetition
RLC – The Ride Across Lake Constance and Other Plays
SBD – A Sorrow Beyond Dreams
SL – Short Letter, Long Farewell
Th – Once Again for Thucydides
V – Voyage to the Sonorous Land, or The Art of Asking and The
    Hour We Knew Nothing of Each Other
WW – The Weight of the World
WV – Walk About the Villages

The Originals:

A – Die Abwesenheit: Eine Skizze, ein Film, ein Gespräch
AT – Abschied des Träumers vom neunten Land
ATE – Die Angst des Tormanns beim Elfmeter
B – Der Bildverlust oder Durch die Sierra de Gredos
BA – Begrüßung des Aufsichtsrats
BE – Ich bin ein Bewohner des Elfenbeinturms
DG – Deutsche Gedichte
DN – In einer dunklen Nacht ging ich aus meinem stillen Haus
EF – Das Ende des Flanierens
FB – Falsche Bewegung
FE – Die Fahrt im Einbaum oder Das Stück zum Film vom Krieg
FM – Am Felsfenster morgens (und andere Ortszeiten 1982-1987)
GB – Die Geschichte des Bleistifts
GD – Gedicht an die Dauer
GW – Das Gewicht der Welt
Ha – Der Hausierer
Ho – Die Hornissen
IA – Die Innenwelt der Außenwelt der Innenwelt
LF – Die linkshändige Frau
LS – Langsam im Schatten
MuS – Mündliches und Schriftliches. Zu Büchern, Bildern und
       Filmen
NS – Nachmittag eines Schriftstellers
PhW – Phantasien der Wiederholung
S 1 – Stücke 1
S 2 – Stücke 2
SN – Sommerlicher Nachtrag zu einer winterlichen Reise
St – Die Stunde der wahren Empfindung
UT – Unter Tränen fragend: Nachträgliche Aufzeichnungen von
       zwei Jugoslawien-Durchquerungen im Krieg, März und April
       1990
WU – Wunschloses Unglück
Wü – Als das Wünschen noch geholfen hat
ZU – Zurüstungen für die Unsterblichkeit
Zw – Aber ich lebe nur von den Zwischenräumen

Handke's Early Narrative Fiction

Thomas F. Barry

PETER HANDKE'S EARLY NARRATIVE fiction comprises the two no-vels *Die Hornissen* (1966; The Hornets) and *Der Hausierer* (1967; The Peddler), in addition to the collection of short prose pieces *Begrüßung des Aufsichtsrats* (1967; Greetings From the Board of Directors). During the 1960s, the young Handke was caught up, as were many students at this time, with the popular currents in socio-cultural and literary-critical theory that characterized the period. As a law student at the University of Graz (1961-65), he was involved with the cultural circle *Forum Stadtpark* and the artists and writers of the Graz Group, as well as with the literary circle around Alfred Kolleritsch and his literary magazine *manuskripte*. Handke gave a number of book discussions from 1964 to 1966 on Austrian radio broadcast on Studio Steiermark under the rubric Book Corner. The list of non-fiction authors reviewed included many of the prominent literary and cultural theoreticians of the 1960s: Freud, Marcuse, Benjamin, Adorno, Lefèbvre, Wittgenstein, and Barthes, as well as the Russian/Czech formalist theorists Roman Jakobson, Boris Ei-chenbaum, and Viktor Sklovskij (Perram 113; 260-61).[1]

The early 1960s were characterized by international movements which questioned the traditional forms of the narrative genre. There was the "death of the novel" group associated with the Iowa Univer-sity Writers' Workshop in America with such authors as Donald Barthelme, Ronald Sukenick, Richard Brautigan, Kurt Vonnegut, and Steve Katz. In Europe there were Roland Barthes' early critical writings (*Writing Degree Zero*, *Mythologies*, *S/Z*) and the French *nouveau roman* movement with such authors as Alain Robbe-Grillet, Michel Butor, Philippe Sollers, and Nathalie Sarraute.

---

[1]Holzinger discusses Handke's early years in Graz and quotes from the manu-scripts of some of the radio book reviews (18-20). Handke has always been, and still is, a voracious reader who is fluent in a number of languages. He has produced a large number of book reviews in his career.

Robbe-Grillet in particular is "the most striking forerunner" of the young Handke's views on literature (Linstead, *Outer World* 31-33). Handke's early narrative texts reflect his involvement with the critical ideas of these postmodern authors and the literary programs of other innovative fiction writers of this era, including the prose and poetry experiments of authors of the Vienna Group and the more radical works of Peter Weiss and Uwe Johnson (Klinkowitz and Knowlton 1-14; Nägele and Voris 7-24; Durzak, *Narziß* 7-25).[2]

His early fiction is highly experimental and focuses on defamiliarizing the act of reading literary texts. It could be characterized as avant-garde attempts at producing "writerly" texts (using Barthes' "writerly/readerly" juxtaposition of postmodern versus traditional narratives from his *S/Z*) which foreground the processes of composition. Handke's early narrative works place emphasis on the artificiality and inauthenticity of the reality depicted in fiction (Perram 134). They are self-referential and focus to a great degree on this analytic deconstruction of language and narration. Literary texts are exposed as representing an inherently ideological (and therefore existentially inauthentic) process that can ultimately falsify the individual's perception of self and reality.[3]

Psychological themes are also present in the early writings and are linked to themes of language. Mixner claims that all of Handke's fictional writings deal with "phenomena of human consciousness" ("Masse" 150). Alienation – estrangement from one's self and from others – and a longing for existential authenticity are consistent issues throughout his works. Handke's later works emphasize a more traditional (and perhaps even modernist) vision of what literature is: the healing dimensions of the magical art of storytelling and the liberation of the self in and through the imagination.[4] The therapeutic magic Handke sees in the activities of reading and writing is a synthetic construction of a psychologically whole, spiritually

---

[2]Klinkowitz and Knowlton (writing in the early 1980s), for example, regard Handke as "a writer who maturely articulates the postmodern aesthetic in German today" (vi).

[3]Perram calls this deconstructive dimension a "didactic obsession with the theme of language as a suspect medium of communication" (30). On language and ideology, see Tabah (24-34).

[4]On the topic of the rehabilitation of storytelling in the later Handke, see Coury and the chapters by Mireille Tabah and Maria Luisa Roli in this book.

healed, and existentially authentic self within a fictional reality, a new textual identity that must be continually reenacted in the activities of reading and writing.[5] These synthetic and analytic movements in Handke's writings are to be understood, however, as being closely connected and complementary methods in his view: there can be no authentic storytelling until the inauthentic ideological distortions of language have been consciously exposed. Both analytic and synthetic aspects are present in varied proportions throughout his fictional writings. There is no gap between the existential dimension and the theme of linguistic formulation in Handke's writings (Bartmann 30-31). Language is to be regarded as a fundamental and inseparable constituent of the perception of self and society.

Despite all the intellectually self-conscious literary theory that informs his early works, Handke is, above all else, a radically subjectivist and autobiographical rather than a politically or socially committed writer, whose only theme is the exploration of his own consciousness and the reality of his own experience (DeMeritt 141-44).[6] In 1972, Handke said of his work: "Whenever I write I am always simply exploiting my own consciousness" (Linder 33). In a dialectic of inner and outer worlds, his narrative texts are "interspersed with autobiographical material" (Nägele and Voris 25). The outer world of social experience is dominated for Handke by ideo-

---

[5]The use of the spiritual and classical language of Goethe, Schiller, and Hölderlin (and the modernist, postromantic discourses of existentialism in Rilke and Hesse) in Handke's later works has confused many critics. In the novel *Langsame Heimkehr* (1979; *The Long Way Around*, 1985), for example, the character of Sorger feels "a need for salvation" (*LWA* 3) and a longing for "sanctuary" (*LWA* 7). One wonders if Handke is engaging here in playful postmodern citation of earlier literary traditions or if he is seriously pretentious. It is, as with many examples of his writing, probably a bit of both: a deconstruction of historical discourses and a simultaneous attempt to reconstruct or rehabilitate their potential meaning in a postmodern era that deforms and cheapens language, most especially in the media and in popular culture that Handke so vehemently decries.

[6]Perram's observation on Handke's early writings bears citation here: "The one truly consistent theme in Handke's œuvre that has survived virtually unchanged from that period up to the present has been his continued absorption in the theme of the individual and the manner in which he responds to the reality of his existence and confronts the more disturbing elements in his own psyche" (252).

logically distorted language and the existential inauthenticity of popular culture, whereas the inner world of personal experience is, in ideal and utopian terms at least, the domain of an authentic and liberated existence. He would seem to be of the conviction that the only subject-matter that a writer can treat with any degree of certainty and realism, with existential validity, is his or her own personality and experience.[7] In 1979, Handke again asserts his rejection of a socially engaged literature and affirms his commitment to writing that is existentially grounded in his experience: "I find it silly to write a social novel – for me. It may be that this is possible for someone, but everything, every tree that I describe, must also be myself. I cannot imagine writing any other way than that through which I achieve an expansion of self" (Schlueter 172). To be sure, postmodern literary theories inform his early writing to a great degree; however, for him all contrived plots and characters that serve extrinsic motives (including the enactment of a literary theory) only distort the perception of reality.

Many of Handke's critics do his early texts somewhat of a disservice by presenting them as if they were solely abstract illustrations of a literary theory when the theory is actually more of a logical extension of the author's existential experience. Durzak, for example, claims Handke's early writing is guided by his uncritical and naïve acceptance of Wittgensteinian precepts (*Roman* 314).

---

[7]Given the degree to which Handke's personality and personal experience are reflected in his writings, a psycho-biographical discussion of the texts is appropriate. A solely text-based approach would overlook important thematic dimensions and psychological resonances within his texts. A reading of Kafka without a discussion of his father and family circumstances would certainly be impoverished. The case of Handke raises the issue of the place of existential themes, which are by definition perennial subjects, in modernist and postmodernist literature. It also makes problematic the question of how an author like Handke might be classified in literary history. Is he a postmodern on the cutting edge of fiction writing (as he has been received in the United States) or is he a post-romantic modern with a traditional existentialist focus? The move towards a mystical-spiritual experience of reality in his more recent writings is not easily integrated into a postmodern framework. The existential terms 'authentic' versus 'inauthentic' are used in this essay and the reader can find useful discussion of their meanings in Cooper (109-25; 168-72). For a discussion of Handke in the context of post-Romantic German literature and intellectual history (with special attention to existential themes), see the book by Eifler.

Language that is actually a product of ideological and political interests but presents itself as reality distorts the individual's perception of objective reality. This obsessive concern with the self and existential authenticity in Handke's writings extends to a rejection of all conceptual and generalizing language in social discourse, especially that found in the pervasive bourgeois media.[8] The political and existential domains are viewed here as inseparable aspects of human experience. The structuralist dismantling of narrative conventions and clichés serves for Handke an existential and even psychotherapeutic purpose: to ground an unstable and traumatized identity that is seemingly constantly beset by debilitating feelings of shame, fear, anxiety, and unreality in a vision of a healed and more authentic self both in and through narration and the literary text. Thus, Handke's first novel *Die Hornissen* has been described as the (albeit unsuccessful) attempt "to construct a viable identity through the power of the imagination" (Perram 189).

Handke's characters usually undergo some crisis or trauma, which sets them out on a quest to achieve a state of psychological wholeness and integrity. Indeed, one might argue – in spite of some definitions of postmodernism that exclude any notion of transcendence as being a specifically modernist and existentialist concept – that they seek what can only be termed a form of spiritual transcendence. The major influences on the early Handke – the French *nouveau roman* and certain aspects of Romanticism – are "deeply concerned with the irrational aspects of man's nature" (Perram 113). These concerns point to the "existential concerns of the protagonists" throughout his writings (Perram 121), to characters "troubled by non-specific anxiety and fear that appears to have its source in a dread of death and annihilation" (Perram 252). The nature of psychological trauma can be described in one sense as the overwhelming of the self by a simultaneous flood of external and internal events, which produces chaos, disorientation, loss of control, and the experience of powerlessness. The therapeutic reprocessing of these events in the practice of writing/narration is a (re-)

---

[8]This critique of the bourgeois news media and their falsifying language of concepts and generalizations, which masquerade as the truth in his view, lies at the heart of Handke's attacks on the negative depiction of Yugoslavia and the Serbs in German newspapers and magazines.

composing of the self in the act of recollection. Remembering as a repetition of past events is a sequential activity, which establishes order and orientation and the restoration of the individual's sense of personal power and control over past events. In analogy to Descartes, Handke might well assert: "I narrate, therefore I am." His early fiction is marked by crisis and trauma for the narrators, which triggers "a fragmented or associative narrative style" (Perram 143) involving both imagined and reprocessed memories. The act of recovering memories – comparable to Proust – is the force that propels the majority of Handke's early texts (Nägele and Voris 25).[9]

*

Begrüßung des Aufsichtsrats is a collection of short prose pieces written during the early 1960s when Handke was a law student at the University of Graz. Almost all the pieces evidence the author's concerns with the themes of alienation and language criticism (Nägele and Voris 35). They show the young writer's experiments with the language and the discourses of fictional texts: his conscientious and at times awkwardly self-conscious and overly didactic working through of the ideas from a variety of intellectual and aesthetic influences. Concerns with problems of narration and description in traditional realist and mimetic literature are prominent in all the pieces. They illustrate "the probing of reality through a constant reorientation of narrational perspectives" and many of the pieces foreshadow "the narrative structure of individual episodes" of his first novel (Perram 135, 145). Their psychological themes show the degree to which subjectivity (especially in the memories, dreams, visions, and unconscious impulses of disturbed and marginalized individuals) influences perception, and "in virtually every one of these early works the reader, the protagonist, or the narrator becomes the victim of illusion or delusion" (Perram 181). The themes of anxiety and fear (and associated acts of violence) that structure so many of Handke's writings are to be found in numerous pieces of the collection (Klinkowitz and Knowlton 27; Nägele and Voris 34).

Included in the collection are two studies, "Die Hornissen" (1963; The Hornets) and "Der Hausierer" (1963; The Peddler),

---

[9]Although it does not discuss the early works, Volker Michel's book on the poetics of memory in Handke is recommended here.

which prefigure the themes and styles of Handke's first two novels. "Die Hornissen" is a darkly tinged seven-page text that describes a violent and cruel father figure, an army deserter who has driven a servant girl to kill herself, told from the point of view of his injured and feverish son (who has possibly also attempted suicide) and from that of a woman to whom he has fled. The shifting and lyrical narrative perspectives suggest the influence of Faulkner (Firda 43; Holzinger 14) and the story certainly owes a debt to Kafka (Nägele and Voris 34), not only in its negative image of the father. It also depicts the Kafkan experience of an alienated consciousness and its vulnerability to its repressed feelings in the moment of awakening:

> I was awake. I was awake before you came in and cried out softly. However, I did not wake up from sleep or from some other awareness, I woke from my own consciousness, I woke from my own consciousness that tormented itself on the bed with my body that was confined there. Yet, my body fell out as you put the blanket on it and bent over me and took my head in your hands. I had closed my eyes and became aware of how my body fell out of my consciousness as it fell into that yellow water, into that dark snow; I awoke from my consciousness and could hear everything that was happening around me and also everything that was not happening. Your name is ... your name was ... I have forgotten your name. (*BA* 22)

The shock to consciousness and the loss of body ego experienced by the abused son leads here to forgetting and the loss of language (names), a pivotal event of disorientation in many of Handke's texts which prompts the act of remembering the past and reconstructing the dislocated self. This portrait of a violent father has autobiographical overtones to Handke's stepfather, a German soldier who was stationed in Austria. It will also appear in several of the later writings, both as an abusive father (specifically in *Die Hornissen* and *Wunschloses Unglück,* 1972; *A Sorrow Beyond Dreams,* 1974) and in the guise of fascist authoritarian figures (the police in *Der Hausierer* and the old man who paints the swastika in *Der Chinese des Schmerzes,* 1983; *Across,* 1986). In the piece entitled "Der Hausierer," the narrator describes the meaning of the word 'peddler' in several contexts, namely in a film and in a stage play, but the narration slowly proceeds from simple description of the action to complete omniscience as the narrator recounts what the figures on stage are thinking and feeling. As do most of the texts in the collection, "Der Hausierer" plays with the reader's perception of the reality presented in the discourse of traditional realistic literature.

Kafka also figures in another piece in the collection, "Der Prozeß (für Franz K.)" (1965; The Trial [for Franz K.]), a brief plot summary of Kafka's novel *Der Process* (1935; *The Trial*, 1968). Handke's point concerns the nature of all writing, namely, that the act of retelling is implicitly an interpretation – and a linguistic de-formation – that should not be confused with the original (Nägele and Voris 36). Handke's paraphrase is a highly reduced version that pointedly refuses the "rambling style of literary narration" (Firda 45). The existential themes of shame and self-delusion that figure so prominently in Kafka's text are also present in Handke's speculative version and point to the latter's emotional identification with the former. The title piece of the collection, "Begrüßung des Aufsichts-rats" (1964) recalls the "black humor of Franz Kafka's parables" (Firda 42). Its theme suggests the way in which language can distort the perception of truth or reality.

Like Kafka, Handke was a law student, and the piece entitled "Das Standrecht" (1964; Martial Law) is another exercise in the defamiliarization of the realities generated by texts, that is, the formulaic and antiseptic style of a proscriptive legal discourse is juxtaposed with the existential realism Handke uses to describe the institutionalized and legalized violence it justifies. It is a parody that creates its effect through the tension between these very different types of discourse (Linstead, *Outer World* 37). The textual process here is similar to another piece in the collection called "Der Galgenbaum" (1964; The Gallows Tree) which contrasts an emotio-nally distanced and technical history of execution by hanging with a realistic description of mob violence and a lynching taken from an American western movie with Gary Cooper. The point is didactic: to illustrate the different realities generated by linguistic texts through a process of defamiliarization. Both pieces implicitly con-demn the violence that is institutionalized and legalized by society and thus they share in the spirit of the social and political protest that characterized the youth culture of the 1960s. Two other pieces, "Prüfungsfrage 1" and "Prüfungsfrage 2" (1965; Test Question 1; Test Question 2), also deal with the legal language. Absurdist and surreal parodies of law school exam questions, they are reminiscent of some of the short anecdotal pieces of Heinrich von Kleist (Firda 44).

The disjuncture between objective reality and textual reality is an idea featured in many of the texts in the collection. The questioning of the truth or factual value of words is a concept from the philosophy of fellow Austrian Ludwig Wittgenstein that influenced the young Handke. The text called "Die Überschwemmung" (1963; The Flood) is also found in the novel *Die Hornissen* with a somewhat different narrative perspective but with the same theme, that is, an "estranged linguistic process" (Firda 42) that plays with the truths or fictions generated by words. A second text, "Über den Tod eines Fremden" (1963; Concerning the Death of a Stranger), suggests the beginnings of a story about a boy who discovers a man hiding in an abandoned World War II bunker. The text undercuts the supposed facts of this story and leaves the reader wondering what is fact and what is fiction. The piece seeks to defamiliarize for the reader aspects of traditional realist narrative.

Handke has always been an avid student of popular culture and the movies, and "Sacramento (Eine Wildwestgeschichte)" (1964; Sacramento. A Story of the Wild West) is taken from Sam Peckinpah's western film *Ride the High Country* (1962). It is another exercise in narration and the perception of reality presented in and through texts. Initially, the narrator appears to be recounting his experience of a violent episode involving his sister. Through subtle inconsistencies in the storytelling, the reader gradually becomes aware that the text is actually a retelling of the movie from the point of view of an audience member who has been emotionally drawn into the action of the film and has identified with one of its characters. As he would assert with respect to *Die Hornissen* and *Der Hausierer*, Handke later rejected the experimental and didactic artifice of the pieces published in *Begrüßung des Aufsichtsrats* and appeared more concerned with the elements of memory and forgetting that the act of writing held for him at the time (Arnold 17).

*

Die Hornissen is undoubtedly the most difficult to read of Handke's narrative works, yet it "contains within it one of the most complex and starkly impressive worlds one could find anywhere in German literature" (Perram 157). It is a highly experimental text, which deals with formalist/structuralist issues of perception and the construction of meaning both in the mediated realm of literary works and in the immediate domain of phenomenological experience. As a postmodern exercise in the indeterminacy of a text, it subverts traditional notions of linear plot development and a stable narrating self, thus rejecting, as do the pieces in *Begrüßung des Aufsichtsrats,* "the suppositions of realistic storytelling" (Klinkowitz and Knowlton 20). The novel consists of 67 separate episodic sections with such enigmatic titles as "The Insects on the Horse's Eyes" and "The Names of the Sounds." The sections challenge the reader to create a linear storyline from this complex mosaic of often highly descriptive fragments, each of which "tends to encapsulate an experience, a memory or piece of fantasy, or some synthesis of these" (Perram 145). Handke's dilemma in this highly self-referential novel is to narrate despite the intrinsic distortions, ideological and otherwise, of all acts of narration, to hover between a Wittgensteinian silence about those (sometimes traumatic) things one cannot express through words and the inevitable falsification of experience inherent in all linguistic formulations.[10]

As many of the early, very negative reviews noted, *Die Hornissen* is so inaccessible that a paperback edition included a brief summary (written by Handke) concerning the novel's overall narrative intentions.[11] One critic calls the text "an obscure, labyrinthine,

---

[10] A detailed discussion of the novel has been delivered by Perram. Darby discusses the multifaceted narrative and heavily embedded discourse structures of the novel, which involve the reader in an uncertain process of "both attrition and the addition of new narrative elements" (259) that render the text ultimately inaccessible. Barry ("Search") highlights how this early text foreshadows the imagery and themes in Handke's later texts: this first novel exhibits the concept of art/imagination as a medium of transcendence that has constituted what Handke has called "an entirely clear continuity" (Durzak, *Gespräche* 332) in his writings. Göttsche presents a detailed analysis of both the novel's deconstructive processes and the author's attempt to lay a constructive groundwork for a viable, more authentic narrative. Haslinger's monograph on Handke's childhood provides valuable biographical insights. Widrich's article discusses *Die Hornissen* in the context of Handke's birthplace.

[11] Handke also gives a summary of sorts in an interview with Durzak (*Narziß* 49). Some of these early negative newspaper reviews can be found in Scharang (17-37). Quotations are from the Suhrkamp edition, for which Handke undertook some revisions of his original text (published by Rowohlt but no longer in print).

piecemeal montage" (Schlueter 13) and another emphasizes its "mosaiclike dispersal of narrative elements and episodes" (Firda 52). The apparent plot concerns the origins of a novel, which may or may not be Handke's *Die Hornissen* itself. It is a narrative which deals with a seemingly blind man, possibly named Gregor Benedikt, who, as he lies awake in bed, is trying to reconstruct the circumstances related to his apparent loss of sight when he was a child, presumably during a wartime bombing.[12] The narrator's blindness is also seemingly connected to the simultaneous disappearance of his brother Hans after the accidental drowning of their brother Matt. At the same time, Gregor also attempts to remember a novel he read (or may have read) a long time ago but has largely forgotten. The penultimate section of *Die Hornissen*, entitled "The origin of the story," gives the reader some idea of the story of the forgotten novel:

> The book tells of two brothers, one of whom later, searching alone for the other lost brother, goes blind; it does not emerge clearly from the story what event causes his blindness; it is stated several times that it is wartime; but all the details of the misfortune itself are omitted, or he has forgotten them. The story begins with the blind brother, now a man, waking up one Sunday and being reminded by something, which eludes him when he tries to think of it, of his missing brother. From that point the bits he thinks he can remember go through his brain, but without any semblance of order. (*Ho* 272)

The plot of this book, however, is only vaguely remembered and the narrator must make up the parts he has forgotten:

> Even the place and time of year in which the plot is set elude him. Because he does not know all this any more, or rather is only in possession of bits of it here and there, because he is

---

[12]The name Gregor appears in several of Handke's texts and should not be construed solely as a playful reference to Kafka. It is more likely homage to the author's maternal grandfather with whom Handke had a close relationship and, more importantly, to his maternal uncle who went missing during the war and whose letters from the front were highly prized within the family. This uncle, beloved by Handke's mother, may have been a major impetus behind Handke's desire to become a writer and to please thereby his mother. Other characters in *Die Hornissen* are an abusive father, a mother who dies midway through the text, and a sister. There is also a man carrying a duffel or sea bag who appears at various points in the text and is possibly the narrator's missing brother Hans.

certain that he read the book at some time he is spurred on and wants to know the whole story. This is what set him off on his long quest. But things remembered are not things proved; what he has conjured up need not be true in the sense that it corresponds plausibly with events in the book, but it does have to be possible and imaginable by being credible in its own right, any false or unnatural utterance would be spurned and rejected by experience. (*Ho* 275).[13]

The blind brother thus (again possibly) becomes identical with the narrator of (and the reader of) *Die Hornissen* itself, although there are discrepancies between the forgotten text and the text the reader confronts. Tabah sees the contrived plot – a novel within a novel – as a parody of traditional mimetic narration and provides an explanation of the story (81-89).

There are quotations (presumably from the missing novel) scattered throughout Handke's text. The fictional events of this long forgotten lost text, however, seem to have merged in the narrator's mind with the forgotten or repressed memories of his real childhood. The story material of the book is probably a deconstruction of the events presented in the quotations (Perram 153). Handke's work effectively conflates here the activities of reading and writing in "a narrative about the construction of a narrative" in which the acts of reading and writing are repeatedly interchanged (Darby 261). The self that narrates the lost text that is *Die Hornissen* (as well as the self of the critic that reads it) echoes what Barthes described four years later in *S/Z* as the "I" that reads texts the sources of which have vanished: "The 'I' which approaches the text is already itself a plurality of other texts, of codes which are infinite or, more precisely, lost (whose origin is lost)" (10). The literary-critical thrust of Handke's "writerly" novel is precisely to make readers conscious of the infinite linguistic codes, public and private, verbal and nonverbal, which they bring to a text in the activity of reading and creating meaning. The fiction of a lost book that lies between the events of the narrator's objective reality and his memories of them is a technique designed to illustrate the distortions of literary language inherent in the traditional mimetic narrative (Tabah 100-01). The lost book suspended between past events and memories

---

[13]The translation of these two passages is taken from Rorrison's article (265-66).

becomes a complex interplay of mediated and unmediated visions of reality. Handke's textual play compels readers to become simultaneously also the writers of *Die Hornissen* through a movement in which they must abandon completely the construction of any traditional discursive meaning and must embrace their own constructions of a story from the intuitive and lyric flow of the text.

The multiple imbedded narrative refractions of Handke's book also beg the questions of narrative organization and meaning as well as the existential status of both fictional texts and of the phenomenological workings of memory and forgetting. The equation of memory and forgotten text in the plot of a novel about a novel suggests that the recovering of memory is portrayed here as being largely a fictional process. This novel of deconstruction is also about the issue of reconstructed memories, "the problematic area of the reflective self" (Perram 221), that is, the ontological dilemma of all human memory as a grey zone between the reality of past events and one's imagined reenactment of those events. In this Proustian remembrance of things/texts past, the process of remembering is also very much a process of fictionalizing, reconstructing the past as a lyric repetition of past experience mediated and directed by the narrator's fluid, highly personal, and private language of images and words. Implied in this view of consciousness is the idea that the psyche itself is a fictional construct. Handke speaks of *Die Hornissen* and his other early narrative texts as being lyrically-toned "epic poems" with existential content: "There is no expansion of character or plot, but an 'I' is writing a narrative poem about the time in which he lives, about the self, and about others" (Schlueter 173). Handke's first novel participates in the modernist tradition of lyrical reverie literature that includes Joyce's *Ulysses* (1922) and Faulkner's *As I Lay Dying* (1930). *Die Hornissen* – and much of the other early fiction – is also influenced by the postmodernist phenomenological depictions of (often deranged) consciousness in the French *nouveau roman* of Alain Robbe-Grillet and Nathalie Sarraute.[14]

The novel's difficulties exist because the text does not treat any positivistic notion of reality – the verifiable facts and events found in the mimetic narrative – but focuses exclusively on the narrat-

---

[14]See the discussion of perception in Handke and Robbe-Grillet by Wellershoff.

or/writer's phenomenological reality.[15] The text consists of an intense interplay of "direct experience, memory, imagination, and images from the unconscious" that has been decoupled from the laws of time and space that characterize traditional narrative storylines (Perram 52). The narrator's blindness creates a dependence on sounds and smells. It thus engenders an original mode of description that constitutes a defamiliarized attempt at a genuine realism (Tabah 102). Sounds and smells also serve prominently as triggers of memory. The existential quest of Handke's writings, the definition or grounding of his identity, is here closely tied to the intimate act of remembering as a kind of archaeology of the self, a search for the origins of his personality in the fragmented memories of his childhood.[16] In this sense, then, Handke's first novel partakes in the turn towards personal and existential themes in German literature that later would be called the movement of the New Subjectivity, a decided rejection of the social and political concerns that dominated the German academic and intellectual culture of the 1960s.[17] The novel's first and last sections, "The beginning of memory" and "The suspending of memory," frame the memory and reverie processes that constitute the intervening sections of this disjointed text. Handke's concern with the representation of reality stems not only from a formal critique of literary language and realist fiction but also from an autobiographical exploration of his own consciousness.[18] Language in this work (and all Handke's texts) is regarded as "the existential core of literature" (Sergooris 34).

---

[15]Marschall (19) sees Handke's text as being more concerned with the phenomenological exploration of a writer's consciousness than with the repetition of a traumatic event in the narrator's past. Durzak, by contrast, finds that guilt is the unconscious impetus that drives the narrative forward (*Narziß* 58).

[16]Wesche comments that in Handke's writings, art might be defined as an "archaeology" in a world that has been deluged by signs (330). Archaeology in Handke's texts is a discipline of both the deconstruction and reconstruction of memory (reality) and textual fragments (fictional reality).

[17]Linstead ("Handke") situates Handke within the context of German literature of the 1970s in general and Zeyringer discusses him in Austrian literature of the 1980s. Ryan places him within newer trends in the Austrian novel in specific, and DeMeritt in the 1970s' movement of New Subjectivity.

[18]Renner (180) asserts that an "autobiographical center" of preoccupations with childhood memories underlies all of the author's works, as does Haslinger (19-20).

Handke considers *Die Hornissen* a "symbol for my beginnings" and decries the "literary artifice," that is, the analytic and didactic deconstruction of the traditional mimetic narrative that characterizes this recondite and contrived text. He calls the reality depicted in the book "a magical world," one that is "the world of my childhood" (Durzak, *Gespräche* 326, 327), an authentic portrait of his childhood experiences in rural Austria. The novel is full of the author's "semi-processed material – experiences and memories" – which are also reprocessed in his later works (Perram 118). Elsewhere, Handke again speaks highly of the images of his childhood in this first novel and of how his memories are "preserved" (Arnold 17) – or suspended, nullified, transcended as the German word "aufgehoben" indicates – in what he had then written. He further claims he would like to take up this text again and to show in a possible "revised" version how such images originated in his consciousness (Arnold 19). In these interviews, Handke rejects the self-conscious artifice of the experimental narrative mode of the novel (perhaps as an excess of his youth) but affirms the personal and existential importance for him of its thematic content. The fragmentary images of Handke's Austrian childhood in this first novel are decidedly negative; they depict a world of desolation, monotony, and loneliness (Gabriel 53).

Indeed, in the appropriately named novel of 1986, *Die Wiederholung* (*Repetition*, 1988), Handke returns to the theme of his Austrian childhood – as he did in the 1972 memoir of his mother's life and suicide, *A Sorrow Beyond Dreams* – and to many of the images that occur in *Die Hornissen*. As such, this later text deserves discussion here as a possible revision of the first novel, this time narrated in a more traditional style with a defined beginning, middle, and end. It is the story of the twenty-year-old Filip Kobal, narrated by the older Filip some twenty years later, who sets out over the Yugoslavian border from his Austrian village to find his "missing brother" (*R* 3), who is named Gregor and is blind on one eye. At one point, Kobal offers commentary on what he had felt when he was twenty and it serves well as Handke's own self-critical review of his first novel: "What I felt within me were mere impulses … a general surge that found no beginnings, jolts in the void, a confused epic without a name, without the innermost voice, without the coherence of script" (*R* 73).[19]

Kobal continues his reflections and links this notion of script to storytelling and to memory as repetition. Remembering past experiences allows him to feel the past in a more "realized" manner as a form of "narrative": "... in being remembered, it first became known to me, nameable, voiced, speakable; accordingly, I look on memory as more than a haphazard thinking back – as work; the work of memory situates experience in a sequence that keeps it alive, a story which can open out into free storytelling, greater life, invention" (*R* 73). Kobal's remarks speak not only to the narrative intentions, however devoid of a unifying "script" and thwarted they may be by the "literary artifice" of the younger author behind the fragments that make up the "confused epic" *Die Hornissen*, but to the creative impetus of memory process behind many of Handke's fiction.

The continuity in Handke's writing has always been towards an ideal of reading and storytelling as a process that seeks to stabilize and situate a traumatized childhood self that has been perceived as shamed, mute, and isolated. This entails a therapeutic reprocessing of memories. Thus, *Die Hornissen* "is about memory, the creation of a literary work out of memory, as well as attempting to deal with one's present existence" (Perram 151). The most important dimension of "this highly complex literary text is the gradual and at times convoluted exposure of the crisis of the individual who is attempting unsuccessfully to come to terms with his own identity, and with his sense of separateness from others" (Perram 209). Handke has expressed his feelings of estrangement: "Unease, dissatisfaction, and anxiety – these [emotions] occur much more frequently in me, then the self appears like some kind of cancerous growth and that is for me in and of itself very unpleasant" (Linder 36). This image of

---

[19]The notion of "script" is first introduced in the novel *Die Lehre der Sainte Victoire* (1980; *The Lesson of Mont Sainte-Victoire*, 1985; *LSV* 178). It becomes important in Handke's later writings and refers to both the reading and writing of literary texts as the aesthetic creation of spiritual mythology. It refers to both the idea of narration and to the physical act of writing by hand with a pencil. Here it is synonymous with a coherent story as well as the lending of coherence to phenomenological experience, narration as a synthetic and existential, rather than an analytic and formal, activity.

the body ego of the self as a "cancerous growth" appears in several of the author's texts, a startling image of existential estrangement in which his own consciousness is perceived as being "dis-eased," that is, not at ease with being in the world. Remembering as repetition is, in the activity of narration, a therapeutic "re-membering" of that shamed and fragmented self.[20]

The childhood images depicted in *Die Hornissen* are far from idyllic; they are dominated by often extreme feelings of anxiety and unreality, displacement and isolation, guilt and denial, withdrawal and shame. These traumatic emotions – Haslinger calls them a "childhood wound" (19) – shape all of the characters in Handke's writings. These feelings undoubtedly stem from a variety of sources, including a series of certainly rather harrowing moves during the war between Berlin and his birthplace in the village of Altenmarkt/ Griffen (in southern Carinthia) as well as repeated Allied bombings in both Berlin and Altenmarkt and a childhood in a very poor rural family. Perhaps most important, Handke experienced an abusive, often drunk stepfather prone on occasion to acts of domestic violence and abuse. The home situation was dysfunctional and seems to have been particularly traumatic for the young child. In a 1973 interview, Handke made the following comment: "There must have been some kind of a primal shock. Many times, I think, there were feelings of anxiety ... when my parents were not at home and then returned and, screaming, beat each other in the room and I hid myself under the blanket" (Haslinger 22).[21] Reading became for him, especially during his years at the Catholic seminary, a salutary means by which he could cope with and escape from this ontolog-

---

[20]The notion of repetition here also suggests an element of ritualized behavior that figures in many of Handke's later works. On the general theme of repetition in Handke, especially the later works, see Bonn.

[21]Handke had recounted this primal scene almost verbatim in the conversation with Christian Linder (36). He also depicts it in a more extended description in *A Sorrow Beyond Dreams*. In an unpublished transcript of a question and answer session with University of Southern California students and faculty dated May 11, 1976, he explicitly associates his interest as an adolescent in language and literature (reading and writing) with the experience of an "existential shock" and an "existential anxiety." Handke spent three days at USC in May 1976 under the auspices of the Max Kade Institute under the direction of Cornelius Schnauber. I thank Professor Schnauber for permission to quote from the session transcripts.

ical anxiety: by generating another perspective on his own life and thereby viewing himself and the world around him in a new (and presumably less threatening) way.

This primal scene with the parents fighting first appears in *Die Hornissen* in the section "Die Reden des Gendarmen" (The Policeman's Speeches). Here the body of the drowned brother Matt is returned to the family. The scene of domestic violence is repressed here like a shameful family secret as a first-person parenthetical memory of the blind narrator Gregor as he lies in bed at night:

> (I sometimes lay awake and listened as my father beat, as best as he could, my mother in the big room; at first I understood the everyday words my parents exchanged behind the wall and I easily distinguished the slapping of the blows, although next to me my brothers began, amid howling and laughing, to beat each other in imitation of our parents; but then I became, as he beat her more vigorously, paralyzed and stupefied, and the veins in my head popped out and numbed me so that I became deaf to all sounds and heard only the raging blood within me.) (*Ho* 27-28)

This primal situation is typical of the dysfunctional family. The child's realization that the parents who are supposed to be in control are in reality out of control prompts feelings of helplessness and abandonment. This initiates a psychic process of emotional denial and a defensive withdrawal into an intellectualized vision of the self. Thus, the narrator of *Die Hornissen* suffers from "some form of essentially intellectual alienation from the natural world" (Perram 217). The list of psychological difficulties that have apparently plagued Handke's personality and that are evidenced in many of his fictional characters is quite substantial: insomnia, depression, and extreme fatigue, chronic states of fear and anxiety, panic attacks and feelings of unreality, an almost painful sensitivity to external stimuli such as sounds and smells, moments of speechlessness and almost autistic, dissociative withdrawal, excessive dependence on the mother and the inability to sustain relationships (particularly with women), debilitating shame and compensatory feelings of grandiosity, and a pronounced narcissistic personality structure. These issues are symptomatic of such traumatic childhood experiences in a troubled family, and many of them are evidenced in various sections of *Die Hornissen*.[22]

The passage from an earlier short story entitled "Die Hornissen" also points to a traumatic incident that is linked to the image of the helpless child in bed and, significantly, to his primal experience of the dissociation and repression of his consciousness (and to the absence of the mother who, in the novel, apparently dies). The bed in these two passages points to its centrality in *Die Hornissen* and it certainly carries here all the weight of Kafkaesque allusions to the place of dreams and nightmares, sexuality, and hence the unconscious and irrational. The bed is the place where narration often begins in *Die Hornissen* and in many of the stories by Kafka. It is the locus of repression where names are forgotten and must be recalled later in narrative texts. In the negative image of the father in the novel, especially in the man's "brutish behaviour and appetites" (Perram 218), we find a further similarity between the sensitive Kafka, who could not reconcile with his own apparently rather gruff father, and Handke.

Although Handke ascribes the narrator's loss of sight to a bomb attack (Durzak, *Narziß* 50-51), one surmises that the origin of the affliction might also be psychosomatic, a repressive response to the chronic fear and anxiety of the narrator's childhood circumstances. The perception of existence in the novel reflects that of a child at a pre-logical level (Perram 173). This may also be seen as an arrested state of development resulting from trauma. Indeed, the distorted and fragmented narrative style, the "literary artifice" of *Die Hornissen*, appears to be more than a consummate formalist exercise in

---

[22]For example, "Die Verführung" (The Seduction; *Ho* 168-74) and "Die Frau" (The Woman; *Ho* 179-83) suggest the storyteller's paralyzing fear of and attraction to the mother/women, a theme that is prominent in several of Handke's other works. There are no long-term romantic relationships with women in Handke's texts. The relationships that are depicted are often abusive. On the other hand, several of Handke's texts have women as the central characters, although they are idealized figures who act as projections of the author's own psyche. There is a decided ambivalence towards the women figures in his writings. Hammer treats the fixation with the mother and the psychosexual issues at play in Handke's texts. Handke was extremely close to his mother and, as Haslinger intimates (52), part of his desire to become a writer may well stem from his intimate correspondence to her, begun in October 1961 when he enrolled at the university in Graz.

poststructuralist literary theory, as it has been interpreted by almost all of its readers. Rather, its deliberately confusing and oblique story line of a poorly recollected text – its radical narrative indeterminacy – might well be read as a deliberate and defensive gesture, as the denial and repression of a deep childhood trauma, the shameful family secret. It is endured by the narrator and hidden within and beneath the protective blanket of his "fictions" of his supposed blindness and of a "forgotten novel" he once read.[23] In this manner, the narrator, "who emerges as the main protagonist in what appears to be a search for a way out of a psychic cocoon, creates a narrational labyrinth into which he ultimately withdraws" (Perram 151). At the same time he fails in his attempt to reestablish his identity because "he is unwilling to confront past events, or aspects of his own identity which are all part of his own reality" (Perram 189). The narrator's presumed blindness serves as a metaphor for his "disturbed relationship to reality" and his "loss of identity" (Sergooris 41).

In a section tellingly called "Der Zwiespalt" (Inner Conflict), it is suggested that Gregor Benedikt's blindness and the entire narrative is a subterfuge in order to "protect" the storyteller "from his own story/history" (*Ho* 229). At another point, a quotation from the forgotten novel is cited that suggests the narrator's duplicity: "'Gregor Benedikt is a liar'" (*Ho* 126).[24] In all of Handke's writings, language and literature have always been presented ambivalently as both distorting reality by transforming it into ideology and as a restorative access to and rehabilitation of reality through the creative imagination. In *Die Hornissen*, both modalities are present simultaneously – as they are in most psychotherapeutic situations – as both a calculated hiding and a healing disclosure of traumatic experience. Denial is a major response by the victim to psychological trauma, especially in the context of domestic vio-

---

[23]A quotation from Maurice Blanchot, cited in Rushkin's book on family secrets and narrative, might also be read as an apt characterization of what is occurring in the convoluted plot structure of *Die Hornissen*: "Narration reveals, but in revealing hides a secret: more accurately it carries it" (64).

[24]Durzak argues that Gregor is a liar because in reality he, and not his brother Hans, was present at the drowning of their brother Matt. Gregor's blindness and the fiction of a forgotten novel are a result of his guilt which he seeks to conceal (*Roman* 327-31).

lence. One suspects that Handke's preoccupation with authenticity in his writings is, in part, a response to the atmosphere of psychic denial that lingers in, and indeed subverts, many of his texts. This first novel is an attempt to create a text as a constructive and synthetic response to trauma (domestic abuse, the loss of a family member, the terrors of war), but it fails, in the opinion of most readers and even the author himself, under the weight of its own analytical but contrived deconstructive processes.

The toll on the narrator exacted by the repression of the trauma is made clear in the section entitled "Das Erwachen" (Waking Up). Here the vulnerability of his consciousness to its repressed contents is at its highest and self-control is at its weakest: "... while I lay, still in the short time (in the monstrous time, my brother said) between the waking of consciousness and the waking of the senses, without defenses amongst my thoughts" (*Ho* 58). The psychological stance of the narrator of Handke's first novel is decidedly defensive. As a "panicked subject" (Bartmann 168), the narrator is beset – as are both the author and most of his fictional characters – by pervasive fears that the reality he perceives will suddenly reveal itself to be completely other than what he had thought, thus leaving the self radically destabilized. This occasions a profound psychic dissociation and a frightening loss of an existential center, a state of mind in which the self appears as something alien and monstrous, a cancerous growth. This is often signaled by the experiences of a jolt or shock to consciousness and moments of speechlessness, motifs well known to Handke readers. The narrator of *Repetition* describes the experience in a way that applies directly to Handke's first novel and to his other early texts as well. It is a basic paradigm in Handke's writings:

> And then another jolt, which was at the same time recollection.... Sometimes as a boy I had encountered myself in that way, usually on waking, and always at times when I felt threatened. My anxiety turned to terror, as if the end had come, and my terror into a dread with which, reduced to a tumor, I waited – unable to stir a muscle – for the tumor to be removed. But it wasn't. Instead, an utter stranger appeared and that stranger was I. (*R* 177)[25]

---

[25]This passage in *Repetition* continues to explain that the (here negatively depicted) experience of dissociation becomes suddenly positive, leaving the

In *Die Hornissen*, this abyss of the irrational revealed in the "jolt" is presented in the final chapter, "Das Aussetzen der Erinnerung" (The suspending of memory), in which the narrator describes his missing brother as the latter walks over a field of snow, suddenly breaking through the ice (*Ho* 276). The final image of the novel has existential overtones as "there is no escape from the dilemma of existence" (Perram 220-21). The image of breaking through the ice is repeated in Handke's play *Der Ritt über den Bodensee* (1971; *The Ride Across Lake Constance*, 1973) where it again suggests the sudden eruption of the irrational that lies beneath the surface of everyday reality. The narrator's almost obsessively detailed descriptions of objects in the novel seem to serve a salutary purpose in that they provide a calming influence on his agitated and disoriented psyche. These descriptions "add a very static dimension to the novel which in other aspects seems to be in a state of flux and dominated by uncertainty" (Perram 184).

The dissociation of the self becomes apparent in the section entitled "Das Wort 'sich verstecken'" (The word 'to hide oneself') in which the blind narrator asserts: "I do not need to hide myself from myself because I cannot see myself; for I am blind, that is, my eyes are blind, that is, my eyes are not eyes, that is, so to speak, I

---

self open to new, revitalized visions of the personality as "pure listening" (*R* 178). Handke's early writings to the mid-1970s are dominated by the negative dimensions of this experience of the dissociated self. His later texts seem to indicate a reversal in that they stress the spiritual aspects of this dissociation as an openness to the world and to his experience of it, evidenced in an attitude of slowness. This psychological stance of slowness – most readily observable in his journals – becomes in practice a patient attentiveness to both external events and the processes of the consciousness that perceives (and constructs) them. It resembles certain aspects of Buddhist meditation. During the mid-1970s when he was living in Paris, Handke reportedly experienced several episodes of panic attacks (and tachycardia) and was hospitalized for a brief period, reflected in some of the journal entries in *Das Gewicht der Welt* (1977; *The Weight of the World*, 1984). The attacks were caused by high levels of stress resulting from his mother's suicide, his divorce, and his life as a single parent. At this time, he began his journal writing – perhaps a result of psychotherapy – and shortly thereafter experienced the illumination of slowness that he mentions in the quotation on the back cover of the essay collection edited by Fuchs and Melzer. I thank Handke's translator and commentator Michael Roloff for this biographical information and for his helpful comments on the translations in this essay.

am not. But I can, while I hide myself, make fun of myself and forget myself" (*Ho* 200). The text also claims enigmatically at several points that something has been (purposefully) left out of the reconstructed narrative as in the final words of the section called "Die Entstehung einer Episode beim Frühstück" (The origin of an episode at breakfast): "Something in the description has been forgotten. No. It has not been mentioned intentionally. No, it has been forgotten. No. I don't know about what" (*Ho* 94). In this deliberately indeterminate manner, Handke is playing with the reader a game of narrative hide and seek that also represents a serious psychic withdrawal from painful events. Although the narrator seems at times to be seeking a stable sense of self, there is "a deliberate attempt to mislead the reader about the person of the narrator and to obscure the perception of his identity" (Perram 215). The psychological etiology of such feelings of unreality, dissociation, shame, and self-alienation (often accompanied by panic attacks) is to be found in the repression of traumatic childhood experiences. Handke has made his anxiety productive as a literary text, "a very complete and complex portrayal of the unsuccessful attempt of an individual to re-establish his own identity and own sense of wholeness after a past shadowy event that traumatized him" (Perram 189).

The fiction of the narrator's supposed blindness represents a psychological denial and withdrawal, a radical retreat of the wounded self into a constructed world of inner visual images.[26] The figure of Gregor is "obsessively introspective" and "is caught be-

---

[26]Blindness also links *Die Hornissen*, in part at least, to *Der Bildverlust oder Durch die Sierra de Gredos* (2002; The Loss of Images, or Across the Sierra de Gredos) which is about the loss of mythological vision – of life-sustaining and enhancing magical or poetic images – in the dehumanized, materialistic, and destructive reality presented in the political and social ideologies of postmodern American and Western European cultures. This loss of poetic discourse is most obvious to Handke in the deadening language of facile concepts and the unfounded, and therefore irresponsible, generalizations found in the mass media. These are for him ideological distortions of reality. Handke's imagination is decidedly eidetic and he is highly prone to so-called hypnogogic states, i.e. transitional stages between sleep and wakefulness when the individual visualizes a flood of spontaneously occurring, almost hallucinatory images. This is represented in *Die Hornissen* and in numerous other texts as the state of semi-sleep.

tween the desire to order and control his existence (as well as to make sense of it), and the inability to deal with the irrational elements which well up into the consciousness when he attempts to do this" (Perram 212). It is, to play upon the title of Handke's 1969 book of poems, the domain of 'the inner world of the outer world of the inner world' where images, of memories and dreams, of real objects and words, exist in a fluid play. In this vein, the insects of the novel's title serve as "a metaphor for the random images and thoughts and memories emerging from the narrator's unconscious" (Perram 213). Given that Handke is afflicted by a partial color blindness and an apparent hypersensitivity (bordering at times on nausea) to visual stimuli, his writings have revolved around the theme of vision, both as a distorted and as an authentic seeing of what is. The author's association in this novel of the blind narrator with the blind seer of ancient Greece (Teiresias and Homer) and therefore with the mythical-magical imagination of the writer as visionary priest – the *poeta vates* – is obvious and deliberate (Durzak, *Roman* 326): "In many tales, it is precisely the blind man who is a seer" (*Ho* 274). For Handke, the visions of the priest-poet are essentially spiritual acts in that they give meaning to and sustain life. The author of the forgotten novel himself is also associated with the notion of blindness in that he remains invisible to the reader. *Die Hornissen* is composed from a point of radical inwardness where the inner and outer worlds become inseparable.

The section concerning the recreation of an episode from the forgotten novel "at breakfast," centers on the blind narrator's processes of visualization and reads as if it were a film script. It serves as a key to understanding how Handke's text is generated.[27] It begins with a quotation from the lost text and proceeds with the blind narrator's apparent reconstruction of the text. He is lying in bed at night – again with all allusions to the bed as the locus of dreaming and the irrational – listening to the disembodied sounds around him. He assigns word-images to the sounds of the trains and trucks he hears (*Ho* 84-86) in what appears to be an increasingly compulsive attempt to give coherence to his sightless and fragmented perception of the world. His efforts immediately depart

---

[27]In his interview with Peter André Bloch, Handke points to this scene as being the experiential "starting point" of his text (172).

from the reality of his experience. They become an imaginative and self-generating flight of images and visual-aural metaphors, a film, as it were, on an inner movie screen with the narrator himself as its would-be director: "I assigned sounds that I did not hear to the pictures" (*Ho* 82).

At the water fountain of an imagined train station in his inner film he creates the image of a man: "I now assigned a man standing next to the fountain" (*Ho* 87). It is the mysterious man with the sea sack who appears throughout *Die Hornissen* and who may be the missing brother, Hans, or even an alter ego of the blind narrator himself. The image reappears in the later novel *Repetition* and may be a biographical reference to one of Handke's two maternal uncles (named Gregor) who went missing during the war. Here, significantly, the flow of pictures becomes self-directing, independent of the narrator's rational control, "against my will" (*Ho* 87), and approaches the imagery flow of "the automatic writing of the surrealists" (Perram 169) or that of the unconscious dreaming process: "I have the man drink more quickly. The image of an electric clock follows by itself. I extinguish this image." The narrator relinquishes here the control of his inner film – "I give myself over to these images" (*Ho* 87) – and is overcome by the involuntary narrative flow of dream images: "What I see then overpowers my will" (*Ho* 89). This cinematic flow of images is "a conscious attempt to order the unconscious," however, the "attempt at a rational ordering of the past (often in a very reduced form) is overpowered by irrational images that disturb the order" (Perram 188). What then emerges (*Ho* 88-91) is the genesis of a surreal narrative, one productively guided by the unconscious imagery of a hypnogogic state, the semi-sleep or dream reverie, in which the man with the sea sack, whose eyes turn "white like an enamel glaze," appears to merge with the blind narrator in his bed as he finally falls asleep. The reconstruction of the forgotten text ends with another quotation from the lost novel – "'He is sleeping'" (*Ho* 91) – in which the forgotten past text and the remembered present text become essentially one text, the one that the reader confronts, the text that is *Die Hornissen* itself.

*

Just as *Die Hornissen* might be read as a didactic deconstruction of the typical elements of the village novel, a subgenre of *Heimat* literature, Handke's second extended prose work, *Der Hausierer*, is a structuralist dismantling of the "standard methodology of the murder mystery ... a book demonstrating literary method, not a text of fiction" (Firda 57).[28] Handke summarizes in italicized sentences that are "expository, rational, objective and analytical in nature" (Perram 119) the various narrative elements to be found in a typical murder story – "Die Ordnung vor der ersten Unordnung" (The Order before the First Disorder) or "Die Verfolgung" (The Persecution) – and then provides the reader with model or possible sentences that might be found at the various stages of the unfolding story of any given mystery text. The style here is "formal, detached, and legalistic, parodying not only typical narrators of the genre but also the style Handke himself learned as a law student in Graz" (Schlueter 14). It is a kind of paradigmatic proto-mystery, "a synthesis of all possible mysteries" (Klinkowitz and Knowlton 23) from which the reader might construct a storyline. More overtly and systematically than *Die Hornissen*, the work plays with the themes of the mediated and unmediated depiction of reality (Tabah 113-14).

The sample sentences form, again much like in *Die Hornissen*, a disjointed and indeterminate narrative in which the peddler emerges as the chief suspect and/or witness to several murders. The intention of this text, in part at least, is to illustrate the literary-theoretical background espoused in Handke's early essays and in his charge of "impotent description" ("Tagung" 29) leveled at the members of the Group 47 during its 1966 meeting at Princeton University. Handke's structuralist (and Wittgensteinian) lesson is simple: language can never be used innocently as if it were a clear pane of glass, as was demanded by Sartre and the 1960s radicals, who, naively in Handke's opinion, called for a politically and socially engaged literature. The meaning of words is always relative as determined by their context, and never absolute. Literature is, in its essence, always "unrealistic" and "romantic" (Handke, "Literatur" 50), more a mirror that reflects the situation of the writer (and his or her

---

[28]Koepnick discusses *Der Hausierer* in a similar manner as an anti-mystery, a postmodern novel that is intended as a critique and deconstruction of traditional narrative forms (100, 124) and genre conventions, and thus thwarts the act of communication between author and reader (101-02).

personal history, society, culture, gender, social class, etc.) than a transparent window pane looking out onto objective reality. To paraphrase Nietzsche, metaphors should never be confused with the things of the world, even though they have been mixed up in the (often ideologically motivated) dialectics of truth and lie throughout human history.[29]

The significance of the sample sentences Handke provides for each chapter is determined by their context within the overall structure of the traditional murder story. In the structuralist model of Roman Jakobson, the structural elements of the typical murder mystery plot provide the syntagmatic axis of the placement or order of the text's individual formulations, and the sample sentences delineate its paradigmatic axis, the sets of possible formulations. Since the prototypical crime story deals with issues of order (everyday normal reality) and disorder (an act of violence), the novel also broaches the ideological criticism – from Barthes and others – that informs Handke's thoughts on language in his early writings. The issue is the creation of a normative social reality in and through unreflected language, that is, language that reflects an ideological point of view and not objective reality. The political, social, or cultural entity that controls words ultimately regulates the reality of those who are compelled to use them and as such may be viewed in many instances as an act of social violence.[30]

Similar to *Die Hornissen*, *Der Hausierer* also reflects the more autobiographical and existential themes that are consistent throughout the author's writings. It is a deconstruction of the murder mystery genre and a construction of the fear and loathing of violence

---

[29]In his well-known essay fragment of 1873, "On Truth and Lie in an Extra-Moral Sense," Nietzsche deconstructs the notion of truth as a lie, as a product of language that has become confused with reality: "... truths are illusions which one has forgotten that this is what they are: metaphors, which are worn out and without sensuous power" (47). These aesthetic lies are, however, necessary for human existence in Nietzsche's view because the horrible truth of human suffering is unbearable and leads to self-destruction. For Nietzsche, the concept of God is one such fundamental but life-sustaining illusion, a lie that has become sacred. For a discussion of Handke and Nietzsche, see the essay by Pütz as well as the chapter by Andrea Gogröf-Voorhees in this book.

[30]All of the discussions of the novel in the secondary literature illuminate the deconstructive and structuralist dimensions and the ideological criticism that dominate Handke's early writings.

and abuse found in this genre. It is an exploration of Handke's own memories, and he has downplayed, as he has done with his first novel, its structuralist elements, its "literary artifice," as it were. In his essay "Ich bin ein Bewohner des Elfenbeinturms" (1967; I am an Inhabitant of the Ivory Tower), written as he was working on *Der Hausierer*, he explains that the latter text deconstructs or defamiliarizes clichéd plot mechanisms primarily so that one might experience one's own emotions of terror, fear, and anxiety in a new, more vital or authentic way. He goes on to assert that the analytic deconstruction of literary clichés was not the main point of the text: "I was not concerned with the 'unmasking' of clichés ... rather with the aid of the clichés of reality to come to new conclusions concerning (my own) reality" (*BE* 28). In a short essay, "Über meinen neuen Roman *Der Hausierer*" (About My New Novel 'The Peddler'), Handke explains that he felt he had to deconstruct the mystery genre analytically because its generic conventions had come to condition the perception and expression of his own emotions. The work explicitly contrasts the mediated and stereotypical expressions of terror and fear in the mystery genre with Handke's attempts to describe his own immediate experience of these feelings. The sample sentences that make up the disjointed story of the peddler are decidedly "experiential, irrational, subjective and undifferentiated," and the novel manifests "the clearest split in any of Handke's texts between the rational and the irrational elements of the human psyche" (Perram 119, 222). This clearly delineated split in the self presented in this text must also be viewed as a therapeutic attempt to evoke and contain the repressed psychic contents that threaten the stability of everyday reality.

Der Hausierer also deals with traumatic events, specifically murder, that must be repressed. Murder and, significantly, the issue of violence against women is an important aspect of *The Goalie's Anxiety at the Penalty Kick* when the disturbed Joseph Bloch strangles the movie cashier Gerda in Vienna and flees to the Austrian provinces. The language used to describe the murder of the woman in the eighth section of *Der Hausierer* entitled "Die zweite Unordnung" (The Second Disorder) anticipates Bloch's act. In *Die Stunde der wahren Empfindung* (1975; *A Moment of True Feeling*, 1977) Gregor Keuschnig's wanderings through Paris are occasioned by his dream of having murdered an old woman. In some of Handke's characters, issues of guilt, intimacy, and sexuality evoke repressed psychological conflicts and the eruption of violence.[31] In these latter two novels, the murders are connected to radical shifts in the characters' consciousness to unexpected moments of estrangement. These are again the well-known sudden shocks or jolts to awareness that are common in numerous Handke texts. Many of these experiences of overwhelming anxiety in the early texts are what Tabah calls "anticipation anxiety" (128), a fear of an unknown and ominous event that will suddenly overcome the individual. A distinct lack of causality defines many of the events depicted in the early narrative writings (Perram 173, note 29) and this unpredictability contributes to the atmosphere of anxiety and dread.

Handke himself again eschews the structuralist aspects of *Der Hausierer* and emphasizes its psychological dimensions: "In the *Goalie's Anxiety* novel, these moments of alienation are quite glaring and also in *Der Hausierer*, these are actually only moments of estrangement, not really so much the unmasking of clichés" (Durzak, *Gespräche* 333). The consciousness of the peddler, as he undergoes interrogation and persecution by the police, is in many respects a precursor of Joseph Bloch, especially in the latter's paranoid perception in which random objects take on special figurative meanings. The police interrogation episode is about "the relationship between abusive power and force" (Firda 60). Indeed, this atmosphere of fear and violence in the face of authority figures brings to mind the situation of the domestic abuse of the mother and the children at the hands of the father in *Die Hornissen* and *A Sorrow Beyond Dreams* and points again indirectly to a primal childhood experience within the dysfunctional family. The existential crisis that afflicts so many of Handke's protagonists seems to stem from their problematic social relationships marked by latent hostility toward others and their latent or overtly self-destructive behavior (Perram 124).

---

[31]The themes of violence and murder – the sudden eruption of the irrational into everyday reality – are again undoubtedly tied to Handke's own repressed anger and guilt associated with his childhood trauma, the resulting psychosexual conflict, and, in the case of the murdered old woman in *A Moment of True Feeling*, with his feelings of remorse that he may have neglected his mother Maria in the time prior to her suicide in 1971.

These sudden occurrences of alienation are often linked to certain specific harsh, abrupt sounds such as clapping, slapping, banging or exploding, with these words and related vocabulary occurring frequently throughout *Der Hausierer* and *The Goalie's Anxiety at the Penalty Kick*. In the former text, just before that murder occurs, the plot commentary states: *"Everyday reality is so complete that it must come to an explosion. The murder proceeds such that it precipitates a break with this reality"* (*Ha* 26). Handke describes his experiences of estrangement as representing an abrupt shift in his awareness, a destabilizing realization of the alienation of his consciousness from the world. These episodes were apparently common in his childhood; what he perceived to be reality would suddenly seem to him quite different from what he had thought:

> Or a feeling I had that this [reality] was not all there was, ... that there was another existence, that the world around me would explode. As a child, I always had the feeling that I would be playing out in the street and suddenly realize: all of this makes no sense at all, everything up to now has been wrong, some other person was coming. (Durzak, *Gespräche* 334).

The peddler is constantly exposed to "apparently a-causal experiences" that make him unsure of his reality (Perram 154). This aura of an ominous unreality – that people, objects, and events are unreal or more than what they appear to be at first glance – is again a symptom of the person who grows up in a disturbed family and it is obviously a structural component of the murder mystery genre, cloaking the secret crime and its perpetrator at its center.

In the tenth section of *Der Hausierer*, entitled "Die Ruhe vor der Entlarvung" (The Quiet before the Disclosure), there is discussion of the objects (as clues) that surround the murder investigation, especially the one clue that remains unclear: *"What is actually the case only reveals itself to him in incomplete sentences, sentences in which one word is missing. Something has been forgotten. The meaning of one detail has not been recognized"* (*Ha* 176). The second sentence here echoes the previously quoted passage in *Die Hornissen*, where "[s]omething in the description has been forgotten.... It has not been mentioned intentionally. No, it has been forgotten" (*Ho* 94). The similarity evokes the dialectics of forgetting and remembering, denial and recovery, that emerges as a major psychological theme in many of Handke's later writings and prompts the reader to inquire about the repressed core mystery of the shamed self.

In *Der Hausierer* (and especially in *The Goalie's Anxiety at the Penalty Kick*), the collapse of everyday reality prompts a profound feeling of being unconnected and the breakdown of signs in which the signifier is separated from the signified. In the seventh section of the former text which deals with the social order as perceived by the suspected peddler after the murder has been committed, the commentary explains this collapse of linguistic order and the loss of coherence:

> *However, the order that is revealed to him now makes him uncomfortable because he can no longer establish any relationships among the objects of this order. It makes him uncomfortable that every object exists only in and of itself.... Through the fact that he lacks any connection, he loses all other connections to objects. Reality becomes unreal for him. Because it is not settled, [reality] falls apart into individual entities that, for him, no longer have anything to do with each other. He can no longer connect the knife with the bread, the room with the door, the horizontal with the vertical.... (Ha 127)*

This inability to connect is a failure in the ability to generate comparisons or connections among objects, a collapse of the capacity for metaphor, in the most general terms. Handke points to this breakdown of the perception of reality, which he terms a "metaphoric feeling," experienced in the wake of some of his own personal traumatic experiences (his divorce and the death of his mother), as being the primary "religious" and therapeutic impulse behind his involvement with literature as both reader and writer. It is an important early statement of the continuity in Handke's project as author.

> Often – mostly – it was a metaphoric feeling, whenever I had changed, or rather a feeling that I had entered another country and did not understand the language and looked at everything anew and things appeared totally new to me through the language because I always had to think about what this or that [thing] might be called. Above all, there were situations that were concerned with the future, that people previously would have termed religious. So then: a longing for a new system of connectedness for my own actions and for my own consciousness, something that I had lacked before then and from which I had suffered.... (Linder 34)

This restorative longing for a "system" of new connections is expressed by Handke in and through the fictional text, encountered in the processes of reading and writing, and ultimately in the act of generating metaphor and narrative, the creation (in the text) of a coherence that is perceived as being absent from real life.[32] All meaning and significance – in structuralist terms – is ultimately the product of comparison in the interplay of similarity and difference. Like Bloch after his traumatic break with reality, the peddler, in order to stabilize his disoriented consciousness through the activity of creating new sign systems, seems compelled to view objects as figurative messages, as metaphors, as "stories": "In each object he tries to read a story, the longest one possible" (*Ha* 131). The plot commentary that follows would seem to suggest that the peddler functions here as a writer (and one akin in method to the author Handke): "*In order to move the story along, he tries all possible kinds of sentences*" (*Ha* 131). The equation of both character and author as storytellers here is both ironic and a clue for the reader as to the secret hidden in the text.

The last section of the novel notes the reestablishment of the order of everyday reality in which the traumatic event has become history, vaguely remembered, and in its final embodiment, it is a game played by children: "The children are already playing [reenacting] the murder" (*Ha* 201). This last sentence appears to be deliberately ambiguous, suggesting both that the murder has been trivialized in/as the formulaic language of a game, and, alternatively, that it has become creative play. Reenacted as aesthetic event, the violent trauma has been sublimated and transformed (or "aufgehoben" as in *Die Hornissen*) into a fictional narrative, namely *Der Hausierer* itself. Handke's deconstruction of the murder mystery paradigm itself depicts in its ending the existential thrust of his writings: the therapeutic transformation of his own distressing feelings of terror and anxiety into creative text that serves as a grounding of an identity perceived anew.

---

[32]Gregor Keuschnig in *A Moment of True Feeling* also longs for a new "system" (*M* 10) for his consciousness and finds it in his magical perception of three random objects in a Paris park as a message. The conclusion of the novel suggests that, like the peddler and Joseph Bloch, Keuschnig too becomes a writer. For a discussion of Bloch as storyteller, see Barry ("Language").

Works Cited

Arnold, Heinz Ludwig. "Gespräch mit Peter Handke." *Text und Kritik* 24/24a. Ed. Heinz Ludwig Arnold. 3rd ed. Munich: edition text + kritik, 1976. 15-37.

Barry, Thomas F. "In Search of Lost Texts: Memory and the Existential Quest in Peter Handke's *Die Hornissen.*" *Seminar* 19.3 (1983) 192-214.

—. "Language, Self, and the Other in Peter Handke's *The Goalie's Anxiety at the Penalty Kick.*" *South Atlantic Review* 51.2 (1986) 93-105.

Barthes, Roland. *S/Z.* Trans. Richard Miller. New York: Farrar, Straus and Giroux, 1974.

Bartmann, Christoph. *Suche nach Zusammenhang. Handkes Werk als Prozeß.* Vienna: Braumüller, 1984.

Bloch, Peter André, and Alexander Jon Schneller. "Peter Handke." *Der Schriftsteller und sein Verhältnis zur Sprache, dargestellt am Problem der Tempuswahl: Eine Dokumentation zu Sprache und Literatur der Gegenwart.* Ed. Peter André Bloch. Bern, Munich: Francke, 1971. 170-78.

Bonn, Klaus. *Die Idee der Wiederholung in Peter Handkes Schriften.* Würzburg: Königshausen & Neumann, 1994.

Cooper, David E. *Existentialism.* Oxford: Basil Blackwell, 1990.

Coury, David. *The Return of Storytelling in Contemporary German Literature and Film – Peter Handke and Wim Wenders.* Lewiston, NY: Edwin Mellen Press, 2004.

Darby, David. "The Narrative Text as Palimpsest: Levels of Discourse in Peter Handke's *Die Hornissen.*" *Seminar* 23.3 (1987) 251-64.

DeMeritt, Linda C. *New Subjectivity and Prose Forms of Alienation: Peter Handke and Botho Strauss.* New York, Bern: Peter Lang, 1987.

Durzak, Manfred. *Peter Handke und die deutsche Gegenwartsliteratur. Narziß auf Abwegen.* Stuttgart: Kohlhammer, 1982.

—. "Für mich ist Literatur auch eine Lebenshaltung. Gespräch mit Peter Handke." *Gespräche über den Roman. Formbestimmungen und Analysen.* Frankfurt am Main: Suhrkamp, 1976. 314-43.

–. *Der deutsche Roman der Gegenwart.* Stuttgart: Kohlhammer, 1971.

Eifler, Margret. *Die subjektivistische Romanform seit ihren Anfängen in der Frühromantik. Ihre Existenzialität und Anti-Narrativik am Beispiel von Rilke, Benn und Handke.* Tübingen: Niemeyer, 1985.

Firda, Richard Arthur. *Peter Handke.* New York: Twayne, 1993.

Gabriel, Norbert. *Peter Handke und Österreich.* Bonn: Bouvier, 1983.

Göttsche, Dirk. *Die Produktivität der Sprachkrise in der modernen Prosa.* Hochschulschriften Literaturwissenschaft 84. Frankfurt am Main: Athenäum, 1987.

Hammer, Stephanie Barbe. "Just Like Eddie or As Far As a Boy Can Go: Vedder, Barthes, and Handke Dismember Mama." *Postmodern Culture* 6.1 (September 1995). Electronic Journal. http://www.iath.virginia.edu/pmc/textonly/issue.995/hammer.995.

Handke, Peter. "Ich bin ein Bewohner des Elfenbeinturms." *Ich bin ein Bewohner des Elfenbeinturms.* Frankfurt am Main: Suhrkamp, 1972. 19-28.

–. "Die Literatur ist romantisch." *Ich bin ein Bewohner des Elfenbeinturms.* Frankfurt am Main: Suhrkamp, 1972. 35-50.

–. "Über meinen neuen Roman *Der Hausierer.*" *Peter Handke.* Ed. Raimund Fellinger. Frankfurt am Main: Suhrkamp, 1985. 36-37.

–. "Zur Tagung der Gruppe 47 in den USA." *Ich bin ein Bewohner des Elfenbeinturms.* 29-34.

Haslinger, Adolf. *Peter Handke. Jugend eines Schriftstellers.* Salzburg, Vienna: Residenz, 1992.

Holzlinger, Alfred. "Peter Handkes literarische Anfänge in Graz." *Peter Handke.* Ed. Raimund Fellinger. Frankfurt am Main: Suhrkamp, 1985. 11-24.

Klinkowitz, Jerome, and James Knowlton. *Peter Handke and the Postmodern Transformation: The Goalie's Journey Home.* Columbia, MO: U of Missouri P, 1983.

Koepnick, Lutz. "Zwischen Avantgarde und postmodernem Antidetekivroman. Eine Revision von Peter Handkes *Der Hausierer.*" *VerLockerungen: Österreichische Avantgarde im 20. Jahrhundert.* Ed. Wendelin Schmidt-Dengler. Vienna: Edition Praesens, 1994. 95-127.

Linder, Christian. "Die Ausbeutung des Bewußtseins. Gespräch mit Peter Handke." *Schreiben und Leben. Gespräche mit Jürgen Becker, Peter Handke, Walter Kempowski, Wolfgang Koeppen, Dieter Wellershof.* Cologne: Kiepenheuer & Witsch, 1974. 32-45.

Linstead, Michael. *Outer World and Inner World. Socialization and Emancipation in the Works of Peter Handke, 1964-1981.* Frankfurt am Main: Peter Lang, 1988.

–. "Peter Handke." *After the "Death" of Literature. West German Writing of the 1970s.* Ed. Keith Bullivant. Oxford: Berg, 1989. 246-62.

Marschall, Christine. *Zum Problem der Wirklichkeit im Werk Peter Handkes. Untersuchungen mit Blick auf Rainer Maria Rilke.* Bern: Haupt, 1995.

Michel, Volker. *Verlustgeschichten. Peter Handkes Poetik der Erinnerung.* Würzburg: Königshausen & Neumann, 1998.

Mixner, Manfred. "Die alte Masse – Handkes Genauigkeit im Erzählen." *Aporie und Euphorie der Sprache. Studien zu Georg Trakl und Peter Handke.* Ed. Heidy M. Müller and Jaak De Vos. Leuven: Uitgeveru Peters, 1989. 149-61.

Nägele, Rainer, and Renate Voris. *Peter Handke.* Munich: Beck, 1978.

Nietzsche, Friedrich. "On Truth and Lie in an Extra-Moral Sense." *The Portable Nietzsche.* Trans. Walter Kaufmann. New York: Viking Press, 1954. 42-47.

Perram, Gavin. *Peter Handke. The Dynamics of the Poetics and the Early Narrative Prose.* Frankfurt am Main: Peter Lang, 1992.

Peter Handke. Ed. Gerhard Fuchs and Gerhard Melzer. Graz: Droschl, 1993.

Pütz, Peter. "Handke und Nietzsche: 'Kein Marterbild mehr malen.'" *Peter Handke.* Ed. Gerhard Fuchs and Gerhard Melzer. Graz: Droschl, 1993. 63-77.

Renner, Rolf Günter. *Peter Handke.* Stuttgart: Metzler, 1985.

Rorrison, Hugh. "The 'Grazer Gruppe,' Peter Handke and Wolfgang Bauer." *Modern Austrian Writing.* Ed. Alan Best and Hans Wolfschütz. London: Wolff, 1980. 252-66.

Rushkin, Esther. *Family Secrets and the Psychoanalysis of Narrative.* Princeton, NJ: Princeton UP, 1992.

Ryan, Simon. "New Directions in the Austrian Novel." Ed. Keith Bullivant. *The Modern German Novel.* Oxford: Berg, 1987. 36-56.

Schlueter, June. *The Plays and Novels of Peter Handke.* Pittsburgh, PA: U of Pittsburgh P, 1981. Contains "An Interview With Peter Handke." 163-77.

Sergooris, Gunther. *Peter Handke und die Sprache.* Abhandlungen zur Kunst-, Musik, und Literaturwissenschaft 270. Bonn: Bouvier, 1979.

Tabah, Mireille. *Vermittlung und Unmittelbarkeit. Die Eigenart von Peter Handkes fiktionalem Frühwerk (1966-1970).* Frankfurt am Main: Peter Lang, 1990.

Wellershoff, Irene. *Innen und Außen. Wahrnehmung und Vorstellung bei Alain Robbe-Grillet und Peter Handke.* Munich: Fink, 1980.

Wesche, Ulrich. "Fragment und Totalität bei Peter Handke." *German Quarterly* 62 (1989) 329-34.

Widrich, Hans. "*Die Hornissen* – auch ein Mosaik aus Unterkärnten." *Peter Handke.* Ed. Raimund Fellinger. Frankfurt am Main: Suhrkamp, 1985. 25-35.

Zeyringer, Klaus. *Innerlichkeit und Öffentlichkeit. Österreichische Literatur der achtziger Jahre.* Tübingen: Francke, 1992.

Place, Autonomy and the Individual: *Short Letter, Long Farewell* and *A Sorrow Beyond Dreams*

Robert Halsall

THE TWO NOVELS by Peter Handke which were published in Germany in 1972, *Der kurze Brief zum langen Abschied* (*Short Letter, Long Farewell*, 1974) and *Wunschloses Unglück* (*A Sorrow Beyond Dreams*, 1975), illustrate the importance of place in Handke's work from two very different perspectives: the former ends in an exaltation of America as the realization of the utopian dreams of its European narrator, the latter in a dystopian condemnation of the negative influence of his Austrian homeland on the life of the narrator's mother and its contribution to the events leading to her suicide.

The two novels have been seen by some critics as an illustration of two seemingly contradictory aspects of the author's poetics: the former a subjectivist future-oriented mythical projection, the latter a past-oriented striving for "authenticity" in the depiction of real events (Durzak 124). The contrasting interpretations of the narrative position, style, and the relationship between fiction and reality in the two novels illustrate divergent critical attitudes towards Handke and his writing. *Short Letter, Long Farewell*, and Handke's works of the 1970s in general, have in some respects received a more favorable reception in America than in German-speaking countries, principally because of the negative reaction of some German critics to his "inwardness" or "subjectivity" (Barry 107). On the other hand, the overwhelmingly positive reaction of many of the same German-speaking critics to *A Sorrow Beyond Dreams* stems from the fact than many saw in this novel a turning away from the inwardness of his earlier works towards a new realism, a Handke who, as one critic put it, had, in this work, "come to his senses" (Weber as quoted in Heintz 59).

Two central aspects of *Short Letter* are immediately introduced on the book's original German cover. The title alludes to the novel's apparent intertextual reference to detective fiction, in particular Raymond Chandler's *The Long Goodbye* (1953). This seems to be confirmed by the plot and subject matter: the narrator, an Austrian writer, has come to America to escape from a marital crisis. Soon after arriving in America, however, he receives a letter from his estranged wife, Judith, threatening him with death. His ensuing journey across America thus corresponds to the plot of a detective novel: a pursuit and counter-pursuit with the aim of carrying out a threat of murder typical of that genre. Although the conventions of detective fiction are employed in *Short Letter*, these function more as a quotation in the sense of an "appropriation and transformation of a set repertoire, whose attraction lies in playful quotation" (Krajenbrink 94). This playful intertextual reference to other genres, both literary and non-literary, of which there are many instances in the novel, is a key feature which has led critics to label the novel postmodern.

The presence of a map of America showing the journey of the narrator from east coast to west immediately suggests that America itself and the narrator's journey across it is not just a setting for the novel, but that this is a journey of confrontation with an idea which America represents for the narrator, and, through this, a confrontation with himself. This view of the role and significance of America is confirmed by Handke in an interview. America as depicted in *Short Letter*, rather than being a true, mimetic representation, is, according to Handke, "a pretext, the attempt to find a more distanced world, in which I can become more myself" (Karasek 87).

The America depicted on the cover is, in terms of the narrator's personal development, a "Versuchswelt" (Schlueter 94), an experimental world through which he can, during the course of his journey, overcome his feelings of alienation and, in Handke's terms, "become more himself." In Handke's work in general, place is of central importance for the inner development of the principal character. The significance of the motif of the journey – both geographically and in terms of inner development – is indicated by Handke's epigraph taken from Karl Philipp Moritz's novel *Anton Reiser* (1785; trans. 1997). While in *Anton Reiser* the tendency of the principal character "to confine the traveler's attention to the road he was going to travel," hence to subsume all his experiences of place under a pre-conceived ideal, prevents a real interaction with place, this same trait is apparent in the narrator of *Short Letter*.[1] Journeys such as the one depicted in *Short Letter* are particularly significant in Handke's works. The journey usually represents a process by means of which the subject, through putting himself into a strange environment, is able to develop an attentiveness to the outside world through perception of the places visited, and to transform these into an inner experience (Wefelmeyer 674; Bartmann 116). Particularly cities play an essential part in that process (Bartmann 126). This differentiates the significance of the journey in Handke's novels from that in Gerhard Roth's *Winterreise* (1978; trans. 1980), for example, as in the latter the protagonist carries the perceptions of his familiar world with him as projections onto the places encountered on the journey. In Handke's novel, it is not just the change of place but the attitude toward place, which undergoes a transformation during the journey (Melzer 382).

The American cities through which the narrator travels, particularly in the first part of the novel, are an apt illustration of this change in attitude. His journey starts in Providence. The opening description of Jefferson Street, which "circles round the business section, changes its name to Norwich Street in the South End, and leads into the old Boston Post Road" (*SL* 3), indicates a city seen by an outsider through a pre-conceived mental image, as if on a plan viewed from above. In a later passage, the description of the street layout of New York is once again crucial. A stranger in the city, the narrator feels disorientation, and, having set out one way, has to go back in the opposite direction (*SL* 25). This disturbing inability to orient himself in a strange environment is also an opportunity for him to see things anew, to gain a new perspective on reality (Nägele, "Welt" 394; "Amerika" 112). The experience of disorientation in the city here could be described as a dialectic of perception of detail and overall context. Because the narrator has lost the overall context (initially provided by his mental image of the city) through disorientation, he focuses obsessively on detail: "In unfamiliar surroundings … I tried to deceive my own sense of ignorance and inexperience

---

[1]At least this holds true for the early stages of the journey, but is overcome by the narrator in its course by means of his inner development (Kraus 175).

by dissecting the few activities within my reach as though speaking of momentous undertakings" (*SL* 26).

This disorientation brought about by place marks the first step in moving from a passive perception of environment to the "active deformation of reality" (Nägele, "Amerika" 113). Experiencing the city, particularly the unfamiliarity and anonymity of the American cities for the European narrator, is an essential part of this transformation. The beginning of this process is evident in a later scene, where the narrator is sitting in a restaurant in Central Park (*SL* 35-37). Here he is at a distance from the city – he is aware of the sounds of traffic and sirens outside the restaurant – and begins to become tired after his earlier frenzied exploration of the city streets. The phenomenon of tiredness alluded to here, to which Handke would later devote an entire essay, is a prerequisite of his overcoming of preconceptions and beginning to truly perceive the city around him: "As I sat motionless, something began to move back and forth in my head in a rhythm resembling that of my wanderings about New York that day" (*SL* 36).[2] The rhythm of the city, previously a strange, disorienting phenomenon, here becomes internalized – something he no longer resists but accepts: "It was only then that I saw inside me the city that up until then I had almost overlooked" (*SL* 36).[3]

This reduction of resistance to allow a full perception of place and the accompanying inner transformation can be seen as the principal significance of the journey motif in Handke's work. The process through which the subject suddenly frees himself from a predetermined categorization towards a free perception of the unfamiliar environment has been described as a "key, an open sesame experience of the unfamiliar environment" (Wefelmeyer 674). The New York restaurant scene is crucial for the narrator's inner development as a whole, as at the end, the city has become "a landscape that was open as far as the eye could see" (*SL* 37).

---

[2]The role of tiredness as a positive factor in Handke's poetic philosophy, that weakens the subject's prejudice (understood as the tendency to classify and judge places according to a pre-exisiting categorization) when confronted with a new environment is confirmed seventeen years later in *Versuch über die Müdigkeit* (1989; *Essay on Tiredness*, 1994).

[3]Bartmann argues that, for this reason, cities for Handke are "utopian, postmodern and timeless conceptualizations of space" (125).

The relationship between the city and nature is also notable in this novel and Handke's work as a whole. The removal of the threatening aspect of New York City means that "the compressed, still-rumbling city became for me a gentle panorama of nature" (*SL* 37). The narrator comes from the country, but does not identify with it; in fact he sees it as oppressive, something to be escaped from (*SL* 40). In this sense, the narrator of *Short Letter, Long Farewell* is the opposite of the hero of Gottfried Keller's *Der grüne Heinrich* (1854-55; *Green Henry*, 1960), the novel which he is reading on his journey and to whose protagonist he often compares himself. While Henry "found freedom in nature," the narrator finds it "hard to imagine that nature could free anyone from anything" (*SL* 40). Whereas for Henry the outside world, particularly nature, is a "place of release" (from inner alienation), for the narrator it is "an image of his own alienation" (Pakendorf 173). It would therefore be inappropriate to apply the model of inner development through the contemplation of nature in the literary models of Keller and Moritz to the narrator of *Short Letter* (Pakendorf 157). In fact, it can be argued that the binary opposites of city and nature which have dominated modernist literature from the Enlightenment through Romanticism are deconstructed in Handke's novel into a postmodern hybrid.

This modernist bipolarity of city and nature, in which everything lacking in the city is projected as a positive idyll onto nature, is rejected: "I detested stubble fields, fruit trees, and pastures, there was something repulsive about them" (*SL* 40). The narrator's repulsion stems from the fact that he was born into a rural environment, and the economic necessity of having to go "about in rubber boots, chasing pissing cows in the rain" (*SL* 40) is sufficient to destroy any idealistic view of nature. The landscape of his childhood provided him with no fantasy, no freedom: "in my nature days I could never do as I pleased" (*SL* 41). The city, on the other hand, is a free and open environment "where there were more forbidden things to be done" (*SL* 40).[4]

On the journey along Interstate 76 from Philadelphia to Pittsburgh the rural merges into the urban to a point where the two become indistinguishable. The pervasive industrialization of agricul-

---

[4]This non-idealist view is even more strongly emphasized in *A Sorrow Beyond Dreams* in the description of the mother's life in an Austrian village.

ture means that "every inch of the ground looked as if it had just been cultivated, there wasn't a living soul in the fields, which were impersonating unspoiled nature" (*SL* 59). There is, in other words, no real nature here, only an illusion or simulacrum.[5] Similarly, the urban phenomena of roads and cars dominate the rural landscape to such an extent that they become a postmodern nature: "the asphalt glittered peacefully; the cars drove slowly, no one did more than seventy" (*SL* 59). This deconstruction of the signifiers of the urban and the rural within the novel is part of a "postmodern aesthetic": nature in modernist terms is a place where signifiers are already classified into a system (*SL* 104; Klinkowitz and Knowlton 47). Cities, and American cities in particular, on the other hand, are "provisional," there to be interpreted, but "with every signification self-apparent" (Klinkowitz and Knowlton 47).

The postmodern aspect of America becomes manifest in that "signs are nothing but themselves" (Klinkowitz and Knowlton 46). This is reflected in the narrator's journeys through the urban and rural landscapes of America, for instance that to Philadelphia by train (*SL* 41-42). Here the images of gloomy urban desolation in the suburbs, with their garbage heaps, chimneys, and houses with boarded-up windows, are seen at a distance – to the narrator they do not signify any of the conditions of urban America – and are interpreted at the level of surface rather than depth.[6] There is virtually nothing to be seen in the American landscape. At one point the narrator takes photographs from the car window but discovers that his photos are mostly indistinguishable from each other. When he arrives in Indianapolis he states: "I didn't want to see the city. As though it had disappointed me in advance and I already had enough of it ..." (*SL* 77). In another, postmodern, sense, however, this emptiness and indistinguishability is full of meaning: the signs which the narrator sees on his journey serve to confirm themselves as part of the myth of America in which the narrator believes (Nägele, "Amerika" 114).

---

[5]Renner points out that there is no "unmediated relationship to nature" and that "civilization" (here the hybrid American landscape) can become a "second nature" (78).

[6]For a similar account of the postmodern aspects of the American landscape from a European perspective see Baudrillard (*America* 69-70, 95-99, 104-05).

America in *Short Letter* can also be identified as a postmodern myth in that it represents a challenge to linear thinking and rational individualism (Meurer 65). This challenge to rationalism is conveyed througth the depiction of a nature that bears archaic, totemic qualities (Meurer 66). The American landscape, in the words of the painter in St. Louis, "'had meaning only if something historical had happened in it. A giant oak tree in itself wasn't a picture: it became a picture only in association with something else, for instance, if the Mormons had camped under it on their way to the Great Salt Lake'" (*SL* 101; Meurer 67). In this sense the child Benedictine epitomizes the postmodern myth of America, for when she saw one of these pictures "she never thought of asking whether there was really such a scene ... because the copy had replaced the original forever" (SL 99).[7]

In order to understand the function of America as symbol in the novel, Bakhtin's notion of chronotope, the fusion of space and time in literary images can be employed, whereby time seems to be frozen and space takes on a kind of emotional coloring (Brüggemann 5-6). In *Short Letter*, the chronotope America figures as an ahistorical utopia in which "the unconnectedness of tangible things is transcended, where people and nature, present, past and future stand in a perceptible unity to each other" (Brüggemann 135). The significance of experiencing the landscape through the journey, then, is to awaken in the narrator the awareness of the possibility of the connectedness of his individual perceptions, together with images from film, popular culture and literature, in an overall utopian unity called 'America.'

That many of the images of America presented in the novel stem from clichéd and stereotypical notions, such as the historical scenes depicted on the curtains in the hotel room in Providence (*SL* 18), the images produced by the painter in St Louis (*SL* 99-101), and the epiphanic sensation caused by the Mississippi steamer (*SL* 102-3), has been interpreted as a deficiency of the novel: that the utopian myth consists of "highly idealized (and thus to some degree falsified) representations of American history" (Elstun 145). This ten-

---

[7]Baudrillard defines a "third order simulacrum," characteristic of postmodernity, as a state where the sign "bears no relation to reality whatever: it is its own pure simulacrum" ("Simulacra" 173).

dency towards cliché can be seen in terms of the therapeutic value of the images in the narrator's inner development, in particular the process of overcoming alienation (Elstun 146). On the other hand, it is also a symptom of the uncritical, apolitical intentions of the author himself, leading to the creation of a "false atmosphere of kitsch," especially in the final scene (Nägele, "Welt" 406; Nägele and Voris 54). Similarly, the kitsch-like nature of Handke's America can be attributed to the author's "overstating his case" in an attempt to distance himself from the dictates of an engaged European modernist literature, as in his critique of Group 47 in Princeton (Fickert 40).

A further, more plausible view, however, is that the connection between literature, film and popular culture evident in *Short Letter* is part of a more general questioning of the notion of heroism and the possibilities of identification with heroic figures in the literature of the 1970s (Burdorf 233-34). The identification of the narrator with the heroes of popular culture, such as those in John Ford's films, is a reaction against this loss. The risk of kitsch and artificiality in the deployment of images from popular culture is a risk which Handke is prepared to take to demonstrate that heroism, although not possible in the real world, is still possible, at least in fictional form, in the mythical world of American popular culture, through identification with the simplicity of the heroic film character (Burdorf 255).[8]

The crux of this debate, perhaps, is the degree to which critics of Handke's depiction of America are engaged in a misplaced criticism of the novel's apparent lack of realism from the point of view of a modernist rather than a postmodernist aesthetic. A key area in this respect is the extensive use of intertextual references to film at two levels. Firstly, there are the numerous literal references to films, in particular the films of John Ford, such as *Young Mr. Lincoln* (1939; *SL* 114-17). The narrator's fascination with sentimental Hollywood

---

[8]In the interview with Hellmuth Karasek, Handke addresses the criticism that, in pursuing these mythic images, he has ignored the present political reality of America, replying that his narrator strives not to use his perceptions of America as "pieces of circumstantial evidence" with which to construct a generalized condemnation of American society. Handke's defense is a familiar indirect criticism of 'engaged literature' and its tendency, in his view, to use details merely to confirm a prior ideological conviction of the author (Karasek 89-90).

films, which culminates in his pilgrimage to and conversation with
Ford, is once again a reflection of the rejection of the search for a
reality beneath the confusions of language which characterizes most
Austrian writing of the time (Kersten 156). This belief that the
superficial reality of the Hollywood film character is preferable to
the search for a deep interior life is borne out by the narrator's reactions to the characters in *Young Mr. Lincoln*: "The longer I watched,
the more eager I became to meet only people like those in the
picture; then I would never again have to pretend; like them I would
be fully present in body and mind" (*SL* 114).

The surface presence of popular culture, such as in the Hollywood film character, is contrasted with the depth of the figures of
European 'high' art, as in the conversation about the performance of
Schiller's drama *Don Carlos* (1787) in St. Louis. For Claire, the
voice which makes general statements about America and the
American way of life (Nägele, "Amerika" 113), American historical
figures, in contrast to those in Schiller's play, "haven't any biography, they're trademarks for what they did …, we're not interested in their lives" (*SL* 125). The dramaturge, in contrast, says of
Don Carlos, "Schiller isn't portraying historical figures but himself;
under their names, he acts out the adventures into which they
themselves put so little charm and dignity" (*SL* 125). The figures of
European drama are, in other words, metaphorical, and their surface
presentation stands for something else at a deeper level. American
characters, on the other hand, have predominantly metonymic
features: they refer simply to other signs at the surface level (Pakendorf 164).

The attraction of what, from a European modernist perspective,
may seem to be the predictability and lack of depth of popular
cultural genres such as the Hollywood film and detective fiction
used in the novel resides for Handke in the assumption that within
genres such as these the audience is aware of their fictionality: that
what they are seeing is a model and they thus know what to expect.
Handke's preference for the genre film as opposed to the European
art film confirms this: "a film … is already accepted as a model, in
which every viewer accepts and indeed expects as a norm that
everything depicted in the film is constructed" (Handke, "Proble-

me" 84; Kersten 162).[9] Popular culture in *Short Letter* fulfills a particular function for the narrator in that "he can confront feelings and circumstances, which in 'real life' he might dread, within the privileged, artificial world of the film viewer" (Kersten 155).

A second level of intertextual reference to film is Handke's tendency to use filmic techniques as a stylistic element. This is typified by Handke's preference for landscapes, moments and situations over past history of characters or development of story (Kersten 161). This can be traced not only in Handke's landscape depictions which are reminiscent of the cinematography of the road movie, but also in his illustration of epiphanic moments which have distinctive filmic qualities. The use of filmic elements is a metafictional technique, by which one fictional medium, film, comments on another, the literary narrative, the former calling the latter into question (Kersten 156).[10]

The prominence of chronotopic moments of stasis in which time stands still and space takes on a particular meaningfulness is epitomized in the novel's moments of epiphany (*SL* 17-18, 26-27, 78-79, 102-03), which not only fulfill a structural function but also mark decisive episodes in the narrator's inner development. The principal issue about these episodes which has dominated much of the discussion of Handke's text is their literary ancestry as such.[11] The question arises as to their phenomenological nature, and whether they have a progressive or retrogressive function within the narrative; whether they constitute an attempt by the narrator to escape from or in some way constitute a new reality.

Some critics have emphasized the mystical element of epiphanic experiences that constitute only a momentary escape from reality.

---

[9]Kersten (156) calls statements in which Handke seems to privilege commercial genre films above art films as a form of "inverted snobbery" in which he is attempting to distance himself from the pretensions of depth of some of his European contemporaries.

[10]Brüggemann also notes the influence of filmic elements in the novel, in particular in the development of the chronotope America. She sees the employment of filmic techniques as a means of "depicting the inner space of the text as a model for the external space, America ... an inwardly directed symbol of the attempt to make a perception of reality understandable as a narrative" (141).

[11] Durzak (115) locates the literary ancestry of these epiphanic episodes clearly in the tradition of literary modernism, orginating in Joyce.

The fleeting nature of this escape is compensated in that this feeling of mystical oneness with the world can be extended beyond the momentary in the projected utopia of the closing scene (Bartmann 135). Other critics similarly locate the relevance of these moments in relation to the utopia of a timeless, ahistorical dream of America as chronotope, the motif of the Golden Age realized at the end of the novel (Brüggemann 136).[12]

The first of these episodes, the dice-throwing in a bar in Providence, takes place as if in "a time other than the time in which I ordinarily lived and thought backward and forward" (*SL* 17). The dimension of time is fused in this state with the dimension of place, "places different from any present place, in which everything must have a different meaning than in my present consciousness" (*SL* 17), thus clearly indicating the closeness of the sensation to the definition of chronotope (Brüggemann 8). The nature of the first epiphany as a moment of sudden unity of inner feeling and outer perception (Frietsch 59) is accompanied by a feeling of inadequacy on the part of the narrator as regards his present life: "There had to be something more than the life I had been living up until now!" (*SL* 18).

A second epiphanic episode, in which the narrator observes two girls in a phone booth in New York, again points to a sudden unity of feeling and perception. Watching the girls' movements, he feels a "paradisiacal state of lightness, a state in which one has the desire to see, and in which to see is to know" (*SL* 27). While the first two episodes take place in a state of isolation and alienation for the narrator, the third occurs on his journey through America with Claire, and can be understood as part of a nascent process of inner development. The third epiphany accordingly indicates less a desire to escape the world than a symbolic desire for intersubjectivity. The narrator internalizes the rhythm of the tree swaying in the breeze

---

[12]Phenomenologically, Heintz sees the nature of these experiences as moments of new spontaneity, ahistorical and utopian in character, in which existing systems of meaning are suspended. These constitute a mystical "virginal" state, in which, having been rid of its preconceptions, the subject is in a state of receptivity to new impressions (123). Heintz questions the interpretation of the epiphanies as purely moments of mystical escape from the world, since the subject himself reflects on them, rejecting his own desire to escape from the world inherent in them (126-27; see also Marschall 47).

outside, increasingly identifying with the object to a degree of self-oblivion (*SL* 78). That this forgetting of the self here is more a state of receptivity to the world rather than escape is indicated by the "sense of will-less well-being" that he feels. His overcoming of his habitual categorizing of perception in the "feeling that I no longer offered resistance" leads to the realization that "I was superfluous" (*SL* 79). The initial significance of place on the journey through America has faded: "It no longer mattered to me where I was ..." (*SL* 79). Now that the feeling of well-being generated by the "will-less" perception of the object is theoretically possible in any place (thus pointing forward to its utopian quality), place is immaterial.

The third epiphany is immediately put in this developmental context by means of a conversation between the narrator and Claire regarding Keller's *Green Henry*. Claire criticizes him for his detachment from the world and categorization of emotions as being similar to that of the protagonist of *Green Henry*: "'He let experience pass before his eyes and never got involved'" (*SL* 80). The narrator agrees with her: "'When I see something and it enters into my experience, I think, yes, this is it. This is the new experience I needed!'" (*SL* 81). His disposition to recognize these inner processes as part of a preordained development is recognized by Claire as a prejudgment or categorization which prevents the narrator from really being present in his current environment. This epiphany is important in relation to the aims of Handke's poetics: that the poetic observation of the world (we must remember that the narrator is a writer) can only occur through letting something happen without intention rather than through an act of will (Marschall 49).[13]

---

[13]This utopian idea of the intentionless objective perception of the external world is likened by Kleist to a "value-neutral, positivistic view of the world" in which criticism is misplaced (99-100). Surely the equation of this tendency with positivism is itself misplaced. Although Handke's poetics certainly attempt to get to the objects themselves rather than our preconceived notions of them, this does not imply a dismissal of metaphysics, as positivism does. In fact, the epiphanic experiences arguably often constitute a metaphysical imbuement of everyday objects. The reluctance to judge implicit in this, which, according to Kleist, ultimately results in "indifference" where nothing matters (102), could rather be seen as more a case of letting the objects speak through a breaking down of the concepts which surround them and which prevent them from impacting on us in a poetic way.

In the subsequent reflections on his epiphanies and their significance, the narrator rejects the temptation inherent in them to enter
"another world that I only had to enter to be rid at last of my fear-
ridden nature and its limitations," as he now perceives this as an
"empty world" (*SL* 84).[14] The desire to escape to a place where
there would be no limitations is now replaced by the desire to fit
experiences "into an order and mode of life that would do me
justice and enable others to do me justice" (*SL* 84).

The epiphanies in *Short Letter* are concerned with finding "an
order and mode of life" which does not involve the extremes of
fear-dominated alienation, on the one hand, which has dominated
his life up to now, or the escape into a timeless, placeless world
envisioned in the first epiphany, on the other. What we see here is
evidence of "the art of living in the everyday" (Barth 55), in which
the subject can maintain his autonomy without either withdrawing
from the world or being totally determined by it. In Handke's works
of the early 1970s we see the beginning of a theme which dominates
his later works (Barth 55), culminating in *The Weight of the World*
and later in the essay *Versuch über den geglückten Tag* (1991;
Essay on the Successful Day, 1994). The narrator is aware of the
need to find "a form of life of one's own" (Winkelmann 145), a
form of autonomy between alienation and the emptiness of withdrawal from the world. In this interpretation, the epiphanies would
constitute an "ecstatic feeling of being outside oneself" (Winkelmann 139), which creates a counterbalance to his self-obsession and
forms part of his development towards the desired goal of harmony
with the outside world.

The fourth epiphany is somewhat different: While the actual
place is specified in greater descriptive detail, the epiphany is dominated by the idea of place as presented in film and popular American culture, and thus its mythical quality. The narrator is aware of
both aspects of this – on the one hand, the poetic qualities of the

---

[14]Marschall (48) argues that the narrator's criticism of his own desire to escape
from the world is called into question by the novel's conclusion which recalls
many of the epiphanic qualities of the earlier scenes, including the desire to
return to an "other time." This motif also recurs in later works, such as *Die
Stunde der wahren Empfindung* (1975; *A Moment of True Feeling*, 1977) and
Das Gewicht der Welt (1977; *The Weight of the World*, 1984), albeit in
different guises.

image, on the other, the prosaic reality, namely that this is simply a tourist trap full of tourists "holding beer cans, Coca-Cola bottles, and bags of popcorn" (*SL* 102). The theatricality of the scene, "in which the things around me ceased to be unrelated, and people and landscape, the living and the dead, took their places in a single painful and theatrical revelation of history" (*SL* 102), overrides the awareness of its artificiality.

What differentiates this epiphany from the others is that the distinction between surface and depth, kitsch and the genuine, between myth and reality, has been deconstructed by the narrator's cumulative impressions of America, a mythical America by means of which "people, things, landscapes are put into a certain order, brought into unity" (Frietsch 77). While in the first two epiphanies the sought after "place beyond place" or "time beyond time" existed in an abstract realm, here the mythical corresponds with an actual place, albeit a place whose very artificiality might appear to be the incarnation of the desire to escape from reality. The epiphanic experiences in the novel, then, are not just and not primarily mystical moments of escape but part of the narrator's realization that fantasy and reality are inescapably interrelated (Renner 84). The utopian qualities of this intermixing of reality and fantasy in the fourth epiphany are carried forward into the final scene of the novel.

The relationship between the narrator and the two principal female characters, his estranged wife Judith and the woman who forms a counterbalance to this relationship, Claire, is the central character relationship of the novel.[15] Psychoanalytic readings of the novel concentrate on the threat of Judith's sexuality on the narrator's enclosed world, as shown in the focus of their relationship on external objects rather than on feelings (Fulde 157). The narrator remembers that Judith had "no sense of time," relationship to money, or sense of direction, while he himself is almost obsessed

---

[15]This relationship has been analyzed in psychoanalytic terms as the narrator's "narcissistic attempt to come to terms with being left" by his wife (Fulde 154). Her pursuit of him, while on the one hand provoking serious psychological reactions on his part, is, on the other, like "a game between two people who are angry with each other, but can't quite give each other up" (Fulde 155). This is perhaps partly due to the nature of the playful intertextual references to the detective novel referred to above, partly to the strange nature of their previous relationship as recounted by the narrator.

with time: "I went to the phone almost every hour to find out what time it was" (*SL* 12). This can be interpreted in terms of a male/female dichotomy, in which the "sense of order" of the man is upset by the "sensuous and bodily" nature of the female (Fulde 158). Thus, the threat Judith's reappearance in America represents for the narrator is a fear of his own sexuality.

If his failed relationship with Judith represents an unacknowl-edged admission of fear of his own sexuality, then the narrator's re-lationship with Claire represents the opposite pole to this, where the woman is "de-personalized, robbed of her subjectivity," and be-haves "according to his needs" (Fulde 161, 163). Claire satisfies the narrator's narcissistic sexual needs in that "she never talked about herself, and it never occurred to me that there could be anything to say to her" (*SL* 47), so that he is then comfortable talking about himself. Claire also takes on a confessional role: because he does not feel threatened by her sexuality he can confess the inadequacies of his earlier life with Judith (*SL* 105-11), and she can take on a role in his inner development through her analysis of his desire to live his life according to the scheme of a *Bildungsroman*, a novel of identity formation or developmental novel. Similarly, the couple with whom Claire and the narrator stay in St. Louis functions within this framework to confirm the problems with his earlier relationship with Judith. Their obsession with objects organized into a perfect system contrasts with the freedom he finds in the uncommitted relationship with Claire (*SL* 97; Schlueter 101).[16]

The problem of the narrator's autonomy in relation to this pro-cess of development raises the fundamental question whether the novel should primarily be seen as a *Bildungsroman* in the line of the classical German model. This sometimes sterile debate, which has occupied critics of the novel at length, takes its origin in the clear intertextual references to Moritz's *Anton Reiser*, Keller's *Green*

---

[16]Fulde sees the polarity in the narrator's own sexuality and projections of the female in the two figures Judith and Claire as an illustration of a deeper prob-lem in Handke's work in general and his use of language in particular. She rightly points to a problem which brings us to the heart of the process of inner development in the novel: that the protagonist conceives his autonomy in terms of a dilemma of complete inwardness, on the one hand, and a total surrendering to the outside world (heteronomy), on the other. Sexuality constitutes a major aspect of this.

Henry and Fitzgerald's *Great Gatsby* (1925), the first two of which fit into the classical genre.[17] The three constitutive elements traditionally ascribed to the *Bildungsroman* can be identified as the experience of nature, the motif of the theatre, and the "developmental conversation," in which the central character is involved in a conversation with a formative character who changes his view of the world (Elm 354). While some evidence of these three elements can be found in *Short Letter*, the form in which they occur differentiates the novel from the traditional genre. As previously noted, nature does not fulfill its traditional formative role (Elm 356), because of the narrator's own rural background and his aversion to nature and because the binary opposition of nature and civilization has been deconstructed in the postmodern American setting of the novel.

Theater has a place in the novel in the performance and discussion of *Don Carlos*, but the theatrical spectacle here has a function opposite to that in the *Bildungsroman* – the narrator wants to escape the role-playing of the stage and prefers the metonymic surface of American film characters to the metaphoric depth of stage characters (Elm 362). The novel does contain a "developmental conversation," in the form of the conversation with John Ford at the end of the novel, but although Ford assumes the role of the "wise old man" giving advice as in the traditional model (Elm 367), there is neither direct nor implicit didacticism, nor apparent Enlightenment ideal of harmonization.[18]

More fruitful than debating whether the novel fits a specific literary genre is perhaps the question whether the protagonist progresses toward Handke's ideal state of autonomy and what this state is. As the narrator's reading of the literary models of the *Bildungsroman* demonstrates, development "as portrayed in these models" is not possible for him. What is still possible, however, is development abstracted from its concrete literary representation (which is pre-

---

[17]The focus of this debate has been Handke's remark that what he had wanted to portray in the novel was "the fiction of a developmental novel ... that one could gradually develop in such a way [as portrayed in such novels]" (Karasek 88).

[18]The lack of concreteness of a utopian ideal propagated by John Ford at the end of the novel leads Elm to categorize it more as a "socially-conscious contemporary novel" than a *Bildungsroman* (372).

sumably what Handke meant in his comment). The narrator's reading of the novels is something which he is less and less able to
apply directly to his life, but his very freeing himself from this
inclination seems to open himself to possibilities of development in
relation to the world which he inhabits.[19] His reading of the *Bildungsroman*, then, is a dialectical process: the recognition of the
need for a fictional model of development, only to realize the necessity of distancing himself from the model presented (Nägele and
Voris 54). The importance of the *Bildungsroman* lies not at the level
of content, but at a metafictional level: it constitutes a possible
narrative to which the novel makes intertextual reference to show
the necessity of the construction of such a narrative in the narrator's
own life (Pakendorf 170). This acceptance of the necessity of finding a way of narrating one's life is only realized at the end when
John Ford asks Judith (who, significantly, takes over the narrating
role in this scene, thus making the story which has been related just
as much their story as his): "Is that all true … None of it's made
up?," and she replies: "No, … it all happened" (*SL* 167).[20]

The nature of the final scene itself has called forth various interpretations. The figure of John Ford is highly stylized and aptly described as a "dying Messiah" to whom the relationship of the narrat-
or and Judith is that of disciples (Burdorf 255). The pedagogical
role of Ford consists of opposing the European concept of the
egotistical self with the American concept of "we." America, as
represented here, then, is the realization of the intersubjective utopia
envisaged by the narrator in the Mississippi steamer epiphany, "the
experience of a unity of people, nature, present, past and future"

---

[19]Heintz rightly points to the parallels here with *A Sorrow Beyond Dreams*,
where the narrator's mother, on being recommended books by her son as part
of his role in her "character formation," finds she cannot apply what she has
learned from them directly in her life (118). The mother's failure, at least as
attributed to her by the narrator-son, mirrors the narrator's attempt in *Short
Letter* to live purely according to a literary model. Nägele speaks in this respect
of a "misunderstanding" of the *Bildungsroman* by the narrator, which is "consistent with his character," namely that he sees self-development as only taking
place at the risk of loss of self ("Welt" 404).
[20]Durzak (108) interprets Judith's reply as indicating the "moral truth" of the
depicted events and thus equivalent in function to the narrator's claims in *A
Sorrow Beyond Dreams* of authenticity in the act of writing.

(Brüggemann 135). This is amplified by the description of the landscape of Bel Air, Los Angeles, which, Ford says, gives him "a feeling of eternity" that lets him forget "that there's such a thing as history" (*SL* 162). The landscape description has clear epiphanic or chronotopic elements which place it in the line of development of the previous epiphanic moments in the novel.

Once again, although this landscape might appear to be an idyllic idealization of pure nature at the expense of civilization, Ford is aware of its artificiality. When Judith points out that the orange trees which Ford has just described as if an idyll of nature are in fact planted, he replies that "[w]hen the sun shines through and plays in the leaves, I forget that" (*SL* 162). The utopian landscape depicted, as it were, as the myth of America in general, might be a fiction, a utopia without any definite content (Elm 371-72), but it is one which is aware of its own fictionality and artificiality.[21] This is further emphasized by the fact that Ford talks about his own stories, his films, as if they were true: "Nothing is made up.... It all really happened" (*SL* 165). What counts, and this could be a motto for Handke's novel, is that the story is told and that its narrator testifies to its possibility, whether unrealistic utopia or not.

*

If America in *Short Letter, Long Farewell* represents for Handke a utopia, a place where possibilities of the future are opened up for the individual, then the setting for *A Sorrow Beyond Dreams*, the Austrian rural environment of Carinthia, from which Handke himself originates, could almost be said to be its equivalent dystopia. This is a place where no such possibilities of individuality and freedom exist, where the environment determines the life chances of the individual to such an extent that there is seemingly no possibility of escape. Where physical escape is not possible, escape by suicide, as in the case of the narrator's mother, presents itself as the only alternative. Austria as dystopia is, although in the background, of relevance in *Short Letter*, where the narrator's Austrian background served a geographical correlate for the "poverty of experience and

---

[21]This surely invalidates the criticism that the utopia presented by Handke is artificial because it is "an esoteric rather than a practical experience" (Fickert 40), as it would certainly not be part of Handke's view of the task of literature to present such a practical utopia.

isolation" of his childhood (Gabriel 61).[22] The geographical and mental distance of the narrator of *Short Letter* from his homeland makes it easier for him to deal with its negative effects (Gabriel 63). In *A Sorrow Beyond Dreams*, the narrator has to confront his past and the constellation of adjoining problems in a much more direct way through the death of his mother.[23]

The narrator's unresolved mental conflict regarding his homeland is reflected in his depiction of his mother's life, which is characterized by a "deterministic pathos" (Mecklenburg 110). He projects his negative feelings toward Austria onto his mother in that she is allowed no possibility of autonomy given the overwhelming determining influence of the place of her birth. Handke's portrayal of these determining circumstances in his account of her life, it has been argued, is thus characterized by "abstractness" and a failure to question underlying social and historical realities dialectically (Mecklenburg 119-20). Although the basis of this critique might be that Handke has not in fact written the social realist novel he seems to have set out to write given his choice of subject matter (and that although it appears that the narrator wishes to examine his own background through that of his mother he has not in fact done so), it does point to the importance of the relationship in the novel between individual autonomy, social circumstances and place.

The determinism of place is introduced in the first sentence of the mother's life story: "Well then, it began with my mother being born more than fifty years ago in the same village where she died" (*SBD* 6). Although she has intermittently lived away from the village, the circumstances into which she was born have accompa-

---

[22]It should be noted that Handke, in common with a succession of postwar Austrian writers such as Thomas Bernhard and Gerhard Roth, is seeking a dialogue not just with Austria as a geographical location but with its history and the inability of present-day Austria to come to terms with it. However, Handke deals with this in a much less polemical and overtly political fashion than the latter two writers.

[23]The narrator's rural Austrian childhood and the biography of his mother has been placed in the context of the wider literary phenomenon of "province" or "regionalism" (Mecklenburg 105), the tendency of postwar writers from the provinces of Austria to exhibit their ambivalent feelings towards their homeland. In Handke's work as a whole, Mecklenburg (106, 108) argues, one can detect feelings which oscillate between abuse and insult on the one hand and an idealized affirmation on the other.

nied her and ultimately brought her back to the same place in which she will die. Handke's explanation of this determinism given three pages later places the reasons for this primarily in her position as a woman: "For a woman to be born into such surroundings was in itself deadly. But perhaps there was one comfort: no need to worry about the future.... No possibilities, it was all settled in advance" (*SBD* 9-10). Handke is attributing the reasons for the determinism to the social position of women, and appends an almost sociological examination of gender roles in rural Austrian society.[24] That the predetermined nature of social roles is apparently the main element of this determinism is further emphasized by the children's game "based on the stations in a woman's life: Tired/Exhausted/Sick/Dying/Dead" (*SBD* 10).

This apparent new-found realism of *Sorrow* has led some commentators to see Handke's project as almost a form of historical/ social documentation of the role of women, which would fit ill with the writer's previously avowed dislike for "engaged" writing (*BE* 35-50). Handke had finally "come to his senses," one critic claimed (Heintz 59). The realism adopted in *Sorrow*, however, is different from Lukácsian realism. Although Handke uses the requisites of everyday life to portray the circumstances of the mother's life, he describes these using a strategy of "linguistic defamiliarization" (Miles 377) – for example by capitalizing adjectives which, while giving us access to the mother's mind and the stereotypes which determine it in a realistic mode, at the same time show the narrator's distance from these modes of thinking, resulting in a "systematic dis-illusionment" of the reader (Miles 377).

Although the social milieu figures significantly in Handke's depiction of his mother's life, place itself and the form of life which is possible in it has an equally important part in this determinism. The principal element is what could be called a metaphysics of place. This becomes evident in the depiction of the passage of time in the village, which

---

[24]Wigmore, for instance, argues: "Although Handke's account of his mother's life cannot be regarded as a direct product of the women's movement, it was nevertheless largely in tune with the attitudes which developed out of the new-found interest in women's lives and women's history then emerging in feminist circles in western Europe" (9).

was marked by church festivals, slaps in the face for secret visits
to the dance hall, fits of envy directed against her brothers, and
the pleasure of singing in the choir. Everything else that happened in the world was a mystery; no newspapers were read
except the Sunday bulletin of the diocese, and then only the
serial. (*SBD* 10-11)

Desires and feelings have to adapt to the place, its rhythms, its lack
of activity and isolation (what Mecklenburg calls "provincialism").
Handke emphasizes this by his description of how, in this environment, one's inner character becomes a mirror of the outside world:

> Rain–sun; outside–inside: feminine feelings were very much de-
> pendent on the weather, because "outside" was seldom allowed
> to mean anything but the yard and "inside" was invariably the
> house, without a room of one's own....

> No possibility of comparison with a different way of life:
> richer? less hemmed in? (*SBD* 11)

Clearly, this is reminiscent of the same determinism of place which
characterized the memories of the Austrian childhood of the narrator of *Short Letter*: a dystopia in which nature has no idyllic qualities, forcing the subject to adapt to it. The full force of this determinism is implicit in the novel's German title: the environment forces
the individual to suppress desires and wishes in order to fit in.

That these reflections on place are colored by the consciousness
of a narrative voice which itself has escaped this environment is
evident despite the analytic nature of the description of the mother's
life. The point of view of the outsider is one which the mother is
also potentially able to adopt, at least temporarily, as she moves
from the rural environment to the town, once to a provincial city
and later to postwar Berlin. The city brings with it the possibility of
autonomy, of life as an individual: "In the city my mother had
thought she had found a way of life that more or less suited her, that
at least made her feel good" (*SBD* 20). Beginning to think as an
autonomous individual in the city, however, is something which
cannot be taken with her when she returns to the village: "In this
rural, Catholic environment, any suggestion that a woman might
have a life of her own was an impertinence: disapproving looks,
until shame, at first acted out in fun, became real and frightened
away the most elementary feelings" (*SBD* 20).

Life in Berlin, although affected by the difficulties of life in the
aftermath of the war, still gives her the freedom to find an identity

denied in her home environment. Her rural background, however, sets her apart from other city dwellers. Her desire to find an identity in the city leads her, instead of becoming a true autonomous individual, "to become, not a different person, but a TYPE: to change ... from a country bumpkin to a city person.... In thus becoming a type, she felt freed from her own history" (*SBD* 25-26). Although, in the narrator's view, she may have been deceiving herself regarding the freedom she had in Berlin, when she returns to her native environment, she nevertheless brings with her certain characteristics of the city dweller: "She no longer took any nonsense from anyone. In the old days her only reaction had been a bit of back talk; now she laughed" (*SBD* 32). On the one hand, her sojourn in the city now sets her apart from the others in the village; on the other, the new-found autonomy makes it doubly difficult for her to obey the dictates of conformity which she was able to accept more readily before her period away.

Handke's depiction of the possibility of development in his mother's life reflects his desire to maintain, in the face of all the pessimistic realism of his deterministic portrayal of her circumstances, the possibility of autonomy. Clearly, Handke does not wish to contribute to the genre of the *Mutterroman* (maternal novel) in which the mother's life is totally determined by external conditions, and which, as the narrator describes it in one of the passages of self-reflection, becomes a "literary ritual in which an individual life ceases to be anything more than a pretext" (*SBD* 28).[25]

The key factor in Handke's portrayal of his mother's life vis-à-vis autonomy and individuality seems to be the question, subject to extensive reflections within the text, of *how* to portray the life of an

---

[25]Wieshahn attempts to classify Handke's novel into this very category, comparing it unfavorably with other entries of the genre, on the basis that the mother's "self-realization is difficult, if not impossible to reconcile with serving others" (41). Handke's attachment to a model of individual autonomy which cannot be reconciled with a role-based relationship to others, then, means that the only assertion of individuality possible is through suicide, which is seen positively by Handke (Wieshahn 49). Wieshahn attributes this aspect of the mother/son relationship to "bias in gender socialization" (48). Handke, in other words, as her son, cannot see that his mother's life, despite its restrictions, might have been worth living because of her role as a mother and through her relationships with others.

individual. The mother, despite being almost totally determined by external circumstances, is still an individual, not just, as Handke puts it in his criticism of Karin Struck's *Die Mutter* (1975; The Mother) "a person cheated out of their life by their being allotted a role" (Handke quoted by Bohn 147). A work of literature which just aimed to show that social determinism is solely responsible for the tragedy would just be a confirmation of what the reader already knew and therefore would be, in Handke's view, "without poetry" (Handke quoted by Bohn 147). What differentiates *A Sorrow Beyond Dreams* from a *Mutterroman* is that, all determinism aside, the author wants to depict his mother as an individual whose life is a potential poetic subject, and thus maintain the autonomy of the work of literature. However, in order to justify the use of the biography and death of his own mother as an *aesthetic* subject in this way, the narrator must reflect on the *ethical* validity of his own writing, and these reflections form an integral part of the novel.

A further controversial element of Handke's portrayal of his mother's life is the link between her self-realization and the Nazi period when individual freedom was suppressed. It is Handke's implication, it has been argued, that fascism contained emancipatory elements in that it freed women such as Maria Handke from the confines of the life they had lived before (Schindler 41). The question is whether the correspondence of the mother's new freedom with this chapter in Austria's history is merely a coincidence or a "causal relationship" (Schindler 45). Handke portrays his mother as someone who "went along [with fascism] opportunistically" (Schindler 48) rather than someone who understood anything about the political significance of the events. What may appear on the surface to be a favorable portrayal of aspects of fascism could, when viewed in terms of the novel's strategy of "systematic disillusionment," in fact be read as a condemnation of the conditioning of the masses in pre-fascist rural Austria, which made people like Maria Handke susceptible to its attractions. For she has no conception of herself as an individual before fascism: "That period helped my mother to come out of her shell and become independent" (*SBD* 15). Still, this does not mean that fascism had positive aspects, but that, given the poverty of her existence until then, even this time, at least at the level of her individual story, constituted a certain period of independence in comparison to what went before and what was to come after.

This leads to the question of the relationship between the individual and history in general in the novel. As stated above, Handke does not wish the portrayal of his mother to be reduced to nothing but a "pretext." The relationship between history and individual story, then, is one in which the individual life (or lack of it) is paramount, and the latter cannot just be deduced from the movements of history. *A Sorrow Beyond Dreams* shows "a strong aversion against the conception of the individual as a historically determined entity" (Schmidt-Dengler 260). Despite the apparent determinism of historical circumstances there is always some element of potential autonomy in the depiction of the mother's life. This writing of "individual history against general history" (Schmidt-Dengler 262) does not mean a denial of history, but an assertion of individual autonomy despite overwhelming historical circumstances. Handke's intention in this respect has been termed a "post-ideological aesthetics," the desire not to analyze and explain in terms of ideological categories (as, in Handke's critique, an engaged literature might attempt to do), but to write "from the point of view of a silent and excluded minority." The novel should therefore not be seen as an "escapist withdrawal from society's needs," but rather as an "attempt to personalize societal suffering," despite the lack of a language in which this can be expressed (Konzett 47).

The period of fascism and the depiction of the mother either as a passive "fellow traveler" or active participant illustrates the more general theme of the antithesis of conformity and rebellion which determines the structure of the mother's life (Stoffel 43, 51). This antithesis ultimately results in the possible interpretation of her suicide as either an act of conformity or a final expression of her individuality, or both. A crucial passage in this respect is the description of the preparations for her suicide (*SBD* 61-63), a "voyeuristic" scene in which Handke spares no details from the reader (Paver 469). The methodical nature of her preparations, writing letters to husband and son, her journey to the town to get the supply of sleeping pills, putting on clothing to ensure that her suicide does not cause an unnecessary mess, could be interpreted as "an act of cruelty," an "act of compassion and love," or "an act of protest" (Paver 469). The degree of authenticity in representing the body of the mother in this scene and the following one in which the son is present at the deathwatch before her funeral (*SBD* 64-65) exposes her to the "gaze of his readership" (Paver 468), once again posing the ethical question as to the justification of Handke's aestheticization of his mother.

The central narratological problem of the novel focuses on the reconciliation of the individual (the dignity of the mother) and the general (depicting this in a way the readership will find interesting) (Bohn 144). The narrator's desire for authenticity illustrates this from the outset: to relate the truth regarding his mother's life, notwithstanding the pain this might cause her son in relating it. This desire for truth is expressed in a continual debate about the ethics of writing itself and the adequacy of language to express this truth.[26] The "crisis of language" in this novel differs in nature from that in Handke's earlier work, in that linguistic skepticism is not employed here as a formal quality of innovation, but as part of the drive for authenticity (Göttsche 279-80). The narrator's reflections on the legitimacy of his language are directed towards the readers – to convince them of the authenticity of the narrator's search for truth.

Another interpretation of these reflections is that their function is primarily therapeutic. They are the narrator's way of coming to terms with his own grief and speechlessness on hearing the news of his mother's suicide (*SBD* 3; cf. Sergooris 66). The opening reflections confirm the therapeutic function Handke ascribes to literature in that they show him writing in the face of overwhelming grief. On the one hand, he has doubts about the communicability of these experiences: "I need the feeling that what I am going through is incomprehensible and incommunicable; only then can the horror seem meaningful and real" (*SBD* 4). On the other, he has a heroic determination to detach himself from this grief and narrate the events: "Now that I've begun to write, these states seem to have dwindled and passed because I try to describe them as accurately as possible" (*SBD* 5). The use of the word "accurately" (*genau*) here is significant in describing this heroic attempt, because at the end of

---

[26]The general narratological problem raised here, that of truth-telling in ethical narratives, that is narratives seemingly motivated by a strong confessional desire to tell an ethical truth, has been the subject of theoretical reflection by theorists in the deconstructive tradition (see De Man and Miller).

the novel, using the same word, the narrator admits that this attempt has failed, deferring the delivery of the truth which his ethical narrative promised at the beginning: "Someday I shall write about all this in greater detail" (*SBD* 70).[27] The opening self-justification of writing, and what is ultimately an aestheticization of his mother's life contains, then, all the elements of an ethical struggle to deliver the truth.

The narrator's apparent heroic stance in attempting to communicate his grief despite his doubts about the ability of language to do so points to the identity between authorial self and narrator, a premise widely accepted in the secondary literature.[28] Taking the narrator's words as representative of the author's own reduces the novel to a case study of the son and his own inability to overcome the difficulties in his relationship with his mother, rather than making it a case study of the mother herself.[29] In contrast to a reading of *Sorrow* as a therapeutic narrative, the narrator's will to truth and objectivity indicates, rather than evidence of being emotionally affected by the death of the mother, "an immense distance between author and narrator" (Mauser 88).

Strong evidence for this reading is the narrator's professed modesty in describing his mother's life. He feels qualified to write about her, not because he identifies emotionally with her plight, but simply because "I think I know more about her than any outside investigator who might, with the help of a religious, psychological, or sociological guide to the interpretation of dreams, arrive at a

---

[27]The translation renders "Genaueres" (*WU* 105) as "in greater detail," though "more accurately" would convey more forcefully the narrator's failure to meet his own intentions in terms of relating ethical truth. Bohn (162) also highlights the "exactness" or "accuracy" which the text seeks.

[28]For example by Kreyenberg and Lipjes-Türr (125). A notable exception is Mauser, who points out that if we accept this simple equivalence, "the first-person narrator is understood as a figure who acts as a representative of the author in recalling a mother-son relationship burdened by problems" (88).

[29]Love's interpretation in particular focuses on the question of the narrator's identification with his mother. Love reads the scene in which the mother is looking at the son from her bed as if he "were her BROKEN HEART" (*SBD* 52) as "a moment of exception" to the general rule that his attempt to identify with her ultimately fails (143). Rey, on the other hand, sees the identification of the mother with the son implicit in this scene as evidence that he is "the only person who understands her" (294).

facile explanation of this interesting case of suicide" (*SBD* 5). The irony of the distancing here sets the tone for what follows – a continual movement between the emotional identification necessary to understand her as a human being and the autonomy deemed necessary to fulfill the demands of objectivity as a writer. This fluctuation is reflected throughout the novel in the use of "man" (literally "one" in English, usually rendered in translation by impersonal or passive constructions) on the one hand and "she" on the other (Rey 299). The impersonal "man" is used to depict the norms and rituals of the provincial society from the distance of an "outsider" (Rey 299). The latter part of the story, in which the mother's increasing awareness of herself as an individual is accompanied by despair that those around her, with the exception of her son, do not understand this, is accompanied by a move from the impersonal pronoun to the personal "sie."

There is a third level of distancing and identification which refers to a "common ground" not based on "social norm," but on "something common to all human beings" (Rey 300), as expressed in the narrator's reflections on the pain of the mother's death at the beginning of the novel. When others express their sympathy at his grief, he says: "I would turn away or cut the sympathizer short, because I need the feeling that what I am going through is incomprehensible and incommunicable" (*SBD* 4). In the English translation, the impersonal and distancing "man" of the original German has been replaced with the personal pronoun 'I' for stylistic reasons. By using "man" rather than "ich," the narrator can imply two things: on the one hand, he is able to express a very personal feeling of the incomprehensibility and incommunicability of grief and the inadequacy of others' expressions of sympathy. On the other hand, as everyone would, in their own case, feel that same incommunicable grief, that grief becomes paradoxically communicable. The narrator must thus assert his autonomy and distance from other human beings (including the reader) in order to reconnect with them at the end of the novel.

Ultimately, the reader is faced with a contradiction in relation to language at the very heart of the novel: the experience which the narrator wants to communicate is defined from the outset as incommunicable; language, the only vehicle by which this feeling can be communicated, is defined as inadequate to the task. This paradox expresses itself at the end, where the narrator has to admit failure[30]: "It is not true that writing has helped me.... Writing has not, as I first supposed, been a remembering of a concluded period in my life, but a constant pretense at remembering, in the form of sentences that only lay claim to detachment" (*SBD* 66). The realization that the "process of postponement" of the truth which the end represents is not just a failed or postponed therapeutic "work of mourning" but a realization that writing itself necessarily represents a process of deferral: that the inability to capture the truth is in fact the basis of writing as such (Renner 86). This opens up the possibility of a deconstructionist reading, in which the essence of the act of writing and its relationship to the truth is foregrounded. The nature of writing, according to Derrida, is *différance*: "The sign is conceivable only on the basis of the presence that it defers and (is) moving toward the deferred presence that it aims to re-approriate" ("Différance" 61). By its nature, writing cannot fully capture the presence or logos of the phenomena being described, it can only differ from and defer this presence (both meanings are present in Derrida's French term). This inability to capture presence, however, has for Derrida a positive aspect: it is the very reason for writing itself.

In *A Sorrow Beyond Dreams*, one can argue that what the narrator is trying to capture in writing is the "presence" of his mother, a presence which is defined from the outset as incommunicable in

---

[30]Critics have interpreted this apparent failure of the project of writing defined at the beginning of the novel in various ways. Some have emphasized the ending of the novel in relation to the role of linguistic crisis in Handke's earlier works. Sergooris sees the ending as representing a "literary overcoming of the speechlessness which (in his previous works) had led to a passive sterility" (77). For Rey, the failure of the act of writing is a confirmation that the process of narration is "endless" and must go beyond the end of the novel (293). Similarly, Nägele and Voris see the failure of the therapeutic narrative as positive in that the narrator's attempt to overcome fear must go on (60). Love, on the other hand, basing her interpretation on the premise that the primary function of the narrative is its therpeutic dimension, argues that its failure means that "the classical claim of art (to express truth) is called into question" (145). Varsava sees the narrator's acknowledgement of failure at the end through his confession of being a liar nevertheless to have "achieved something more than dissimulation through his admission" (121) in that his recognition of failure has more impact than would a claim to have fulfilled his aim.

language. It is a hopeless task, moving from the narrator's "speech-lessness" after the news of her death (*SBD* 3), through his admission that "At best, I am able to capture my mother's story for brief moments in dreams ... the moments ... in which extreme need to communicate coincides with extreme speechlessness" (*SBD* 31), to his final admission of failure (*SBD* 66). Although, in his own words, writing has "failed" to capture the presence of his mother, his final realization is that this is a failure which is in the nature of writing itself. Writing must nevertheless continue, the attempt to capture this presence has been deferred, but will continue: "Someday I shall write about this in greater detail" (*SBD* 70). The failure of the act of writing, when thus viewed from a deconstructionist or post-struc-turalist perspective, confirms that for Handke "the important point is not what is written *about* but what is produced by the *act* of writing" (Klinkowitz and Knowlton 55). It is not as a failed attempt to describe reality but part of an (implicitly incomplete) act of writing that the book should be seen.

Both *Short Letter, Long Farewell* and *A Sorrow Beyond Dreams* share the preoccupation with the relationship between the individu-al, place and autonomy, which forms an important characteristic of Handke's later work. Place assumes a key role in the development of autonomy and the inner development of the protagonist in both novels, either in the form of a dystopia to be escaped from or a utopia which incorporates all the perceived freedom lacking in the former. The ultimate significance of place within Handke's poetics, however, lies in the process by which, through overcoming the ten-dency to prejudge and categorize perception, alienation can be over-come and the self opened up to the poetic possibilities implicit in the everyday world.

Works Cited

Barth, Markus. *Lebenskunst im Alltag. Analyse der Werke von Peter Handke, Thomas Bernhard und Brigitte Kronauer.* Wiesbaden: Deutscher Universitätsverlag, 1998.

Barry, Thomas F. "America Reflected: On the American Reception of Peter Handke's Writings/Handke's Reception of America in

His Writings." *Modern Austrian Literature* 20.3-4 (1987) 107-15.

Bartmann, Christoph. "'Der Zusammenhang ist möglich': *Der kurze Brief zum langen Abschied* im Kontext." *Peter Handke*. Ed. Raimund Fellinger. Frankfurt am Main: Suhrkamp, 1985. 114-39.

Baudrillard, Jean. *America*. 1986. Trans. Chris Turner. London: Verso, 1989.

–. "Simulacra and Simulations." *Jean Baudrillard. Selected Writings*. Ed. Mark Poster. Cambridge: Polity, 2001. 169-87.

Bohn, Volker. "'Später werde ich über das alles Genaueres schreiben': Peter Handkes Erzählung *Wunschloses Unglück* aus literaturtheoretischer Sicht." *Peter Handke*. Ed. Raimund Fellinger. Frankfurt am Main: Suhrkamp, 1985. 140-67.

Brüggemann, Aminia. M. "Peter Handke: *Der kurze Brief zum langen Abschied*." *Chronotopos Amerika bei Max Frisch, Peter Handke, Günter Kunert und Martin Walser*. Studies in Modern German Literature 70. New York: Peter Lang, 1996. 123-52.

Burdorf, Dieter. "Helden fur einen Tag: Zur deutschsprachigen Prosa nach 1968." *Der unzeitgemäße Held in der Weltliteratur*. Ed. Gerhard R. Kaiser. Jenaer Germanistische Forschungen 1. Heidelberg: Carl Winter, 1998: 231-56.

De Man, Paul. *Allegories of Reading*. New Haven: Yale UP, 1982.

Derrida, Jacques. "Différance." *A Derrida Reader*. Ed. Peggy Kamuf. Hemel Hempstead: Harvester Wheatsheaf, 1991. 59-79.

–. *Of Grammatology*, Trans. Gayatri Chakravorty Spivak. Baltimore: Johns Hopkins UP, 1986.

Durzak, Manfred. *Peter Handke und die deutsche Gegenwartsliteratur: Narziß auf Abwegen*. Stuttgart: Kohlhammer, 1982.

Elm, Theo. "Die Fiktion eines Entwicklungsromans: Zur Erzählstrategie in Peter Handkes Roman *Der kurze Brief zum langen Abschied*." *Poetica: Zeitschrift für Sprach- und Literaturwissenschaft* 6 (1974) 353-77.

Elstun, Esther N. "Images of America in Peter Handke's Bildungsroman, *Short Letter, Long Farewell*." *The Image of America in Literature, Media, and Society*. Ed. Will Wright and Steven Kaplan. Society for the Interdisciplinary Study of Social Imagery: University of Southern Colorado, Pueblo, CO, 1999. 144-48.

Fickert, Kurt. "The Myth of America in Peter Handke's *Der kurze Brief zum langen Abschied.*" *German Studies Review* 21.1 (1998) 27-40.

Frietsch, Wolfram. *Die Symbolik der Epiphanien in Peter Handkes Texten. Strukturmomente eines neuen Zusammenhangs.* Sinzheim: Pro-Universitate, 1995.

Fulde, Ingeborg. "Sprache ohne Leidenschaft. Die sexuellen Beziehungen in Peter Handkes *Der kurze Brief zum langen Abschied.*" *Literatur und Sexualität.* Ed. Johannes Cremerius, et al. Würzburg: Königshausen & Neumann, 1991. 153-72.

Gabriel, Norbert. *Peter Handke und Österreich.* Bonn: Bouvier, 1983.

Göttsche, Dirk. "*Wunschloses Unglück* – Literarische Sprachskepsis und Authentizität." *Die Produktivität der Sprachkrise in der modernen Prosa.* Hochschulschriften Literaturwissenschaft 84. Frankfurt am Main: Athenäum, 1987. 274-82; 420-22.

Handke, Peter. "Die Literatur ist romantisch." *Ich bin ein Bewohner des Elfenbeinturms.* Frankfurt am Main: Suhrkamp, 1972. 35-50.

—. "Probleme werden im Film zu einem Genre." *Ich bin ein Bewohner des Elfenbeinturms.* Frankfurt am Main: Suhrkamp, 1972. 83-87.

Heintz, Günter. *Peter Handke.* Munich: Oldenbourg, 1976.

Miller, J. Hillis. *The Ethics of Reading: Kant, De Man, Eliot, Trollope, James, and Benjamin.* New York: Columbia UP, 1989.

Kann, Irene. "Leben im Augenblick und Sehnsucht nach Dauer: Peter Handke." *Schuld und Zeit. Literarische Handlung in theologischer Sicht: Thomas Mann – Robert Musil – Peter Handke.* Paderborn: Schöningh, 1992. 167-252.

Karasek, Hellmuth. "Der kurze Brief zum langen Abschied. Ohne zu verallgemeinern." Gespräch mit Peter Handke. *Über Peter Handke.* Ed. Michael Scharang. Frankfurt am Main: Suhrkamp, 1972. 85-90.

Kersten, Lee. "Film Reference as an Imaginative Model in Handke's *Der kurze Brief zum langen Abschied.*" *AUMLA: Journal of the Australasian Universities Language and Literature Association* 56 (1981) 152-66.

Kleist, Jürgen. "Die Akzeptanz des Gegebenen: Zur Problematik des Künstlers in Peter Handkes *Der kurze Brief zum langen Abschied.*" *Modern Austrian Literature* 21.2 (1988) 95-104.

Konzett, Matthias. "Cultural Amnesia and the Banality of Human Tragedy: Peter Handke's *Wunschloses Unglück* and its Post-ideological Aesthetics." *Germanic Review* 70.2 (1995) 42-50.

Klinkowitz, Jerome, and James Knowlton. *Peter Handke and the Postmodern Transformation: The Goalie's Journey Home.* Columbia, MO: U of Missouri P, 1983.

Krajenbrink, Marieke. *Intertextualität als Konstruktionsprinzip. Transformationen des Kriminalromans und des romatischen Romans bei Peter Handke und Botho Strauß.* Amsterdam, Atlanta: Rodopi, 1996.

Kraus, Cristine. "Literarische Vorbilder in Peter Handkes Roman *Der kurze Brief zum langen Abschied.*" *Österreich in Geschichte und Literatur (mit Geographie)* 22 (1978) 174-80.

Kreyenberg, Regina, and Gudrun Lipjes-Türr. "Peter Handke: *Wunschloses Unglück.*" *Erzählen, Erinnern: Deutsche Prosa der Gegenwart – Interpretationen.* Ed. Herbert Kaiser and Gerhard Kopf. Frankfurt am Main: Diesterweg, 1992. 125-48.

Love, Ursula. "'Als sei ich ... ihr GESCHUNDENES HERZ.' Identifizierung und negative Kreativität in Peter Handkes Erzählung *Wunschloses Unglück.*" *Seminar* 17.2 (1981) 130-46.

Marschall, Susanne. *Zum Problem der Wirklichkeit im Werk Peter Handkes. Untersuchungen mit Blick auf Rainer Maria Rilke.* Bern, Stuttgart: Haupt, 1995.

Mauser, Wolfram. "Peter Handke: 'Wunschloses Unglück' – erwünschtes Unglück?" *Der Deutschunterricht* 34.5 (1982) 73-89.

Mecklenburg, Norbert. "Provinzbeschimpfung und Weltandacht: Peter Handkes ambivalente Heimatdichtung." *Wesen und Wandel der Heimatliteratur: Am Beispiel der österreichischen Literatur seit 1945.* Ed. Karl Konrad Polheim. Bern, Frankfurt am Main: Peter Lang, 1989. 105-34.

Melzer, Gerhard. "Dieselben Dinge täglich bringen langsam um: Die Reisemodelle in Peter Handkes *Der kurze Brief zum langen Abschied* und Gerhard Roths *Winterreise.*" *Die andere Welt: Aspekte der österreichischen Literatur des 19. und 20. Jahrhunderts: Festschrift für Hellmuth Himmel zum 60. Geburtstag.* Ed. Kurt Bartsch, et al. Bern: Francke, 1979. 373-93.

Meurer, Reinhard. *Peter Handke: Der kurze Brief zum langen Abschied.* München: Oldenbourg, 1992.

Miles, David. H. "Reality and the Two Realisms: Mimesis in Auerbach, Lukács and Handke." *Monatshefte* 71 (1979) 371-78.

Nägele, Rainer. "Amerika als Fiktion und Wirklichkeit in Peter Handkes Roman *Der kurze Brief zum langen Abschied.*" *Die USA und Deutschland: Wechselseitige Spiegelungen in der Literatur der Gegenwart. Zum zweihundertjährigen Bestehen der Vereinigten Staaten am 4. Juli 1976. Amherster Kolloquium zur modernen deutschen Literatur.* Ed. Wolfgang Paulsen. Bern: Francke, 1976. 110-15.

–. Nägele, Rainer. "Die vermittelte Welt: Reflexionen zum Verhältnis von Fiktion und Wirklichkeit in Peter Handkes Roman *Der kurze Brief zum langen Abschied.*" *Jahrbuch der Deutschen Schiller-Gesellschaft* 19 (1975) 389-418.

–, and Renate Voris. *Peter Handke.* Autorenbücher 8. Munich: Beck, 1978.

Pakendorf, Gunther. "Der Realismus der entfremdeten Welt: Peter Handke, *Der kurze Brief zum langen Abschied.*" *Acta Germanica: Jahrbuch des Germanistenverbandes im Südlichen Afrika* 14 (1981) 157-74.

Paver, Chloe E. M. "'Die verkörperte Scham': The Body in Handke's *Wunschloses Unglück.*" *Modern Language Review* 94 (1999) 460-75.

Perry, Petra . "Peter Handkes *Wunschloses Unglück* als Kritik der Biographie: Geschichte und Geschichten." *Orbis Litterarum: International Review of Literary Studies* 39.2 (1984) 160-68.

Renner, Rolf Günter. *Peter Handke.* Stuttgart: Metzler, 1985.

Rey, William H. "Provokation durch den Tod: Peter Handkes Erzählung *Wunschloses Unglück* als Modell stilistischer Integration." *German Studies Review* 1 (1978) 285-301.

Schindler, Stephen K. "Der Nationalsozialismus als Bruch mit dem alltäglichen Faschismus: Maria Handkes typisiertes Frauenleben in *Wunschloses Unglück.*" *German Studies Review* 19 (1996) 41-59.

Schmidt-Dengler, Wendelin. "Peter Handkes *Wunschloses Unglück.*" *Bruchlinien: Vorlesungen zur österreichischen Literatur 1945 bis 1990.* Salzburg: Residenz, 1995. 254-68.

Schlueter, June. *The Plays and Novels of Peter Handke.* Pittsburgh: U of Pittsburgh P, 1981.

Sergooris, Gunther. *Peter Handke und die Sprache*. Abhandlungen zur Kunst-, Musik- und Literaturwissenschaft 270. Bonn: Bouvier, 1979.

Stoffel, G. M. "Antithesen in Peter Handkes Erzählung *Wunschloses Unglück*." *Colloquia Germanica* 18 (1985) 40-54.

Weber, Werner. Rev. of *Wunschloses Unglück. Neue Zürcher Zeitung* 22 Oct. 1972.

Wefelmeyer, Fritz: "Die Naturschrift der Reise bei Peter Handke." *Reisen im Diskurs. Modelle der literarischen Fremderfahrung von den Pilgerberichten bis zur Postmoderne. Tagungsakten des internationalen Symposions zur Reiseliteratur, University College Dublin 10.-12. März 1994.* Ed. Anne Fuchs and Theo Harden. Neue Bremer Beiträge 8. Heidelberg: Carl Winter, 1995. 660-79.

Wiesehan, Gretchen. *A Dubious Heritage: Questioning Identity in German Autobiographical Novels of the Postwar Generation.* Bern, Frankfurt am Main: Peter Lang, 1997.

Wigmore, Juliet (ed.). *Wunschloses Unglück.* By Peter Handke. Manchester: Manchester UP, 1993.

Winkelmann, Christine. *Die Suche nach dem 'großen Gefühl.' Wahrnehmung und Weltbezug bei Botho Strauß und Peter Handke.* Frankfurt am Main: Peter Lang, 1990.

Varsava, Jerry A. "Auto-Bio-Graphy as Metafiction: Peter Handke's *A Sorrow Beyond Dreams*." *CLIO: A Journal of Literature, History, and the Philosophy of History* 2 (1985) 119-35.

The Quest for Authenticity, a Trilogy:
The Goalie's Anxiety at the Penalty Kick,
A Moment of True Feeling,
The Left-Handed Woman

Frank Pilipp

SINCE HIS EARLIEST WRITINGS, Handke's major theme has been the manipulation and suppression of individuality by what is universally considered true, hence undeniable (Nef 1241). Particularly in his prose works of the 1960s and 70s, Handke has been preoccupied with the ways linguistic and cultural codes pre-shape our perception of inner and outer world. In Handke's view, humans don't live authentic lives but surrogate ones due to their unquestioning adherence to a system that is taken for granted. Behavior and thought, meanings and values, customs and communication are automatic functions governed by a familiar normalcy that is never challenged or disputed. The protagonists of the three texts under discussion here "find themselves unable to respond 'normally' to the routine linguistic and visual messages" (Linville and Casper 14) with which they are constantly bombarded. They respond with anxiety, anarchy, or anti-social behavior as a means to forego automated and taken-for-granted patterns of behavior and thought.

The catchy title of Handke's first novel of the 1970s undoubtedly contributed to its immediate commercial success. The iambic *Die Angst des Tormanns beim Elfmeter* (1970; *The Goalie's Anxiety at the Penalty Kick*, 1972) deftly combines the popular appeal of the game of soccer with the existential motif of fear. The sensationalism thus generated instantly stirred the readers' curiosity, which was largely responsible for the success of the novel by the newly prominent author-rebel after its release in early 1970 (Pütz, "Angst" 148-49). Furthermore, after the highly self-reflexive and experimental *Die Hornissen* (1966; The Hornets) and *Der Hausierer* (1967; The Peddler), *The Goalie's Anxiety at the Penalty Kick* marked, at first sight, Handke's emergence as a more conventional storyteller.

The novel features a realistic storyline within a concrete spatial-temporal narrative context (Durzak 66). Joseph Bloch, a former professional soccer goalkeeper and meanwhile a construction worker, interprets a gesture by his foreman as his dismissal. Already divorced from his wife, estranged from his child, and marginalized by society, the loss of his employment is concomitant with his loss of an anchor in a reality shared with others, and sets in motion a chain of events with fatal consequences. Wandering aimlessly through the city of Vienna for a few days, he ends up at the movies where he befriends Gerda, the cashier. After spending the night with her, Bloch strangles her to death. He then travels to Austria's south-eastern border where he takes up accommodations. With the police on his trail, Bloch, seemingly unaffected and indifferent, but persistently plagued by his unrelenting perception of signs, bides his time in a border village. In the final scene, he is shown watching a local soccer match while explaining the goalie's reasoning before a penalty to another spectator.

On the surface, the linear narrative of *The Goalie's Anxiety* bears a certain resemblance to the detective novel. Indeed, Handke deliberately employs that genre's characteristics as a façade but "exposes and destroys the clichéd reality of the mystery novel while leaving the genre itself intact" (Klinkowitz and Knowlton 26). In the end, he mocks the conventions of the detective novel when he mercilessly shatters its fundamental rule and denies the reader any resolution of the murder case (Pütz, "Angst" 150; cf. Heintz 111). The narrative model of the detective story, the brand of unreflected, neo-realist writing Handke denounced during the 1966 meeting of Group 47 in Princeton as naïve and as literary impotence (Handke, "Tagung" 29), is parodied, if not negated, and in the process of telling the story, its conventions are deconstructed (DeMeritt, "Antigeschichten" 201; Nägele and Voris 50; Göttsche 273).[1] In line with the protagonist's loss of context and continuity, the narrative lacks the causal motivation of an actual plot,[2] and its "illogicality and dis-

---

[1]For the most exhaustive discussion of Handke's transformation of the detective genre, see Krajenbrink (51-87).
[2]The terms 'story' and 'plot' are used here according to their definition by E. M. Forster (30, 87), in order to differentiate a temporal sequence of events (story) from a sequence of causal connections (plot).

continuity result in a type of monotonous sequentiality" (DeMeritt, *Subjectivity* 159; cf. Heintz 115).

Within the acausal sequence of events the murder does not serve as a narrative focus or catalyst, although Handke employs it dexterously as a structural device, not only to sustain reader interest but also to provide a context in which many of the protagonist's seemingly paranoid perceptions and thought processes become explainable (Pütz, "Angst" 150-51; cf. Krajenbrink 73). Throughout the narrative, Bloch remains strangely detached, disinterested and unconcerned about the looming prospect of being taken to task under legal parameters. Capture, trial and punishment do not even represent a possibility to him (*GA* 93), although he reads in the newspaper that "an important lead in the Gerda T. case was being followed into the southern part of the country" (*GA* 82). Contrary to a fugitive's attempt to remain inconspicuous, he repeatedly seeks arguments and brawls with strangers (*GA* 56, 59).[3] Yet, while he attentively follows the search for him in the newspapers (*GA* 93),[4] any psychological or ethical issues connected with the murder (such as guilt or emotional trauma) are excluded.[5] The narrative evades (or transcends) any moral or ethical issues anchored within a traditional value system. Instead, Handke seems to situate his char-

---

[3]Göttsche (270) makes a valid point when he explains this behavior as Bloch's attempt to revert to a more immediate, i.e. physical, mode of perception, unmediated by language.

[4]When Bloch wipes the objects after the murder, this is not rational behavior (as claimed by Mixner 138 or Klingmann 169), but subconscious and automatic conformity to (stereo)typical behavior patterns of fugitives (cf. Pütz, "Angst" 152-56). After all, Bloch does not erase his traces very carefully and leaves a coin next to the body of his victim. As Demetz states, Bloch appears like "a schizophrenic killer who actually wants to be caught" (223) – or, one might add, doesn't care one way or the other. Demetz, like a number of critics, among them Mixner, Durzak, Sebald, Heintz, Summerfield, Reinhardt, and, most compellingly, Tabah (*Vermittlung*), bases his reading of the novel on Handke's statement that he had studied Klaus Conrad's theoretical work on schizophrenia (see Handke, "Angst" 45). A second group of critics endorses an approach to the novel based on semiotics (White, Schlueter, Renner, Bohnen), while a third (Klinkowitz and Knowlton, Adams, O'Neill) advocates a postmodernist reading. As these approaches are rather complementary than contradictory, this reading seeks a synthesis of critical voices.

[5]This contradicts Klingmann (169), who overemphasizes Bloch's deliberate preparations of his escape and his feelings of guilt.

acter in an amoral, or pre-moral, state reminiscent of Robert Musil's prostitute murderer Moosbrugger from *Der Mann ohne Eigenschaften* (1931; *The Man Without Qualities*, 1953) and Ingeborg Bachmann's patricide Wildermuth in the eponymously titled short story (1961; trans 1987), in whose worlds there exist no categories for valuation.[6]

The Goalie's Anxiety at the Penalty Kick has earned critical acclaim first and foremost as a postmodern novel in which "[d]eterminacy and transcendence, the twin goals of modernism," fade into the background in favor of a "self-conscious system of differences rather than identities" (Klinkowitz and Knowlton 5). Differently put, the novel reflects the postmodern realization that words cannot be considered stand-ins for the objects they are supposed to signify. Handke's deconstruction of modernist literary precepts is primarily reflected through his protagonist's worldview. Not only does Bloch, who is oversensitive to external stimuli, appear to inhabit a world which is a semantic vacuum until humans create meaning, he is also characterized by a radical lack of psychology and motivation (Rossbacher 94). As a synthetic entity, the appellation Joseph Bloch is a hybrid in itself,[7] making him a postmodern character without character, whose ostensibly arbitrary behavior consists exclusively of random, disconnected, and "inscrutable actions" (Schlueter 80).

Another essential condition of the postmodern, the blurring of *Sein* and *Schein*, of reality and illusion, is suggested early in the text. When Bloch "pretended to be startled," though "in reality he was startled" as well (*GA* 10), simulation becomes equivalent to reality. Regardless of whether Bloch's display of fright is real or feigned, the narrator tells us that "in reality" Bloch *was* frightened. That Bloch feels compelled to act out his fright illustrates how he automatically conforms outwardly to an inner sensation, by translating it into (body) language. This puts into question the objectivity and reliability of the "reality" depicted in the text by an uninvolved

---

[6]See also Adams, who calls Bloch "an a-moral player" (5). As to the analogy with Moosbrugger, see the article by Herzmann.

[7]Generally, critics suggest the names Joseph K. and Block from Kafka's *The Trial* (Adams 8; Brown, "Names" 63), although the latter of the two is more likely to refer to the real estate broker Bloch in Thomas Bernhard's novel *Verstörung* (1967; *Gargoyles*, 1970) on which Handke has written a short essay (*BE* 211-16; see Bohnen 398-99, note 10).

and non-committal yet omniscient narrator who casually mediates the limited point of view of the character entrusted to him.

Still, it is not only the derisive deconstruction of genre, character, narration, and realism itself that lends *The Goalie's Anxiety* the self-reflexive quality of a postmodern meta-narrative. Handke's text also reverberates with echoes of a number of literary precursors.[8] While it initiates literary allusions to such authors as Robbe-Grillet, Sartre, Camus, Büchner, Döblin, Hofmannsthal, and Bernhard, two other seminal figures in Austrian literature seem to be of particular relevance. On the one hand, there is the legacy of Franz Kafka, who is especially prominent in Handke's early prose works. In *The Goalie's Anxiety*, it is above all the narrative perspective which, like Kafka's, remains tightly connected to the point of view of his alienated and isolated anti-hero and loyally reflects his perceptions, deliberations and interpretations. Furthermore, the opening scene, where the protagonist's decision to leave his job is based on his subjective interpretation of a gesture, creates an atmosphere strongly reminiscent of Kafka's *Der Process* (1935; *The Trial*, 1968). Both authors introduce "a guilty, isolated hero [who] attempts to understand the nature of his relationships," and "create a surreal atmosphere seemingly resistant to interpretation" (Schlueter 79). On the other hand, the circumstances surrounding the murder case are perhaps best understood with reference to Ingeborg Bachmann's narrative "A Wildermuth," to which *The Goalie's Anxiety* exhibits striking parallels.[9]

---

[8]These have been mentioned or investigated by a number of critics. For a summary, see O'Neill (293), but also Adams, who illustrates with regard to Kafka how literary citation "becomes integral to [Handke's] writing" (2).

[9]Handke greatly admires both of these authors. During his formative years as a writer the fictional universe of Franz Kafka fascinated him. One of his earliest fictional texts, published in an Austrian newspaper in 1959 and later reprinted in Haslinger's biography of Handke's youth and adolescent years (38-42), bears the title "In der Zwischenzeit" (In the Meantime), and Handke admits it is written "like Kafka" (Haslinger 91). The influence of Kafka can be traced in virtually all of Handke's prose writings of the 60s and 70s (see Pilipp, "In Defense"). For a detailed analysis of the multifaceted aspects of *The Goalie's* indebtedness to Kafka's *The Trial*, see O'Neill (294-95) and the astute essay by Jeffrey Adams, who comments that the "reconstruction [of Josef K. and Block] in the name 'Josef Bloch' is a rhetorical device by which Handke re-members his anxiety of influence, cutting to pieces the precursor's text and reassembling

Arguably the dominant aspect of *The Goalie's Anxiety* lies in its mediation of the protagonist's alienation and disorientation, and thus reflects a major theme in Handke's writing, namely the problematic relationship between the subjective self and the outside world as well as how the former reads meaning into the latter. Much of the text centers on the (mis)perception of incidents, the interpretation of signs, the appearance of gestures, the explanation of words, and how Bloch is continually "engaged in the attempt to construct from language a coherent and meaningful relationship with the world outside his consciousness" (Barry, "Language" 98; similarly, Bohrer 64). Although Bloch constantly and compulsively questions and analyzes what, how and why he perceives, he remains undisturbed by the fact that most of his interpretations are neither accurate nor rational. Unable to engage in productive communication with others, he only feels at ease in anonymous spaces: in cinemas or in front of a television set, in a soccer stadium or on the telephone (Summerfield 104-06). There he finds himself facing a reality he is not forced to interpret.[10]

As a former goalkeeper he is conditioned to decode the action of the game constantly in relation to his own reactions and to interpret the opponent's body language, which, in view of the unpredictable nature of the game and its players, invariably cannot always be done successfully.[11] Dictated not by an objective causality but by its main character's insistently subjective filtering of his surroundings, the novel abounds with the terminology of (frequently false) perceptions and (often frustrated or defective) communication. This becomes illustrative of a critique of (human) consciousness as the primary driving force behind the "proliferating meaninglessness"

---

it" (8). Likewise, Handke has immense respect for Ingeborg Bachmann, to whom he dedicated his Büchner Prize award speech of 1974 (*Wü* 71-80).

[10] A similar tendency is evidenced by Bloch's obsession to size up objects by counting them or by classifying them by their price (cf. Tabah, *Vermittlung* 273).

[11] Cf. White's similar comment that Bloch "interprets the world around him like an anxious goalkeeper awaiting the penalty-kick" (249), which echoes Durzak's remark that Bloch reacts to reality as a goalkeeper to the game (71-72). In that sense, the titular penalty kick is representative of an external (non-subjective) occurrence, while the goalie's anxiety stands for the internal realm of the subjective.

(O'Neill 287) of the depicted events.[12] When Bloch returns to his workplace three days later to pick up his papers and they are not ready, this confirms the misinterpretation of his presumed release and his "los[ing] step with the semiotic system of his world" (Klinkowitz and Knowlton 40).[13] Quite appropriately, critics have termed Handke's novel a fictional account of Ferdinand de Saussure's theory of semiotics (Renner 22), a "fictional exegesis of Wittgenstein's inquiry into language" (Firda 63), and "the story of a fall from hermeneutic grace, an expulsion from a semiotic Eden" (O'Neill 296). Once again accentuating the predominance of the subjective, it elevates the protagonist to the "author of the world's text, and shifts the reader's attention from the created to the creative world, from product to process" (Klinkowitz and Knowlton 39).[14]

Although several critics have taken Handke's reference to schizophrenia in connection with his goalie as the basis for a psychological reading of the novel, Handke merely suggests an analogy. His comments that "a schizophrenic perceives the objects around him as word games, which essentially constitutes the principle or structure of this narrative ... except for the fact that this principle is *not* applied to a schizophrenic but to a 'normal' protagonist" should make it abundantly clear that it would be reductive to take schizophrenia as the basis for interpreting the text.[15] Even more significant is Handke's following statement: "This process of viewing objects

---

[12]Verbs such as to (mis)interpret, perceive, notice, understand, misconstrue, recognize, comprehend, convey, mean, impart, think, believe, explain, signify, denote, insinuate, quote, allude, translate, refer, remind, descry, discern, gather, conclude, and respond occur along with their corresponding nouns. Even if the story seems to trace Bloch's gradual mental disintegration into schizophrenia (Demetz 223), Handke seeks to destroy any objective category by which Bloch's actions could be explained and is more preoccupied with showing that causality is "determined solely by the subjectivity of a consciousness for whom all naturalness and systematic objectivity have become questionable" (DeMeritt, *Subjectivity* 159).

[13]Klingmann (165) calls it Bloch's "auto-release," emphasizing his social failure due to his acute state of alienation as the central theme of the narrative.

[14]This is essentially also O'Neill's thesis, whose 1991 reading of Handke's novel as a postmodern text is heavily indebted, though without reference, to Klinkowitz's and Knowlton's book of 1983.

[15]Equally insufficient is a reading of Bloch's alienation as a result of society's manipulations. See Arnulf Lenzen, who attributes Bloch's state of alienation exclusively to social conditions (esp. 401, 406).

as *norms* is not supposed to be presented as *pathological* and thus harmless, but rather as typical: the laws do not begin with the Judicial Code but with the objects themselves" (Handke, "Angst" 45; also quoted by Kanzog 158-59). What Handke is getting at is that humans automatically translate objects into signifiers, which is why the objects themselves already assume prescriptive meanings. Bloch, too, views, or, more appropriately, reads (cf. Göttsche 269) the objects around him "literally,"[16] transforming them automatically and obsessively into linguistic signs. This obsession irritates Bloch until he is "disgusted with talking" (*GA* 91), has "to keep his guard up against words" (*GA* 93), and is consumed by a "loathsome word-game sickness" (*GA* 96; cf. Rossbacher 98). In a Nietzschean fashion, this irritation is synonymous with a loathing (*Erkenntnisekel*) about the shortcomings of a deficient mode of communication that has become automated (Durzak 73) and controls how we view the world.

Because these signifiers prove as arbitrary as they are undeniable (*GA* 30), Bloch becomes increasingly insecure in using language to communicate and "can no longer employ words, phrases, and constructions taken for granted by the rest of society" (DeMeritt, *Subjectivity* 156; cf. also Wellershoff 47-48; Sebald 49; Zeller 134; Göttsche 269). Instead of having command of language, language has command of him (Wolf 35). He realizes how linguistic structures enslave the speakers by shaping their thinking and their perceptions of what is (Demetz 219). While other characters feel at home in their reality and in the shared usage of language, Bloch "is dominated by the subjective and has lost contact with the storehouse of socially accepted meanings" (Barry, "Language" 98). Nonetheless, he alone seems to recognize how humans are trapped in a pre-

---

[16]This, as are other crucial elements associated with Bloch's manic efforts to create meaning, is missing in the translation (see *GA* 102). The original has: "Buchstäblich war alles, was er sah, auffällig. Die Bilder ... sprangen ... einem buchstäblich in die Augen" (*ATE* 87), translated inadequately as: "Everything he saw was conspicuous. The pictures ... jumped out at you" (*GA* 102). Admittedly, a precise translation is problematic, since "buchstäblich" carries a double-entendre here. Therefore the last sentence can be read as: "The images literally jumped at you"; or: "The images jumped at you as letters." Equally inadequate renderings or omissions are found on *GA* 10, 95, 103, and 127. – Bloch had previously become aware that he "as if compelled, was thinking of the word for each thing" (*GA* 58).

formulated grammar of perception (Bohrer 66; cf. Hamm 165) and how everyday behavior patterns and relationships are dictated by the signifiers that make up society's rules (Nägele and Voris 49, 50; Rinner 172). As in soccer, where every participant has a role to play, a function to perform, and must adhere to prescripted rules, society assigns us roles that perpetually stand in the way of authentic existence (Klingmann 164).[17]

Bloch's revulsion to the "word games" (*GA* 95), especially in the name of ruling ideologies of society's brainwashing industry, results in a state of resignation that makes everything "unbearable" (*GA* 57) without escape: "In fact, his nausea was the same kind of nausea that had sometimes been brought on by certain jingles, pop songs, or national anthems that he felt compelled to repeat word for word" (*GA* 58). In the vast linguistic landscape of continually self-referential "insinuations" (*GA* 94) creating an endless chain of *différance* (Krajenbrink 77, note 65), the infinite deferral of meaning is concomitant with a loss of wholeness and identity which leaves behind an acute feeling of disempowerment. Since Bloch cannot grasp, control, or recreate reality with words, his hands take over and he strangles Gerda (Klinkowitz and Knowlton 38). Bloch's assault may be seen as a reflex (Zürcher 39) in reaction to her disturbingly "unselfconscious use of language" (Adams 9),[18] a "necessary act of release for a feeling of intense irritation" brought on by the nagging consciousness of the "tyranny of words"

---

[17]Cf. Also DeMeritt: "For Handke all of life is regulated, manipulated, and controlled, be it by means of language, roles, habits, conventions, ideologies or institutions" (*Subjectivity* 145). While other characters lack the awareness of this control and are in fact 'played' by the signifiers (Hartwig 15), Bloch resists. Several passages are symptomatic for Bloch's hyperconsciousness, his "Überbewußtheit" (Klingmann 165, 166). Repeatedly this becomes apparent when he focuses his attention away from an action to its imminent goal or result; e.g. not the bird but the spot for which it heads (*GA* 33); not the drop running down the glass but the spot on the table it is going to hit (*GA* 34); not the dog but the man it is running toward (*GA* 101); not the striker but the goalie (*GA* 132). This shows Bloch's constant attempt to assume control by anticipating an outcome in advance (cf. O'Neill 289).

[18]Zürcher (39) comments that Gerda reuses Bloch's utterances matter-of-factly and thus deprives him of the last vestiges of his identity, though he clearly overemphasizes *The Goalie's Anxiety* as the story of an identity crisis (40).

(Schlueter 88).[19] First and foremost, however, the murder is a desperate and panicked action against being linguistically usurped by Gerda's language and marks Bloch's definitive rejection of the linguistic code as a means of human interaction (Marschall 28).

Here the link to Ingeborg Bachmann's narrative "A Wildermuth" comes to the fore. Her title character (whose name literally translates as 'wild temper') undergoes a similar crisis as Bloch and experiences "the greatest difficulty in making head or tail of these nebulous sentences" (Bachmann, "Wildermuth" 164). Like Bloch, Wildermuth rejects human communication through language as "[i]ndolent, apathetic word set on agreement at all costs" ("Wildermuth" 169). The main connection between Handke's and Bachmann's narratives, however, consists in the conspicuous fact that Wildermuth's wife is named Gerda and is primarily characterized through her constant 'idle talk' in which her husband discerns a nauseating hypocrisy. He concludes that the nature of language is self-referential[20] and realizes that true essence can only be achieved through a congruence of "object and word" ("Wildermuth" 169). Bachmann's Gerda, too, represents the mendacious language that can only operate

---

[19]With regard to Bloch's impulsive act of killing, Lenzen's socially-minded approach does offer a valid argument in that Gerda's question whether Bloch is "going to work today" (*GA* 20) reminds him of his social uprootedness and isolation, and thus causes his discontent to explode into aggression (Lenzen 403; cf. also Sergooris 51, Tabah, *Vermittlung* 278, and Thornton 50). Like Mixner in his insistence on psychological realism, Lenzen (402), too, takes the issue of unemployment expressed in the sentence "He had been idle too long" (*GA* 84) to have central significance. A rather forced realist explanation largely based on hypotheses is offered by Russel Brown, who believes that Bloch commits murder to establish a new self-identity in order to reclaim his "lost sense of self" as a goalkeeper ("Handke's *Die Angst*" 298). And, in her rather general and often arbitrary textual exegesis based on free association, Dixon submits that Bloch wants to silence the chatty Gerda (86).

[20]He makes this recognition after an erotic encounter with Wanda, a gypsy woman, who lets him experience unfathomable depths of ecstasy and passion. Significantly, not one word is ever spoken between them, Wanda being characterized by "speechlessness" ("Wildermuth" 162) and an overwhelming pre-intellectual and untainted, and at the same time uninhibited physicality. In contrast to the mendacious verbosity of Handke's and Bachmann's Gerda, Wanda possesses a sincere, if amoral, sensuality and communicates non-verbally. At the verge of unconsciousness, Wildermuth finds himself in perfect unity with a body not his own, a corporeal harmony speechless with passion.

within the universe of a binary value system created by human consciousness – for Bachmann a highly inadequate mode of expression
and communication. That Handke's Gerda is the victim of Bloch's
sudden outburst of aggression may well be an allusion to Bachmann's
narrative, for, akin to Bachmann's Wildermuth, he, too, has lost all
faith in the expressibility of meaning and communication of essences
through language.[21]

Language, Bachmann and Handke agree with Wittgenstein, who
equates the limits of human perception with the limits of language
(*Tractatus* 5.6), is incapable of expressing anything external to its
system and is therefore tautological and self-referential. Consequently,
it becomes apparent to both Bachmann's Wildermuth and Handke's
Bloch that signifier and signified are continually breaking apart and
reattaching in new combinations, thus revealing the inadequacy of
Saussure's model of the sign, according to which a signifier and its
signified relate as if they were two sides of the same coin. Instead of
pointing to some ultimate presence, essence, truth or reality, language
achieves precisely the opposite function, namely that of obscuring
possible meanings ("Wildermuth" 163). While both Bloch and Wildermuth yearn for a correspondence between "object and word, feeling and word, deed and word" ("Wildermuth" 169), between language
and everything external to it, words simply cannot be considered
reliable referents to a meaning, because meanings are never stable but
vary with the context of the signifier. And since language is something
humans are made out of, these characters realize that the whole idea
that they are stable, unified entities must also be a fiction.

In Handke's and Bachmann's narratives, the murder cases exemplify the unreliability of the signifier and the absence of stable meaning, once considered the fundamental condition of human existence.
Yet the inefficiency of language is merely indicative of the innate
shortcomings of human intellect, which is limited to constructing
pseudo-realities. Handke goes one step further: his murderer is not

---

[21]Bachmann herself always insisted that true identity can only be experienced
intuitively or emotionally, a state that is marked by "speechlessness and
silence" ("Musik" 60). Compare also the similarity of the following sentences
describing the respective protagonist leaving with his new acquaintance. In
Handke, "[t]hey walked along together a while, but keeping their distance, not
touching" (*GA* 16), and in Bachmann, they "went away together, without a
word, without touching each other" ("Wildermuth" 163).

held accountable, neither ethically nor judicially, his act is not even at the center of the fictional events. Like Moosbrugger, Bloch stands outside of any ethical-moral code, and Gerda's murder, Handke seems to indicate, was committed in an extra-moral sense, "in a world without consequence ... detached from any final signification" (Klinkowitz and Knowlton 35). Again, this would be in line with Bachmann's narrative, where it is not the title character Wildermuth who commits murder but his *alter ego* of the same name. The other Wildermuth has killed his father, while the title character, a judge who is to sit in judgment over his namesake, must now question the applicability of ethical norms in light of his own upbringing and values. He must accept that language proves inefficient in providing a sensible, stable, and accurate account of the crime. Located in a realm "before all moral" (Bachmann, "Fragen" 192), the perpetrator's sincere and compliant nature and his free admission of his deed create the impression that the murder is beyond all moral judgment and that it was committed as if in a state beyond good and evil. And when moral verdicts can no longer be passed, even language loses its grounding, and the patricide, analogous to Bloch's offense, must be located beyond all taboo boundaries, namely in the truth that lies beyond language (Pilipp, "Tabus" 67).

Another nod to Bachmann and her utopian concept of a new language may be seen in Bloch's journey "to the border" (*GA* 24), which is not only to be understood as the literal (Austrian) border but also, metaphorically, as the border between language and silence, between reason and insanity, the border of language itself.[22] What Bloch encounters in the border village provides an "example of language in its most problematic state" (Klinkowitz and Knowlton 42). It is therefore not surprising that it is the social outsider Bloch himself who detects the corpse of the missing boy (*GA* 71) who had "had trouble talking" (*GA* 32). At first the boy appears to be a "mute" (*GA* 83) brother of Kaspar Hauser – the legendary

---

[22]Russel Brown calls it the border "between insanity and morality, between life and death, freedom and capture" ("Names" 72). In the wake of Wittgenstein's adage, *"The confines of my language* are the confines of my world" (*Tractatus* 5.6), Bachmann expressed the same skepticism about the limits and limitations of language in many of her early short stories (esp. those of the collection *Das dreißigste Jahr* (1961; *The Thirtieth Year*, 1987) and uses the trope of the border in several of them.

uncivilized and nearly speechless 'wild child' that one day turned up in Nuremberg in 1828 – to whom Handke had dedicated his stage play *Kaspar* in 1967 (trans. 1969). Before society can completely impose its symbolic order on him, he is brutally assassinated. The speechless boy's death in *The Goalie's Anxiety*, however, is alleged to have been an accident (*GA* 127). Still, the comment that all children, "more or less, have a speech defect" (*GA* 105), and that their speech consists merely of "memorized stuff that they rattle[] off by rote" (*GA* 104), suggest that humans are programmed to acquire language mechanically, robot-like, and as an artificial means of communication deemed authentic (cf. Pütz, *Handke* 44; Meier 44).[23] That Bloch perceives signs as "regulations" (*GA* 116, 129) reflects Handke's own skepticism of the symbolic order and its processes of signification. Again language is exposed as that system by which everybody is manipulated, leveled, controlled, and conditioned to play a societal role (Sergooris 61).[24]

It is precisely this societal role against which Bloch rebels when his maddeningly intense consciousness climaxes in his self-perception of a grotesquely metamorphosed creature – a scene later reprised in *A Moment of True Feeling*:

> For a moment it seemed as if he had fallen out of himself. … A cancer. He became aware of himself as if he had suddenly degenerated. He did not matter any more. No matter how still he lay, he was one big wriggling and retching; his lying there was so sharply distinct and glaring that he could not escape into even one picture that he might have compared himself with. The way he laid there, he was something lewd, obscene, inappropriate, thoroughly obnoxious. "Bury it!" thought Bloch. "Prohibit it, remove it!" He thought he was touching himself unpleasantly but realized that his awareness of himself was so intense that he felt it like a sense of touch all over his body; as though his consciousness, as though his thoughts, had become palpable, aggressive, abusive toward himself. … Nauseatingly his insides turned out; not alien, only repulsively different. It had been a jolt, and with one jolt he had become unnatural, had been torn

---

[23]Göttsche (271), too, draws attention to the novel's prevalent theme of misunderstandings, misperceptions, and miscommunication (e.g. *GA* 3, 5, 42-43, 74, 97). Cf. also Sergooris's main thesis that Bloch's alienation and isolation is caused by the clichés and norms that constitute human language (58).

[24]Sergooris (62) comments that language takes on the dimension of a Freudian super-ego, the principal manifestation of society's authority over the individual.

out of context. He lay there, as impossible as he was real; no
comparisons now. His awareness of himself was so strong that
he was scared to death. (*GA* 80-81)

Here, Bloch's alienation reaches a temporary climax as he undergoes a temporary transformation akin to Kafka's Gregor Samsa in
Die Verwandlung (1970; *The Metamorphosis*, 1971; cf. Barry,
"Poetics" 72). Bloch can no longer resort to metaphor in order to
express his condition through language, instead he substitutes a
chain of metonymies ("cancer" → "retching" → "obscene" → "insides turned out" → "repulsive" → "unnatural" → "impossible").
Pushing language to its limits, he tries in vain to express something
that has no equivalent in human experience or language. While a
hint of the authentic self is revealed behind its socially (and
linguistically) conditioned façade, it remains of no consequence, as
Bloch's perception continues to be determined by self-awareness.

The jolt also signals another parallel to Bachmann, who uses it
in a similar fashion as the catalyst for a heightened awareness of her
protagonists, allowing for an elevated, new perspective.[25] This new
mode of cognition would then no longer have to be based on the
symbolic order of a linguistic code but would consist of a more immediate perception, similar to what Bloch achieves when he momentarily eludes preformulated reality and perceives "everything
with total immediacy, without first having to translate it into words,
as before, or comprehending it only in terms of words or word
games." However, he is also aware that this perception is fleeting
and illusory and is a subjective perception of a "state where everything *seemed* natural to him" (*GA* 111; emph. add.) induced by
extreme fatigue. Only moments later when "all things reminded him
of each other" (*GA* 116), the endless chain of self-referential signifiers has reasserted its dominance.[26] Bloch's semantic crisis culminates in a scene where he reads the objects in his room from left to

---

[25]In her lectures on poetics, Bachmann speaks of a "moral-cognitive jolt"
("Fragen" 192) effected by an explosive, new consciousness.

[26]Bloch's "neurotically self-conscious" (Vannatta 610) and out-of-kilter perception of reality as a meta-reality of language is referred to repeatedly, for
example when he perceives things "like a simile for something else" (*GA* 71),
when "it began to seem that every word needed an explanation" (*GA* 66-67),
when "it seemed as if he should be seeing all this only in a figurative sense"
(*GA* 74), or "as if the parts he saw stood for the whole" (*GA* 88).

right as signifiers, indicated by the words in quotation marks, and then from right to left as images, indicated in the text by their pictographs (*GA* 124-25). It illustrates again how arbitrary the process of signification has become for Bloch. Even this purely visual way of registering objects as "mental hieroglyphics" (White 248) separated from their signifiers (Göttsche 271) and reminiscent of the "cartoons with no words" he prefers to 'read' (*GA* 14) cannot last,[27] and eventually changes into a perception where everything "seemed to have been newly named" (*GA* 130).[28]

The ending shows a way out of Bloch's dilemma and reinforces the analogy between the game of soccer and the symbolic order of human existence as classic examples of a tripartite communication model consisting of sender, message and receiver. In both cases, the participants or players are forced to adhere to preset rules. While successful communication through language is dependent on the observance of grammatical, syntactic, and lexical structures, soccer is delimited by rigid rules as well as spatial demarcations. And just as the successful transmission of a verbal message depends on productive and receptive skills of sender and receiver, in soccer, too, the skills and techniques of the players are imperative in the handling and passing of the ball. The crucial difference, however, is that language – as Handke agrees with Wittgenstein and Bachmann – cannot achieve transcendence because it is no substitute for objects. In soccer, however, transcendence is possible. When the ball, which constitutes the essence of the game (Wolf 34) but carries no intrinsic meaning itself (Thornton 46), passes the goalkeeper and crosses (transcends) the goal line, it has fulfilled its hitherto hollow

---

[27]Similarly, Schlueter suggests that this "immediacy" is illusory and merely a result of Bloch's utter "physical and mental exhaustion" (89; cf. also Wolf 36). Heintz views this "radical consequence" (115) negatively, arguing that Bloch now lacks knowledge of the signifiers to capture their signifieds intellectually. He equates Bloch's temporary loss of speech with a loss of "Lebensunmittel-barkeit" (116), of a purer, first-hand experiential knowledge. However, the opposite is the case, as Handke makes it clear that language "is the most central and pervasive barrier to a personalized apprehension of reality" (Linville and Casper 14).

[28]Rossbacher (105, note 30) mentions the parallel to Peter Bichsel's short story "Ein Tisch ist ein Tisch" (A Table Will Be a Table, 1969), where the renaming of objects causes a man increasingly to lose touch with reality.

purpose and brings the game to a momentary climax of orgasmic proportions for the scoring team and its fans.

Since a goalie's identity is based on his successfully preventing the game from being interrupted by a goal against his team, i.e. preventing transcendence, it is perfectly sensible for Bloch to inscribe himself in the symbolic order again where he can be sure that no transcendence is possible. Thus it is not surprising that, in an ultimate turning point (Krajenbrink 82), Bloch eventually resubmits to the linguistic code as an inescapable means of communication (or, to use another soccer analogy, of passing the ball) when he finds himself on familiar grounds by a soccer field. It is here that he discovers his speech again and relates the psychology or, rather, the semiotics between soccer goalie and striker to another spectator. By doing so, he once again embraces the system that, analogous to the game of soccer, defines and delimits identity. Only in his role as goalie can Bloch experience identity, can he cope with the signifiers (Renner 22) and find a sense of liberation in language (Bohrer 65).[29] The text ends with an image of a goalie who saves a penalty by remaining motionless, which – just as the image of the defeated goalie in the beginning – allows for various interpretations.[30] In this way, Handke keeps the free play of signifiers alive until the end, "avoiding the closure of meaning appropriate to a strictly realistic novel" (Klinkowitz and Knowlton 43; cf. Thornton 63). In fact, as Bloch narrates, he himself becomes part of his narration through his identification with the goalkeeper he is witnessing (Marschall 38).

---

[29]Cf. Barry: "A former construction worker, Bloch begins to 'construct' with language his own alternative 'reality,' to narrate his own story complete with dialogue within the context of Handke's text" ("Language" 101). Krajenbrink (83) speaks of Bloch's new sovereignty that makes his preferred hyperconscious meta-perspective appear "ridiculous" (*GA* 133) even to himself. For Tabah, too, the ending is positive, as she sees it as Bloch's recovery (*Vermittlung* 296).

[30]Landfester also points out that the final image becomes an allegory of reading (427). Indeed, Handke already opened every possibility for interpreting the goal scored in the dictum preceding the text. It need not be interpreted as the goalie's failure (as by Tabah, *Vermittlung* 267-68 and Bohnen 399, note 16), but rather as the fault of his defenders or the sheer brilliance of the opposing player(s). Surprisingly, the most recent article on Handke's novel (cf. Watson) disregards most of the previously published scholarship and thus has little to contribute to its critical discussion.

The self-referential nature of the signifiers becomes evident one more time as goalie and striker obviously follow the same train of logic that dead-ends in a missed/saved penalty. This is neither, as has been argued, the goalie's triumph by reacting instinctively and masterfully (Thuswaldner 30), nor the striker's failure (Renner 22), but rather a lucky coincidence which topples all rational contemplation and confirms the arbitrariness of semiotic processes (Kann 183).[31] Far from being a metaphor of restored harmony and the goalie's final vindication and overcoming of his *Angst* (cf. Linstead 99), it is actually "the punch line of a joke on the level of discourse, unrelentingly provoking the reader to renewed reflection" (O'Neill 298; cf. Henschen 78). Deceived and disillusioned by the aborted detective story, the reader enters the viciously self-referential cycle of interpretation in order to solve the conundrum, essentially mimicking the conjecture between striker and goalie which Bloch has illustrated (Landfester 428).[32] In the end, Handke passes the ball into the reader's hands.

In this way, Handke mocks "our emotional attachments to the meaning-centered standards of literary modernism [and] mimetic promises of unexamined language itself," thus invalidating reader

---

[31]Since the chances of saving a penalty are rather slim, a goalie cannot be expected to do so. The pressure is actually on the striker who is expected to score. In fact, the striker's anxiety at the penalty kick by far exceeds the goalie's.

[32]Similarly Schlueter: "That the reader is finally left with the task of interpretation is, of course, a perfectly appropriate conclusion to a novel which has been analyzing the process of interpretation throughout and gradually transferring the responsibility to the reader, who for Handke has always been as much a creator of a novel as the author himself" (91). Klingmann (165) sees the missed penalty as the climax of the theme of misreading reality, Renner (22) as a statement that communication is always skewed, and Göttsche (266) argues optimistically that the ending signals a new normalcy for Bloch who has acquired a new consciousness. Largely the productive outcome of his schizophrenic perception that is now no longer automatic or mechanical, it is based on linguistic self-consciousness and skepticism that still allows communication. Another upbeat conclusion is Wellerhoff's reading of the final scene as mirroring Bloch's new equilibrium, as the world is now focused on him and fulfills his every wish (69), or that the goalie's ultimate victory points to a way out of Bloch's vicious cycle of compulsive interpretation (Wolf 37). While for Perram the ending is merely ambiguous (161), Marschall (37-38) offers a more differentiated and subtle interpretation of the final scene as an indication of a beginning process of Bloch's incipient identity formation.

expectation ranging "from moral argument and meaning to the very existence of content" (Klinkowitz and Knowlton 16). Still, he not only shatters outmoded (modernist) reader expectation, he also proves that, after these conventions are tossed aside, one can still tell compelling stories (Klinkowitz and Knowlton 34). It becomes clear that Handke "endeavors to free the reader from the patterns of perception and societal conventions by means of the experience of alienation" (DeMeritt, *Subjectivity* 141; cf. Marschall 37). Handke exposes the state of human communication after its 'Fall from Grace' and focuses in *The Goalie's Anxiety* on human existence as one of isolation, alienation, and as a perennial odyssey in a symbolic universe.

*

Die Stunde der wahren Empfindung (1975; *A Moment of True Feeling*, 1977) may be seen as a continuation of the theme of the individual's alienation and domination by automatized categories of cognition (Nägele and Voris 61). As in *The Goalie's Anxiety*, this alienation has its basis in a linguistic code (Klinkowitz and Knowlton 60) that casts the protagonist at the center of a ubiquitous presence of signs. Other similarities between *Moment* and *Goalie* exist in the pervasive presence of literary echoes,[33] the sudden crisis of alienation accompanied by a loss of totality, the murder as catalyst, the acausal, fragmented storyline and its discontinuous thought processes as the constitutive feature of the narrative (Zürcher 52; Krajenbrink 127).

A Moment of True Feeling serves as a prime example of 1970s subjectivist literature in that it illustrates Handke's self-proclaimed agenda to explore *his* reality (*BE* 25) and his insistence on subjectivity as a means to transcend preconceived patterns of description and thought. The text focuses on the inner life of Gregor Keuschnig, an Austrian press attaché at the Paris embassy, his fears, dreams, desires, as well as his highly subjective, often erratic, at times frivolous, and

---

[33]Although critics have discussed its affinity to Sartre's *La Nausée* (1938; see Nägele and Voris 63; Critchfield, "Parody" 45-51), and Rilke's *Die Aufzeichnungen des Malte Laurids Brigge* (1910; *The Notebooks of Malte Laurids Brigge*, 1972; see Blasberg 520-35; Marschall 66-86; Saalmann), especially on the grounds that they all share a disgusted protagonist roaming the streets of Paris, Handke's narrative, at least its thematic and structural premise, is conceived in conspicuous analogy to Kafka's *The Metamorphosis* (Fickert; Binder 262-63; Pilipp, "Kafka").

by far not always coherent or logical sensory perceptions, associations, and thought processes.

The catalyst of the story is the main character's abrupt disconnection from his previous existence. All social, indeed all human, values have suddenly become meaningless as he finds himself in an identity crisis of existential proportions, initiated by a dream in which he has become a murderer. The dream shatters Keuschnig's reality and prompts him to construct a "new system of signification" (Klinkowitz and Knowlton 67). The (original German) title intimates the synthesis of the subjective (sensibility) and the objective (truth) (Pütz, *Handke* 79), summarizing an essentially Nietzschean premise: that truth can only be perceived from an elevated platform of consciousness, but that in order to attain this position the old one must be abdicated and left behind. This is the course initiated by Keuschnig's dream.[34]

As with Joseph Bloch after his presumed release, Keuschnig's life is ruled by a pervasive feeling of isolation and disorientation, and it is this negativity and his rejection of any system that forms the thematic basis for a narrative that essentially consists of the protagonist's quest for an affirmative, authentic existence. *A Moment of True Feeling* illustrates the main character's odyssey from the disillusionment about the way humans function in unreflected conformity to patterns of behavior, cognition, and expression to a changed worldview that provides the prerequisite for a sensibility freed from preset conventions. Tied to the protagonist's vision of the world via a subjective narrative perspective that is again reminiscent of the point-of-view style in Kafka's novels, the reader accompanies Keuschnig on his routes through Paris, with stops at home, at work, at his girlfriend's, and at a press conference, over a period of two days.

Parallel to Kafka's opening scene, Gregor Keuschnig awakens from an unsettling dream only to find out that "he had ceased to belong" (*M* 4).[35] The awakened consciousness that struggles with the (unchanged) human body both constitutes an ironic twist on Gregor

---

[34]The sole validity of subjective perception as a 'truer' layer of reality is expressed in Keuschnig's statement: "My dream was true ..." (25).

[35]Without specifying or pursuing these links, David Roberts ties the beginning of *Moment* to Kafka's *The Metamorphosis* and *The Trial* (89), while Manfred Jurgensen, in his socially-minded approach, presumes that Handke aspired to imitate Kafka's novella, concluding: "In both texts the socially isolated individual is abandoned by his family" (103).

Samsa's awakening, whose (unchanged) human consciousness is trapped within his transformed body. It is the occurrence of the out-of-the-ordinary, of the unthinkable, that has come to typify the Kafkan experience. In Handke's text, too, reality is suddenly disabled and conventional norms no longer apply. However, Handke goes beyond Kafka in that the altered consciousness reflects on itself and its previous constraints and entrapment. It adjusts to the strange situation and inaugurates a change of perspective required to establish a rapport with the world, something which Kafka's characters could never accomplish.[36]

What Handke adopts from Kafka is the idea of the instant of awakening as a critical existential moment; a moment of entering, embracing, and reconnecting with everyday reality, or one of exiting and being disconnected from it. During the transition between the two stages time stands still, and one is most vulnerable to being estranged from the everyday and runs the risk of waking up to a changed reality where previously existing precepts are no longer valid. This is the moment when the consciousness of the awakening person is jolted out of its familiar habitat and is confronted with the unfamiliar (or defamiliarized) and incomprehensible. For Kafka, the disconnection from the familiar was synonymous with a confrontation of the individual with an overwhelming, arresting, surrealistic force or authority, but one that laid bare previously alienating conditions and implied unfathomable possibilities for self-fulfillment. For Handke, this jolt also exposes an ossified routine (DeMeritt, *Subjectivity* 164) that stifles creativity and prevents self-actualization, even as it opens the possibility for genuine reorientation. Reversing Kafka, however, it is not Keuschnig who is perceived to be strange; rather, the world is perceived as "alien" (*M* 130) by him. Whereas in Kafka's tale it is Gregor who becomes the object of repulsion, in Handke's, Keuschnig is repulsed by the world outside.[37]

---

[36]That Handke associates the 'true feeling' with Kafka is underscored by an entry in his diary identified as a quote from Kafka: "('I should have to search for a year to find a true feeling inside me' – K.)" (*WW* 65). Keuschnig's metamorphosis leads exactly to that new feeling and existential reorientation.

[37]Binder (263) summarizes the parallels between the two texts as follows: "The first name Gregor, the nightmares, the awakening, the perception of a change of conditions, the survey of the room, the horizontal position in bed, the futile attempt to fall asleep again, the thoughts of murder ..., the alarm clock, the

Furthermore, in both texts, the flight back into sleep to fend off the changed reality is no longer possible. The opening depicts the moment of awakening where the protagonist realizes an unexpected change that took place during the night, defying all logic. While Keuschnig begins immediately to reflect on his transformation, Samsa simply seems to take it as a matter of fact, as if he were certain that the new situation is unchangeable (Gabriel 128-29). While Kafka's characters are arrested in a paralyzing inertia, Keuschnig's life will eventually take on a new outlook.

Clearly, Gregor Samsa served Handke as the prototype of the hapless victim who does not cross over too well into the familiar territory of wakening consciousness. The "bourgeois comfort" of Keuschnig's "usual life" (*M* 3) is shattered into "no kind of life" (*M* 7). In a sudden reversal of values, the former "harmony that was drummed into" him (*M* 25) has turned into an "eternal hubbub of absurdity" (*M* 32). Contrary to Samsa, who obstinately clings to his human background in a desperate attempt to reverse his transformation, Keuschnig immediately realizes that his metamorphosis can "never be undone" (*M* 4). While, akin to his Kafkan cousin, Keuschnig, too, worries about "the disgrace to [his] family" (*M* 4), he recognizes a causality Samsa would not see. He reflects critically on the regulatory and conditioning mechanisms of society at large and with regard to his work routine which consists of rather meaningless and superfluous duties. He reads French newspapers and corrects the image of Austria according to official "guidelines" (*M* 12),[38] a job that leaves him "not a free moment, every move [is] mapped out until ... he would switch off his bedside lamp" (*M* 24). Before his ominous dream, Keuschnig, like Samsa, had been leading merely a vicarious existence with a "self-image formulated by others" (Schlueter 139). Still, it is not only his self-image that was imposed by the outside world, but his entire worldview – thoughts that "were not his own" (*M* 60). The dream serves as a sort of reality check and initiates in Keuschnig a mental "jolt" (*M* 25),

---

morning train, the inflation of the body – this is the sequence of the motifs in the original that Handke has taken up."
[38]On Keuschnig's stupefying work role, see Pilipp ("Österreichbilder" 214-18).

creating first a "neither/nor in his head" (*M* 10),[39] soon followed by an inkling of another, liberated life (Klug 161).

In the interim, however, this "new life will consist solely in pretending to live as usual…. I can't live *like* anybody; at the most I can go on living 'like myself'" (*M* 8). This prospect fills Keuschnig with such nausea that he undergoes a virtual metamorphosis: "In the next moment he felt as though he were bursting out of his skin and a lump of flesh and sinew lay wet and heavy on the carpet" (*M* 8). Handke presents the metamorphosis as a psychological conflict; he adopts Kafka's theme without getting Kafkaesque. Later, in an effort to describe the indescribable, the process of metamorphosis itself is graphically illustrated:

> … Keuschnig, in full consciousness, had an experience he had never before encountered except in occasional dreams: He felt himself to be something BLOODCURDLINGLY strange, yet known to all – a creature exhibited in a nest and mortally ashamed, IM-MORTALLY DISGRACED, washed out of the matrix in mid-gesta-tion, and now for all time a monstrous, unfinished bag of skin, a freak of nature, a MONSTROSITY, that people would point at…. (*M* 78)

If Gregor Samsa, in his "unsettling dreams" that preceded his meta-morphosis, glimpsed a parasitical existence as vermin, one might claim that his vision contained an ambivalent thrust, that is, repulsion and enticement. After all, Samsa's sensations, which are dominated by fear, anxiety, and disgust, are sporadically interrupted by moments of unadulterated enjoyment. The same point can be made for Gregor Keuschnig. His dream of a "sex murder" (*M* 33) involving an old woman seems repugnant at first, even to himself, as it breaks with ultimate societal taboos. In fact, Keuschnig views this breach as the "unimaginable" (*M* 26), as some sort of perverse utopia for which there exists no word. Nevertheless, the crime is one of lust, and Keuschnig chooses to see it as the "first sign of life since God knows when" (*M* 25), even as his "dream of life" (*M* 26). In that respect, it is this dream, the signifier yet to be discovered (cf. Klug 163-65), that constitutes the titular moment of truth (Roberts 83), as the alienated self breaks out of its shell (Krajenbrink 133). The voidance of

---

[39]Cf.: "Everything had lost its validity, he could imagine nothing" (*M* 5). Later, everything appears to Keuschnig "equally unreal" (*M* 11); the original has "gleich ungültig" [equally invalid] (*St* 17).

traditional social norms and morals now provides a *tabula rasa* in need to be filled with new content.

On this Nietzschean quest for a revaluation of values (cf. Saalmann 503), the status quo has to be torn down before a new order can be erected. Keuschnig still has no clue for reorientation, but he has become all too conscious of the automatic and unquestioning conformism that shaped his persona. While he used to live this "role" (*M* 20) without opinion or reflection, he now has become an actor who plays it on the stage of the world and loathes every aspect of it.[40] His wish to "cross it all out" (*M* 14) and "abolish everything" (*M* 63) primarily refers to the prescriptive signs surrounding him: the symbolic order of language, especially media language, which forms the ideological foundation of human cognition.[41] The frequent capitalization of words and the italicizing of phrases in the text draw attention to the arbitrariness of meaning of a linguistic code that "has become its own reality" (Klinkowitz and Knowlton 69) and is used automatically.[42] Everything around him seems to occur according to preset rules and conventions that are neatly tied to normative linguistic patterns. Hyperconscious, Keuschnig puts everything into question, denigrates everything as trivial and predictable.[43]

Similar to Gregor Samsa, whose otherness implies untested potential for self-actualization, truth is explored in pre-moral (Mixner 220, 222) and socially tabooed forms of behavior as a fundamental protest

---

[40]Pütz (*Handke* 76) sees loathing as a leitmotif in *Moment*, especially regarding the threat of ossified perception so prevalent in Handke's own previous works. DeMeritt speaks of "regulatory meanings, patterns, and systems" (*Subjectivity* 165).

[41]Cf. the sentence: "I observe as if I were doing it for someone else! thought Keuschnig" (*M* 45). No doubt, Handke uses the verb *wahrnehmen* (to observe, perceive) here as a double-entendre to convey the idea of recognizing the real, the ultimate, and objective, in short: the true (*wahr*) meaning of things.

[42]An example would be the phrase "the fountain pen POISED in his hand" (*M* 39) ["die in seiner Hand GEZÜCKTE Füllfeder" (*St* 52)]. This example illustrates why signification seems random and questionable to Keuschnig. In German, the verb *zücken* describes a fast drawing motion of such weapons as knives and swords, but it is also used in a metaphorical sense in reference to writing utensils, a meaning that seems to puzzle Keuschnig.

[43]The following passage is typical of Keuschnig's negativism: "Now, he thought, they'll be putting their preposterous arms around each other, looking into each other's pitiful eyes, kissing each other's pathetic cheeks, left and right. And then imperturbably they'll go their senseless ways" (*M* 29).

against the process of acculturation and socialization (Renner 97). Whereas it is the fear of desire that constitutes the disturbance in *The Metamorphosis*, Handke highlights the forbidden desires of his protagonist. Sneering at the "high towers of civilizations" (*M* 34), Keuschnig, in a series of regressive behavior patterns (Klug 157), tears down traditional taboos: his exhibitionistic whims (*M* 9, 50, 52), the reviving smell of urine (*M* 14), the "sudden impulse to bare his teeth" (*M* 15), the enjoyment of emitting "a loud fart" (*M* 23), the desire to "howl" (*M* 16, 108), to "bellow" (*M* 52) or "to go mad" (*M* 117), his letting out "an animal cry" (*M* 120), the sheer pleasure of "[m]ere breathing, even swallowing" (*M* 129), the contentment of smelling "his own sweat" (*M* 120); all of this illustrates the culturally subversive potential underlying his urges, underscored also by the frequent depiction of aggressive tendencies, sexual and scatological situations.[44] Thus, Handke's protagonist realizes the positive potential of his metamorphosis and eventually inculcates in himself a sensibility that makes everything "bearable" again (*M* 130).[45] In contrast to *The Metamorphosis*, which ends with the death of the pitiful creature and reconfirms the patriarchal order, Keuschnig breaks with the repressive system (Klug 156). He can muster his free will and find an artistic gaze to adopt a new lease on life. When Keuschnig exclaims: "'I can change'" (*M* 64), the emphasis lies clearly on the power of the self.

The titular moment of true feeling is generally seen in the episode when Keuschnig espies three objects in the grass: a chestnut leaf, a piece of a pocket mirror, and a child's barrette. In a sudden moment of absolute clarity and naïve vision, they appear to him as "miraculous objects" (*M* 63) and reveal "the IDEA of a mystery" (*M* 64). No doubt this passage is central to the narrative and marks a turning point in Keuschnig's disposition, for it is here that he experiences a momentary freedom from, as one critic put it, the "intellectual terror-

---

[44]Very appropriatley, Klug (152, 156) speaks of a schizoid rebellion of Keuschnig's repressive super-ego against his internalized feelings of guilt and shame with constructively subversive consequences that eventually lead to what Bartmann (185) has termed a second socialization. Linstead comments that "Keuschnig's repressed inner world breaks through, in all its brutality and sexual aggression" (153; cf. also Krajenbrink 137, note 31).
[45]This translation is not quite accurate. The original has "erlebbar" (*St* 162), meaning that something can be experienced.

ism of the technocratic rationality, ideological functionalism, and metaphysical escapism of the modern world" (Tabah, "Structure" 160). In the tradition of Joyce's concept of epiphany, Virginia Woolf's "moments of being" and Musil's "other state," Handke grants his protagonist a moment of pure sensation, where the perceiver is not concerned with meaning but rather views the perceived object divested of meaning and context.[46] In this moment he "evokes their authentic nature by clustering them in a timeless constellation" (Pizer 88) and Keuschnig gains revelatory insight into his interconnectedness with a world previously perceived as meaningless (Rey 396). It is essentially a mystical experience,[47] "divorced from any social context," that takes place on that value-free basis which is the foundation for a new innocence (Pütz, *Handke* 78) and makes possible a new curiosity for and relationship with the world: "'Who said the world has already been discovered'" (*M* 63).[48]

After this epiphany, Keuschnig feels "so free" and experiences a "magical proximity" (*M* 64) between inner and outer world that the future seems desirable again. At this point in the narrative, his emotions move away from an exclusively negative thrust and begin to oscillate between disgust and newfound contentment. While at one moment he perceives life around him as occurring "year in year out with the same inexorability, predictability, mortal tedium, and deadly exclusivity" (*M* 62), he can sense in the next instant "a new, calm life feeling" (*M* 63). This seesawing rhythm (DeMeritt, *Subjectivity* 170-74) dominates the second part of the text, time and again highlighting the random nature of Keuschnig's perceptions legitimated simply by

---

[46]While it seems sensible that Handke chose the number three to illustrate the mystical effect of the objects in question, I agree with Linstead (161) that it would be futile to try to decode a meaning of these objects. As Fickert writes, it is "precisely the insignificance of these random objects which allows them to be transformed" (106). By contrast, Frietsch is at pains to explore the symbolic significance of the number three (106-11).

[47]According to Handke's own statements in the interview with Arnold (29).

[48]Wagner sees this as the novel's main weakness and states with unveiled irony: "The alienated employee has turned into a vigorous world conquerer" (234). Scherpe and Treichel suggest that Keuschnig's occupation as a bureaucrat can hardly obscure the artist's gaze (193). Similarly, Bartmann argues that Keuschnig's aesthetic rediscovery of the world will lead to a rediscovery of social meaning, signifying a new beginning after his experiment in negation (191).

the exclusive validity of a subjective individual sensibility. This alternation of joy and loathing becomes the constitutive feature of the second half, until the balance eventually shifts toward unyielding optimism. When Keuschnig overcomes his previous "disgust," "hate," and "horror" (*M* 107) he realizes the idea of the world as mystery: "In becoming mysterious to him, the world opened itself and could be reconquered" (*M* 121). In acquiring a defamiliarizing and innocent gaze that accepts the world as "alien" (*M* 130) and coincidental, it regains its naïve character as a mystery.[49] The mystery does not have to be expressed; it reveals itself to the beholder in the guise of coherence, union, and harmony.[50] Sudden desire, longing and imagination congeal into an inner steadfastness through which Keuschnig acquires the serenity to rediscover a continuity that lets him envisage a "more sustained yearning" for a non-alienating kind of "work, the outcome of which would be as valid and unimpeachable as a law" (*M* 129).

In this subjectively willed fashion – the vision of the meaningfulness of his work within the human community exists only in Keuschnig's imagination – the protagonist gains a new, albeit tentative (Sergooris 89), equilibrium that solidifies into a "conviction with which he can work, thereby transforming happiness into a more lasting state."[51] Keuschnig's aesthetic socialization by way of the power of imagination (Jurgensen 116) will determine his continuing efforts to rediscover "a world made inaccessible by means of the systems and explanations which eradicate its strangeness and secrecy" (DeMeritt, *Subjectivity* 169). Not entirely without justification, Handke has been taken to task for this unscrupulous insistence on inwardness and capriciousness. The novel has been called a narcissistic hall of mirrors (Durzak 127) in which the protagonist "experiences alienation or enthusiasm according to his private disposition" (Linstead 157), a state upon which the protagonist is unable or unwil-

---

[49]This attitude corresponds to Wittgenstein's adage that the mystery of the world is not what it is like but rather *that* it is (*Tractatus* 6.44).

[50]Again, the parallel to Wittgenstein is conspicuous: "There exists indeed the inexpressible. This will *reveal* itself. It is the mystical" (*Tractatus* 5.522).

[51]Weber (197) criticises Handke's text for its fairy-tale ending, because it illustrates the depoliticization of Handke's writing and his inability to draw consequences from the fragmentation of reality that implicitly banks on the reader's acquiescence to the status quo of a world of contradictions.

ling to reflect (Pakendorf 135). Under criticism was also the awkward creation of a fictional context (Durzak 126) in which the depicted events emerge as a conglomerate of gratuitous epiphanies, vapid banalities, and pretentious pseudo-insights (Nägele and Voris 64-65).

The narrative, some scholars have argued, lacks motivation, psychology (Wagner 230; Buselmeier 58), authenticity (Durzak 134), and fails to illustrate believable interpersonal and social causes underlying the protagonist's crisis and his mysterious overcoming it (Bullivant 29; Améry 470). The relevance given to a social and historical context fades completely (Scherpe and Treichel 199), instead full emphasis is placed on the protagonist's inner workings as unquestionable and absolute (Wagner 231). This results in a fragmented narrative stream consisting of an unconnected series (Roberts 99) of microelements and interchangeable perceptions.[52] Consequently, the rapid succession of fleeting conditions or phases (Bartmann 183) never coalesce into a meaningful whole (Wagner 232; Durzak 134) nor point to a meaning that might transcend the narrated events. Hence, the 'moment of true feeling' is simply one experience in a chain of random and sudden experiences contingent on the protagonist's subjective disposition. It remains one episode among many and therefore arbitrary, impetuous, and inconsequential (Bartmann 190).[53]

At any event, the outcome of Keuschnig's transformation is hinted at in the final paragraph of Handke's text. Determined to meet the unknown woman whose telephone number he previously copied off the pavement, he evidences a fresh sense of orientation based on a shared feeling of an affirmative existence (Wellershoff 60) and a desire to reintegrate himself into a social community with others.[54] But again, the process of negating the negative status quo,

---

[52]Handke himself states that every object and perception becomes interchangeable in its emotional value and therefore everything has lost validity (Arnold 22-23; cf. DeMeritt, *Subjectivity* 171).

[53]Contrarily, Klug sees this as a process mediated with psychological subtlety and differentiation (155).

[54]Klug even calls this Keuschnig's "euphoric return to the fellowship of humanity" (165). Quite contrarily, Goettsche comments that, in view of the uncertainty of his personal circumstances, Keuschnig's social reintegration is by far not guaranteed (286). Roberts calls the ending an inevitable dead-end street (98), and Pakendorf sees it as an awkward and artificial solution in light of the status quo (141). In contrast to the majority of the critics, Saalmann (506) considers the novel's conclusion compelling and true to reality, as he sees

of looking at the outside world as defamiliarized and mysterious, does not generate a consciousness-raising dialectical process (Scherpe and Treichel 203). Until the end, the text makes it abundantly clear that Keuschnig's serenity rests on unstable feelings the scope and durability of which are by no means guaranteed. His ability to come to his own "Platonic rescue" and effect his own "aesthetic redemption" (Pizer 79) by converting his feeling of alienation into one of happiness seems fickle and capricious at best, incredible at worst. The undeniable lack of a 'real' experience is covered up by attributing sole legitimacy to the illusive act of the art of perceiving (Scherpe and Treichel 204).[55]

In the end, Keuschnig is shown as having "reinvent[ed]" (*M* 116) himself as that "new man" (*M* 88) he had envisioned earlier and has managed to transform his resolution to die (*M* 116) into a new aesthetic beginning in that the epiphanizing gaze becomes applicable (Goettsche 285-86). The narrative perspective is now removed from Keuschnig's vision and reflects the outside stance of a seemingly omniscient narrator. In keeping with Handke's theme of gaining a fresh perspective, this narrator would still be Keuschnig, who has now attained that plateau he was striving for since his liberating dream and which is the paradoxical synthesis of a subjectively perceived objective vantage point. Clues earlier in the story repeatedly point to Keuschnig's vision of himself as the protagonist of an unheard-of event.[56] As "the hero of an unknown tale" he walks "resolutely" (*M* 133) toward the café where the unknown woman is presumably waiting.[57] While Keuschnig could be seen here as an anonymous individual disappearing in the masses (Bartmann 192), and his new anonymity as essential for the restitution of his personality (Saal-

---

Keuschnig successfully overcoming the social, economic, and political parameters that had previously defined him.

[55] Again, Klug assesses this outcome in positive terms and maintains that through the process of alienation, Keuschnig has achieved a change of consciousness and gained a new receptivity to the world (164).

[56] The translation renders "eine unerhörte Geschichte" (*St* 145) as "a most extraordinary experience" (*M* 115).

[57] Fickert writes: "His manner of dressing indicates that he has achieved independence, but not at the price of having to exhibit antisocial behavior. The man with murder in his heart has become the circus clown ... – his ultimate transformation" (113). Critics have also pointed out that Keuschnig's clothes reflect the colors of Goethe's Werther (cf. Klug 165; Blasberg 534).

mann 511), he, like his predecessor Bloch, becomes the protagonist on the meta-fictional level of the story about to begin (Jurgensen 119).

The protagonist's sudden insight into the deceptive conventions of what humans have come to call reality and the concomitant loss of connectedness can be read as an analogy to the end of innocence. Now Keuschnig is no longer *keusch* ("nig" is related to "nicht" [Fickert 92]), whereas his daughter Agnes (Latin for 'lamb') serves as a counterfigure, whose natural innocence and lack of guile mystify him.[58] He subsequently embarks on an odyssey marked by skepticism, disgust, depression, and aggression. Ironic allusions to major literary motifs of the Romantic period manifest themselves when Keuschnig can no longer comprehend the lost meaning of the gurgling water in the gutter, "relat[ing] to an almost forgotten event" (*M* 22). Furthermore, repeated references are made to a rustling sound (*rauschen* or *rieseln*) usually heard outside[59] that seems to contain some essential message Keuschnig is unable to decipher because he is no longer in touch with his origins.

His loss of coherence stands in stark contrast with Agnes, whose "self-sufficiency" ("Fürsichsein" [*St* 141]) illustrates that she lives an existence of genuine harmony: the pride she exudes has a quality that is "objective"; living in a original state of naïveté, she is, to use a Nietzschean phrase, a law unto herself, an autonomous entity living in a state of truth in which Keuschnig cannot partake: "If only he could perceive with her!" (*M* 112). Perhaps his finally "steering a westerly course" (*M* 127) implies that, after the failed attempt of a

---

[58]This is why later Keuschnig envisions relief through "[c]hildren's voices" (*M* 103). They represent the Romantic harmony he knows is lost but enjoys as a "feeling that one could return home on foot from any point whatsoever" (*M* 121). Jurgensen (116) calls this impression, quite appropriately, an "aesthetic formula for a neo-Romanticism."

[59]This is, for example, a favorite motif of Eichendorff. Further references are: "the leaves ... could be heard rustling" (*M* 4); "... that swishing sound – where did it come from?" (*M* 57); "murmuring trees" (*M* 61); "the plane trees ... murmured" (*M* 62); "no rustling, only a soft, almost eerie breathing" (*M* 82); "the roar of cars" (*M* 83); "The trees set up a rustling" (*M* 116). In Handke's film book *Falsche Bewegung* (1975; False Move), too, Wilhelm takes a copy of Eichendorff's novella *Aus dem Leben eines Taugenichts* (1826; *Life of a Good-For-Nothing*, 1988) with him, so Eichendorff is clearly a reference for Handke and his protagonists.

direct return to Eden "eastward" (*M* 117), he is ready to make the journey (westward) around the world and re-enter it, as Kleist would have it (345), through the back door.[60] That Keuschnig moves "weightless[ly]" (*M* 118) suggests that he has found his natural grace again (cf. Kleist 342). While this is simply playful, postmodernist Romantic irony, the parallels to Romantic literature are not too far-fetched. Most notably in the works of Eichendorff and Tieck, the disturbing aspect of this so-called reality is that it systematizes, regulates, limits, confines, and controls the protagonists who then begin to explore the darker sides of life.[61]

But there is another important aspect pertaining to this adventure about to begin with Keuschnig as the hero. Earlier when Agnes suddenly disappears, Keuschnig speaks with a parking lot attendant: "Calmly and deliberately, as the guardian *would testify later on*, he gave him his addresses ..." (*M* 117; emph. add.). The future testimony of the attendant intimates that more ominous, though untold, events are to follow. While it is uncertain whether they concern the disappearance of Agnes or Keuschnig's encounter with the woman (the latter is more likely since the story to follow is leading up to it), it seems that they will involve the police. Earlier hints in the narrative – especially Keuschnig's positive interpretation of his dreamed *Lustmord* as the first sign of (a new) life that promised unheard-of gratification, his frequent explorations of breaking societal taboos, and his imagined metamorphosis into a grotesque and monstrous being – suggest that, now that his daughter is gone, he has divested himself of all ties to his former existence and actually becomes that murderer he already was in his dream, thus giving in to a mode of existence that used to deter him.

This would mean that Gregor Keuschnig actualizes what Gregor Samsa could never accept: to renounce all societal and familial, moral and ethical, indeed all human considerations and commit (to) the indescribable, inexpressible, and unthinkable. After establishing a new *Wertfreiheit* (freedom of and from values), Keuschnig will put into practice that "idea of a mystery" he gained earlier in the park. In that sense, his initial dream would serve as the catalyst for divesting

---

[60]Cf. Buselmeier (50) who also mentions the analogy to Kleist's essay "Über das Marionettentheater" (1811; "On the Puppet Theater," 1982).
[61]Esp. in such stories as Tieck's "Der Runenberg" (1810; "The Runenberg," 1985) or "Das Marmorbild" (1819; "The Marble Statue," 1985).

himself of his old consciousness, the scene in the park as the catalyst for the discovery of a higher consciousness, and the untold (and untellable) story as the actual experience of the "moment of true feeling." Whatever offense Keuschnig is to perpetrate, it will be committed as if in a societal vacuum, in an extra-moral sense, as it were, outside of any depictable system, but in that "other state" which lies beyond language and therefore cannot be communicated, but which is the only sphere that allows true sensation.

*

Although similar in theme to *The Goalie's Anxiety* and *Moment*, the slender narrative *Die linkshändige Frau* (1976; *The Left-Handed Woman*, 1977) makes for a markedly different reading experience. No longer does a personal narrator privy to the protagonist's inner workings mediate the fictional events. Instead, Handke employs a neutral narrative voice (Handke, "Tür" 240) that exercises rigorous restraint and does not purport to possess superior insight into the characters (Pütz, *Handke* 88). The interior perspective of the earlier narratives is now replaced with an exterior one where the depicted events speak for themselves (Linville and Casper 16). In that the characters are "observed with the sober, objective eye of the camera" (Linstead 168), the narrative technique resembles a film script. Indeed *The Left-Handed Woman* was initially conceived as a screenplay and Handke himself subsequently directed the film of the same name in 1977.[62]

After a brief exposition, the narrative lacks any further plot development, as the idea of a story in the traditional sense seems to have become superfluous (Schlueter 155). Unspectacular and entirely without extreme situations – there are neither actual nor dreamed murders – the novella mainly depicts a succession of unconnected scenes from everyday life (Sandberg 65), mostly moments of perception and meditation (Renner 108) lending it a deliberately quiet and static quality (Linville and Casper 17; Bartmann 222).[63] When the narrative does focus on movements, these are usually "routines that appear automatic and ritualized, yet strange and awkward"

---

[62]Bleicher (126) comments that reading the text is like watching a film, for "the text shows everything one can espy."

[63]Bartmann (226) comments that the narrative process with its deliberate detachment from the subject constitutes an ideal continuity in itself, as opposed to the narrated discontinuity and fragmentation of Keuschnig's story.

(Linville and Casper 15). Due to its ostensible renouncement of motivation, psychology, and characterization (Renner 104) and its "elliptical style" that moves abruptly from scene to scene (Linville and Casper 16), any action is minimized and the characters and their movements reduced to unusually flat representations (Corrigan 261). This is underlined by the characters' direct speech which appears contrived and purposely artificial (Klein 245). Having the protagonist appear as if in a still life or a cinematic mise-en-scène (Pütz, *Handke* 89) underlines Handke's shift to an aesthetic of the visible and audible, the expressivity of gazes, gestures, postures, and speech.

The narrative strategy of *The Left-Handed Woman* is to illus-trate, almost entirely without authorial commentary, that what is externally perceptible is the effect of inner turmoil (Mixner 231; Renner 109) and complex psychological processes (Nägele and Voris 66). The only commentary is provided by the characters themselves, whose monologues and dialogues almost exclusively center around loneliness and isolation (Brokoph-Mauch 75). Sidestepping insinuations of any underlying causal patterns, Handke frustrates reader expectations (Nägele and Voris 69) and redirects the focus to the everyday and insignificant – the woman is often shown reading or sewing or just gazing –, thus substantiating the appended Goethe quote, "as though nothing were wrong" (*LW* 89) ["als ob von nichts die Rede wäre"; *LF* 133]. In this way, the narrative discontinuity creates gaps to be filled, thwarting habitual reader responses (Linville and Casper 17).

As in *The Goalie's Anxiety*, the catalyst for the story is reminis-cent of the titular theme of Ingeborg Bachmann's collection *The Thirtieth Year*, where the protagonists, sparked by a sudden burst of consciousness, embark on a year of crisis and transition. Handke, too, has his thirty-year-old heroine experience an "illumination" (*LW* 12, 13; a central motif, similar to the abrupt "jolt" in *Moment*, for Handke as well as for Bachmann), which initiates sudden in-sights into the web of dependencies governing her life. Marianne recognizes that she leads an "average middle-class bourgeois" exist-ence (Ingalsbe 3) where everyone is in unquestioning conformity with traditional gender roles.[64] While she plays the triple role of homemaker, wife and mother, Bruno plays the roles of husband, businessman and father, though his first and foremost concern is his professional career for which he seems to spend most of his time on business trips. Beyond that, the mechanisms of their marital relationship are anchored in the dynamics of her subservience to his dominance.[65] Thus, she acts as chauffeur to the airport, and as an attentive waitress-servant at home (*LW* 9). In order to parade her like a trophy, Bruno has her wear a "low-cut dress" (*LW* 10) to dinner, and in the hotel restaurant he requests a room, announcing: "You see, my wife and I want to sleep together right away" (*LW* 11). Oblivious to her feelings, Bruno revels in unadulterated narcissism, declaring enthusiastically how he enjoys being waited on, as if all his happiness depended on it (*LW* 12). In this way, their marriage mirrors a feudal master-servant relationship (Ingalsbe 6-7), but one where the master lives under the delusion that by imposing his needs on his servant-wife he fulfills hers as well (Linstead 167).

As a rule, all decisions concerning the family are his, and Bruno makes it clear that his happiness depends on 'having' her and being assured of her devotion to him. His self-identity is based on the subjugation of her mind and body – besides having sex with her at will, he threatens her (*LW* 48), gets "rough" (*LW* 21), hits her, and even murders her symbolically when he burns her photograph under

---

[64]Like Bachmann, Handke references here Nietzsche's thirty-year-old Zarathustra, who is struck by a flash of awareness about the duplicitous nature of human affairs and consequently severs all relationships in order to withdraw into a hermitic existence of reflection.

[65]A very similar constellation is found in Bachmann's narrative "Ein Schritt nach Gomorrha" (1961; "A Step Toward Gomorrha," 1987), where the female protagonist's acquiescence to the rigid structures of a male-dominated society is challenged while her controlling husband Franz is on a business trip. An ironic reflection of Franz's inflexible views may be seen in the character of Franziska in *The Left-Handed Woman*. In general, the characters who attempt to exert some kind of influence on Marianne are male: husband, father, editor, potential lover, and her friend Franziska, the 'masculine' feminist. The patriarchal master-servant or tormentor-victim dichotomy is also played out in other character constellations, e.g. between the publisher and his chauffeur, and, although only playfully, between Marianne's son and his friend. As Linville and Casper (18) point out, however, Handke does not tie this representation of society to neo-Marxist concepts, just as Marianne resists the ideas of the women's support group.

her nose (*LW* 22). In short, he reduces her to "an object acted upon" (Klinkowitz and Knowlton 72), exemplifying a culture where a woman is the "object of psychological and physical abuse" (Critchfield, "Abuse" 33). At work, Bruno practices tactics of intimidation, such as a "power stare" (*LW* 40), a gaze that, contrary to Marianne's, is self-centered, unreceptive and manipulative, and underlines his rigid and intolerant personality and obsession with power mechanisms (Nägele and Voris 68). Marianne's pose, on the other hand, is yielding ("nachgiebig" [*LF* 10], awkwardly translated as "she seemed to bend to her thoughts" [*LW* 5]), receptive, and indiscriminating. Her gaze constitutes a dynamic between inner and outer, subjective and objective world, where what is outside is absorbed into the self and the inner world projected into the images observed.[66] Handke portrays his protagonist as a person possessing extraordinary inner, spiritual strength and an almost mystical aura exuding an unsurpassed empathy, gentleness and serenity that has a soothing effect on others (*LW* 73).[67]

Marianne's illumination[68] occurs while performing her quotidian duties, prompted by her son's writing assignment on "my idea of a better life" (*LW* 4). Determined to try out a (not yet resolved) alternative to the extant male ideology of rationalism, instrumentalism, performance and domination (Tabah, "Weiblichkeit" 127), the thus illuminated housewife asks her husband to leave her. Since he, too, is engaged in constant role-play and theatrics (*LW* 55), she wishes he would also embark on a path to self-discovery. It becomes clear that liberation is perceived as "the transcendence of fixed and rigid definitions of social roles, be they of women or men" (Critchfield, "Abuse" 34). By ending their mutual acquiescence to pre-scripted roles, however, Bruno's identity seems to fall apart and for most of the narrative he appears aimless and confused in his efforts to reconquer her (Linstead 167) and reassert his male

---

[66]Handke himself speaks of the "interpenetration of self and world" ("Paar" 141).

[67]Nägele and Voris (71) as well as Tabah ("Weiblichkeit" 127) note that Handke, by endowing the woman with this mystifying aura, succumbs to the cliché of the feminine 'other' as a masculine conception.

[68]The eye/light-motif is introduced on the first page and recurs when her eyes "light up" (*LW* 3), "shine" (*LW* 26), or "glisten" (*LW* 46); in one passage her entire face "lit up" (*LW* 11).

authority (Brokoph-Mauch 72). In contrast to Marianne, he does not recognize the possibility, let alone the necessity, of unalienated, authentic relationships with others and oneself.[69]

The main focus of *The Left-Handed Woman*, then, may be seen as the "stoic resistance" (Corrigan 263) of an awakened consciousness to public discourses and "the conventional phallocentric norms which determine the parameters of her existence" (Ingalsbe 5). Nevertheless, Handke completely detaches his narrative from social reality (Wagner 237; Linstead 168; Brokoph-Mauch 79), thus illustrating that Marianne's voyage of self-discovery can only succeed by withdrawing from any ideological discourse of valuation and domination (Tabah, "Weiblichkeit" 127). The story of Marianne is not so much a social critique of a woman's emancipation reflecting on the coercive role patterns of a patriarchal society (Tabah, "Weiblichkeit" 126); rather, her protest is an intuitive rejection of the given (Renner 106).[70] Discarding all fixed images, judgments, and opinions formed by others about her, the only authenticity for Marianne lies in the prospective actualization of her potential (Pütz, *Handke* 95). The consistent reference to her as "the woman" (as opposed to the use of her husband's proper name) emphasizes that potential, for to "be recognized as an individual and not as a functional part of someone else's system is her demand" (Klinkowitz and Knowlton 74).

Other than in *A Moment of True Feeling*, Marianne's goal is not work-related or dependent on societal conditions. Society at large fades into insignificance (Nägele and Voris 68), and on the few occasions where Marianne does come in contact with external reality (*LW* 42-43), it is "overshadowed by the spectre of insults and injuries" (Critchfield, "Abuse" 32). Set against a "background of aggression and hostility," the outside world is portrayed as "so brutal, male-oriented and collectively organized that her self-isolation is bound to appear as an 'emancipation' in itself" (Linstead 168-69). That Marianne consequently perceives her surroundings as

---

[69]Tabah comments that this is a utopian projection without a concrete societal basis, but as such it is a dream of a not yet realized possibilty ("Weiblichkeit" 127).

[70]See also Handke's comment that the "possibility of a different kind of society" implied in his story, lies first and foremost in the "negation" of the status quo ("Paar" 142).

an ongoing "long-lasting catastrophe" (*LW* 42) – this psychological insight represents one of very few authorial interventions – emphasizes her desire for escape and liberation (Runzheimer 126). But her "dreamlike withdrawal into long, nearly catatonic silences" (Schlueter 148) – the impression of her as a "mystic" of sorts (*LW* 22) is not unbefitting – defies any kind of intersubjective connectivity. Like Bloch's impassive non-participation in society or Keuschnig's impetuous rebellion against the cultural super-ego, Marianne's insistence on inner, private freedom and imagination,[71] epitomizes the essence of the literary current of the 1970s' New Inwardness. And as any inwardness, Marianne's, too, is marked by a good deal of narcissism attested to by her frequent gazes in the mirror and her avowed enjoyment in engaging in, even overdoing, sessions of intra-subjective communication (Bleicher 125) as attempts at self-orientation.

Another means to mediate the heroine's self-searching is the insertion of secondary texts that indirectly comment on her situation (Pütz, *Handke* 93). Thus, the titular left-handedness, celebrated in the lyrics of Jimmy Reed's country song, accentuates, on the one hand, Marianne's unique individuality and her refusal to conform to a prescribed order or system (Wagner 239).[72] On the other, it serves to connect her uniqueness with a like-minded 'other,' yearning for a future harmony together in an "unknown continent." The undiscovered, unpredictable, and undefined, which harks back to Gregor Keuschnig's encounter with the unknown woman at the end of *Moment*, is also central to the French biography Marianne is translating. As in the title song, that author's expectation that in "the land of the ideal" a man should love her for what she is and what she "shall become" (*LW* 35) matches that of Marianne.[73]

---

[71]Wagner (239) views this as anti-social, hence negative, claiming that the subject is left to engage exclusively with herself with no possibility for interaction.

[72]Cf. also Ingalsbe: "The left-handed individual implies a direct contrast with the right-handed norm, those around whom society has regulated itself. With its clearly defined rules of conduct and conventional thought, bourgeois society has forced the Left-handed Woman to conform, to go through the motions of life in a manner contrary to her true self" (3).

[73]However, as Brokoph-Mauch points out (75), Marianne's gesture – she shrugs her shoulders – seems to express a rejection of these statements and therefore infuses a note of ambiguity into her expectation from a potential life partner.

The translation Marianne is working on seems like a companion text (Haberkamm 383), as it mirrors her own life in greater detail. Like Bruno, the husband in the French text wants his wife to be strong, though only to perform those domestic tasks in which he is not interested, while otherwise destroying her (*LW* 36). Consequently, that author speaks for Marianne again: "'The man I dream of is the man who will love me for being the kind of woman who is not dependent on him" (*LW* 47). The emphasis on the flexible, independent, and not-to-be-determined individual – a notion of a relationship prior to humankind's fall from grace (Haberkamm 382) – is central to her idea of a future mate: "Even if I were always with him, I wouldn't want to know him" (*LW* 54), for knowing him would be synonymous with forming a fixed image and not loving the other for what he or she may be(come).

The narrative, then, is an exploration of solitude as a prerequisite for personal integrity and new autonomy (Pütz, *Handke* 87), an autonomy that, as Handke himself comments, allows Marianne to escape her multiple roles ("Tür" 240). While the idea of breaking out of an existence ostensibly predetermined by patriarchal discourses (cf. Corrigan 264) has been inconceivable to her before, it now becomes imperative (Klinkowitz and Knowlton 62). Still, a new, livable existence has yet to be discovered. Reminiscent of Gregor Keuschnig's predicament after his dream caused by the "neither/nor in his head" (*M* 10), Marianne's dilemma is a similar one, for the text that initiates her illumination, her son's essay, inadvertently breaks down the fundamental logic of human existence (cf. Ingalsbe 5). His naïve wish that the weather be "neither hot nor cold" (*LW* 4) puts into question a universally accepted binary value system.

In limbo between the rejected status quo and a yearned-for, yet uncertain, ideal, between reality and utopia, Marianne sets out to find a new basis for self-determination. Like Keuschnig, she undertakes the dissolution and subsequent reconstitution of a coherent sense of self (Bartmann 222). Despite well-meant warnings and counsel from those close to her about the torments of self-isolation and of living "in the wrong direction" (*LW* 59), she is unwilling to make concessions. Shunning all social relationships and insisting on a meditative and aesthetic space for herself, she settles for the "peace of an asocial world" (Schlueter 152; cf. Brokoph-Mauch

74).[74] Inevitably she chooses to tread her path solitarily – in "powerful isolation," as Handke remarked ("Paar" 143) –, and any synthetic systems, such as a women's support group whose assistance she is offered, must prove deceptive. In fact, her friend Franziska, that group's leader, appears dictatorial and intolerant, spouting political slogans and platitudes that remain shallow and sentimental (Ingalsbe 10; Haberkamm 383; Critchfield, "Abuse" 31). Her feminist brand of emancipatory ideas, which demand a dogmatic change of roles and automatic opposition in line with the "historical conditions" (*LW* 22), is ridiculed rather than validated (Renner 108).[75] Marianne refuses to exchange one ideologically determined role for another, declaring the only political action acceptable to her the anarchic option of "run[ning] amok" (*LW* 55).

At times she appears lost in a spatial-temporal vacuum "as if in a trance" (*LW* 5) or, akin to the epitome of purity and innocence, Keuschnig's daughter Agnes, entirely self-sufficient ("für sich" [*LF* 12, 16, 50; cf. *St* 141], translated as "self-possessed" [*LW* 6] and "to herself" [*LW* 9, 31]).[76] The central scene that epitomizes her resolute protest takes place in front of the mirror where she engages in soliloquy: "I don't care what you people think. The more you have to say about me, the freer I will be of you.... From now on, if anyone tells me what I'm like, even if it's to flatter or encourage me, I'll take it as an insult and refuse to listen" (*LW* 23). Quietly

---

[74]In this withdrawal, Corrigan recognizes the "central paradox" of the narrative: the "definition of a *social* space only as it is produced by an individual's demand for a private space" (273).

[75]Critchfield comments: "She is, above all, the prototype not so much of the woman in revolt, but of those who pay lip service to her. The satirical portrayal of Franziska creates a ludicrous figure, if not a caricature of an avowed feminist" ("Abuse" 32). Hence Schlueter remarks that "Handke is not constructing a feminist myth so much as he is deconstructing it" (150). And Tabah adds that, like Bruno, Franziska stands for a male fixation on predetermined patterns of thought and behavior ("Weiblichkeit" 126).

[76]Schlueter (152) sees Marianne "return[] to a pure self, a symbolic childhood representative of a self which has not yet been subsumed by the demands of civilization." Marschall speaks of a "harmony of nature and culture" (113). In the text, Marianne sees children as an aid for existential self-reflection (*LW* 85).

and persistently, completely without aggression,[77] and with un-
matched "spiritual energy" (Marschall 113), she persists in her protest against unquestioned, "limiting and, above all, coercive"
(Critchfield, "Abuse" 34) role patterns, indeed against any non-subjective identity-determining forces. With unconditional self-reliance
and self-assertion, this heroine rejects to live what Handke has
termed a predetermined biography ("Paar" 140; cf. Linstead 164).

At the end, the heterogeneous group of disconnected characters
introduced in the course of the narrative is united at a party at Marianne's. It is a "communal, conciliatory coming together ... made
possible by the special magnetism of the woman whom all expected
to find alone" (Linville and Casper 20). Almost magically, all social
hierarchies are temporarily transcended (Linstead 165) and gender-
roles seem discarded (Ingalsbe 11), as Handke has his figures express themselves honestly without defining themselves or each
other by assuming role patterns (Knowlton and Klinkowitz 73).[78]
Thus, in stylized scenes of "unaffected spontaneity" (Ingalsbe 11),
individual essences can determine the structure of existence and not
the other way around. Toward the end, Marianne is proud to have
successfully preserved her integrity and can tell her mirror image:
"You haven't given yourself away. And no one will ever humiliate
you again" (*LW* 87).

The sum of her subsequent 'actions' – pouring herself a drink,
rolling up her sleeves, relaxing comfortably, and beginning to draw
– subtly suggest Marianne's new self-confidence and determination.
By letting the outside world enter her (cf. the emphasis on her dilat-
ing pupils), she can sketch herself as an integral part of the immediate and wider surroundings. In fact, her personal space becomes an
integral part of *space*, as the sketch proceeds from her toes to the
room to the window to the starry sky (*LW* 87): the self as a part of,
but also as an autonomous entity in the universe. This marks the

---

[77]Only once is she momentarily overcome by a bout of violence and starts to
throttle her son, but, as Handke states, this merely shows Marianne's emotional
stress as a consequence of her self-isolation ("Tür" 239).

[78]Linville and Casper comment aptly: "It is as if, for a brief period, that inner
integrity that Marianne increasingly acquires has drawn the others into an orbit
and exerts an inexplicable fascination, paradoxically offering a respite from
inner isolation to those characters now gathered around this woman who has
chosen social isolation" (20; see also Critchfield, "Abuse" 34)).

culmination of a gradually evolving process in creativity and self-actualization (Pütz, *Handke* 100). Her progression from sewing to translating to drawing, an act of creating art, may be seen "as a metaphor for the beginnings of her new life" (Critchfield, "Abuse" 35). She is "now in control of her surroundings rather than allowing them to control her, yet she does not steal from their individuality, either" (Klinkowitz and Knowlton 75).

An artistic-creative process, her drawing preserves the objects' uniqueness while maintaining her personal integrity and freedom from determining forces.[79] In antithesis to societal discourses, this constitutes her non-verbal discourse of self-definition. A brief epilogue reinforcing an optimistic ending concludes the narrative. The static image of the beginning, where Marianne is sitting fixedly with a blanket over her knees has changed to an image of levity, contentment, and motion that shows her moving gently in a rocking chair, with fir trees swaying in the breeze. No longer in need of a synthetic security (blanket), she lifts her arms as if in victory. This final image hints at Marianne's successful transformation into a new autonomous, authentic self that has rediscovered sensibility, sensuality, and imagination as part of her previously suppressed (feminine) existence (Tabah, "Weiblichkeit" 128).

As in the case with *A Moment of True Feeling*, the reception of *The Left-Handed Woman* has not been unequivocal. Contrasting with the majority of favorable assessments, Handke has been sharply criticized for having lost sight of social reality and for employing a pretentiously poetic diction that oscillates between deliberate simplicity and artificial pathos (Durzak 145). Thus, the novella's style has been classified as trivial literature (Durzak 144), its content disqualified as insignificant (Lüdke).[80] It seems more likely, however, that *The Left-Handed Woman*'s indebtedness to trivial literature, as well as to fairy-tales, is intended.[81] Handke often uses traditional literary genres, only to transform them in his narratives:

---

[79] Again, Wagner (239) views this outcome as negative, calling it a speechless and anti-social escape from societal constraints.

[80] Contrarily, by adducing the split reception of Handke's novella of the feuilleton reviewers, Eschbach and Rader demonstrate that a universally valid classification as trivial is impossible.

[81] Michael Klein (esp. 239-47) has elucidated numerous structural and formal parallels between *The Left-Handed Woman* and the German *Volksmärchen*.

the detective novel in *The Goalie's Anxiety*, the *Bildungsroman* (novel of identity formation) in *Falsche Bewegung*, and the woman's novel in *The Left-Handed Woman* (Pütz, *Handke* 98). While the woman's novel generally ends with the protagonist's yearned-for union with the male 'other' who is needed to complete her, Handke's ironic transformation of that genre leads to the liberating separation for the female protagonist.

*

In *The Goalie's Anxiety*, Handke exposes the process of identity formation on the basis of a systematically linguistic world as arbitrary yet inescapable and shows how individuals are enslaved by a confining, one-dimensional system of normative signification. In *A Moment of True Feeling*, he illustrates an individual's attempt at ridding himself of a thus constructed identity and the ensuing search for an existence beyond universally accepted conventions (Tabah, *Vermittlung* 298). Keuschnig's self-discovery is shown to succeed by his withdrawal into the realm of the subjective, aestheticizing and poeticizing the objective and rejecting the conventional in terms of moral, ethical, social, and linguistic parameters. In *The Left-Handed Woman*, freedom from systematic definition and personality-delimiting forces also proceeds from finding sanctuary in a solitary and meditative state where one detaches oneself from any external encroachments to achieve and preserve personal integrity.

The Goalie's Anxiety at the Penalty Kick, *A Moment of True Feeling* and *The Left-Handed Woman* attest to Handke's own statement that his "primary literary intent is the destruction of predetermined systems and concepts of reality" (*BE* 20). Handke is writing against an internalized normative order which produces meanings not intrinsic to the things themselves (Tabah, *Vermittlung* 300) and for the "freedom from that captivity of consciousness produced by the alienating verbal and cultural patterns which filter daily existence" (Linville and Casper 21).[82] Each of the texts presents an individual who has recognized these patterns as artificial constructs, and illustrates the rebellion against cultural forces that seek to cement normative modes of perception.

---

[82] Or, as DeMeritt adds, "the power of the code to perpetuate itself depends solely upon the individual's unwillingness or perhaps inability to question it" (*Subjectivity* 146).

Once more, the analogy to Ingeborg Bachmann's stories in *The Thirtieth Year* becomes apparent. Although Bachmann has her protagonists' quest for transcendence constantly end in failure, she insists on the constant striving for the unattainable. Convinced that we don't live in the only possible of all worlds, she continuously stresses that by engaging in the dialectical interplay of status quo and utopia, the possible and the seemingly impossible, we expand "our capacities" ("Wahrheit" 276). It is up to us to generate the tension of this dynamic that aims for a higher level of consciousness and more authentic forms of expression. Handke's texts, too, in their appeal to the reader's critical faculties, imply a utopian perspective of a freer and unmanipulated form of living in a world where humans would dare transcend the normative power of words and objects and would cease to obey a seemingly inescapable routine of living under the alienating rule of a symbolic universe and its ideologically prescriptive schemes.

Works Cited

Adams, Jeffrey. "The Undoing of *Angst* in *Die Angst des Tormanns*: Handke's Creative Response to Kafka.." *Carleton Germanic Papers* 22 (1994) 1-14.

Améry, Jean. "Grundloser Ekel: Marginales zu Peter Handkes neuem Buch *Die Stunde der wahren Empfindung*." *Merkur* 29 (1975) 468-71.

Arnold, Heinz Ludwig. "Gespräch mit Peter Handke." *Text und Kritik* 24. Ed. Heinz Ludwig Arnold. 3rd ed. Munich: edition text + kritik, 1976. 15-37.

Bachmann, Ingeborg. "A Wildermuth." *The Thirtieth Year.* Trans. Michael Bullock. New York: Holmes & Meier, 1987. 133-70.

–. "Fragen und Scheinfragen." *Werke* 4. Ed. Christine Koschel, Inge von Weidenbaum, and Clemens Münster. Munich, Zurich: Piper, 1978. 182-99.

–. "Musik und Dichtung." *Werke* 4. 59-62.

–. "Die Wahrheit ist dem Menschen zumutbar." *Werke* 4. 275-77.

Barry, Thomas F. "Language, Self and the Other in Peter Handke's *The Goalie's Anxiety at the Penalty Kick*." *South Atlantic Review* 51.2 (1986) 93-105.

–. "Kafka and Handke: Poetics from Gregor to the Gregors." *The Legacy of Kafka in Contemporary Austrian Literature*. Ed. Frank Pilipp. Riverside, CA: Ariadne, 1997. 61-90.

Bartmann, Christoph. *Suche nach Zusammenhang. Handkes Werk als Prozeß*. Vienna: Braumüller, 1984.

Binder, Hartmut. "Metamorphosen: Kafkas 'Verwandlung' im Werk anderer Schriftsteller." *Probleme der Moderne: Studien zur deutschen Literatur von Nietzsche bis Brecht*. Festschrift for Walter Sokel. Ed. Benjamin Bennett, Anton Kaes, and William J. Lillyman. Tübingen: Niemeyer, 1983. 247-305.

Blasberg, Cornelia. "'Niemandes Sohn'? Literarische Spuren in Peter Handkes Erzählung *Die Stunde der wahren Empfindung*." *Poetica* 23 (1991) 513-35.

Bleicher, Thomas. "Filmische Literatur und literarischer Film: Peter Handkes Erzählung 'Die linkshändige Frau' und Sembene Ousmanes Film 'Xala' als Paradigmata neuer Kunstformen." *Komparatistische Hefte* 5-6 (1982) 119-37.

Bohnen, Klaus. "Kommunikationsproblematik und vermittlungsmethode [sic] in Peter Handkes *Die Angst des Tormanns beim Elfmeter*." *Wirkendes Wort* 26 (1976) 387-400.

Bohrer, Karl Heinz. "Wo hören und sehen vergeht." Rev. of *Die Angst des Tormanns beim Elfmeter. Über Peter Handke*. Ed. Michael Scharang. Frankfurt am Main: Suhrkamp, 1973. 64-68.

Brokoph-Mauch, Gudrun. "Fiktion und Wirklichkeit in Peter Handkes *Wunschloses Unglück* und *Die linkshändige Frau*." *In Search of the Poetic Real. Essays in Honor of Clifford Albrecht Bernd*. Stuttgarter Arbeiten zur Germanistik 220. Stuttgart: Heinz, 1989. 67-79.

Brown, Russel E. "Names in Handke's *Die Angst des Tormanns beim Elfmeter*." *Literary Onomastics Studies* 12 (1985) 63-73.

–. "Peter Handke's *Die Angst des Tormanns beim Elfmeter*." *Modern Language Studies* 16.3 (1986) 288-301.

Bullivant, Keith. "Möglichkeiten eines subjektiven Realismus. Zur Realismusdiskussion der 70er Jahre. Zu Peter Handkes 'Die Stunde der wahren Empfindung' und Uwe Timms 'Kerbels Flucht.'" *Subjektivität, Innerlichkeit, Abkehr vom Politischen? Tendenzen der deutschsprachigen Literatur der 70er Jahre*. Ed. Keith Bullivant, et al. Bonn: Deutscher Akademischer Austauschdienst, 1986. 19-34.

Buselmeier, Michael. "Das Paradies ist verriegelt." *Text und Kritik* 24. Ed. Heinz Ludwig Arnold. 3rd ed. Munich: edition text + kritik, 1976. 57-62.

Corrigan, Timothy. "The Tension of Translation: Handke's *The Left-Handed Woman* (1977)." *German Film and Literature: Adaptations and Transformations*. Ed. Eric Rentschler. New York: Methuen, 1986. 260-75.

Critchfield, Richard.. "From Abuse to Liberation: On Images of Women in Peter Handke's Writing of the Seventies." *Jahrbuch für internationale Germanistik* 14 (1982) 27-36.

—. "Parody, Satire, and Transparencies in Peter Handke's *Die Stunde der wahren Empfindung*." *Modern Austrian Literature* 14.1/2 (1981) 45-61.

DeMeritt, Linda. "Handkes Anti-Geschichten. Der Kriminalroman als Subtext in *Der Hausierer* und *Die Angst des Tormanns beim Elfmeter*." *Experimente mit dem Kriminalroman. Ein Erzählmodell in der deutschsprachigen Literatur des 20. Jahrhunderts*. Ed. Wolf Düsing. Studien zur deutschsprachigen Literatur des 19. und 20. Jahrhunderts 21. Bern, Frankfurt am Main: Peter Lang, 1993. 185-203.

—. *New Subjectivity and Prose Forms of Alienation: Peter Handke and Botho Strauss*. Studies in Modern German Literature 5. New York: Peter Lang, 1987.

Demetz, Peter. "Peter Handke." *After the Fires: Recent Writing in the Germanies, Austria, and Switzerland*. San Diego, New York, London: Harcourt Brace Jovanovich, 1986.

Dixon, Christa K. "Peter Handke: *Die Angst des Tormanns beim Elfmeter*. Ein Beitrag zur Interpretation." *Sprachkunst* 3.1 (1972) 75-97.

Durzak, Manfred. *Peter Handke und die deutsche Gegenwartsliteratur: Narziß auf Abwegen*. Stuttgart: Kohlhammer, 1982.

Eschbach, Achim, and Wendelin Rader. "Ist die 'linkshändige Frau' trivial? Überlegungen zur literarischen Wertung." *LiLi: Zeitschrift für Literaturwissenschaft und Linguistik* 27/28 (1977) 104-16.

Fickert, Kurt. "The Other Gregor: Peter Handke's *A Moment of True Feeling*." *The Legacy of Kafka in Contemporary Austrian Literature*. Ed. Frank Pilipp. Riverside, CA: Ariadne, 1997. 91-116.

Firda, Richard Arthur. *Peter Handke*. Twayne's World Author Series 828. New York: Twayne Publishers, 1993.

Forster, E. M. *Aspects of the Novel*. 1927. New York: Harcourt, Brace & World, 1954.

Frietsch, Wolfram. *Die Symbolik der Epiphanien in Peter Handkes Texten: Strukturmomente eines neuen Zusammenhanges*. Sinzheim: Pro Universitate, 1995.

Gabriel, Norbert. *Peter Handke und Österreich*. Bonn: Bouvier, 1983.

Göttsche, Dirk. *"Die Angst des Tormanns beim Elfmeter* – Dezentrierung und Versprachlichung des Bewußtseins." *Die Produktivität der Sprachkrise in der modernen Prosa*. Hochschulschriften Literaturwissenschaft 84. Frankfurt am Main: Athenäum, 1987. 264-74; 418-20.

–. *"Die Stunde der wahren Empfindung* – Epiphanie und Krise." *Die Produktivität der Sprachkrise in der modernen Prosa*. Hochschulschriften Literaturwissenschaft 84. Frankfurt am Main: Athenäum, 1987. 282-94; 422-25.

Haberkamm, Klaus. "Linkshändig, nicht links: Die von Goethes *Wahlverwandtschaften* vorgegebene Links-Rechts-Dichotomie in Handkes *Linkshändiger Frau*." *Mutual Exchanges*. Ed. Dirk Jürgens. Frankfurt am Main: Peter Lang, 1999. 370-85.

Hamm, Peter. "Handke entdeckt sich selbst." *Über Peter Handke*. Ed. Michael Scharang. Frankfurt am Main: Suhrkamp, 1973. 159-66.

Handke, Peter. "Die Angst des Tormanns beim Elfmeter." *Text und Kritik* 24. Ed. Heinz Ludwig Arnold. 2nd ed. Munich: edition text + kritik, 1971. 45.

–. "Durch eine mystische Tür eintreten, wo jegliche Gesetze verschwunden sind." *Peter Handke*. Ed. Raimund Fellinger. Frankfurt am Main: Suhrkamp, 1985. 234-41.

–. "Ich bin ein Bewohner des Elfenbeinturms." *Ich bin ein Bewohner des Elfenbeinturms*. Frankfurt am Main: Suhrkamp, 1972. 19-28.

–. "Und plötzlich wird das Paar wieder denkbar." *Der Spiegel* 10 July 1978: 140-44.

–. "Zur Tagung der Gruppe 47 in den USA." *Ich bin ein Bewohner des Elfenbeinturms*. 29-34.

Hartwig, Heinz. "Peter Handke und die Sprache. Sprache und Wirklichkeit oder *Kaspar*." *Peter Handke: Sechs Beiträge*. Ed.

Ivar Sagmo. Osloer Beiträge zur Germanistik 11. Oslo: Repro-sentralen, 1986. 2-24.

Haslinger, Adolf. *Peter Handke: Jugend eines Schriftstellers.* Salz-burg, Vienna: Residenz, 1992.

Heintz, Günter. *Peter Handke.* Stuttgart: Klett, 1971.

Henschen, Hans-Horst. "Die Reklame der Gegenstände für sich selber." Rev. of *Die Angst des Tormanns beim Elfmeter. Über Peter Handke.* Ed. Michael Scharang. Frankfurt am Main: Suhrkamp, 1973. 74-78.

Herzmann, Herbert. "Der Tormann Moosbrugger. Über Musil und Handke." *Wirkendes Wort* 34.2 (1984) 67-76.

Ingalsbe, Lori Ann. "Woman beyond the Myth: A Feminist Reading of Peter Handke's *Linkshändige Frau.*" *New German Review: A Journal of Germanic Studies* 7 (1991) 1-14.

Jurgensen, Manfred. "'Die zuständig gewordene Poesie'? Peter Handke: *Die Stunde der wahren Empfindung.*" *Handke: Ansätze – Analysen -- Anmerkungen.* Ed. Manfred Jurgensen. Queensland Studies in German Language and Literature 7. Bern: Francke, 1979. 101-20.

Kann, Irene. "Leben im Augenblick und Sehnsucht nach Dauer: Peter Handke." *Schuld und Zeit. Literarische Handlung in theologischer Sicht: Thomas Mann – Robert Musil – Peter Handke.* Paderborn: Schöningh, 1992. 167-252.

Kanzog, Klaus. "Die Standpunkte des Erzählers und der Kamera. Peter Handkes und Wim Wenders [sic] *Die Angst des Tormanns beim Elfmeter.* Point-of-View-Probleme im Film-Text und in der Text-Verfilmung." *Erzählung und Erzählforschung im 20. Jahr-hundert.* Ed. Rolf Kloepfer and Gisela Janetzke-Dillner. Stutt-gart: Kohlhammer, 1981.157-68.

Klein, Michael. "Peter Handke: 'Die linkshändige Frau': Fiktion eines Märchens." Ed. Johann Holzner, Michael Klein, and Wolf-gang Wiesmüller. *Studien zur Literatur des 19. und 20. Jahrhun-derts in Österreich. Festschrift für Alfred Doppler zum 60. Geburtstag.* Innsbrucker Beiträge zur Kulturwissenschaft, Ger-manistische Reihe 12. Innsbruck: Kowatsch, 1981. 235-52.

Kleist, Heinrich von. "Über das Marionettentheater." *Sämtliche Werke und Briefe.* Vol. 2. Ed. Helmut Sembdner. Munich: Hanser, 1961. 338-45.

Klingmann, Ulrich. "Handkes *Die Angst des Tormanns beim Elfmeter*: Buchtext und Filmtext." *Germanic Review* 70 (1995) 164-73.

Klinkowitz, Jerome, and James Knowlton. *Peter Handke and the Postmodern Transformation: The Goalie's Journey Home.* Columbia, MS: U of Missouri P, 1983.

Klug, Christian. "Peter Handkes frühe Postmoderne: Desintegration als Befreiung in *Die Stunde der wahren Empfindung* (1975)." *Der deutsche Roman nach 1945.* Ed. Manfred Brauneck. Bamberg: Buchner, 1993. 152-66.

Krajenbrink, Marieke. *Intertextualität als Konstruktionsprinzip. Transformationen des Kriminalromans und des romatischen Romans bei Peter Handke und Botho Strauß.* Amsterdam: Rodopi, 1996.

Kurz, Paul Konrad. "Sprach-Exerzitien als Gegenspiel." *Über moderne Literatur.* Vol. 4. Frankfurt am Main: Knecht, 1973. 9-52.

Lenzen, Arnulf. "Gesellschaft und Umgebung in Handke: *Die Angst des Tormanns beim Elfmeter.*" *Wirkendes Wort* 26 (1976) 401-06.

Linstead, Michael. *Outer World and Inner World: Socialization and Emancipation in the Works of Peter Handke, 1964-1981.* European University Studies Series 1, German Language and Literature 1024. Bern, New York, Paris: Peter Lang, 1988.

Linville, Susan, and Kent Casper. "Reclaiming the Self: Handke's *The Left-Handed Woman.*" *Literature/Film Quarterly* 12.1 (1984) 13-21.

Lüdke, Martin W. "Als ob von nichts die Rede wäre: Notizen zur Wahlverwandtschaft einer 'linkshändigen Frau.'" *Goethes Wahlverwandtschaften: Kritische Modelle und Diskursanalysen zum Mythos Literatur.* Ed. Norbert W. Bolz. Hildesheim: Gerstenberg, 1981. 52-63.

Marschall, Susanne. *Zum Problem der Wirklichkeit im Werk Peter Handkes. Untersuchungen mit Blick auf Rainer Maria Rilke.* Sprache und Dichtung 43. Bern, Stuttgart, Vienna: Haupt, 1995.

Meier, Elisabeth. "'Abgründe dort sehen lernen, wo Gemeinplätze sind.' Zur Sprachkritik von Ödön von Horváth und Peter Handke." *Sprachnot und Wirklichkeitszerfall. Dargestellt an Beispielen neuerer Literatur.* Ed. E. Meier. Düsseldorf, 1972. 19-61.

Mixner, Manfred. *Peter Handke.* Kronberg: Athenäum, 1977.

Nägele, Rainer, and Renate Voris. *Peter Handke.* Autorenbücher 8. Munich: Beck, 1978.

Nef, Ernst. "Peter Handkes neue Schriften und seine Entwicklung." *Universitas* 31 (1976) 1241-45.

O'Neill, Patrick. "The Role of the Reader. Signs and Semiosis in Peter Handke's *Die Angst des Tormanns beim Elfmeter.*" *Seminar* 27.4 (1991) 283-300.

Pakendorf, Gunter. "Empfindungen eines entfremdeten Individuums. Zu Peter Handkes Geschichte des Gregor Keuschnig." *Handke: Ansätze – Analyse – Anmerkungen.* Ed. Manfred Jurgensen. Frankfurt am Main: Suhrkamp, 1979. 121-44.

Perram, Garvin. *Peter Handke: The Dynamics of the Poetics and the Early Narrative Prose.* Frankfurt am Main: Peter Lang, 1992.

Peter Handke: Sechs Beiträge. Ed. Ivar Sagmo. Osloer Beiträge zur Germanistik 11. Oslo: Reprosentralen, 1986.

Pilipp, Frank. "In Defense of Kafka: The Case of Peter Handke." *The Legacy of Kafka in Contemporary Austrian Literature.* Ed. Frank Pilipp. Riverside, CA: Ariadne, 1997. 117-50.

–. "Österreichbilder in Peter Handkes *Die Stunde der wahren Empfindung.*" *Modern Austrian Literature* 30.4 (1997) 213-21.

–. "Peter Handke's Coming to Terms With Kafka: *Stunde der wahren Empfindung.*" *Modern Austrian Prose: Interpretations and Insights.* Ed. Paul Dvorak. Ariadne: Riverside, CA, 2001. 107-28.

–. "Tabus und Utopie: Aspekte zur sprachphilosophischen Identität österreichischer Autoren." *Modern Austrian Literature* 29.3/4 (1996) 57-74.

Pizer, John. "Phenomenological Redemption and Repressed Historical Memory: Benjamin and Handke in Paris." *Monatshefte* 81 (1989) 79-89.

Pütz, Peter. "Die Angst des Tormanns beim Elfmeter." *Deutsche Bestseller – Deutsche Ideologie.* Ed. Heinz Ludwig Arnold. Stuttgart: Klett, 1975. 145-56.

–. *Peter Handke.* Frankfurt am Main: Suhrkamp, 1982.

Reinhardt, Stephan. "Handkes 'Tormann,' Handkes Skrupel." *Text und Kritik* 24. Ed. Heinz Ludwig Arnold. 2nd ed. Munich: edition text + kritik, 1971. 50-55.

Renner, Rolf Günter. *Peter Handke.* Stuttgart: Metzler, 1985.

Rinner, Fridrun. "Der Erzählwandel bei Handke: Beschreibung als Reflexion." *Erzählung und Erzählforschung im 20. Jahrhundert.* Ed. Rolf Kloepfer and Gisela Janetzke-Dillner. Stuttgart: Kohlhammer, 1981. 169-77.

Roberts, David. "Peter Handke: *Die Stunde der wahren Empfindung.*" *Handke: Ansätze – Analysen – Anmerkungen.* Ed. Manfred Jurgensen. Frankfurt am Main: Suhrkamp, 1979. 83-100.

Rossbacher, Karlheinz. "Detail und Geschichte: Wandlungen des Erzählens bei Peter Handke, am Vergleich *von Die Angst des Tormanns beim Elfmeter* und *Der kurze Brief zum langen Abschied.*" *Sprachkunst: Beiträge zur Literaturwissenschaft* 6 (1975) 87-103.

Runzheimer, Doris. *Peter Handkes Wendung zur Geschichte: Eine komponentialanalytische Untersuchung.* Beiträge zur Neuen Epochenforschung 8. Frankfurt am Main: Peter Lang, 1987.

Saalmann, Dieter. "Subjektivität und gesellschaftliches Engagement: Rainer Maria Rilkes *Die Aufzeichnungen des Malte Laurids Brigge* und Peter Handkes *Die Stunde der wahren Empfindung.*" *Deutsche Vierteljahrsschrift für Literaturwissenschaft und Geistesgeschichte* 57 (1983) 498-519.

Sandberg, Beatrice. "Text und Film *Die linkshändige Frau.* Zu Handkes Darstellungsweise." *Peter Handke: Sechs Beiträge.* Ed. Ivar Sagmo. Osloer Beiträge zur Germanistik 11. Oslo: Reprosentralen, 1986. 56-72.

Scherpe, Klaus R, and Hans-Ulrich Treichel. "Vom Überdruss leben: Sensibilität und Intellektualität als Ereignis bei Handke, Born und Strauß." *Monatshefte* 73 (1981) 187-206.

Schlueter, June. *The Plays and Novels of Peter Handke.* Pittsburgh, PA: U of Pittsburgh P, 1981. (The chapter on *The Goalie's Anxiety at the Penalty Kick,* pp. 79-92, is a slightly revised reprint of the author's article "Handke's 'Kafkaesque' Novel: Semiotic Processes in *Die Angst des Tormanns beim Elfmeter.*" *Studies in Twentieth Century Literature* 4.1 [1980] 75-88.)

Sebald, W. G. "Unterm Spiegel des Wassers – Peter Handkes Erzählung von der Angst des Tormanns." *Austriaca* 16 (May 1983) 43-56.

Seibert, Thomas-Michael. "Gerechtigkeit als Kampf um Sprachzugang: Bemerkungen zu Ernst v. Steffen, 'Rattenjagd,' und Peter Handke, *Die Angst des Tormanns beim Elfmeter.*" *Autor und*

Täter. Ed. Klaus Lüderssen and Thomas-Michael Seibert. Frankfurt am Main: Suhrkamp, 1978. 53-97.

Sergooris, Gunther. *Peter Handke und die Sprache.* Abhandlungen zur Kunst-, Musik- und Literaturwissenschaft 270. Bonn: Bouvier, 1979.

Summerfield, Ellen. "Die Kamera als literarisches Mittel: Zu Peter Handkes *Die Angst des Tormanns beim Elfmeter.*" *Modern Austrian Literature* 12.1 (1979) 95-112.

Tabah, Mireille. "Structure et fonction de l''épiphanie' dans l'oeuvre de Peter Handke à partir de *La courte lettre pour un long adieu* et *L'heure de la sensation vraie.*" *Etudes Germaniques* 47.2 (1993) 147-66.

–. *Vermittlung und Unmittelbarkeit. Die Eigenart von Peter Handkes fiktionalem Frühwerk (1966-1970).* Frankfurt am Main: Peter Lang, 1990.

–. "Weiblichkeit im Werke Peter Handkes. Zur Darstellung einiger Frauenfiguren des Autors." *Geschlechterdifferenz in der Literatur: Studien zur Darstellung der weiblichen Psyche und zum Bild vom anderen Geschlecht in zeitgenössischer Dichtung.* Ed. Michel Vanhelleputte. Europäische Hochschulschriften Series 1, Deutsche Sprache und Literatur 1473. Frankfurt am Main: Peter Lang, 1995. 119-30.

Thornton, Thomas K. *Die Thematik von Selbstauslöschung und Selbstbewahrung in den Werken von Peter Handke.* Europäische Hochschulschriften Series 1, Deutsche Sprache und Literatur 659. Frankfurt, Bern, New York: Peter Lang, 1983.

Thuswaldner, Werner. *Sprach- und Gattungsexperiment bei Peter Handke.* Salzburg: Verlag Alfred Winter, 1976.

Vannatta, Dennis. "Wittgenstein, Handke's *Goalie's Anxiety at the Penalty Kick*, and the Language of Madness." *The Literary Review* 28 (1985) 606-16.

Wagner, Karl. "Peter Handkes Rückzug in den geschichtslosen Augenblick." *Literatur und Kritik* 134 (1978) 227-40.

Watson, Scott B. "One Guess is as Good as Another: Reading Life Into Handke's Soccer Goalie." *Aethlon* 18.1/2 (Spring 2001) 47-56.

Weber, Norbert. "Peter Handke: Die Stunde der wahren Empfindung." *Das gesellschaftlich Vermittelte der Romane österreichischer Schriftsteller seit 1970.* Europäische Hochschulschriften

Series 1, Deutsche Sprache und Literatur 345. Frankfurt am Main: Peter Lang, 1980. 185-201.

Wellershoff, Irene. *Innen und Außen. Wahrnehmung und Vorstellung bei Alain Robbe-Grillet und Peter Handke.* Munich: Fink, 1980.

White, J. J. "Signs of Disturbance: The Semiological Import of Some Recent Fiction by Michel Tournier and Peter Handke." *Journal of European Studies* 4 (1974) 233-54.

Winkelmann, Christine. *Die Suche nach dem 'großen Gefühl.' Wahrnehmung und Weltbezug bei Botho Strauß und Peter Handke.* Frankfurt am Main, Bern: Peter Lang, 1990.

Wittgenstein, Ludwig. *Tractatus Logico-philosophicus. Logisch-philosophische Abhandlung.* 1921. Frankfurt am Main: Suhrkamp, 1969.

Wolf, Jürgen. *Visualität, Form und Mythos in Peter Handkes Prosa.* Opladen: Westdeutscher Verlag, 1991.

Zürcher, Gustav. "Leben mit Poesie." *Text und Kritik* 24. Ed. Heinz Ludwig Arnold. 3rd ed. Munich: edition text + kritik, 1976. 38-56.

Handke's *Slow Homecoming* Tetralogy

Karl Wagner[*]

LIKE HARDLY ANY OTHER contemporary author, Peter Handke has developed a keen and discerning perception in using images illustrative of the passage of time as well as dimensions of time, which assume a particular function with regard to structure and rhythm of his texts. In his works as in his writing routine Handke counters the constraints of measured time with a different measure: the sequence of the seasons, of night and day and of parts of the day, thereby illustrating their succession and transition. Handke thus celebrated emphatically the completion of *Kindergeschichte* (1981; *Child Story*, 1985) – at the end of the book he indicates "Salzburg, Spring and Summer 1980" as the time and place:

> I've just now completed *Child Story* – "and now off to the wine bar!" I have never been so far from death – and if I had to die tonight! Under the elder bush two snorting hedgehogs circle one another, a Greek sun glistens on their spines, like on fur. In the summer wind, the entire house stands there like an hour glass. The jasmine leaves whirl through the garden like snow. The lime blossoms sway out of the cypress. The torn-out stinging nettles smell like "Wild Woman." The plantain, light-green, cools the childhood wounds anew; and the brightest green in the garden comes from the apple tree. Today is summer! Today the pencil's point is a towering mountaintop from out of the clouds! 'Carry me into the sunset,' says the Lady from Shanghai. And I've made a clean sweep for my next decade. (*GB* 229)

The threefold repetition of "today," the epitome of summer and of the moment of bliss and triumph, fans out into the sphere of nature so significant for Handke's writing (elder, jasmine, cypress, stinging nettle, apple tree, plantain) and whose iridescence visualizes the yearly cycle ("like snow"; "lime blossoms"). The author's past and future life appear in harmony, and the new decade is inaugurated with an erotic promise. Through the sequence of descriptive details a context materializes. The description of the sun as "Greek" under-

---

[*]Translated by David N. Coury and Frank Pilipp.

scores the image of happiness and points to the just completed work, which, after all, invokes the Greek historian Thucydides as the chief advocate of narrative structure and cohesion (cf. *GB* 227 and motto of *Child Story*). Although Handke reaffirms Thucydides' practice of writing historiography at the end of the subsequent decade in *Noch einmal für Thukydides* (1990; *Once again for Thucydides*, 1998), this does not adequately characterize the 1980s as a homogeneous entity, neither with regard to Handke's biographical circumstances nor his literary output.

The years from 1979 to 1987 were "settled and domestic" years (*FM* 5) for Handke, during which, after five years in Paris, he lived in Salzburg with his daughter Amina, born in 1969 from his first marriage, so as to allow her an education in her native language. The Salzburg years came after Handke's sojourn in the United States (1978-1979). In terms of his writings, a crucial and conscious change occurred, which Handke himself has reflected upon on several occasions. The narrative *Langsame Heimkehr* (1979; *The Long Way Around*, 1985), written mostly in the United States and expanded upon in quick succession by *Die Lehre der Sainte-Victoire* (1980; *The Lesson of Mont Sainte-Victoire*, 1985), *Child Story* and *Über die Dörfer* (1981; *Walk About the Villages*, 1996) to form a tetralogy, caused sharp controversy like no other of his previous works and changed Handke's public stature as a writer.[1]

Handke has always been aware of this. Shortly before concluding *The Long Way Around* he writes in his journal *Die Geschichte des Bleistifts* (1982; The Pencil's Story): "With my earlier works I still experienced myself under the protection of the others, the pioneers. With my current work, however, I am entirely on my own (though without being a pioneer). But in writing there probably are no pioneers, only repeaters. And the repeaters are the loneliest

---

[1]The connectedness of the works in the tetralogy no doubt eludes the English-speaking reader. What Ralph Manheim translated under the title *Slow Homecoming* (1985) is a trilogy, consisting of *The Long Way Around, The Lesson of Mont Sainte-Victoire* and *Child Story*. While one cannot assume that this practice of publishing occurred without the author's permission, one also shouldn't overemphasize the genre aspect of the tetralogy. On the dust jacket of the first edition of *Über die Dörfer* one reads: "First the story of the sun and snow; then the story of names; then the story of a child; now the dramatic poem: altogether they should be called *Slow Homecoming*."

people on earth; repetition is the loneliest occupation" (*GB* 128). He notes something similar during the genesis of *Child Story*: "Wherever I write, I am (in the meantime) completely alone. But with me are all of the good spirits" (*GB* 227). This entry accentuates the solitary role of the writer, who is aware of the loss of his "charisma" (cf. *FM* 473) but sees himself in the diachronic context of a literary tradition that sets the standards for him (but also in synchronic relation to a number of other contemporary authors). The awareness of being exposed and the risk of exposing one's self in the process of writing, traumatically experienced as the loss of language in the writing process, leaves its mark on the tetralogy as a whole.

Handke's intentional and highly precarious transformation of his previously successful writing method manifests itself in a postulatory rhetoric and in an at times imperiously prophetic tone – no doubt a tribute of sorts to his reading of Heidegger and Nietzsche during these years. At the same time, Handke's public statements, both verbal and written, consist of disgruntled and brusquely self-righteous tongue-lashings. As 'threshold texts' to a new, ever more serene series of works that reached an undisputed climax in 1986 with *Repetition*, the tetralogy nevertheless assumes a programmatic significance – a significance, however, that is much more easily recognizable in retrospect than immediately after the individual texts appeared between 1979 and 1981.

Central to this writing approach is a heightened self-reflection and self-examination that can be seen in the individual texts as well as in his notes on reading and writing from 1976 to 1980 collected in the journal *Die Geschichte des Bleistifts* and continued with *Phantasien der Wiederholung* (1983; Fantasies of Repetition) and *Am Felsfenster morgens* (1988; Mornings at the Natural Arch). Handke even draws upon his own translations. As in the case of Ralph Manheim's translations into English, the rendition of his work by someone else enables Handke to gain a serene distance from and, at the same time, to receive a strong confirmation of his own writing. Via the linguistic work of the translator, that of a foreign language, the author's own language becomes accessible and workable yet again: "In any case, the English sentences of my translator Ralph Manheim will be an even stronger guiding principle for my German prose in the future!" (*MuS* 32). Handke pledged in his eulogy of his deceased translator.[2] In retrospect, this not only confirms the urgency of Handke's new beginning but also intimates the panic of his search at that time: "Exactly those elements of my work that were foreign to him (especially the religious – or hysterical – search for place in *The Long Way Around*) did not repulse him, the Jewish cosmopolitan ladies' man and garden lover, but rather inspired him to reify it in his wonderfully dry, yet flexible and light, even painterly English" (*MuS* 31).

Handke himself forcefully announced this critical change of his writing approach, with particular mention of Franz Kafka (which has been used repeatedly in the critics' polemic against Handke). As the literary critic Reinhard Baumgart points out in his recollections of Handke's oft-recounted appearance at the meeting of Group 47 in Princeton, Handke placed his birth as a writer on the world's stage in relation to Kafka: "Then a small young man in a dark-blue suit stood up, a man whom nobody there knew, but who proclaimed at the Empire State Building in front of the rolling NBC cameras a few days later: I am the new Kafka. His name was Peter Handke" (Baumgart 242). Handke introduced his new writing project in, of all places, the speech he gave upon being awarded the Kafka Prize (and in accompanying notes), placing himself, as he did in other reflections and observations of the time, in a different relation to Kafka. The portentous statement, "I hate Franz Kafka, the eternal son" (*PhW* 94), should not obscure the fact that in the Kafka Prize speech he states: "Franz Kafka has been for me, in the period of my life as a writer, sentence for sentence the authority" (*EF* 156). And, with regard to his new writing project, Handke states: "In striving for the forms for my truth, I am after beauty – after unsettling beauty, after the unsettling *through* beauty; indeed, after the classical, universal, which according to the teachings of the great painters, only takes form through constant contemplation of and immersion into nature" (*EF* 157-58).

With reference to one of these great painters, the "poet-painter" Paul Cézanne, Handke bid farewell to Kafka and took the chance of changing his writing, in order to learn from Cézanne the "transformation of the visible world into a still-life," as the poet Durs

---

[2]That does not exclude Handke's dissatisfaction with individual decisions of his translator (cf. Jungk 10).

Grünbein argues with regard to other writers interested in Cézanne (Grünbein 45). To be sure, Handke later used a phrase from Francis Ponge on several occasions to depict the "monde muet" (the mute world) as our sole homeland: "My homeland is the wordless world" (*FM* 29; cf. *FM* 483; cf. Ponge 197).[3] In correspondence with Cézanne's paintings of the Sainte-Victoire, which, like the painter Roderer in Stifter's *Nachkommenschaften* (1864; Descendants), Cézanne painted in ever new attempts, Handke seeks to uncover a literary tradition of storytelling (or at least make it accessible to the German-speaking world through his translations). This tradition, in the wake of Goethe and Hölderlin's *Hyperion* (1797-99; trans. 1990) is on the one hand determined by a succession of writers, especially Flaubert, Stifter, Grillparzer, Rilke, Hofmannsthal, Emmanuel Bove, Francis Ponge, Walker Percy, Ludwig Hohl, Hermann Lenz[4] among others (without discounting Handke's earliest, renewed and attested reading experiences with Faulkner, Chekhov, Robbe-Grillet and others). On the other hand, it is determined by Handke's aggressive rejection of the classical-modernist novel (Proust, Joyce, Musil). Like Cézanne, Handke distances himself from his own beginnings marked by catastrophes; with Cézanne he continues to explore what he had already begun in *The Long Way Around*, namely what he considers the 'real': "Real was what was peaceful" (*LH* 128), he states emphatically. The references to Stifter in *The Lesson of Mont Sainte-Victoire* once more affirm Stifter's "gentle law" and defend it against its narrative method prescribed by the time and indebted to catastrophe: "His reality became the form he achieved, the form that does not lament transience or the vicissitudes of history, but transmits an existence in peace" (*LSV* 147).

   The Lesson of Mont Sainte-Victoire not only recounts aspects of the history and conception of *The Long Way Around* and its sequels, it has also been read as an outline of Handke's poetics in narrative form (cf. Bartmann). The main portion of this narratological sketch deals with fundamental questions, namely the possibility of a litera-ry realization of Cézanne's concept of art and, consequently, the

---

[3]In the 1980s, Handke translated Francis Ponge's *Das Notizbuch vom Kiefern-wald* (1982) and *Kleine Suite des Vivarais* (1988).
[4]*The Lesson of Mont Sainte-Victoire* is dedicated to "Hermann Lenz and Hanne Lenz with thanks for January 1979."

continuation of a different modernist tradition. Not until the final chapter, "The Great Forest," is the lesson of the French painter, the revered "teacher of humanity" brought to life. This is accomplished through the account of a walk through the Morzg Forest near Salzburg inspired by a Ruisdael painting in the Vienna Kunsthistorisches Museum. Paradoxically, this walk through the forest is not a story, rather, as the use of the present tense indicates, a description of a scenery, more of a portrait of a landscape than a narratively conveyed experience of nature. Embedded in his script-image – and Handke accomplishes this with consummate ingenuity – is an image methodically prepared and recurring within the text, which expands the topography of the forest near Salzburg into a universal world landscape and illustrates the coexistence of historical epochs, of antiquity and present.

Significantly it is at the transition, on the "threshold between forest and village, [that] the cobbles of the Roman road reappear" and another "woodpile" can be seen. Its representation – "You stand there and look at it" – is more than an image-within-an-image technique. With the provision of a "certain look" of the "beholder," namely "extreme immersion and extreme attention" (*LSV* 210), the pure matter of the woodpile transforms itself, in a "breath," into a play of colors, while "the forms come later": "At first it looks like a scarred piece of malachite. Then the numbers of color charts appear. Then night falls on it and then it is day again. After a while the quivering of unicellular organisms; an unknown solar system; a stone wall in Babylon. World-spanning flight, a concentration of vapor trails, and finally, a unique blaze of colors, taking in the entire woodpile, reveals the footprint of the first man" (*LSV* 210-11). This moment of great concentration and attentiveness is followed by the six-fold repetition of "back to" – back to the places of distraction and the noise of civilization, a return that Handke subsequently refers to in several of his works, for example at the end of *Die Abwesenheit* (1987; *Absence*, 1990) or in the finale of *Das Spiel vom Fragen oder die Reise zum sonoren Land* (1989; *Voyage to the Sonorous Land, or The Art of Asking and the Hour We Knew Nothing of Each Other*, 1996). The critics' verdict, provoked by Nova's final sermon in *Walk About the Villages*, that Handke was an agrarian romantic, is invalidated simply through this deliberate 'Return to Civilization.' In addition, the act of perceiving nature is aesthetically prefigured in *The Lesson of Mont Sainte-Victoire*, though one might criticize Handke's over-determination of the act of perception. The retracing of the paths in Cézanne's Provence and the allusion to Petrarca's climbing Mount Ventoux recalls the modernist history of the aesthetic conception of nature as landscape, though Handke does not content himself with merely revisiting this tradition.[5]

The image of the woodpile in the landscape description of the Morzg Forest is a Handkean symbol, which is to connect the history of the aesthetic representation of nature with Handke's own story – a connection that "cannot be explained but can be told" (*LSV* 173). The woodpile also intertwines the legend of St. Alexius (in connection with the child's hiding place under the staircase in the parents' house in *The Hornets*), the life story of the Georgian painter Pirosmani, who, unknown in his lifetime, "earn[ed] a livelihood chiefly by painting the signboards of inns," and Handke's ideal as a writer "to become with my writing a corduroy road for someone else (who could, however, be myself) or, precisely, a light-colored, tightly packed woodpile" (*LSV* 174).[6] Considering this forced combination, Handke's demand of the production and reception of the work of art becomes manifest. At a stage in history where art has attained autonomous status, art is to touch all aspects of life; that is its mission. Literature and art can hardly be taken more seriously than that, and every criticism of Handke's position must be measured against this seriousness. This passage is significant with regard to Handke's writing method because – despite all attempts at periodization – it determines not only the levels of meaning of an individual work but is worked into the later texts as a recurring motif. Just as the passage refers back to his first novel, so too does the reference to Pirosmani anticipate the configuration in *Die Wiederholung* (1986; *Repetition*, 1988). In *The Lesson of Mont Sainte-Victoire* one reads of the "fantasy" that "my ancestors, about whom I knew next to nothing, came from Georgia" (*LSV* 173) and of the hope that "in the East I would learn something of his origin" (*LSV* 173-74) –

---

[5]Cf. the seminal essay by Ritter.
[6]Wiethölter underscores the psychological implications of this "conservative poetic" (428). Köhnen ties the tribute to postmodern play. The two detailed works dealing with the image-text relationship are by Schlieper and Kurz.

referring to Andreas Sorger in *The Long Way Around*. In both cases Pirosmani's paintings function as a point of reference.

In *Repetition*, Filip Kobal departs on a search in the East for his lost brother. In the account of the protagonist's childhood in the village, a time marked by disorientation and life on the fringes, the figure of the roadmender, who is also a "sign painter," plays a crucial role:

> As I watched him adding a shadowy line to a finished letter with a strikingly slow brushstroke, aerating, as it were, a thick letter with a few hair-thin lines, and then conjuring up the next letter from the blank surface, as though it had been there all along and he was only retracing it, I saw in this nascent script the emblem of a hidden, nameless, all the more magnificent and above all unbounded kingdom, in the presence of which a village did not disappear but emerged from its insignificance as the innermost circle of this kingdom, irradiated by the shapes and colors of the sign at its center" (*R* 33).[7]

In retrospect, the emphasis with which Handke equates the real and the peaceful in *Slow Homecoming* must be placed into its context. Outside the arena of literature it was part of the peace movement of that time and the protest against NATO's plans for rearmament. Within his texts, Handke opposes the then-rampant apocalyptic visions, which he repudiates in his polemic with Wolfgang Hildesheimer and also in *Child Story*: "Then he realized that the modern times that he had so often cursed and rejected did not exist, and that the 'end of time' was also a figment of the brain. The same possibilities were reborn with every new consciousness, and the eyes of children in a crowd – just look at them! – transmitted the eternal spirit. Woe unto you who fail to see those eyes" (*CS* 273). This biblical pathos, however, is coupled with the violence that mercilessly unfolds in the text. Nowhere else is Handke's transformation of his writing, which claims to be indebted to the desire for appeasement so relentlessly connected to the

---

[7]Georgia, Pirosmani's home, comes into play in another way in the genesis of *Repetition*. Regarding Handke's thoughts on the epic, his lecture on the Georgian epic *The Man in the Panther's Skin* (1966) by Shota Rustaveli is relevant. See also the notes in *Am Felsfenster morgens* (*FM* 90-91). On Handke's reflections on the epic and the genre, see Werner Michler, "Teilnahme, Gattungsreflexion und Epos bei Peter Handke" (to appear in the proceedings of the Klagenfurt Symposium for Handke's 60th birthday).

feeling of guilt as in *Child Story*. The violence against the child – "he struck the child in the face with all his might, as he had never in all his life struck anyone" (*CS* 237) – becomes an existential moment of a utopia of storytelling, in which, according to Handke's self-imposed imperative, there is no place for catastrophe. *Child Story* is arguably Handke's most disturbing text, particularly with regard to his settling scores with the former rebels of the 1968 generation, who after all accosted him with equally confounding symbolic violence. Since then, "false animosities" have, it appears, become unavoidable on both sides.[8] In contrast to the dramatic poem *Walk About the Villages* with its assigned speaking parts, the narrative voice in *Child Story* is characterized by the acknowledgement of violence and the announcement of eternal peace. Differently put, ignoring violence would be tantamount to a misrepresentation of both the world and the self.

Walk About the Villages obscures the social ills of the petty-bourgeois village community – those that destroyed his mother's life in *A Sorrow Beyond Dreams* – by stylizing poetic speech to the point of becoming incomprehensible. At this point Handke tries to save his poetic view of the world by labeling his critics with biblical wrath the "deserted ones" and the "false scribes" (*WV* 70). Obviously, this cannot abolish the negative status quo, but it does underline the urgency of the redemptive message. The encouragement of the audience (*Publikumsermutigung*) – Nova announces at the end of the piece, as a *dea ex machina* of sorts and despite and beyond all conflicts, the "spirit of a new age" (*WV* 99) – exhausts itself in a continuously postulatory speech culminating in the message that the world is good: "Yes, imbued, yearning for form, hand on the hale world – snide laughter about this lacks all awareness. (Laughter is the wrong word: it is the soul cadaver's death rattle.)" (*WV* 105-06). With these words directed to the audience, the trivial conflict of the poem-play, which exists in the siblings' dispute over their inheritance, is laid to rest.

On his return from overseas, Gregor, who is to be conceived of as a writer, renounces his inheritance in order to allow his sister to secure her economic independence as a shop owner, although he does not approve. This is completely in keeping with Nova's

---

[8] See, among others, the essays in the collection edited by Scharang.

advice: "a hoot for the tragedy, spit on misfortune, laugh conflicts to smithereens" (*WV* 18). The mere desire for reconciliation will not remedy the flawed reality. The victims of this reality, in particular Gregor's brother and his colleagues from work, are to be "transformed" (*WV* 28), at least for the duration of the play. The staged festivity, ostensibly overcoming all everyday conflicts, is to return dignity to the workers. In contrast, the "signifying word" (*WV* 37) of scientific studies and the documentary literature[9] would merely reduce them to objects. Gregor's gaze has the "power to transfigure" (*WV* 62) and is thus capable of seeing the "sufferers" as the "authentic humanity" (*WV* 61-62). With Hans, Gregor's brother, the play plainly speaks out against the literary journalism of the documentary literature: "Once someone came here with a tape recorder and camera in the name of the public, bemoaned us and expected us to bemoan ourselves. But we want to appear differently. We want to be acclaimed" (*WV* 25). With this view, expressed elsewhere as well (*WV* 29), the text distances itself from the intellectual positions of the 1960s and 70s, where the search for the revolutionary subject effecting historical change degraded the proletarian to object status.

As for the thematic context of regionalism, one is reminded of Franz Xaver Kroetz, who after a number of folk plays (*Volksstücke*) published the *Chiemgauer Geschichten* (1974; Chiemgau Stories), a series of interviews with Bavarian villagers, in order to understand their everyday social struggle – which is obviously not in line with the dramaturgy of his plays. While Kroetz's documentation is sustained by an optimistic outlook, namely that the story of the exploited masses, in Marxist terms, is to be brought to a happy end, Nova's festive speech remains skeptical. Three times she repeats her insight, which she knows also includes herself: "Of course there is no gainsaying that our whole history lacks foolproof consolation" (*WV* 108, cf. 99, 108). At the moment of greatest aloofness (from the quotidian but also, in a concrete spatial sense, from the elevated platform of the cemetery wall), the "exploited, the downtrodden and insulted" (*WV* 37) remain caught up in their history of suffering. An escape into a utopian time appears no longer possible. Comfort,

---

[9]Handke refers to Marxist theories of alienation, which exhaust themselves in analyses without effecting change.

however, shall remain: "Nature is all I can promise you – the only foolproof promise" (*WV* 101). In place of a utopia to be found in history, a spatial utopia appears: "The village is great...Walk about the villages" (*WV* 110). Nova has the last word. The elements of resistance of what came before speak through her faltering proclamation, so that Nova's utopia cannot simply be understood as a counterspace to the existing negative status quo, as is the case in the traditional dichotomy of the *Heimat* literature. For while Gregor announces his Faustian dream as a dream of humanity yet to be realized: "I have saved a piece of land. I have saved a piece of sky" (*WV* 64), the "lament" of the old woman about the negativity of village life retains a hint of reality: "Maybe the village never existed.... How alien everything here has become.... How worthless the village is.... I would like to damn this village and its inhabitants" (*WV* 68). She interprets Gregor's longing to return home as a return to the foreign land (*WV* 77). Her evil gaze transforms the landscape into a "terrain for war": "As of now, *this* is the front" (*WV* 78). She expects Gregor to try to prevent this as she sees in him an avenger, who will carry out the concerns of her kind. Gregor, however, apparently aware of the associated political significance and the consequences of such desire, cannot and will not accept this role: "Why don't you finally rid yourselves of the notion that someone might come and atone for some sin or unburden you of some fate, or regale you with marvels of a different place" (*WV* 73).

Gregor's objection to a violent restoration of a world devoid of meaning at some point in the future is an attempt to break the cycle of violence. This is presented in the play by means of mythologizing the present-day state of affairs, a means which in itself appears problematic. For the random ruling of what is to be accepted as positive – poorly illustrated at that through an abundance of indeterminacies – furiously and unconditionally condemns the critical momentum of this negation. The "skeptics far removed from childhood," the "unserious snickerers," (*WV* 102) and the "disillusioned" who "grin evilly" (*WV* 105) – to cite only some examples from the register of name-calling – are condemned and denounced so that the "gods of change" (*WV* 108) remain unharmed: "illusion is the power of vision, and the vision is true" (*WV* 105). This empty but extreme statement receives its justification through the mere fact that it imputes tautological meaning and in doing so foregoes the previous criticism. This practice is reminiscent of Nietzsche, who has left distinctive traces in Handke's work (cf. Pütz 121).[10] The direction – whether progressive or reactionary – of an all-out, total-izing critique that questions everything cannot be determined. In the case of Nietzsche it furthered the radicalization of the counter-enlightenment (Habermas 419). In Handke's case, at least one can recognize that after his break from history in his earlier works, he found refuge in utopian spaces in the *Slow Homecoming* tetralogy. The process of the gradual replacement of a utopia of time through a utopia of space, which Reinhart Koselleck describes as having begun in the middle of the eighteenth century, comes to an end (cf. Koselleck).

In light of the shortfall of progressive theories, Handke no longer projects the 'better world' into a potentially livable, historic-al future. At the same time he is aware that a naïve return to a tradi-tional pre-enlightened spatial utopia is impossible. The tetralogy encompasses half of the globe. The protagonist returns from the wilderness of Alaska, far removed from civilization, via New York, France and Germany to his home village in Austria. This does not mean that the place of his childhood is imagined as a place of happiness in the sense of the traditional quest for *Heimat*. Even within his country he encounters the foreign, while even the foreign can be home. Nova's advice to walk about the villages does not equate origin (*Herkunft*) with future (*Zukunft*); rather, she strives to depict the village as a model for a place of happiness that eludes sociological as well as a topographic determination: "forget the yearning for the holy places and years of times past" (*WV* 107). In her pronouncement that "[o]ur harborage is nowhere" (*WV* 109), this nowhere is to be understood in the context of the tetralogy as everywhere. A better world is latently present in the one that exists. Handke expresses this idea already in the first part, *The Long Way Around*, when Sorger, a geologist specializing in spaces, is intro-duced:

> Sorger needed nature, but not only in its "unspoiled" state; in big cities, for example, he was satisfied to gain awareness of scarcely perceptible asphalt-covered humps and hollows, gentle rises and falls in the pavement, of church floors or stone stairs, worn with the steps of the centuries; or, visiting an unknown

---

[10]See also the article by Andrea Gogröf-Voorhees in this volume.

high-rise building, to fancy himself passing vertically through all the floors of the room from roof to basement, and, finally, to daydream its granite foundations – until, in the end, orientation and the breathing space (and hence self-confidence) indispensable to life endangered each other. (*LWA* 6)

When the leitmotifs of nature and space are henceforth brought together, this imputes the possibility of meaning ("orientation") – a meaning, however, that only the individual with the "ability" (*LWA* 6) to detect the scarcely perceptible or to call upon the 'world-spaces' for help is able to perceive. The discovery of meaning and the significance of the individual are mutually dependent. Consequently it seems logical (and characteristic of Handke's self-image) that the cycle is concluded with an artist as protagonist. Largely eased of the burden of 'reality' (and therefore, like Gregor, with a guilty conscience), the artist is poised to develop his "specialization in sensibility" (Kluge 206) to the highest degree, in order to demonstrate it in his writing.[11]

For the sensitive individual, nature is discernible in all places. Sorger eventually finds it even in the cosmopolitan city of New York. The following passage, which anticipates *Walk about the Villages*, affirms Sorger's previously cited reflection. Suddenly New York takes on traits of his hometown and appears as a landscape:

> Moving on the concrete slabs of the sidewalk intensified his conquest of space and gave it permanence. He experienced the subsoil of the city, which only a short while before had risen into the air from lifeless pavement. Now the buildings no longer seemed to have been plunked down in the landscape, they had become an integral part of it, as though the skyscrapers were really at home on this rocky island. Indeed, the city gradually became a village-like settlement...." (*LWA* 116-17)

What Walter Benjamin argued with regard to the flâneur holds true for Sorger as well: the city drifts apart into its "dialectical poles" (Benjamin 525).

To recognize the contours of the exalted village in the hubbub of the city confirms the ubiquity of the nature principle as a guarantor of meaning. On the basis of its sensibility the subject is able to discern in the present time, as conflict-laden as it may be, the image

---

[11]Kluge objects to the "specialization" of sensibility as it deactivates its societal relevance.

of total harmony and timeless happiness. The artist, who – not unexpectedly – assumes the religious aura of the prophet and the herald,
uses the artistic myth of 'order' to evoke the illusion of harmony.
This is only possible at the cost of a semantic vagueness that glosses
over the specific organizing principles regulating society's mundane
affairs (cf. Piechotta). With its tendency to persistently poeticize the
world, Handke's text makes extensive use of myths of order and
innocence, myths validated by tradition. The village, the child and
nature become such ultimate representations for completeness.
Whereas modernist aesthetics postulate the longing for an ideal of
completeness by means of negating the status quo, Handke, with his
antimodern-classicist turn, deliberately attracts criticisms of being
affirmative. He does, of course, make every effort not to concretize
in any way the substance of his conceptions of order. Nova's interpretation of nature attests to that: "Of course [nature] can be neither
refuge nor escape. But she is the model and provides the measure:
which, however, must be taken each and every day" (*WV* 101). The
same holds true for her advice to walk about the villages, which
does not endorse the narrow-minded view of the village as an idyllic
place. As a result of their factual unreliability, these concepts cannot
remain immune to the criticism of dogmatic positivism. It is the
weakness of Handke's aesthetic method to promote this interpretation, an aesthetic that aims to revalidate the (still) abused promises
of happiness by simply restating them.

This ostracism of the artist and the degradation of his work
illustrate the tensions within the play as well as the distance to
Hofmannsthal's precepts which, during his time, were already
ideologically tainted: "Do you want to perform for the educated or
for the masses? Whoever has the concept of the people in his soul,
rejects this separation."[12] Thus, Handke keeps his distance from
conventional beliefs: "Don't look to the people – nothing can be

---

[12]In contrast to Hofmannsthal's allegory of the social classes in *Das Salzburger
Große Welttheater* (1922; *Great Salzburg World Theater*, 1962) who shape
themselves into 'the people,' Handke's play remains until the end a game of
incongruities, which are not to be validated as delineations of a world model or
of a societal order. Handke's festivity, which is neither simple affirmation of
the status quo nor subversive societal ecstasy or carnivalesque counter-culture
in the Bakhtinian sense, draws on religious and tribal rituals in order to bestow
upon the ordinary an aura of significance.

seen there anymore" (*WV* 34). The humiliated and the deserted want to exploit the "power of the riddle" in a different way: "This evening, let us embody the craft that we have actually learned and whose members once were called 'the people': 'The Carpenter People.' Let's leave announcers and procurers out of the play here – do not the people form of themselves?" (*WV* 39-40). This can be read, on the one hand, as a rejection of Hofmannsthal's stage mechanisms – the announcer of *Jedermann* (1911; *The Salzburg-Everyman*, 1929), for example – and as a critique of the powerful, on the other; those who, in an expression reminiscent of Robert Walser, are seen as the "disenchanted" (*WV* 41) whose children exploit and abuse their cultural privileges by flaunting their own phobia (cf. *WV* 41-42).

The conversion from a specific critique of society to a universal critique of culture also tends to question the validity of a "the carpenter people" as an ideal. In his *Versuch über die Müdigkeit*, 1989; *Essay on Tiredness*, 1994), Handke illustrates this ideal as – to use his poetological vocabulary – recapitulated childhood memories and sets it off against "the unrepentant 'gang of the untired'" (*J* 18). The fading memories of communal craftsmanship (cf. *WV* 55) create a poetic effect which is not the result of the power of stylization but rather of the innocuousness of art as craft. Despite its post-Romantic ossification, Handke uses art as craft to illustrate his critique of alienation, especially when he contrasts craftsmanship and mechanical labor. In a subsequent reflection, Handke attempts to affirm the legitimacy of this image: "The fact is, however, that I have affecting, communicable pictures of manual workers' tiredness, but none (thus far) of a combine operator's" (*J* 16). Without the illuminating penetration of the real world there would only remain empty, poetic illusion (*Schein*) and the collapse of the concept of *Volk* into that ideology, which Handke presented in *A Sorrow Beyond Dreams* by means of "images ... devoid of human content" as the vanishing of political concepts: "oppression as chains or boot heel, freedom as mountaintop, the economic system as a reassuringly smoking factory chimney or as a pipe enjoyed after the day's work, the social system as a descending ladder: 'Emperor–King–Nobleman–Burgher–Peasant–Weaver/Carpenter–Beggar–Gravedigger'..." (*SBD* 15).

If for Handke the predisposition for communal experiences and the projections of an ideal people is critical, so is the awareness that these concepts have become forever precarious due to their abuse during the National Socialist period. In *A Sorrow Beyond Dreams*, Handke clear-sightedly describes the fascination for the rituals of the communal cult of fascism through which life became organized so that "you felt protected, yet free":

> For the first time, people did things together. Even the daily grind took on a festive mood, 'until late into the night.' For once, everything that was strange and incomprehensible in the world took on meaning and became part of a larger context; even disagreeable, mechanical work was festive and meaning-ful. (*SBD* 14)

In *Walk About the Villages* as well, the fragile nature of the imagined festiveness of the "carpenter people" becomes evident. The intensity of the war, the "feast of feasts" (*WV* 88) threatens to absorb it. The "triumph to be lost," the "ecstasy finally to be irreconcilable forever" (*WV* 88) lies as a curse over the trivial family feud that Handke raises to the heights of Greek tragedy, in which, however, "those who went under" bless the "living," instead of ruining "their feasts" (WV 98; cf. *GB* 236).[13]

Handke wants to preserve the utopian nature of the festivity, and not only as a fleeting homage to the context of the Salzburg Festspiele, where Wim Wenders staged the premiere. Looking back at the individual parts of Handke's tetralogy, it is *Walk About the Villages* that illustrates most emphatically the chance Handke took at the end of the 1970s. Out of an almost frenzied search for meaning grew his willingness to risk transforming his writing formula by breaking with an aesthetic of negativity. The four texts that make up *Slow Homecoming* bear the traces of this arduous effort – which, eventually, marks both their strength and their short-comings. Although Handke's ostentatious and often overstated aestheticism mediated by a rhetoric of proclamation and affirmation begs criticism, his achievement deserves respect. Without this *tour de force* Handke's later works surely would not have been as interesting, perhaps not even possible.

---

[13]With regard to similarities between *Walk About the Villages* and dramas of antiquity, see Halter.

Works Cited

Bartmann, Christoph. "Malende Menschheitslehrer. Peter Handke und die Poetik der 'Realisation.'" *Weimarer Beiträge* 41 (1995) 562-72.

Baumgart, Reinhard. *Damals. Ein Leben in Deutschland. 1929-2003.* Munich: Hanser, 2003.

Benjamin, Walter. *Gesammelte Schriften V.1.* Ed. Rolf Tiedemann. Frankfurt am Main: Suhrkamp, 1982.

Grünbein, Durs. *Das erste Jahr. Berliner Aufzeichnungen.* Frankfurt am Main: Suhrkamp, 2001.

Habermas, Jürgen. "Die Verschlingung von Mythos und Aufklärung. Bemerkungen zur *Dialektik der Aufklärung* – nach einer erneuten Lektüre." *Mythos und Moderne. Begriff und Bild einer Rekonstruktion.* Ed. Karl Heinz Bohrer. Frankfurt am Main: Suhrkamp, 1983. 405-31.

Halter, Regine. "Peter Handkes *Über die Dörfer.*" *Deutsches Drama der 80er Jahre.* Ed. Richard Weber. Frankfurt am Main: Suhrkamp 1992. 287-305.

Jungk, Peter Stephan. "Aus meinen Tagebüchern." *Salz: Zeitschrift für Literatur* 28 (Oct. 2002) 8-10.

Kluge, Alexander. *Gelegenheitsarbeit einer Sklavin. Zur realistischen Methode.* Frankfurt am Main: Suhrkamp, 2002.

Köhnen, Ralph. "Zwischen Zeichenspiel und Wahrheiten: Peter Handkes Cézanne-Rezeption." *Intermedialität. Vom Bild zum Text.* Ed. Thomas Eichner and Ulf Bleckman. Bielefeld: Aisthesis, 1994. 185-220.

Koselleck, Reinhart. "Die Verzeitlichung der Utopie. Am Beispiel von Louis-Sébastien Merciers *Das Jahr 2440.*" *Neue Zürcher Zeitung* (overseas edition) 6 Aug. 1982: 25-26.

Kurz, Martina. *Bild-Verdichtungen. Cézannes Realisation als poetisches Prinzip bei Rilke und Handke.* Göttingen: Vandenhoeck & Ruprecht, 2003.

Piechotta, Hans Joachim. "Ordnung als mythologisches Zitat. Adalbert Stifter und der Mythos." *Mythos und Moderne. Begriff*

148 Karl Wagner

und Bild einer Rekonstruktion. Ed. Karl Heinz Bohrer. Frankfurt
am Main: Suhrkamp, 1983. 83-110.

Ponge, Francis. *Le grand recueil. Méthodes.* Paris: Gallimard, 1961.

Pütz, Peter. *Peter Handke.* Frankfurt am Main: Suhrkamp, 1982.

Scharang, Michael (ed.). *Über Peter Handke.* Frankfurt am Main:
Suhrkamp, 1973.

Schlieper, Ulrike. *Die "andere Landschaft." Handkes Erzählen auf
den Spuren Cézannes.* Münster: LIT, 1994.

Ritter, Joachim. "Landschaft. Zur Funktion des Ästhetischen in der
modernen Gesellschaft." *Subjektivität.* Frankfurt am Main:
Suhrkamp, 1974. 141-63.

Wiethölter, Waltraud. "Auge in Auge mit Cézanne: Handkes *Lehre
der Sainte-Victoire." Germanisch-Romanische Monatsschrift 71
(1990) 422-44.

Storytelling in Imagery:
Across, Repetition, and *The Afternoon of a Writer*

Maria Luisa Roli[*]

WITH *DER CHINESE DES SCHMERZES* (1983; *Across*, 1986) and *Die Wiederholung* (1986; *Repetition*, 1988) Handke continues in the direction he began in the *Langsame Heimkehr* tetralogy (1979-81; *Slow Homecoming*, 1985) that emphasizes the visual and spatial dimension in his narratives (Wolf 10, 67-70). Within the body of his recent work, Handke increasingly uses a mythicizing prose, a style aimed not at the reelaboration and the reinterpretation of ancient myths – that is, the "construction of a mythology" (Blumenberg) – but at mythologizing elements of personal history or daily life through the use of repetition as an aesthetic-literary device (*GW* 279; Gottwald 41). This emphasis on distinctive features, which were already present at least partially in the author's earlier narratives, has led some critics to talk about a turn in Handke's production (Hamm 103; Nenon and Renner 104-15), while others have simply identified these elements as a sign of a further develop-ment (Gottwald 35), a shift in emphasis (Melzer 131), or of the possibility of a search for a more binding textual linkage and a more substantial continuity with the past (Bartmann 1).

Like the protagonist of *Die Angst des Tormanns beim Elfmeter* (1970; *The Goalie's Anxiety of the Penalty Kick*, 1972) Andreas Loser, the main character in *Across* and a teacher of ancient lang-uages, decides not to show up for work one day. Loser lives separated from his wife and children (without a real reason) on the outskirts of Salzburg in a small compound near a bus station. Loser, whose family name does not mean the one who "loses" in the English sense, but rather is derived from a popular verb meaning "listen" or "hark" (*Ac* 15), is the narrator of this tale himself. His

---

[*]English version by David N. Coury and Frank Pilipp.

need and desire for emptiness, or, more precisely, for blank shapes, is the premise for the narration; indeed it corresponds, as he points out emphatically, "to the invocation of the Muse at the beginning of an epic" (*Ac* 5). The narrative then develops from Loser's conscious contemplation of his surroundings (Melzer 133): little by little the village where he lives becomes populated with people returning from work in the evening and others who are immersed in their – often ancient – daily activities associated with rural life in contrast to the factories adjoining the village.

Therefore the place where Loser lives does not show the squalid and alienating traits of a large urban city; indeed nature represents a balancing factor in his life, as in the image of the tree branches stirred by the wind, which are compared to a loom moving with a regular rhythm (*Ac* 6). Moreover the wild animals do not feel the human presence as something threatening and can thus move freely around the village. As in Handke's other texts, such as *Die linkshändige Frau* (1976; *The Left-Handed Woman*, 1978), *Das Gewicht der Welt* (1977; *The Weight of the World*, 1984), and *Slow Homecoming*, urban centers and nature, supermarkets and farms become integrated into one natural outline, emerging into "a harmonious utopia of space" (Bartmann 154). The village at the outskirts of the wood yet close to the city is one of Handke's typical locations, as it is a place which affords the protagonist both solitude and a privileged viewing point, distant yet not too far from the world which surrounds him. It is a threshold which is to be understood, as the priest in the narrative explains, as a "precinct" whose significance encompasses the meanings of "transformation, floor, river crossing, mountain pass, enclosure (place of refuge)" (*Ac* 67). Besides being a teacher of languages, Loser is also an archaeologist who, as part of his research, is participating in the excavations of a Roman villa in the suburbs of Salzburg. As such, he views himself as "a thresholdologist (or seeker after thresholds)" (*Ac* 12). The word "threshold" is a key concept in the novel, for it is additionally used by the protagonist to describe an infallible impulse to stimulate his companions to narrate (*Ac* 70).

In some ancient cultures the threshold is the interval separating the inner sacred area of the temple from the external one (Manthey 382). In psychoanalytic terms, a link can be established between the autobiographical nocturnal cry of a child (*Ac* 38) and the motif of the threshold which returns repeatedly throughout the text. Both elements harken back to the Aristaeus myth, which concludes Virgil's *Georgics* (Manthey 377), the book Loser would like to translate and which spurs him to travel to Mantua and the Mincio river.

In the episode told by Virgil, Aristaeus, son of the god Apollo and of the water nymph Cyrene, is a shepherd and beekeeper who has lost his bees through a misadventure with Eurydice. In despair he laments and asks his mother's help, whereupon she welcomes him in the deep river bed, opens a fjord in the waters and says: "Lead him, do, lead him to us, he is permitted to touch the divine threshold" (Virgil 335).[1] As plausible and fascinating as Manthey's reading may be, it contrasts with Handke's concept of myth, which does not consist of a reelaboration of ancient myths, as is the case, for instance, with the myth of metamorphosis in Christoph Ransmayr's novel *Die letzte Welt* (1988; *The Last World*, 1990) or that of Cassandra in Christa Wolf's novel (1983; trans. 1988) of the same title (Gottwald 41), both of which transform myth into ritual through the luminous attention to details, images and scenes (Bartmann 219). To be sure, though, the narration does not assert any connection between the boy's cry and the motif of the threshold, even though the establishment of such a connection clearly falls within the possibilities of interpretation offered by this text.

The narrative also arises from a wider exploration of the territory surrounding Loser which includes not only the city of Salzburg and its neighbourhoods, but extends also to Italy and the region of Mantua – touching particularly on Virgil's birthplace, Andes –, the Mincio river and Sardinia. The observation of space and places lends the text an element of fantasy and allows the aesthetic metamorphosis of the external world. This metamorphosis is brought about through the use of exotic features (Bartmann 155), for instance, the entrance of immigrants into a bar-restaurant that provokes a sense of change:

> And something that had never happened before: the café turned into the garden terrace of a restaurant of the west bank of the Jordan: The terrace was empty except for crackling gusts of sand, the slapping of palm leaves and the sound of music without beginning or end. Eastward lay the Dead Sea depres-

---

[1] The parallels between Handke's text and Virgil's *Georgics* have been illustrated by Feichtinger.

sion; the pregnant woman straightened up in her chair, gathered her long hair together and piled it on top of her head; while the record was playing, she was a woman on the shores of the Dead Sea, an embodiment of the sea itself. (*Ac* 29)

A similar phenomenon is described later: "Man and woman were sitting with their faces close together with solemn expressions, which were giving them Egyptian profiles." These transformations continue and evoke a certain oriental fantasy: "in the darkness, the illumined twin steeples of the Kollegienkirche, which, with the rings of light-colored stone figures on their flat roofs, resemble castles on a chessboard by day, became grimacing Indian idols; the clocks became eye sockets, the window ledges bulging foreheads, and the ring of statues flaming hair" (*Ac* 52). The metamorphoses also appear in rapid succession, thereby becoming a kind of phantasmagoric game. In this way, the mere description exceeds the boundaries of the external world and the possibilities of elaborating on the fabulous seem endless:

> At this point, there is a double bend in the road; this gave me a view of a separate section of the rock face, shaped like a truncated pyramid and topped like a ruin with grass and saplings. Here for the moment lay the ruins of a temple in the jungles of Central America. Then in the lamplight the cliff took on the grey coloration of a wasp's nest, riddled with black cells which seemed abandoned yet alive. The layer of foliage at the foot of the cliff blew back and forth in the storm wind, with eddies, waterspouts and breakers, and the nest with its black holes changed into a chalk-white oyster bed (the oysters being the shell-shaped stones protruding from the cliff). (*Ac* 57)

As in *Slow Homecoming*, the protagonist in *Across*, who in the titles of three parts of the text is referred to as "the observer," builds a subjective topography of space (Bartmann 228), starting with the small village where he lives and moving to the city of Salzburg and to the mountain which overshadows it, the Mönchsberg. If in the description of the small village at the outskirts of the forest the idea of harmony between man and nature prevails, in the second part of the novel, the outcome of the exploration of the Mönchsberg is different. Loser, the observer, experiences a sudden feeling of hatred for an old man who has painted swastikas with a spray can. The tranquility of mind experienced by the observer, whose task it is to convert perceptions into images, is deeply altered by "this sign, this negative image, [that] symbolized the cause of all my melancholy" (*Ac* 51).

The figure of this nostalgic Nazi is emphatically stylized into a superenemy through euphemisms of biblical origin which refer to Satan as the evil one, as well as references to physical traits taken from the iconographic tradition, such as the crocodile foot and colorless eyes. That figure, laden with negative features, is used by the protagonist to dispel and eliminate the violence that had manifested itself in the past in two distinct episodes. To interpret this exclusively autobiographically as a reference to Handke's father (Manthey 378) may be correct,[2] though it disregards its literary contextualization. The word *Unbild* (negative or horrid image) moreover does not appear as "an indication of the desire to erase something from Loser's memory" (Manthey 378), but rather as a negative expression of the deepest contrast to Loser's main activity: the transformation of perceptions into images. *Unbild* might therefore indicate the impossibility of absolute evil being changed into images. Even though just a sign, a historically inno-cent sign like the swastika, can provoke Loser's rage as the "sign of a history of violence which is being perpetuated" (Lorenz 214) and which can only generate more violence.

Loser's initial sensation of triumph in killing the old Nazi is replaced by a feeling of "living in damnation"; in this passage the narrative uses religious terminology such as "guilt" (which Loser states does not affect him) and "perdition" (*Ac* 93). In *Across* one finds several terms referring to Christianity, such as "state of grace" (*Ac* 19), "St. Andrew's Cross" (*Ac* 59), "the ritual of transubstantia-tion," or the sound of bells (*Ac* 103), all of which contribute to the creation of an aura of sacredness. The references to religious sym-bols and rituals in the text cannot clearly be linked to their original connotations, though they are recalled to illustrate the intimate path of Handke's hero and the overcoming of his crisis of orientation and stabilization (Gottwald 70-71). The divine can reveal itself to man only in "the pure immanence, as a product of subjectivity, as a human instrument of establishing meaning in a world deprived of magic and of myth" (Gottwald 73). In this way, a pantheistic con-

---

[2]In the interview with Herbert Gamper, Handke denies having referred to his father and his stepfather in that period. The allusion, according to Handke, was rather aimed at all Germans (*Zw* 23).

ception of the divine, or, rather, of a religiosity in which the
individual is able to transcend the mere materialism of the world, is
delineated (Gottwald 74), and meaning and a magic halo is con-
ferred to the small, seemingly meaningless things in the world. With
this pantheistic conception of the world one can associate the
descriptions of panoramas, characterized not only by visual but also
aural perceptions, which often develop into a spatial bliss (Bartmann 162), where the Mönchsberg represents for Loser the world
and Salzburg becomes the "capital city" (*Ac* 55).[3]

In a penetrating analysis of Handke's works between 1979 and
1989 (excluding *Across* and *Repetition*), Walter Weiss has high-
lighted the uncertain and questioning ways in which Handke employs religious motifs. They no longer serve, he argues, as the reference points consolidated by the Christian tradition but are used to
establish a personal path for contemplation that has developed over
the course of his works. In contrast to the religious revelation
(Weiss, "Motive" 228), Handke's adaptation of religious motifs
approaches the kind of philosophical-religious thinking that is
marked by doubt and in continual evolution.

Some frequently recurring images in *Across*, particularly those
of a void, of light and of a threshold, are linked to the religious and
mystical realm. These moments of enlightenment point to a return
of serenity, a feeling of creativity and the perception of emptiness
within oneself. The consequence of such dispositions is the disappearance of melancholy, expressed by an image that alludes to its
classic iconographic representation in the fine arts: "My forehead no
longer needed a supporting hand" (*Ac* 5). The gesture of the raised
arm and of the head resting on the hand is a sign of meditation and
of musing, and forms an emblematic representation of melancholy
in Greek, Roman and Byzantine arts (Chastel 62). The same motif is
found in the miniature of the *Manessische Liederhandschrift* (Hoff
293) representing Walther von der Vogelweide sitting on a rock
with his head reclining and his cheek leaning on the palm of his
hand, which illustrates the poem "Ich saz uf eime steine" (I sat on a
stone), as well as in Albrecht Dürer's *Melancholia I* (Klibansky,
Panofsky, Saxl 269-374). Additional examples of the same gesture

---

[3]This type of pantheistic-holistic religiosity echoes many of Goethe's and
Stifter's ideas.

can be found both in poetry, in the description of Henry I of Navarra in the seventh canto of Dante's *Purgatory* (Chastel 62) and in painting, from the Chemical Sibyl by Lorenzo Lotto[4] and several figures in Michelangelo's Sistine Chapel (Christ's ancestors) to Cézanne's *The Boy with the Red Waistcoat* (Zurich version 1888-1890) and *The Smoker* (about 1895), or to the more recent *Portrait of Jaime Sabartés*, *The Thoughtful Harlequin* and *The Two Tumblers* (all 1901) by Picasso.

The Chemical Sibyl by Lotto, for example, is portrayed with a book in her hand and her cheek leaning upon the palm of the hand in a melancholic and meditative mood. It becomes apparent that the figure is under the influence of the planet Saturn (Klibansky, Panofsky, Saxl 119-201) which drives the spirit to contemplation of the highest matters, while the book hints at Mercury's influence, which turns man to wisdom. The Sibyl is therefore "almost a portrait of inspiration"[5] that compels all those who are engaged in artistic activities into a melancholic mood. One finds a similar motif of the leaning head in *The Boy with the Red Waistcoat* and in the peasant who posed as model for *The Smoker*: they too are the expression of a melancholic mood, which, particularly in Cézanne's late works, recalls the dark, lonely and meditative mood of the artist and his fear of being unable to attain his goal before his death.[6] Solitude, melancholy and incommunicability are the dominating themes in three of Picasso's paintings of the Blue Period as well. With regard to Handke's reference, his description of the absence of this gesture nevertheless refers to melancholy, whose representation has throughout the history of the fine arts used the same body language to the point of becoming emblematic. In Aby Warburg's words, one might speak of a "pathos formula" (443-54).

Handke himself refers to the protagonist of *Langsame Heimkehr* (1979; *The Long Way Around*, 1985) by quoting the text, stating that he is "a melancholic player" and adds: "For me he is mainly a metaphor of the artist: the melancholic player who was involved in a game about which he does not know at all how much it will cost

---

[4]The Chemical Sybil is a figure from Lotto's cycle of frescoes titled *Storie di Santa Barbara, Brigida, Caterina d'Alessandria e Maria Maddalena*, which can be found in the Cappella Suardi in Trescore Balneario near Bergamo.

[5]Cf. Cortesi Bosco (22-24) and illustration 109 (24).

[6]Cf. Düchting, illustrations 152 and 25.

him" (*Zw* 47). For the artist it is a case of finding the rules of the
game he intends to play in the world around him; it is not a question
of rules which the artist elaborates upon autonomously and imposes
on the world, rather of finding and then following what Handke
calls, with a Stifterian formula, "this gentle law." The mystical
image of enlightenment is therefore connected to the artist's moment of creation which springs from an absence, from the perception of the void not as "an emptiness, but a being-empty; not so
much *my* being-empty as an empty form" (*Ac* 5). And the empty
shape is for the writer by definition the narrative, the story. The idea
of a void is, on the other hand, expressed by the narrator through the
image of "a shallow river crossing" (*Ac* 5), thus revealing its close
kinship with the concept of the threshold, a theme that Handke
expands upon in many variations in the episode of the game of
Tarot, yet is present throughout the novel. Handke then clarifies the
connection between "void" and "threshold":

> ... this void, this fluttering, heavenly, fruitful, enticing emptiness
> never manifested itself in a deserted nature, but always in the
> proximity of people. Therefore it was always on the margins, on
> the margin of a city, for instance, on the border between a forest
> and steppe, for instance, it is strange in fact: always on the
> boundaries, or, more precisely, on the threshold. (*Zw* 113)

The observer Loser works on the threshold, a privileged point of
observation of the world, and the visual nature of his narrative is the
result of this vantage point. The description of the gesture of melancholia is an example of such a method. The key artistic method for
visualizing the narration is therefore that of description. The episode
involving the slaying of the old Nazi is preceded by a description of
the Mönchsberg, which results in a slowing down of the story; yet at
the moment of the killing, the narrative suddenly accelerates. What
distinguished the descriptions in *Across* is that they tend toward the
fantastic, approaching depictions of dreams or visions, as in the
episode of Loser's arrival at the airport on the moon (*Ac* 97).
Another instance of the verbal representation of visual art, the use
of *ekphrasis*, is found in the following description:

> At one table sat four card players, all wearing hats, and at the
> next, three young women, one well advanced in pregnancy, one
> with a faint mustache and hair dyed reddish-brown, the third
> with a dachshund at her feet. A fifth man, keeping the card
> players company, was holding an accordion, on which he softly

accompanied the card game, using different chords for different phases of play. (*Ac* 26)

This description recalls the first version of Cézanne's famous painting *The Card Players* (1890) which presents a similar scene with five figures, four players and two observers. The constellation of this setting is repeated in a subsequent episode in the second part of *Across*: the game of Tarot with five figures, each of whom in turn becomes a spectator.

The players are a clergyman, a politician, a painter (whose short stature and deep-set eyes recall pictures and self portraits of Cézanne),[7] and the master of the house as well as Loser, who is introduced as a teacher. He is the one who then raises the topic of the threshold in order to elicit the players' recollections and associations with the theme, from which a narration with multiple voices develops (*Ac* 68). The card game takes on a metaphorical meaning and there are many details which underscore this hypothesis. First the players are sitting around a table which is imbued with a sacred look as its legs form an X-shaped cross, reminiscent of the cross on which the Apostle Andrew endured his martyrdom. The atmosphere is one of silence marked by the concentration of the players who are almost stiff in their movements. The external world, which can be seen through the windows of the room, is described in detail, with the garden shining in the darkness and the distant sights of the city. From the inside of the house one can hear the subdued noises made by other people and the sound of a violoncello which contrasts with the players' concentration and their silence. The players' concentration becomes so intense that, like Cézanne's players, they are unable to take their eyes off the cards, intent as they are on complying with the rules of the game. The scene shows a subdued setting, separated from the world but, at the same time, rich with tension, in part because of the diversity of the players. The card game could be interpreted as a metaphor of literary creation (Höller 187) which, according to Handke, also requires separation from the outside world, concentration and respect for the rules of the game.

Handke's metaphor for writing, the "rules of a game," and his poetics have certainly evolved since the 1960s. If one compares the

---

[7]As for the relationship between Handke and Cézanne, see Wolf (132-54) as well as the article by Karl Wagner in this volume.

programmatic declarations of such texts as *Ich bin ein Bewohner des Elfenbeinturms* (1967; I am a Dweller of the Ivory Tower) with those found in the writings from the late 1970s, one sees a change in Handke's artistic conception. The aesthetic of antithesis, based on the deconstruction of the conventions of literary genre and on the continuous search for new forms, is replaced by an aesthetic of identity, based on the preservation of certain rules and on repetition (Weiss, "Tendenzen" 136). But the juxtaposition of these two artistic concepts is in fact not as clear-cut as it may first seem, as a close reading of the texts shows.

In *Across* we find a clear example of these aesthetic tendencies: after contrasting the positive meanings linked to the concept of repetition with the negative ones, the storyteller suggests the word "rediscovery" as a synonym for repetition (*Ac* 36). This term suggests a freer and more vital relationship with tradition and is very close in meaning to renewal and re-creation. Handke points out that the Latin root of the Slovenian word for repetition, *ponovîtev*, is *novus* which is related to *Erneuerung* or rediscovery (*Zw* 112). This linguistic affinity echoes in some ways Stifter's dictum that the writer writes of "finding" (*finden*) a form for his subject matter rather than "inventing" (*erfinden*) one.[8] Handke also elaborates on the theme of repetition and on its relationship to the literary tradition (*Zw* 146-47), underlining the importance the study of repetition had been for him during those years. Among the many influences he names are Virgil, Goethe, Thucydides and Stifter.

The narrator's recognition of the fruitful relationship with the literary tradition is one of the most important aspects of *Across*. For instance, in the case of the quotation from Virgil's *Georgics* the narrator is deriving a lesson "for the things that still matter: the sun, the earth, rivers, woods, trees and shrubs, domestic animals, fruits (along with jars and baskets), utensils and tools" (*Ac* 22). Virgil's verses, which like all poetry are "congruent with things" (*Ac* 22), bring those elements alive to the reader, and make them shine with new light. The words in the classical text have, as a consequence, the purpose of sharpening the observer's perception and, at the same

---

[8]Cf. Stifter: "When I give [narrative] form to my subject-matter it is entirely independent of me and only depends on the subject-matter itself; I have to find it [the form], not invent it.... My story has always existed, I only discover it" (266).

time, of telling the story of each word through the *epithetum ornans* which is usually associated with it, as in: "the slow-growing olive trees, the smooth linden, the bright-colored maple" (*Ac* 22). As a contemporary writer, Handke plays with these codified elements in the literary tradition by employing a game of free association and repetition, as evidenced by the name of the woman the protagonist meets at the airport: Tilia Levis is nothing more than the Latin name for linden, along with its characterizing epithet. Such modern adaptation of the tradition also occurs during the journey on foot through the areas where this tradition was born, as in the case of the protagonist's peregrination to the Virgilian places, Andes (Pietole) and the Mincio river in whose waters he enters as if desiring to be baptized.

The aesthetics of contraposition, present throughout the narrative, manifests itself similarly in the previously mentioned episode of the killing of the old Nazi which turns the protagonist into a "criminal" (*Ac* 10) and a "pursuer" (*Ac* 53). Now Loser too belongs to the "nation of criminals" (*Ac* 57). This same aesthetics is evident in the extremely censorious description of the downtown section of Salzburg (Weiss, "Tendenzen" 138), where the buildings close to the mountain erase the boundaries between nature and man's works which only pretend to be nature, as they appear camouflaged in the environment. Loser's criticism here is so fierce that the painter tells him his family name might as well be Spite (*Ac* 79).

In the third part of the story, "The Viewer seeks a Witness," a title which once more underlines the observer's presence within the text, the protagonist acknowledges that with the killing of the old Nazi his own gradual death has begun but that he can still overcome that condition. To that end he must seek a witness and ask for advice. Through the link to the Easter week ritual and the sound of bells the narrative, which had already shown certain references to the sacred is, so to speak, consecrated,[9] which allows a reading based on the thematic categories of death and resurrection. The first character to give evidence to Loser is the woman he met at the airport, whom he asks, after spending the night with her, to describe him. The woman, after remarking that he is "outside ordinary law,"

---

[9]On the other hand, this process of art consecration seems to be typical of Handke's artistic project since the end of the seventies (Egyptien 53).

responds with a parable that describes Loser's unusual situation: A seriously ill man goes to see a friend and, in taking leave, his tense eyes become slits as he tries to smile. His friend then sends him off with the words "Goodbye, my suffering Chinaman" (*Ac* 116). The woman thus becomes Loser's witness in that her parable points to his pain and alludes to his uniqueness.

The most important witness Loser looks for, however, is his son. When he tells him his story, narrating becomes the tool to bestow order on the past, to break with it, and to proceed into the future: "A story meant: it was, it is, it will be – it meant future" (*Ac* 130). Furthermore, an escape from the protagonist's isolation seems possible (Weiss, "Tendenzen" 138). The epilogue of the story deals with one of Handke's favorite places, "wherein nature and civilization together join in a sort of arcade" (*PhW* 55): the bridge over the canal which leads to the compound where Loser lives. The bridge represents the privileged viewing point for the observer; it is a place of separation and of conjunction between city and *hinterland* that allows the people who traversed it to abandon the constraints of their urban roles and to feel at home. From that vantage point close to the dwellings – a threshold by definition – the observer connects the people crossing the bridge over the old medieval canal with the stone figures decorating the church portal in the Old City of Salzburg, creating a fantasy from which flows "peace, mischief, quietness, gravity, slowness, and patience" (*Ac* 138). The attempt to harmonize the lower middle-class world of the small village with that belonging to the city and to eliminate the contradictions, attempted once in *Über die Dörfer* (1981; *Walk About the Villages*, 1996) and repeated here, certainly moves in the opposite direction of *Wunschloses Unglück* (1972; *A Sorrow Beyond Dreams*, 1976) where the suffocating world of the village represents the reality against which the writer's mother struggles in vain and ultimately perishes (Wagner, "Dörfer" 169).

In *Die Wiederholung* (1986; *Repetition*, 1988) Handke resumes the (auto)biographical scheme he began in *A Sorrow Beyond Dreams* but radically changes the documentary approach to create an autobiographical, mythicizing narrative through images. The first person narration appears in fact to begin in the same documentary style as his mother's biography. The scenario is the same: the native village which for Filip Kobal soon changes into the cold and overwhelming Catholic school environment. The return to his parents' home and the concomitant change of having to commute to a public school, does not integrate him into the place of his birth but rather makes the boy unable to feel at home anywhere. Experiences such as the game of telling stories (*R* 32), of observing the artist painting the signboards, or the confused sister who rejoices at his presence cannot "take the place of the village I had lost" (*R* 38). Filip's inability to integrate into a place results in an acute feeling of solitude (*R* 42), to a degree that, paradoxically, he can feel at home just by traveling back and forth from the city to the village.

The mythicization of the story takes shape with the evocation of the story of Filip's ancestor, Gregor Kobal, who in 1713 led a peasant rebellion against the Habsburg monarchy at Tolmin (Tolmezzo) in the Isonzo valley, was subsequently executed and his family exiled. Handke's epic project reveals itself as a contrast to the model of the family sagas that were typical of the great bourgeois novels of the nineteenth and twentieth centuries, representing the crisis of different generations (Wagner, "Epos" 218). The references to Filip's mythical ancestor and to his offspring's persecution helps the reader understand, through the father, the indignation he feels toward the historical events which the narration transforms into an "enthusiasm for geography and the geological formations" (Wagner, "Epos" 215). In the novel, the marks of history can be read and recognized in the landscape as archaeological reports (Wagner, "Epos" 216). They are peculiar ground structures like the empty cow paths, no longer overrun by cattle, the country paths with grass growing in the middle signalling the ancient passage of carts, or other symbols like the blind windows. Those signs become the characteristic traits of a view that reveals its past, its history; that of the Austrian empire in its less conspicuous and more genuine shapes. Two of them, the blind window and the empty cow path, also serve as titles for the first two parts of the tale. The second part recounts Filip's travels to Yugoslavia, his father's country, in search of his brother Gregor, who has been missing since enlisting with the Slovenian partisans.

Filip's arrival in his father's village still takes place under the influence of the night spent in the train tunnel, a veritable rite of

passage marked by darkness[10] and by troubled sleep filled with
shocking dreams – dreams of having to fight a hopeless battle
against the story that turns into a monster until he manages to regain
his narrative ability and utter "two clear sentences, the one following naturally from the other" (*R* 79). In the dream, a child appears in
the same role of the girl in *Kindergeschichte* (1981; *Child Story*,
1985) to correct, but at the same time approve the adult's narration.
The episode of the night in the tunnel assumes the quality of a rite
of passage and therefore of purification, as previously announced by
Filip's history professor. He also tells about the war prisoners'
sacrifice who lost their lives in the construction of the tunnel and of
whom all that is left are the horrible traces of the hardened eye-
lashes in concrete (Roli 286). The presence of a still innocent human would have been enough, according to the professor, to erase
the terrible events of the past.[11] Filip's exit from the tunnel corre-

---

[10]The rite of passage, that is the nightly initiation of young men into adulthood,
is a common tradition in ancient civilizations; see Frazer and van Gennep.
Filip's situation exhibits parallels to this rite.

[11]In a more general sense, Butzer mentions a rite of passage which would consist "in a retrospective contemplation of … [the protagonist's] life" that would
enable him "to enter into the space of Slovenian memory" (285). However,
Butzer does not identify the night and the tunnel as the actual time and place of
the rite of passage marking the novice's symbolic death; instead, he sees it as a
"sojourn in the underworld" (286). It should be pointed out that rites of passage
especially occur in such places as impenetrable forests, where the classical
authors of antiquity, for instance Ovid, Virgil, and later Dante, used to situate
the entrance to the next world. Also, such rites were usually accompanied by
feelings of horror and fear (cf. Propp 92). Consequently Filip's utterance "that
is why I now see the little knot of glowworms in the grass outside the tunnel
blown up into a fire-spewing dragon guarding the entrance to the underworld"
(*R* 81) does not so much identify the tunnel as representing the underworld
itself, but rather indicates the close proximity of an entrance to that world. The
consequence of the rite of passage, therefore, is not the protagonist's
"forgetting of his personal history" (Butzer 286), but his legitimate arrival in
the world of adults and his concomitant appropriation of the world of his
ancestors. With regard to the third part of *Repetition*, Butzer points to "a series
of rites of passage," the first being brought about by the Karst wind that
"baptizes" the protagonist (293). The episodes in which Butzer makes out these
rites – the work at the old woman's in the dolina, drinking with the residents of
the Karst, the wake of an unknown woman, and the metaphorical wedding of
the protagonist and a young woman by means of an exchange of glances – each

sponds to taking possession of a new geographic space which, having passed his rites of passage, he finds he can read as a coherent whole: as text and therefore as the world. In this passage Handke hints at the possibility of overcoming the horrors of the past, "to open the closed space of the post-Holocaust period through writing, meant in the classical sense as expiation" (Höller 183). He is able to accomplish this by remembering the Slovenian language that his father spoke when Filip was a child and an old German-Slovenian dictionary owned by his older brother. In this way, the narrative brings forth the Slovenian cultural background, the culture and language of the region where the protagonist was born (Roli 287).

The recovery of Filip's family history is precipitated by the symbolic retrieval of the family language, that is, of the father's language, Slovenian. The opportunity to retrieve both his language and history comes during the young man's travel to Yugoslavia and the tools at his disposal are his brother Gregor's composition book of fruit-growing and Maks Pletersnik's nineteenth-century dictionary. The words of this lesser-known language acquire a very strong evocative power as they spark an intuition in Filip which transforms into images rather than words. A few notes by Handke entitled "Die Wiederholung, slowenische Wortgeschichten" (1993; Repetition, history of Slovenian words) are very relevant to that effect in that the author here comments on several terms drawn from Pletersnik's dictionary. The words he selects belong to the area of agriculture, and through the search for the corresponding term in German, memories of his childhood return (Roli 288). The reading of the composition book also gives the protagonist the opportunity to recall episodes from his childhood connected with the fruit orchard that was established by his brother. By renaming certain objects, small things in a simple scenario linked to nature and to the cycles of seasons, Filip is able symbolically to "give birth" to them.[12]

In the process of recollection and at the moment when these objects are named, his experiences become speakable and acquire a place "in a sequence that keeps it alive, a story which can open out

---

represent an experience that assumes for him a singular meaning from which he can draw conclusions and gain knowledge.

[12]One should note here the intertextual link of this part of the narration with Virgil's *Georgics* mentioned in *Across*. Such intertextual linkages are common in Handke's narrative.

into free storytelling, greater life, invention" (*R* 73). The narrative therefore establishes the epic order and makes it visible (Wagner, "Epos" 219). The recovery of objects and experiences through recollection and their naming revitalizes them and preserves them for the future, thus preventing their disappearance in a technical world (Cometa 107). What matters most to the now forty-five-year-old narrator is not the reporting of facts as they happened in the past, but the creation of appearance and illusion, an illusion which already springs from his brother's writings, his composition book and the letters to the family, in which the language of images prevails and has a direct impact on the naming of things. This process of creating an illusion in the course of the narrative leads to the unconflicted mythicization of Gregor, who becomes Filip's ancestor par excellence, the guardian he sees kneeling by him and in whom he fully recognizes himself and whom he incarnates. At this point all the implications of the semantics of repetition appear: not just to draw things from the past, but to regain them for memory and to tell of them and restore them (Roli 289), and also to mythicize one's ancestor and oneself by incarnating him.[13]

The act of repetition is nonetheless a constituent element of the myth Handke wants to introduce into literature. It establishes connections that are instrumental to a holistic conception of the world among individual perceptions, meditations and recollections through the analogic processes carried out by the characters (Gottwald 51). In this conception of repetition, Handke echoes and adapts ideas from Kierkegaard's work of the same title (*Repetition: an Essay in Experimental Psychology*, 1941), who stated that repetition and recollection are opposite manoeuvres. Recollection reproduces the object in reverse, generating unhappiness, whereas repetition moves in a forward direction, resulting in happiness (Wagner-Egelhaaf 201-02). With reference to Heidegger the title *Repetition* can be seen as epitomizing a central concept of postmodernism. Accordingly, postmodernism must not be perceived as a nostalgic longing for the past but as a confrontation with the past in order to renew the present (Küchler 151). This notion of repetition, however, clashes with the Freudian interpretation of the term as an urge to

---

[13]Schmidt-Dengler also sees Handke here celebrating his ancestral heritage that cannot be separated from its "political implications" (496).

repeat (Wagner, "Epos" 217). Handke's understanding of the term emerges clearly at several points in the narrative, for example in the episode involving the hike in the mountains where the narrator follows the same path he used to walk with his father as a child. It is not the realization of again taking the same path, but rather the moment of narrating the new experience that lets him experience the peculiar sensation which only later materializes in the act of writing and leads him to meditation (Roli 289). At this stage, the repetition reveals itself as more than a remake or an imitation, namely as something which must be retraced and relived (*R* 176).

Furthermore, the representation of space in Handke's texts is similarly connected to a mythicization of the narration (Renner 125-26; Gottwald 52-54). *Repetition* resumes the theme of the threshold which Handke had touched upon in *Across*. After arriving at the Wochein valley, the protagonist left the village every afternoon for a vast highland, a plateau where he could be alone, yet at the same time not be far from the world and from civilization, a place which for Handke bears the distinctive traits of the zone of the threshold (*R* 139). In its double meaning as highland and writing table, the *Tischebene* as a kind of threshold zone is an ideal place for deciphering Gregor's composition book, an activity which also alludes to the act of writing (Wagner, "Epos" 220). The spatial experiences of Handke's characters since the *Slow Homecoming* tetralogy consist of the subjective processes of perception and orientation (or disorientation) in a natural setting which often bears anthropomorphous traits (Gottwald 53). Those experiences are connected to the theme of the *Wanderung* (hike, peregrination), where the emphasis is not placed on the individual process of cognition and development as it is in the German literary tradition (Roli 290), but on conferring new meanings to natural details through their descriptions with mythicizing and consecrating qualities (Gottwald 53).

An example of that type of spatial description are the so-called "empty forms" (R 159), the empty cow paths and the blind windows. These empty signs are undetermined and have no significance of their own. They refer back to the empty form of narrative, while meaning is created through repetition, the act of storytelling itself (Küchler 155). In Filip's imagination, the empty cow paths become the Mayan pyramids populated with the figures of family members and, at the end, with the figure of the protagonist's alter ego. That figure at first gesticulates in the air which, little by little, becomes a regular movement recalling the act of writing. After recognizing himself in that figure, which is itself a variant of the leitmotif of repetition, Filip remarks: "...like a scientist who is at the same time a manual laborer, I make hatch marks on a sheet of paper lying on the stone-grey steps" (*R* 160). When spoken aloud in the deserted space, the words from his brother's dictionary bounce off the mountain slopes marked by the empty cow paths and cause an echo which Kobal terms "world sound" (*R* 161). They are the words of an ancient language, rich with images, which still possesses its poetic power and which can still be used to express the things of the world.

The protagonist's wandering through the Karst region also serves as an example of the spatial representations that are of central significance. Filip's teacher compares the dolinas, the funnel shaped cavities which are the key feature of this landscape, to the Yucatan countryside with its "overturned shape," which is formed by cone-shaped towers and pinnacles, as though there existed a "basic form" (*R* 213) of landscape replicated throughout different parts of the world. The crossing of the Karst region and the visit to Maribor, the village where the older brother Gregor had attended the agricultural school, reflects a repetition of his brother's trip and affirms the meaning of returning to the country of origin that it had for his brother. The voyage is therefore part of the protagonist's process of identification with his predecessor or "ancestor" and has at its end "the savanna of freedom and the ninth country." This is also the title of the third part of the novel and hints both at the utopian country of origin of the Kobals whom, as Gregor mentioned in his letters, he wanted to join, as well as the sacred Mayan number nine (Egyptien 47).

A spirit of reconciliation dominates this final part, which is considered by some critics a strained happy end that weakens the narration (Czernin 48). The aesthetic reconciliation of the profane with the sacred-religious represents not only the most distinctive trait of Handke's writings, but is also the starting point from which their poetic success can be evaluated (Czernin 49). The poetic efficacy of this reconciliation rests on the basis of a narrative structure consisting of connections and of motifs which interlock to the point of forming a network of links upon which the poetic validity of the text is based and built. In works where that network of links fails to materialize, as in Handke's diaristic texts (Czernin mentions *Am Felsfenster morgens*, 1998; Mornings at the Natural Arch), the setting into which the descriptions of objects or perceptions can be inserted is not present and they appear as a demonstration of the observer's acuteness of perception, but sometimes with an "unintentional comicality" (Czernin 39).

At the end of the narrative, Filip's old teacher highlights the importance of numbers and of counting as elements that moderate, regulate and slow one down, things, on the other hand, which have been tied to poetry since antiquity. *Repetition* ends with an invocation of the act of storytelling, an act that is compared to a spacious vehicle, a chariot capable of carrying the world, replicating and restoring it (*R* 245).

Handke's novelistic text *Nachmittag eines Schriftstellers* (1987; *The Afternoon of a Writer*, 1989) continues the autobiographical meditations that have become typical of his works. Still, the choice of a third-person narration establishes a certain narratorial distance from what is being narrated, so that the text appears to be cohesive and therefore effective from a narrative standpoint. Unlike some of Handke's diaristic and aphoristic texts, the narrative does not become fragmented into a plethora of visual and auditory perceptions.

The story portrays a writer who must overcome the painful experience of writer's block, of the blank page and the inability to produce, something which has in his mind left him with professional and existential fears. The drastic decision to shut himself off in a room to write so as not to be diverted by the external world is not sufficient to overcome the impasse. On the contrary, only contact with a few select places in the external world can promote his return to writing and narrating. These places are Handkean spaces par excellence: a solitary home where the protagonist is the only inhabitant besides a cat, a place where the interior and exterior are in communication and light and darkness break in. But it is only at night, sitting in partial darkness, given the reflection of the city lights, that the writer experiences a "sense of being at home" (*AW* 9). These are the moments when he is happiest, when recollections surface in the room and "his musings merged into equally peaceful dreams" (*AW* 10). The house therefore assumes the meaning of a "space of loneliness" and of a place where the writer's intimacy is located (Bachelard 28). Moreover, the house represents also the place for writing, an activity which gives it warmth and makes it hospitable, as it is carried out on a desk, which for an instant rises to "a place of righteousness or becoming righteous" (*AW* 12). On the other hand it is the space where the humble daily activities of our lives take place.[14]

The centripetal motion towards the house, toward darkness and loneliness is offset by the protagonist's centrifugal motion towards the outside world, which occurs in the daytime and manifests itself only in specific locations. These locations can be divided into crowded places in the city center, which the writer chooses in periods of idleness, and marginal areas without human presence, which he prefers in periods of creativity. Here the allusion to the idea of the threshold is clear, even though the word is not mentioned. In the story, the protagonist's decision to "combine the periphery with the center" (*AW* 16) prevails in that he selects a path which leads from the woods and the outskirts to the center of the city. What makes that path peculiar is that it allows the writer to match distant images ("distance, my thing"; *AW* 20) with closer ones. In his periods of artistic creativity, such images have the tendency to give rise to reveries and to extend their boundaries:

> Surprisingly, it was almost exclusively at times when he was writing that he was able to divest the city he lived in of its limits. The little became big; names lost their meaning; the light-colored sand in the cracks between cobblestones became the foothills of a dune; a pallid blade of grass became a part of a savanna. (*AW* 24)

An additional thought forces the writer to acknowledge that it is not the material that is critical in a narration, but rather the framework or the structure into which that material is inserted. On the other hand, images give strength to the writer: through them he finds the

---

[14]The attention to "daily life" and to the "small things of every day" that Handke mentions in the interview with Gamper (*Zw* 104, 96) as well as the privilege given to the less colorful or even insignificant aspects of things represent a distinctive trait of Handke's writing, which has been correctly compared to that of Stifter (Amann 9) and appears as a characteristic of this story as well. The comparison between Handke and Stifter had already been made by Sebald on the basis of both writers' tendency to create images filled with light that stand in stark contrast to their 'obscure' social origins.

"localization" (*AW* 37) of things and manages to describe them. Another aspect of the writer's life related in this story is his relationship with the public, characterized by timidity and even by shame (*AW* 39). His awareness of being a well-known public figure goes hand in hand with an understanding of his own lack of boldness and of the superficiality of the public's recognition of him. His identification with his image, the writer ironically remarks, fluctuates between that of a wanted poster and a television image. Only in one case does he have the impression of being recognized by a reader, while the vast majority of the people shows a more or less open hostility toward him. That fact together with his loss of self-confidence enables the writer to realize once and for all that the place most congenial to him is the outskirts of the city (*AW* 46) or the home.

In this work the persona of the writer thus appears, in the best tradition of twentieth-century literature, as an outsider, as a life far from normality and out of place in an epoch of materialism, mass production and mediocrity (Pakendorf 82). Like the title character of Rilke's *Die Aufzeichnungen des Malte Laurids Brigge* (1910; *The Notebooks of Malte Laurids Brigge*, 1972), the protagonist of *Afternoon* lives a marginal existence which is silently acknowledged and accepted only by others as marginal as he, by the outcasts: the old retired teacher who has become a poet and who solemnly recites a poem to the writer when he meets him in the street, the old woman with a confused mind who after falling into a bush utters infantile sounds and addresses only the writer among all the people who come to her rescue, and the drunkard in the tavern who speaks to himself in meaningless words, declaring that they are important matters. All of these characters can be considered deformed and grotesque doubles of the writer (Roli 291) and are connected with him not only from an existential point of view, but also from a linguistic one. They are placed not only on the margin of existence, but literally on "the frontiers of language" (*AW* 64), which comes close to the infant's or the poet's babbling (Pakendorf 83).

Related to the idea of the infant's and the poet's babbling, and linked to the very ancient traditions of oracles is the protagonist's experience of the loss of his name, of himself, of the extension of the boundaries of individuality, which makes him a solitary being within the world around him. The harmony with the world acquired

through the loss of individuality represents the experience of the
mystical union with other things (Pakendorf 82) and is itself linked
to the writer's wanderings (Roli 291) outlined in the following passage:

> As he was crossing the open fields by his usual diagonal paths,
> his just acquired namelessness, favored by the snowfall and his
> walking alone, took on substance. This experience of nameless-
> ness might at one time have been termed a liberation from limits
> or from the self. To be at last wholly outside, among things, was
> a kind of enthusiasm, one felt one's eyebrow arching. Yes, to be
> rid of his name was ground for enthusiasm; like the legendary
> Chinese painter, he felt himself disappearing into the picture....
> (*AW* 51)

Besides, the quotation from Goethe's *Torquato Tasso* (1790; trans.
1965) appended to the story – "'tis all there, but I am nothing" (*AW*
87) – seems to refer to an experience of self-effacement and the
concomitant enthusiasm of letting things prevail. It should be
emphasized that the experience is possible only if connected to
specific places, localized in the intermediate territory between city
and country, in the outskirts of the city where the countryside is not
clearly defined and fixed in its meanings. But it also has an open
and free quality, which returns to the realm of fantasy and of
originality (Pakendorf 82).

Two additional doubles for the writer appear in the story: the
first, a writer himself, is at the end of his life and, now unable to
read, has become sadly dependent on the protagonist, his friend,
who tells him about the judgments of the newspaper editors. This
example reinforces the protagonist's determination to remain outside of the cultural world and to rely only on his own strengths. The
other double is an old, former writer who now works as a translator.
He describes the beginnings of his activity as reproducing images of
the world in writing and as listening to a primary text being
transferred onto paper. The operation of transfering those fragments
into writing nevertheless clashed with the problem of connecting the
parts and casting them into a whole. This produced a feeling of fear
in the writer and nightmares about the inability to write. As this episode illustrates, the translator's conception of the verbal art is very
similar to Handke's own. What is missing is the step that moves
beyond the fragmentary character of the perceived representation
which would establish the link between the fragments and thus

create the narrative. This induced the translator to give up the job of writing and to pursue a more modest goal, one without anguish and better fit to his abilities.

The path chosen by the writer is different, though he poses several questions to himself about his mission, the mission of the writer in this epoch. As Rilke's Malte, the protagonist of *The Afternoon of a Writer* realizes that many of the chances afforded writers of the past are no longer present, and storytelling has become truly difficult, if not impossible. If Rilke could still declare that he had access to a "cosmic space" ("Weltinnenraum" [Rilke 113; cf. *NS* 73; *AW* 68]), Handke puts this "existential (and poetological) wish" (Rilke 515) into question, though he, similar to Rilke, evidences an attitude tinged with Romanticism. To preserve their art both chose a life of solitude, of self-exclusion from the social community to which they feel they don't belong. In exchange for that exclusion, Handke at least considers it a possibility – although a questionable one – to "just praise the beloved objects of this planet with a stanza or a paragraph about a tree, a countryside, a season" (*AW* 68).

All those meditations are bound together either by the unity of time which lends the story its title, or by the ordered sequence of places or their partial descriptions (Pakendorf 79) the synthesis of which is reached in the account of the threshold zones between city center and periphery. *The Afternoon of a Writer* ends with a night of rest and with the restatement of the writer's will to continue in his work "as a storyteller" (*AW* 85). Handke here takes up *topoi* of the meditations on poetics of Austrian writers of the twentieth century, such as the loss of language by Hofmannsthal in the letter to Lord Chandos, "Ein Brief" (1902; "A Letter," 1952), as well as the impossibility to narrate, as mediated by Rilke through his character Malte. The solution imagined and adopted by Malte, the visualization of narration, is a very difficult process, but of great poetic expressivity when successfully implemented. Significantly this solution is very similar to the one practised by Handke: to narrate in images.

Works Cited

Amann, Klaus. "Peter Handkes Poetik der Begriffstutzigkeit." *Peter Handke zum 60. Geburtstag* [= *Manuskripte* 42]. Ed. Alfred Kolleritsch and Günter Waldorf. Graz: Styria, 2002. 8-12.

Aspetsberger, Friedbert, and Hubert Lengauer. *Zeit ohne Manifeste? Zur Literatur der siebzigerJahre in Österreich.* Vienna: Österreichischer Bundesverlag, 1987.

Bachelard, Gaston. *La poétique de l'espace.* Paris: PUF, 1989.

Bartmann, Christoph. *Suche nach Zusammenhang. Handkes Werk als Prozeß.* Vienna: Braumüller, 1984.

Blumenberg, Hans. *Arbeit am Mythos.* Frankfurt am Main: Suhrkamp, 1996.

Butzer, Günter. "Rettung: Peter Handke, *Die Wiederholung.*" *Fehlende Trauer. Verfahren epischen Erinnerns in der deutschsprachigen Gegenwartsliteratur.* Munich: Fink, 1998. 271-318.

Chastel, André. "Melancholia in the Sonnets of Lorenzo de' Medici." *Journal of the Warburg and Courtauld Institutes* 8 (1945) 61-67.

Cometa, Michele. *Gli dei della lentezza. Metaforiche della "pazienza" nella letteratura tedesca.* Milano: Guerini e Associati, 1990.

Cortesi Bosco, Francesca. *Lorenzo Lotto. Gli affreschi dell' Oratorio Suardi di Trescore.* Milan: Skira, 1997.

Czernin, Franz Josef. "*Die Widerholung* und *Am Felsfenster morgens*: Zum Verhältnis von Erzählung und Weltanschauung bei Peter Handke." *Text und Kritik* 24. Ed. Heinz Ludwig Arnold. 6th ed. Munich: edition text + kritik, 1999. 36-50.

Düchting, Hans. *Cézanne 1839-1906. La natura diventa arte.* Cologne: Taschen, 1991.

Egyptien, Jürgen. "Die Heilkraft der Sprache. Peter Handkes *Die Wiederholung* im Kontext seiner Erzähltheorie." *Text und Kritik* 24. Ed. Heinz Ludwig Arnold. 5th ed. Munich: edition text + kritik, 1989. 42-58.

Feichtinger, Barbara. "'Glaenz mir auf, harte Hasel. Schweb ein, leichte Linde.' Zur *Georgica*-Rezeption in Peter Handkes *Chinese des Schmerzes. Arcadia* 26 (1991) 303-21.

Frazer, James George. *Il ramo d'oro. Studio sulla magia e la religione*. Trans. Lauro De Bosis.Turin: Boringhieri, 1973.

Gennep, Arnold van. *I riti di passaggio*. Trans. Maria Luisa Remotti. Turin: Boringhieri, 1981.

Gottwald, Herwig. *Mythos und Mythisches in der Gegenwartsliteratur. Studien zu Christoph Ransmayr, Peter Handke, Botho Strauss, George Steiner, Patrick Roth und Robert Schneider*. Stuttgart: Heinz, 1996.

Hamm, Peter. "Die (wieder) einleuchtende Welt. Peter Handkes Buch *Der Chinese des Schmerzes*." *Die Arbeit am Glück. Peter Handke*. Ed. Gerhard Melzer and Jale Tükel. Königstein/Ts: Athenäum, 1985. 102-10.

Handke, Peter. "Die Wiederholung, slowenische Wortgeschichten." Faksimile einiger Seiten aus dem Notizbuch von Peter Handke mit Auszügen aus dem Wörterbuch von Maks Pletersnik. *Slovensko-nemski slovar*. Ljubljana 1894. *Noch einmal vom Neunten Land: Peter Handke im Gespräch mit Jože Horvat*. Trans. and ed. Klaus Detlef Olof. Klagenfurt, Salzburg: Wieser, 1993. 19-40

Hoff, Ursula. "Meditation in Solitude." *Journal of the Warburg Institute* 1 (1937-38) 292-94.

Höller, Hans. "Cosa, immagine, scrittura: *Die Lehre der Sainte-Victoire* di Peter Handke." *Le muse inquiete. Sinergie artistiche nel Novecento tedesco*. Ed. Grazia Pulvirenti, Renata Gambino, Vincenza Scuderi. Florence: Olschki, 2003. 171-88.

Klibansky, Raymond, and Panofsky, Erwin, and Saxl, Fritz. *Saturno e la melanconia. Studi di storia della filosofia naturale, religione e arte*. Trans. Renzo Federici.Turin: Einaudi, 1983.

Küchler, Tilman. "Von blinden Fenstern und leeren Viehsteigen. Zu Peter Handkes *Die Wiederholung*." *Seminar* 30.2 (1994) 151-68.

Lorenz, Otto. *Die Öffentlichkeit der Literatur. Fallstudien zu Produktionskontexten und Publikationsstrategien: Wolfgang Koeppen – Peter Handke – Horst Eberhard Richter*. Tübingen: Niemeyer, 1998.

Manthey, Jürgen. "'Franz Kafka, der Ewige Sohn.'" *Peter Handke*. Ed. Raimund Fellinger. Frankfurt am Main: Suhrkamp, 1985. 375-85.

Melzer, Gerhard. "'Lebendigkeit: ein Blick genügt.' Zur Phänomenologie des Schauens bei Peter Handke." *Die Arbeit am*

Glück. Peter Handke. Ed. Gerhard Melzer and Jale Tükel. Königstein/Ts: Athenäum, 1985. 126-52.

Nenon, Thomas, and Renner, Rolf Günter. "Auf der Schwelle von Dichten und Denken. Peter Handkes ontologische Wende in *Der Chinese des Schmerzes.*" *Text und Kritik* 24. Ed. Heinz Ludwig Arnold. 5th ed. Munich: edition text + kritik, 1989. 104-15.

Pakendorf, Gunther. "Writing about Writing: Peter Handke, *Nachmittag eines Schriftstellers. Modern Austrian Literature* 23.3-4 (1990) 77-86.

Propp, Vladimir. *Le radici storiche dei racconti di fate.* Turin: Boringhieri, 1972.

Renner, Rolf Günter. *Peter Handke.* Stuttgart: Metzler, 1985.

Rilke, Rainer Maria. *Werke. Kommentierte Ausgabe in vier Bänden.* Vol. 2. Ed. Manfred Engel, et al. Frankfurt am Main: Insel, 1996.

Roli, Maria Luisa. "La rinarrabilità della storia. Autobiografia come racconto mitico in 'Die Wiederholung' di Peter Handke." *Il testo autobiografico nel Novecento.* Ed. Reimar Klein and Rossana Bonadei. Milan: Guerini, 1993. 279-92.

Schmidt-Dengler, Wendelin. "Peter Handke (*1942): *Die Wiederholung* (1986)." *Bruchlinien. Vorlesungen zur österreichischen Literatur 1945-1990.* Salzburg: Residenz, 1995. 488-506.

Sebald, Winfried G. "Helle Bilder und dunkle. Zur Dialektik der Eschatologie bei Stifter und Handke." *Die Beschreibung des Unglücks. Zur österreichischen Literatur von Stifter bis Handke.* Salzburg, Vienna: Residenz, 1985. 165-86.

Stifter, Adalbert. *Sämtliche Werke.* 25 vols. Ed. August Sauer, et al. 1901. Hildesheim: Olms, 1972.

Virgil. *Georgiche.* Trans. Antonio Canali. Milan: R. C. S., 1997.

Wagner, Karl. "Über die literarischen Dörfer. Zur Ästhetik des Einfachen." *Zeit ohne Manifeste? Zur Literatur der 70er Jahre in Österreich.* Ed. Friedbert Aspetsberger and Hubert Lengauer. Vienna: Oberösterreichischer Bundesverlag, 1987. 166-80.

–. "'Warum sind wir Österreicher nur solche Arschlöcher?' Handkes 'Epos des Heimatlosen': *Die Wiederholung.*" *Der Schriftsteller und der Staat. Apologie und Kritik in der österreichischen Literatur. Beiträge des 13. Polnisch-Österreichischen Germanistentreffens Kazimierz Dolny 1998.* Ed. Janusz Golec. Lublin:

Wydawnictwo Uniwersytetu Marii Curie-Sklodowskiej, 1999. 213-23.

Wagner-Egelhaaf, Martina. *Mystik der Moderne: Die visionäre Ästhetik der deutschen Literatur im 20. Jahrhundert.* Stuttgart: Metzler, 1989.

Warburg, Aby. "Dürer und die italienische Antike." *Gesammelte Schriften. Die Erneuerung der heidnischen Antike.* Vol. 2. Leipzig, Berlin: Teubner, 1932. 443-54.

Weiss, Walter. "Neueste Tendenzen am Beispiel Handkes." *Zeit ohne Manifeste? Zur Literatur der 70er Jahre in Österreich.* Vienna: Österreichischer Bundesverlag, 1987. 134-40.

—. "Religiöse Motive. Poetik des Fragens bei Peter Handke." *Sprachkunst* 20 (1989) 227-35.

Wolf, Jürgen. *Visualität, Form und Mythos in Peter Handkes Prosa.* Opladen: Westdeutscher Verlag, 1991.

Handke's *Versuche*: Essaying Narration

David N. Coury

IN 1994, THREE NARRATIVE prose works by Peter Handke were published in English translation under the title *The Jukebox and Other Essays on Storytelling*.[1] The curious subtitle given to this collection adds a certain explication to the works which was not present in their original form, but which nevertheless provides insight into Handke's own aesthetics. Early on in his career, Handke was known as an iconoclastic writer who purposely broke with literary traditions, often with the primary goal of provocation. Steeped in the Austrian avant-garde and borrowing heavily from the French *nouveau roman*, Handke's earliest prose fiction[2] dealt predominantly with linguistic questions and given its anti-narrative structures was at times quite abstruse. In the 1970s, however, he helped usher in a wave of self-reflective literature which came to be known as the New Subjectivity. These works of short fiction[3] were very experientially based and in some ways resembled extended interior monologues, in that the narrator recounted his feelings and emotions in a pondering, philosophical style, at times both questioning and answering himself.[4] Not one to remain stagnant, however,

---

[1] The original essays appeared separately under the titles *Versuch über die Müdigkeit* (1989; *Essay on Tiredness*, 1994), *Versuch über die Jukebox* (1990; *Essay on the Jukebox*, 1994), and *Versuch über den geglückten Tag* (1991; *Essay on the Successful Day*, 1994). As such they form a trilogy and were published together in English translation. While the subtitle was added by the translators or the publisher, the publisher's note states that Handke always worked very closely with Ralph Manheim and was thus certainly in agreement with the subtitle.

[2] To this period belong his first two novels *Die Hornissen* (1966; The Hornets) and *Der Hausierer* (1967; The Peddler).

[3] The two most important and which many critics considered Handke's best works are *Der kurze Brief zum langen Abschied* (1972; *Short Letter, Long Farewell*, 1974) and the memoir about his mother's death *Wunschloses Unglück* (1972; *A Sorrow Beyond Dreams*, 1975).

[4] As with most of Handke's works, there exists a very close correspondence between writer and narrator. This stems from Handke's belief that the writer

Handke soon redesigned his narrative structures and completed in the early eighties a tetralogy[5] that exhibited a change in his narrative program, namely the rediscovery of the story as a vehicle for structuring and conveying his ideas.[6] While nature and city spaces receive great attention in these works, the style is still quite self-reflective and subjective. Primary as well are the author's own experiences and emotions, which are echoed by the semi-autobiographical nature of these works. As Handke had written some ten years before, "life writes the best stories" (*BE* 22), a fitting motto for his works from 1970-1981, as they reflect his own journeys, crises, and feelings.

Thus in some ways it comes as little surprise that in 1989 he would turn his attention in a series of essays to the issue of storytelling and narration and how they are linked to the individual's sense of perception. What was unusual, however, was the form that Handke chose to explore the act of storytelling. Unlike his homage to F. Scott Fitzgerald, *Nachmittag eines Schriftstellers* (1987; *The Afternoon of a Writer*, 1989), which in (meta-)narrative form recounts the struggles and thoughts of a writer,[7] Handke decided to expound on the act of telling through an examination of two concepts (tiredness and the successful day) and one concrete object (the jukebox). He also chose an essayistic form which he titled a *Versuch*, which, while literally meaning an "attempt" or "try-out," was also the German translation for Michel de Montaigne's *Essais* from the 1570s that today are considered the basis

---

must draw from life and experience for poetic inspiration. Most critics agree that the narrator usually *is* Handke, although a discretionary caution is of course always in order. Handke would continue with this style and as Paul Konrad Kurz (139) has maintained, this critical self-questioning forms the underlying principle for all three *Versuche*.

[5]*Langsame Heimkehr* (1979; *The Long Way Around*, 1985), *Die Lehre der Sainte-Victoire* (1980; *The Lesson of Mont Sainte-Victoire*, 1985), *Kindergeschichte* (1981; *Child Story*, 1985), and *Über die Dörfer* (1981; *Walk About the Villages*, 1996). See Karl Wagner's chapter on the tetralogy in this volume.

[6]For a more thorough discussion of Handke's embracing of the story in his fiction of the 1980s as well as the theoretical discourse on the overall decline in narration, see Coury.

[7]For an extended analysis of this story, see Pakendorf.

for the modern Western form of the essay.[8] While Handke had written and published many essays before – especially early on in his
career – this particular designation for the form indicates a conscious deviation from the pieces he had previously written and
published.[9] The essay has, of course, a long tradition in German-
language literature. Paul Konrad Kurz has argued more specifically
that, since Hermann Broch's *Schlafwandler* trilogy (1931, *Sleep-
walkers*, 1932) and Robert Musil's *Der Mann ohne Eigenschaften*
(*1930; The Man Without Qualities*, 1953), Austrian literature has in
general exhibited a trend toward the essayistic (133). Both authors,
Kurz writes, believed in the modernist tradition that the world and
human consciousness could no longer be appropriately conveyed
through narration. Handke too questioned the ability of narrative to
convey reality and human experience, a subject he takes up early in
his career beginning with his plays and so-called *Sprechstücke*
(speak-ins). His early novels attempt as well to deconstruct the
narrative act so as to explore the boundaries of language and words
and their ability to function as appropriate signifiers. In "The Essay
as Form," Adorno argued that this was the greatest strength of the
essay, in that as a form it allowed a mediation between art and
philosophy that could result in the elucidation of historical truths.
Handke, on the other hand, uses the form as a means of poeticizing
his speculations on his own experiences, thereby offering an attempt
at narrative. Ingeborg Hoesterey likewise sees a similar connection
between Handke and Musil in that Handke embraces Musil's
dictum that we must live hypothetically, an idea that suggests a
melding of art, life and philosophy (48).

While Hoesterey rejects the term "essay" as an appropriate
translation for the *Versuche*, Gerhard Pfister, in his study of the
critical reception of Handke's works, notes that most critics do
equate the "Versuch" with the "Essay," yet they often fail to state
exactly how they understand the essay (230). Following Gero von
Wilpert, Pfister maintains that indeed the *Versuche* contain most of
the elements of the traditional essay: subjective form, a partial
openness in form, incompleteness, and a style midway between

---

[8]Kniesche (323) makes reference to this as well and Stolz refers to the works
using the French *essai*.
[9]For instance: *Ich bin ein Bewohner des Elfenbeinturms* (1972; I Am an Inhabitant of the Ivory Tower); *Das Ende des Flanierens* (1980; The End of Idling).

academic and poetic prose (230). In particular, critics have emphasized the denotative "attempt" that is inherent in the "Versuch,"
which thereby suggests a degree of incompleteness that the purer
essay does not necessarily connote. As Martina Kurz states: "Handke has termed his latest book 'Versuch' and thereby disavowed
from the outset all claims to a systematic exhaustion of his topic ...
as well as to a closed form."[10] Hoesterey acknowledges this search,
which is very much in the tradition of Montaigne, but argues that
Handke's textuality distinguishes these pieces form the long line of
essays in the German cultural tradition which are infused with a
much greater degree of irony and wit (47). Moreover Handke's
conspicuous avoidance of the term "essay" invites the reader to
focus less on the concrete and more on the speculative, a position
Handke himself takes early in the first piece on tiredness: "tiredness
isn't my subject; it's my problem" (*J* 12).[11] Ernst Ribbat sees this
conundrum as representative of a larger narratological problematic
that is the necessary result of the inability of traditional forms of art
(painting, stories or song) to achieve completeness, or in Handke's
terms, success (or rather a successful day). Only the open structure
of the essay, an "attempt" a "try-out" can approximate the goals and
ends of that which is to be explored (169).

In as much as the "Versuch" conveys the inability to achieve
narrative completeness, so too is it a reflection of the narrative act;
namely an attempt to narrate an idea or emotion (successful day), a
concept (tiredness) or an object (jukebox). Thus the narrative
structures of the essays incorporate a narrative voice distinct from
those found in most essays, which are by nature non-linear and
fragmentary. The author and critic John Berger has similarly maintained that stories are "discontinuous" and based on an implicit
agreement between the teller and the listener about what is *not* said.

---

[10]Martina Kurz, "Plädoyer wider die Putzmunteren," *Trierischer Volksfreund*
12 Oct. 1989 (quoted in Pfister 231).
[11]However, Manheim translates the subsequent line using the word "essay":
"And in dealing with the remaining varieties of tiredness, the non-malignant,
the pleasant, the delightful, which have prompted me to write this essay, I shall
try to remain equally heartless..." This line could perhaps also serve as a
programmatic statement; first, for lack of a better word, it is an *essay*, but one
in which the author will *try* to remain objective, all the while presenting us with
subjective observations.

Berger, whom Handke admires and whose work informs much of Handke's writing from this time, writes in this regard: "The discontinuities of the story and the tacit agreement underlying them fuse teller, listener and protagonists into an amalgam. An amalgam which I would call the story's *reflecting subject*. The story narrates on behalf of this subject, appeals to it and speaks in its voice" (285). This "reflecting subject" is not at all unlike the self-reflective narrator/subjects of Handke's *Versuche*. Indeed, the first-person narrative form, the "I" of each of these three essays, mirrors the narrative technique that Handke praises in Berger: "he [Berger] is at times also the narrator of his own self and sometimes even of himself without role-playing, not a speaker or advocate of others, no longer their self-proclaimed chronicler of history, neither of concepts nor of the self benumbed by knowledge" (*LS* 164) Berger simply does nothing more "than to walk and look … in order to write about it" (164); as such he is the epitome of the experiential writer.

All three of Handke's essays are characterized by this kind of experientiality, a mixture of fictional and autobiographical non-fictional codes, which Hoesterey has termed "autofiction," a term borrowed from the French author Serge Doubrovsky who coined the term for his 1977 novel *Fils* which, she maintains, was an early postmodern attempt at reconfiguring the parameters of the autobiographical genre (48). Kniesche similarly sees the three works as postmodern experimentations with non-representational forms. Handke's poetics at this time, he maintains, consists of deconstructing a seemingly fixed conception of reality through an exact description of its constituent parts, in order to construct a new image that transforms yet synthesizes this reality and frees the viewer from the constraints of the former (316).[12] As such all three are linked, both internally as well as thematically, in that they explore the possibilities of narration. Moser sees each work as a narratological turn, either a turn away from something (as in the case of history in *Jukebox*) or toward something (like tiredness or the successful day) whereby each turn can inevitably only be revealed through the author's own experience and his subjective

---

[12]Samuel Moser (143), in contrast, argues that the *Versuche* are more *Verwerfen* (discarding) than *Entwerfen* (creating).

perceptions of them.[13] The experience though is in the end only made possible by the act of writing itself, for within the act of writing, life and the work are fused (140). This attempt at connecting and fusing life (experience) and text (essay) is apparent in each of the three essays.

In the first, *Essay on Tiredness*, Handke explores the existential state of tiredness as it relates to his own experiences, beginning with childhood and continuing through his life as an adult. In the second, *Essay on the Jukebox*, the interrelatedness between autobiography and text is stated clearly in the opening sentence: "Intending to make a start at last on the long-planned essay on the jukebox, he bought a ticket to Soria at the bus station in Burgos" (47). In the final piece, *Essay on the Successful Day*, Handke chooses to open the narrative with three observations: an artistic one (a painting by Hogarth), a concrete one (the vein in a rock he found at Lake Constance) and an emotional one (a perception he experienced while riding the train in the suburbs of Paris). These three observations, he notes, gave him the impetus to return to his idea of the successful day and the desire "to describe, to list, or discuss the elements of such a day and the problems it raises" (*J* 121-22). Unlike tiredness, the successful day is both subject and problem and as such, he attempts to address the idea narratologically in a manner that is perhaps closest to the traditional form of the essay. As a result, when the three essays are taken together, one can ascertain progress (or even success) in the evolution of his attempt to narrate. First, however, Handke had to overcome the "tiredness," both personal as well as narratological, which he brought to the project from its outset.

After completing work on and the publication of his novel *Die Wiederholung* (1986; *Repetition*, 1988), Handke was, as he himself claimed, exhausted from writing. When his friend and long-time collaborator Wim Wenders approached him to write the screenplay for what would become the film *Der Himmel über Berlin* (1987;

---

[13]To be sure, not all critics viewed the essays positively. Dieter Stolz, in a parody of Handke's self-questioning style, calls *Jukebox* "a perfectly formed, but failed *essai* which lured its readers, patient enough to reach the last page, down a primrose path but failed to deliver its midsummernight's promise. The sensual feast created under the sign of a new poetics of the moment failed to arrive on our table" (270).

Wings of Desire), Handke declined, but then reconsidered and wrote the dialogues for the angels in the film as well as the opening poem, "Lied vom Kindsein" (The Song of the Child).[14] Thus it was only logical that in the first of the three essays, Handke would explore the concept of personal tiredness and exhaustion. As so often in his career, the act of writing would become crucial in his own understanding of the condition. While it appears at first somewhat ironic that Handke would chose the act of writing to comprehend his own fatigue as a writer, his desire for self-understanding is paramount and thus the motivating force behind the essay. Handke has often stated that for him, literature and writing is about his quest for self-understanding and clarification, and the *Essay on Tiredness* is no different.[15] He repeats this claim toward the end of the essay as well: "Tiredness provides teachings that can be applied. What, you may ask, does it teach? The history of ideas used to operate with the concept of the 'Thing in itself': no longer, for an object can never be manifested 'in itself,' but only in relation to me" (*J* 37). The narrator's answer here – to an inquiry as to whether tiredness enables one to act – is at once a philosophical affirmation of post-Kantian idealism as well as an underscoring of the postmodern aesthetics that have informed so much of Handke's work. Objects, so much the subject of inquiry not only in his narrative fictional work but in the non-fiction pieces,[16] not only become relevant but take on meaning only in relation to the narrator's/author's perception of them. The narrator continues his explanation: "What's more: they [the various forms of tiredness] give me the idea along with the concept" (*J* 37). In many ways, this reflection serves as a programmatic statement of Handke's work of the 1980s. Objects in their existential tiredness form the basis for inquiry and inevitably the

---

[14]"I am completed exhausted, I have no words left in me, everything that I had I put to paper." But then, as Wenders recalls, Handke added: "Maybe if you come here and tell me the story, I can help and write some dialogues" (Wenders 135).

[15]Handke opened his famous essay, "Ich bin ein Bewohner des Elfenbeinturms" with a comment in this regard: "Literature was for me for a long time a means to become if not clear than clearer about myself" (*BE* 19).

[16]See especially *The Lesson of Mont Sainte-Victoire* as an example of the former and *Noch einmal für Thukydides* (1990; *Once Again for Thuycidides*, 1998) as exemplary of the latter.

narrative act. As becomes apparent through the course of the essay, Handke inextricably links tiredness with narration and the ability to tell a story. However, in choosing to present this theme, he opts for a form quite unique amongst his writings, namely the dialogue.

The piece opens with a first-person account of the narrator's pre-existing understanding of the subject: "In the past I knew of tiredness only as something to be feared" (*J* 3). From the first line, Handke signals that the form he has chosen for the work is very much in the tradition of the essay; it is in first person, recalls his past experiences with tiredness and indicates that presently he has a different conception of the subject which will be the theme of the following narrative. Yet what follows is quite different from the modern (or even modernist) essay, in that the second line is a question that engages the narrator. Afterwards it becomes clear that the essay is in the form of a dialogue, a Socratic questioning and answering. As Samuel Moser has commented, these are not Platonic but Socratic dialogues, in that meaning and understanding arise through the alternation of question and answering, rather than through the dissemination of knowledge from an authorial figure (142). It is important to note, however, that only the first of the three essays takes this form; the second of the series, *Essay on the Jukebox*, is a much more traditional narrative essay.

In many ways, *Jukebox* is one of the more traditional stories that Handke has written, in that it is told in third person (although the autobiographical elements are, as in most of his works, clearly discernible) and has a more traditional narrative arc, even leading to semi-closure at the end of the essay.[17] *Essay on the Successful Day*, however, returns to the form of Socratic dialogue. While in *Tiredness* the dialogue is between an "I" and a "you," and in *Jukebox* it occurs between the narrator and the protagonist, *Successful Day* exhibits a combination of the two (Kniesche 324). In fact, in *Jukebox*, Handke recounts his thought process with regard to narrative form:

---

[17]Ribbat argues, however, that *Tiredness* and *Jukebox* conform to more traditional constructs of narrative whereas *Successful Day* is unique, in that, with its subtitle "Ein Wintertagtraum" ("A Winter's Day Dream" – oddly, this subtitle is omitted from the English translation) it moves in the realm of the dreamlike associations of the imagination (*J* 167-68).

> When he first had the inspiration ... of writing an "essay on the jukebox," he had pictured it as a dialogue onstage: this object, and what it could mean to an individual, was for most people so bizarre that an idea presented itself: having one person, a sort of audience representative, assume the role of interrogator, and a second person appear as an "expert" on the subject, in contrast to Platonic dialogues, where the one who asked the questions, Socrates, secretly knew more about the problem than the other who, puffed up with preconceptions ... knew the answer. (*J* 80)

Over the course of the trilogy, it becomes clear, Handke's narrator (i.e. Handke himself) evolves in his ability to relate objects to himself as well as in his ability to narrate, so that *Tiredness* reflects the need for dialogic interplay in order to achieve (self-)understanding, whereas with *Jukebox*, the narrator has achieved a sense of autonomy, where the narrative act is enabled solely by the quest for the subject – both physical and narratological.[18] Finally, in *Successful Day* a sense of narrative authority has been reached so that questioning serves not as a means of reaching understanding but as a means of edification.

Handke's attempt at narration in the second essay takes a different form. Toward the end of *Tiredness*, the "I" invites the "you" to sit down and examine nature in closer detail. The neo-romantic strains in Handke's nature writing, evidenced first in *The Long Way Around* and subsequently expounded upon in *The Lesson of Mont Sainte-Victoire*, are apparent again in *Jukebox*. The themes of isolation, nature and narration are continued in this essay, whereby the narrator travels to an isolated region of Spain in order to find the peace and solitude necessary to write. His escape, or "turn" as Moser would have it, is not only from people and the world around him, but also from history, as the narrative time is the same as the actual time of its writing – at the time of the fall of the Berlin Wall. This impetus to "escape history" is one which exemplifies Handke's view of the beguiling nature of the political. In *The Afternoon of a Writer*, the narrator remarks that news and current events are only means of distraction and that the writer should isolate himself from the outside world. In this way, Handke not only echoes the views of

---

[18]Kurz sees a similar yet distinct development as well. *Tiredness* and *Jukebox*, he maintains, present the remembrances of maturation. They show the "stations of coming into consciousness of a young man" and attempt to find the traces of a distant, youthful past (142).

the apolitical writer, which he championed in his early essays, but he also places the writer in the long-standing German tradition of the outsider, removed from society, atop an Olympian perch, able to observe the surrounding world and to write and create, based on these images.

In this context, the narrator's journey, ostensibly to set out to determine if there are any jukeboxes remaining in Spain and then to write an essay on them,[19] becomes in typical Handkean fashion a journey of self-discovery. As so often is the case in this period of Handke's œuvre, the story becomes a meta-narrative as, in another postmodern turn, he problematizes his own creative struggle, in turn writing a story about the process of writing an essay. What he finds and what serves as a source of inspiration throughout his journey are landscapes, both interior and exterior, which reveal to him a rhythm not unlike that heard from a jukebox, that provide him once again with the possibility to narrate. And just as suddenly as he hears these musical rhythms, so too does he find the rhythm of narration: "And now, as he aimlessly checked out trails in the savanna, suddenly an entirely new rhythm sprang up in him, not an alternating, sporadic one, but a single, steady one, and, above all, one that, instead of circling and flirting around, went straight and with complete seriousness in medias res: the rhythm of narrative" (*J* 82).[20] This rhythm of narration enables him once again to become a chronicler of events and experiences, ideally and ultimately leading to an epiphany of true feeling (as well as creativity) and a fusing with the world, which can only be described using the phraseology of his final essay, "a successful day."

Here, as in the first essay, narrative form is once again a central issue. In *The Afternoon of a Writer*, the narrator, in similar dialogic

---

[19]Interestingly, at one point Handke uses the verb "versuchen" to describe his writing process which Manheim renders "and here he wanted to essay the unworldly topic of the jukebox..." (*J* 58).

[20]Handke has always shown a love for music and pop-culture. At one point in the essay he even considers using a song as a structuring principle for the essay: by creating a montage or conglomeration of scenes and feelings, the essay would become like a song or a ballad on a jukebox. The jukebox is a fitting symbol, then, for Handke of the importance of music and a pop culture. Ulrich Schönherr has argued that the narrative search for the jukebox is in fact an allegory for the reconstruction of the "aura" that Benjamin maintained had been lost through modernity.

form, questions his own (pre)occupation: "What was his business, the business of a writer?" He then wonders: "Was there anyone, for example, whose deeds and sufferings cried out not only to be recorded, catalogued, and publicized in history books but also to be handed down in the form of an epic...?" (*AW* 67). Márta Horváth wonders, quite correctly, why the thought of an epic would be attractive to a writer at the end of the twentieth century (231). The answer, she maintains, lies in the fact that inherent in the epic is a mythical world view in which totality of being is present. In *Tiredness*, Handke's narrator speaks repeatedly of the "all in one" and of the "all there together" (*J* 38) revealed in a blade of grass in the middle of the road. According to this poetic, Horváth argues, the world can only be written into a literary work in its entirety (231). Handke, she maintains, "attempts to strive to mythologize the world through his writing and to find the timeless moments of the world that are absent of history" (232). Such moments, devoid of history, are the moments of peaceful existence without war.

Handke expounds upon this idea in the screenplay to Wenders' film *Wings of Desire*, through the figure of Homer, the old man who inhabits the libraries of Berlin and who embodies both history and epic storytelling. At one point Homer states: "My heroes are not the warriors and kings, rather the objects of peace, one as good as the other....Yet no one has been successful in intoning an epic of peace. What is it about peace, that it does not continually excite and seldom allows itself to be told?" (Wenders and Handke 56). For Kniesche this represents a certain utopianism in Handke's writings that mixes the political, the literary and the mythical. History, Handke writes in *Jukebox*, even in 1990 – "the year of history" – seemed as if it could be "a self-narrating fairy tale" (*J* 57). His "epic dreaming," he tells us further, "insistently told him a story; they [these dreams] told, though only in monumental fragments, which often degenerated into the usual dream nonsense, a world-encompassing epic of war and peace, heaven and earth, West and East, bloody murder, oppression, rebellion and reconciliation ..." (*J* 58-59). That history appears to him either as a fairy-tale or an epic dream suggests the irreality of politics and "history" which is then juxtaposed with the "reality" of the narrator's perceptions. Thus, for Handke, "[h]istory is either aestheticized or else it is not brought into the discourse" (Kniesche 320). This is exactly what critics later reproached Handke with in his essays on the war in Yugoslavia. But the desire for an "epic" (which Handke then in 1994 'gave' to the public in the form of his monumental novel *Mein Jahr in der Nie-mandsbucht* [*My Year in the No-Man's-Bay*, 1998]) reflects the importance for Handke not only of narrative but of literature itself.

Handke's reading of Walter Benjamin at this time is crucial to understanding his estimation of stories and narrative.[21] In his 1936 essay entitled "The Storyteller," Benjamin laments the decline of the storyteller and of the art of storytelling in general. One of the primary reasons he gives is the "obvious" one that "experience has fallen in value" (83-84). Moreover, he writes, the earliest symptom of this decline was the rise of the novel. What distinguishes the novel from the story is that it does not come from the oral tradition (like the epic): "the storyteller takes what he tells from experience – his own or that reported by others. And he in turn makes it the experience of those who are listening to the tale" (Benjamin 87). Handke approximates this situation through the dialogic form that he chooses for these three essays or attempts at storytelling. Benjamin goes on to condemn the novelist for having isolated himself from his public and thus for having lost the ability to counsel others. Similarly Handke's protagonist in *The Afternoon of the Writer* recognizes this very issue, but views the situation differently. In answer to his self-questioning about the business of the writer, he comes to the following conclusion: "By isolating myself (how many years ago?) in order to write, I acknowledged my defeat as a social being; I excluded myself from society once and for all" (*AW* 68). While he realizes that he'll never become one of the "others," that is a non-writing member of the public, at the end of the story he is able to reconcile his desire to seek and convey truth with the position of the writer as an isolated being: "I started out as a storyteller. Carry on. Live and let live. Portray. Transmit. Continue to work the most ephemeral of materials, my breath; be its craftsman" (*AW* 85). Clearly, the narrator positions himself in the line of oral tellers whose material is the voice, "my breath." In an interview a few years earlier, Handke had struggled with this very issue: can the novel (or novelist) truly convey the same type of

---

[21]In *Wings of Desire*, one of the texts that the angels (and Homer) are reading is Benjamin's "Theses on the Philosophy of History." Handke mentioned his readings of Benjamin in interviews at the time as well.

truths that the story and teller of tales once could?: "I think that perhaps the novel – well, I don't really know what 'novel' really is, but perhaps a certain narrative stance – can do justice to society. I'm not saying 'novel' rather the stance of the narration, the collective past: 'once upon a time', or 'I went,' 'she,' the woman, 'went'. I believe that that is an eternal and also the freest language. It's not called 'novel' rather it's called the language of storytelling" (Schlueter 165). However, in a postmodern age, Handke struggled with the inability of the narrative to both convey and represent truth and reality and this problem formed the basis for his explorations in narrative method. Moreover, his desire for narrative and descriptive unity, as Kniesche formulates it, is evident in the *Versuche* as he struggles to be content with the reality of what is possible. This too has an effect on his writing process, whereby he is continuously confronted with the impossibility of narration, yet each time he tries anew, he finds another barrier impossible to overcome (Kniesche 335-36). This explains, in part, the fragmentary and incomplete nature of these essayistic "attempts." The result is that "the wholeness of perception and writing that Handke postulates, the self-narrating world, is nothing more than the unity of observation and idea, that utopian idea, which according to Adorno had cele- brated its resurrection in the essay" (Kniesche 336). The problem, Handke's realizes, lies in the narratability of an idea: "But how can an idea be told?" (*J* 129), his narrator asks somewhat rhetorically. The answer is the central question underlying each of the essays.

In the case of *Jukebox*, it is not just the rhythms of music which serve to stimulate narration, rather the landscape becomes both an impulse and a reflection of the narrator's inner-self.[22] The journey in the course of the story from the dry, arid plains of Spain to the moist, precipitous landscapes of the north-central regions where it has begun to snow, mirrors his own creative struggle. His destina- tion in Spain, Soria, is significant not only for being a somewhat desolate area (removed from "history"), but also as the home of the Spanish poet Antonio Machado. For Machado, the arid plains of the area served as a source of inspiration and as the subject of one of his greatest collections of poems, *Campos de Castilla* (1912; *Lands of*

---

[22]See the chapter in this volume by Mireille Tabah on landscape in Handke's work.

Castile, 2002). The irony that Handke is ostensibly searching for the last jukebox, the ultimate symbol of modern mass culture in a small, rural village in central Spain is not lost on him. He recognizes, however, a poetic source stronger than that of modern culture, namely the landscape: "To be able to read the landscape a little in passing grounded one, and he had learned that in Spain geography had always been subservient to history, to conquests and border drawings, and only now was more attention being paid to the 'messages of places'" (*J* 111). This appeal to heed the message of the landscape is a reflection of Handke's conception that the narratives of history should be absent from literature, but present in nature.[23] The permanence of the countryside and the knowledge it holds of past histories should serve as a source book for understanding the narratives of history. Just as one reads a history text, he feels, so too should one "read" the landscape, so as to hear its narrative. In the end, he does not find the jukebox he had sought and must be satisfied with the fact that the only remaining jukebox in Spain is to be found in Andalusia. However, he does not leave disappointed but with the sense that he is just now, after this journey of self-discovery, beginning to understand geography and nature, an understanding of which will provide the material for him to write.

In the third and final essay, *Essay on the Successful Day*, Handke gives no formula for a successful day, but once again ties it inexorably to storytelling and creativity. Hoesterey quite correctly points out a peculiarity of the translation, namely the dual meaning of the term "Glück." The translation of the original title, *Versuch über den geglückten Tag*, places emphasis on "success" as opposed to "happiness," whereas it is clear that the successful day is linked to happiness; that is, the joy of success brings with it a sense of happiness. Thinking in terms of happiness, though, brings with it a human aspect that then probes the registers of an individual's emotions. This links the text to a long line of classical philosophical texts which seek to understand the nature of human happiness. Kurz sees this line of thought as realization of a certain strain of a western thinking that roots happiness both in the Greek *kairos* as well as in Christian thought (143). Toward the end of the essay, Handke

---

[23]This becomes a topic in his essays on Yugoslavia a few years later. He once again chooses the essay form (rather than the novel) and places great weight on the landscape and personal histories.

quotes and alludes to various passages from the Bible.[24] Arguably, Handke's interest in the Bible has less to do with theology than with the "archaic form of this meditative and dialogic language" (Kurz 145) whose rhetorical gestures he imitates toward the end of the essay. In fact, at one point, the narrator asks himself: "And rather than an essay, mightn't the psalm form – a supplication presumed in advance to be in vain – have been more conducive to the idea of such a day?" (*J* 155). But it is not just the Bible that serves as a linguistic source of inspiration, rather the narrator's musings race from one text to another (often in the same sentence): from *Parsifal*, the *Odyssey* and *Don Quixote* to Goethe, Van Morrison and Marilyn Monroe. In this way, Handke continues in the path of *Jukebox*, where the jukebox served as a symbol of the postmodern and "ingeniously links high and low culture and dismantles traditional aesthetic hierarchies" (Hoesterey 53). As a reflection of his personal inclination, it becomes clear that for Handke happiness is found in the high culture of the great literary texts as well as in the pop culture of music and the cinema. In the literary realm, he seeks success while in the realm of pop culture he often finds happiness.

Both lines of thought, success and happiness, do have a decidedly personal side to them, and like the previous two pieces, this essay intertwines autobiography with philosophical reflection. The result is an essay that "offers the reader a more general, quasi-anthropological perspective on happiness as a cultural construct on whose ideological bindings the citizens of the West and other world regions depend" (Hoesterey 56). An underlying motif in this essay is the recollection of a painting by William Hogarth that includes an inscription entitled the "Line of Beauty and Grace," which Handke uses as a symbol of a larger concept in cultural thought. While on the one hand recalling Schiller's eighteenth-century aesthetics, Handke's conception of this "Line" also represents a twentieth-century striving for harmony and order in a fragmentary world. Just as he had earlier sought order through narrative constructs, he now seeks harmony and unity in narration, a desire to produce a narrative of grand import. While in Paris, the narrator feels the need and urge to capture in words the images and feelings of the city

---

[24]Kurz identifies, among others, passages from Hebrews, Romans, as well as various references to Paul's letters.

which he can only sense: "A dream of the all-encompassing, all-absorbing book, long gone from the world, long dreamed to an end – was back again all of a sudden; or renewed? here in the daytime world, and needed only to be written down" (*J* 131). If he were able with one single word to somehow approximate the images he has in mind, he continues, then this would be a successful day. But he realizes that conquering such linguistic challenges, which would be his conception of a successful day, is at best nothing more than a dream. Returning once again to the form of an inner Socratic dialogue as well as to his imaginary dialogue partner, "the other I," he ponders this very same problematic at the end of the essay, realizing this time, however, that although such perfection in writing is a mere dream, there is a difference: "Yes, except that instead of *having* it, I've *made* it in this essay" (*J* 166). Once again, he acknowledges the advantage a postmodern writer has over his predecessors and their inability to overcome a crisis of language and, by association, of narration: by having once again written an essay about writing an essay, he has succeeded in communicating his own conception of inner harmony as well as narrative wholeness by actually producing a written work, albeit a meta-narrative on the ability to achieve happiness through successful narration.

If indeed Handke is, as Horst Steinmetz has argued, exemplary of a larger trend in Western literature of a return to narrating and storytelling (67), one would perhaps wonder, based on Handke's three essays, if that return weren't a somewhat transmogrified return to formless, postmodern, meta-narratives. While these essays structurally give an indication that this may perhaps be the case, Handke's calls in the 1990s for a new modernism seem to be saying that there is a bit more to narration than that (cf. Hage and Schreiber 170). To be sure, he has no conception of what constitutes a successful day. However, he states that the impetus for him to write is an idea and the desire to "tell" this idea. Narration is only possible, he maintains, in the same way that modern life is understandable – through fragmentation, broken thoughts, and digressions. If so, his essays and aesthetics argue for a modernism not unlike that which Benjamin called for in his analysis of storytelling as a means to exchange and communicate experiences. However, Handke's decided emphasis on personal realities and meta-narratives problematizing the creative process adds little to the conception of telling as a means of discourse and communication. Handke seems to be hoping for a return to narratives not only as a means of overcoming the inability to narrate, but also as a bridge to harmony and peace, a theme he explores in greater depth together with Wenders in *Wings of Desire*. This program and aesthetic ideology is one he seeks to clarify with the concept of a "successful day," and one which best represents his self-conception as a writer, namely as an epic story-teller. But to be sure, Handke's embracing of the story has not resulted in a spate of 'traditional' narratives. His texts are still highly personal, self-reflective meta-narratives which more than anything reify the narrative process if not the story itself.

Works Cited

Adorno, Theodor. "The Essay as Form." *Notes to Literature*. Trans. Shierry Weber Nicholsen. New York, Columbia UP, 1991. 3-23.

Benjamin, Walter. "The Storyteller." *Illuminations*. Ed. Hannah Arendt. New York: Schocken, 1969. 83-84.

Berger, John, and Jean Mohr. *Another Way of Telling*. New York: Pantheon, 1982.

Coury, David N. *The Return of the Storyteller in Contemporary German Literature and Film – Peter Handke and Wim Wenders*. Lewiston, NY: Edwin Mellen, 2004.

Hage, Volker, and Mathias Schreiber. "'Gelassen wär ich gern:' Der Schriftsteller Peter Handke über sein neues Werk, über Sprache, Politik und Erotik." Interview with Peter Handke. *Der Spiegel* 5 Dec. 1994: 170-76.

Hoesterey, Ingeborg. "Autofiction: Peter Handke's Trilogy of Try-outs." *The Fiction of the I: Contemporary Austrian Writers of Autobiography*. Ed. Nicholas J. Meyerhofer. Riverside, CA: Ariadne, 1999. 47-60.

Horváth, Márta. "Peter Handkes 'Versuche.'" *Die Zeit und die Schrift: Österreichische Literatur nach 1945*. Ed. Karlheinz F. Auckenthaler. Szeged: Jate, 1993. 229-39.

Kniesche, Thomas W. "Utopie und Schreiben zu Zeiten der Post-moderne: Peter Handke's 'Versuche.'" *Zeitgenössische Utopie-entwürfe in Literatur und Gesellschaft. Zur Kontroverse seit den achtziger Jahren.* Ed. Rolf Jucker. Amsterdam: Rodopi, 1997. 313-36.

Kurz, Paul Konrad. *Komm ins Offene: Essays zur zeitgenössischen Literatur.* Frankfurt: Knecht, 1993.

Moser, Samuel. "Das Glück des Erzählens ist das Erzählen des Glücks: Peter Handkes *Versuche.*" *Peter Handke. Die Langsamkeit der Welt.* Ed. Gerhard Fuchs and Gerhard Melzer. Graz: Droschl, 1993. 137-53.

Pakendorf, Gunther. "Writing about Writing: Peter Handke, *Nachmittag eines Schriftstellers.*" *Modern Austrian Literature* 3.4 (1990) 77-86

Pfister, Gerhard. *Handkes Mitspieler.* Bern: Peter Lang, 2000.

Ribbat, Ernst. "Peter Handkes 'Versuche': Schreiben von Zeit und Geschichte." *"Sein und Schein – Traum und Wirklichkeit": Zur Poetik österreichischer Schriftsteller/innen im 20. Jahrhundert.* Frankfurt am Main: Peter Lang, 1994. 167-79.

Schlueter, June. "An Interview with Peter Handke." *The Plays and Novels of Peter Handke.* Pittsburgh: U of Pittsburgh P, 1981. 163-77.

Schönherr, Ulrich. "Die Wiederkehr der Aura im Zeitalter technischer Reproduzierbarkeit: Musik, Literatur und Medien in Peter Handkes *Versuch über die Jukebox.*" *Modern Austrian Literature* 33.2 (2000) 55-72.

Steinmetz, Horst. "Die Rückkehr des Erzählers. Seine alte neue Funktion in der modernen Medienwelt." *Funktion und Funktionswandel der Literatur im Geistes- und Gesellschaftsleben.* Bern: Peter Lang, 1989. 67–82.

Stolz, Dieter. "'Form, soweit das Auge reichte': A Discussion in Dialogue-Form on the Poetics of Peter Handke's Three-Part Series of *Essais.*" *The Individual, Identity and Innovation: Signals from Contemporary Literature and the New Germany.* Ed. Arthur Williams and Stuart Parkes. Bern: Peter Lang, 1994. 259-71.

von Wilpert, Gero. *Sachwörterbuch der Literatur.* Stuttgart: Kröner, 1989.

Wenders, Wim. "Le souffle de l'Ange." *Die Logik der Bilder.* Frankfurt am Main: Verlag der Autoren, 1988. 133-38.

Wenders, Wim and Peter Handke. *Der Himmel über Berlin: Ein Filmbuch.* Frankfurt: Suhrkamp, 1989.

Handke's Theater

Fritz Wefelmeyer

THEATER AS THEATER: *Publikumsbeschimpfung* (1966; *Offending the Audience*, 1969)

"Play-acting was in your blood, you butchers, you buggers, you bullshitters, you bullies, you rabbits, you fuck-offs, you farts" (*P* 30). These insults, directed at the audience in the theater, are taken from the play *Offending the Audience* with which Peter Handke made his debut as a dramatist in the Frankfurt Theater am Turm in 1966. Handke had originally intended to write an essay or pamphlet against the theater, not the theater in general, but rather the way it had developed historically into an institution (Joseph 28). However, he soon realized that a pamphlet was not the best way to give weight to his opinion. If he really wished to change the theater, he would have to question precisely those expectations and characteristics which were keeping the established theater alive. It was therefore essential for him to turn his critique of the theater into a first-hand theatrical experience. The theater-going public had to be treated not as so many individual readers of a text, but as spectators whose expectations had to be challenged in the theater itself. What logically followed from this aim may at first seem paradoxical. A play had to be devised which would attack the theater by means of theatrical devices.

For Handke, traditional theater is above all a theater of illusion, in which simplifications of reality are presented on stage as if they were indisputable: the stage represents the world, the stage becomes the world, the world theater. Theater-goers regard this world as if it existed independently of them and functioned according to rules which are both comprehensible and universally accepted. Moreover, the actors present this reality in the form of a story as if nobody were watching. However, the fact that this conventional form of presentation might oversimplify the complexity of the real world is never discussed. The audience in this kind of traditional theater is not meant to be troubled by the thought that the "possibilities of reality are limited by the impossibilities of the theater" (*BE* 27).

Rather it blithely accepts the events on stage as a significant chain of events. Theater is expected to have a meaning which is to be communicated by the actors. Whatever happens on stage means something which can be decoded and understood by recourse to so-called reality. In traditional theater, speech and plot form part of a world of illusion which is created by means of the reality of the stage. The public is both objective witness to and judge of this world from which it is, however, strictly excluded by the footlights, because the theater produces reality in such a way that the production process is kept concealed. The spectator is thus subjected to a secret ritual of conventions, accepted attitudes and perceptions, succumbing to what Handke later calls "automatism" (*BE* 28).

In his plays Handke is not, on the other hand, concerned with presenting or imitating social reality beyond the theater, but rather with pointing out how and by what means that reality is produced. His questions are: What do we assume? What do we take for granted? What preconceived patterns does our imagination follow? It is possible, according to Handke, to recognize what is taken for granted and assumed, when what seems self-evident is removed and our assumptions are challenged. For example, the theater's principal convention is that the play is enacted upon the stage, while the audience watches from the auditorium. Stage and auditorium are two separate worlds which belong to one another but are kept strictly apart. Handke has accordingly given himself the task of gradually demolishing the boundary between these two worlds, thereby leading the spectator into a new terrain where none of the old familiar markers are valid. Uprooted and disorientated, the theater-goers are thrown back upon their own resources. The systematic lack of markers in Handke's theater invites the audience to question normal conventions: that at least is the objective which Handke hoped to achieve.

Handke's public was not always inclined to accept this invitation, however. At some of the performances of *Offending the Audience*, there was barracking and near-rioting. Expectations were so emphatically not met that irritation and anger were widespread. The self-questioning that Handke wanted to provoke was not forthcoming from at least part of the audience. But the audience's annoyance and irritation confirmed Handke's thesis that certain expectations and conventions are inherent in the traditional theater.

Indeed, no traditional theater is viable unless it respects these conventions. It therefore demands a considerable effort on the part of the audience to turn their frustration at not having their expectations met into a willingness to question the justification for those expectations. Interestingly, however, this effort can only be effective if it is accompanied by a certain distancing both from events on stage and from one's reactions to them. For the spectator, the crucial factor is the realization that the playwright's intention is not to produce frustration *per se* but rather to promote self-questioning. Rather than engender antipathy for the author and his play, Handke's aim is to make the audience recognize that having their expectations frustrated is part of a game.

Anyone who wishes to disappoint expectations will do well to ensure that the public does in fact anticipate such expectations. Handke achieves this at the beginning of *Offending the Audience*. Even while the spectators are taking their seats, noises can be heard from behind the closed curtain as if props were being carried onto the stage. According to the text of the play, the ushers are required to make sure that the public is smartly dressed and behaving in a manner which is appropriate to such cultural events as theatrical performances. When the curtain finally rises, the spectator is confronted with a completely empty stage. And yet the four actors who then appear and stroll across the stage towards the footlights appear at first to be fully absorbed in a conversation among themselves. This conversation seems to be part of a conventional play which is about to begin. It is not until they address the public directly from the footlights that the last remnant of a world of illusion, a world independent of the audience, is destroyed. From now on, all speech is directed at the public directly, with no deception or half measures. The public is the subject of the play:

> What is the theatre's is not rendered unto the theatre here. Here you don't receive your due. Your curiosity is not satisfied. No spark will leap across from us to you. You will not be electrified. These boards don't signify a world. They are part of the world. These boards exist for us to stand on. This world is no different from yours. You are no longer eavesdroppers. You are the subject matter. The focus is on you. (*P* 8-9)

This quotation sums up well what the play is about. It aims to destroy the theater's illusions by redirecting the spectator's attention to events on stage. The stage is now demolished; the spectator becomes a participant. It is important to realize that this happens according to a methodological process which Handke describes within the play itself as its "dialectical structure" (*P* 13). On closer analysis, the method can be seen as consisting of three separate stages. The first is a process of systematic refusal: the expected play will not be performed. In the second stage this refusal is then linked to the redirection of the audience's attention. The spectators are referred back to themselves. This redirection is accompanied by a reassessment of the traditional roles required by the theater. The spectators are turned into objects for the actors who themselves become spectators. This second step is necessary as more is required than just the simple refusal to perform as actors. Were it not so, the show would be nothing more than a protest movement of actors going on strike for higher wages or simply enjoying the fun of not acting. The purpose of *Offending the Audience* is to raise awareness of those linguistic and cultural habits which the spectators bring with them and which create their reality, habits which are always implicit and assumed. Without them, there is no reality, especially in the world of theater. This last point is worth pursuing before considering the third stage.

The idea of language or a speech act creating reality is a seminal component of all of Handke's plays. In the first detailed studies written about him, Handke was rightly described as a language metaphysician (Schultz 15). Since he appears to hold the view that the significance of what happens on stage depends on culturally acquired linguistic forms, critics have made frequent reference to Ludwig Wittgenstein's linguistic philosophy. Indeed, Wittgenstein had attempted to show that no meaning could be created outside the language we use in our interactions. Language is the *conditio sine qua non* for the recognition of reality. Language games form the transcendental and pragmatic precondition for the constitution of meaning. In such essays as "Die Literatur ist romantisch" (1966; Literature Is Romantic) and "Ich bin ein Bewohner des Elfenbeinturms" (1967; I Am an Inhabitant of the Ivory Tower) in the collection of the same title Handke has expressed views which are reminiscent of Wittgenstein's linguistic philosophy.[1]

---

[1]Handke also refers explicitly to Wittgenstein's theory of meaning (*BE* 37). The whole complex of Handke's relationship to Wittgenstein is dealt with by Schmidt-Dengler.

However, it must not be forgotten that Handke has no desire to use his plays in order to illustrate philosophical propositions. It would clearly be wrong to understand his early plays as philosophy seminars in the theater. They do not have the purpose of pointing out that reality and meaning are not a given but are dependent on the cognitive and cultural activities of human beings. For Handke the issue is rather the need to liberate ourselves from those forms which prevent us from seeing the complexity of reality. In philosophical terms, one might say that it is not the transcendental-pragmatic conditions of speech that are under discussion, but linguistic and cultural assumptions within the theater that can be changed through reflection and self-awareness (Bubner 1-2). Therefore Handke does not, as is sometimes claimed, tackle the problem of language *per se*. For him it is more a question of a particular use and form of language in social contexts (Mixner 62). With *Offending the Audience*, Handke seeks to create a new theater, a new practice of language. If, compared with traditional theater, the play appears artificial, it is nevertheless the training ground for something quite new: "Theater has the possibility of becoming more artificial so that it may appear unfamiliar and unpredictable again" (Schultz 19). This new theater is intended to pave the way for a fresh approach to the world. The established, automatized ways of accessing reality bring no new discoveries or insights. They work rather like some kind of ritual that the spectators unknowingly undergo. Moreover, the familiar mechanisms of illusion-based theater are, according to Handke, a recipe for staleness and boredom.

It is only by analyzing his eminently practical approach to the theater that one can fully appreciate the third stage of Handke's method. If the aim of the second stage was to redirect the spectators' attention towards themselves, the final step is to show the productive side of a language-based self-awareness. The public is led away from the deconstruction of old theatrical forms into the construction of a new reality as the speakers build through language a reality based not on illusions but on conscious and critical foundations. Handke brings the perception and creation of reality to a new level of consciousness from which result some surprising discoveries. Equally surprisingly, some elements from the classical theater are revived.[2] The far-reaching nature of this change of consciousness through new language awareness is emphasized by a statement made by the actors at the beginning of the performance. They define their play as a "prologue." Later they state more precisely that this prologue refers not only to the past, but also to the present and future actions of the spectator, including those taking place outside the theater itself. All aspects of the spectator's life are drawn into the theater. Thus we have here a prologue, both to a history of the theater and to its future development as a theater of spectators. The prologue that the audience listens to is the prologue to their own actions and development since the spectator is to become the actor in the theater of his or her own life. *Offending the Audience* aims therefore at a profound change on the part of the audience. It is the task of the actors to lead the spectators into the pure present of their own consciousness, which has been liberated from preconceived ideas and automatic behavior, and allow them consciously to take part in the process of producing this present. After that they will follow this path to greater self-awareness unaided.[3]

It is possible to misunderstand the concept of action in this context. In the play, actors have concentrated on addressing the public directly and giving them instructions. It is true that no story or plot is being presented on stage, so there is no action in the conventional sense. However, the aim is to show how people act through language. Speaking means actively producing reality. It is not a passive process but an act of intervention and a shaping of reality. The play correctly states that this "prologue" is a "world theatre" (*P* 27). It creates a "world" or reality, but only as the result of a conscious process of construction. This construction and shaping of reality is a universal feature of language. Without spoken communication or cultural content, without setting scenes, allocating roles and prescribing actions, reality does not come into being in everyday life. In Handke's theater this process is presented not as philosophy, but as lived experience as we become witnesses to a

---

[2]Pfister is critical of the idea of a revival and speaks instead of a "redefinition" (248).
[3]Lorenz (181) makes the point that this self-awareness has a considerable potential for creating personal identity and freedom and that the play is thus more than just a rebellious experiment in style.

staging of how reality is constructed.[4] For this reason, it is also important to engage a director and professional actors to present the play in a theater. The play is clearly not a script to be read as a text at home.

Handke called his piece a speech-play or speak-in, a label he also chose for three of his other plays, *Weissagung* (1966; *Prophecy*, 1976), *Selbstbezichtigung* (1966; *Self-Accusation*, 1971) and *Hilferufe* (1966; *Calling for Help*, 1976).[5] With this label, he dissociates himself from all traditional categories, such as drama, tragedy and comedy, and emphasizes that the focal point for him is language in the form of speech as a reality-creating activity. What is more, he dissociates himself from Brecht's epic theater, as well as from Sartre's *littérature engagée* with their direct political commitment (*BE* 43-50).[6] In a short commentary to his speak-ins, Handke states that his plays aim to promote awareness instead of revolution (*P* 308).[7] In Handke's case, speech itself is the subject matter. Speaking (*sprechen*) is here synonymous with *vorsprechen*, speaking in front of someone to show them how something is spoken. Speech is no longer a mere instrument of mimesis, but comes into its own as a means of communication and also as a reflection on itself. It is both presentation and judgment in one. Narrative or epic theater tells a story; a speech-play or speak-in speaks of itself. It is only if language's ability to actively construct reality is recognized that it can bring about social change, as Handke argued at the meeting of the Group 47 meeting at Princeton University in 1966. Instead of acting, he said, "as if it were possible to look through

---

[4]Roelcke (119) analyzes this in terms of dramatic communication and points to the meta-communicative function of all Handke's early plays.

[5]The term 'speak-in' was used in *Offending the Audience* but seems to have gone out of fashion.

[6]The different relationship to the audience is also significant here; see Sauerland (147-51).

[7]Mixner (28-29) discusses this aim in the context of the question as to whether Handke's plays are "anti-theater." This term was much used in the early reception of *Offending the Audience* and even provided part of the catchy title of the first book-length study of Handke's theater in English (Hern). However, Hern already had reservations about the validity of the term (37-38), and most subsequent studies no longer make systematic use of it. Most critics will recognize that Handke is not against theater *per se* but against a certain kind of theater. For this and the question of awareness, see Behse (354-57).

language as if one were looking through a window pane, one should see through the ruses of language itself and, when this is done, show how many things can be manipulated through language" (*BE* 30).

It should be pointed out how Handke proceeds in *Offending the Audience*. After the speakers have presented the general intention of the play, their first step is to destroy paradigmatic or "standard idea[s]" (*P* 11). These relate primarily to what happens on stage. For example, expectations that the words of the speakers can be understood as the significant events of a play form part of these ideas which are gradually frustrated. There is no playing with reality, with props and objects on stage, no presentation of an individual fate, no parable, no didacticism, no storyline or plot which might form a coherent whole, no enlightenment for the audience, no explanations, no entertaining games, no factual reports, no dreams, no roles – nothing is to be taken metaphorically, nothing symbolically: every attempt to give what is happening on stage a meaning runs into a brick wall. There are only denials and refusals. Any kind of meaning is relentlessly destroyed, as is the notion of theater as action on stage. Finally, there is the insulting of the audience, through which any remaining illusion of a barrier between stage and auditorium is removed. Since no past is presented on stage and also no future invoked, only the present time matters. Time is constituted as pure presence in the here and now and the required response on the part of the audience is to be attentive. The speakers thus always direct the attention of the spectators back towards themselves.

It is therefore important to realize that there is a further step following the destruction of meaning. Firstly, the intellectual operations which the spectator carried out in order to follow the destruction of meaning are put under the spotlight. Handke always attempts to bring the spectators back to their own experience. Nothing is to be forced onto the audience: "You have recognized that we negate something. You have recognized that we repeat ourselves. You have recognized that we contradict ourselves. You have recognized that this piece is conducting an argument with the theatre" (*P* 13). Secondly, the method by which the spectators' consciousness is changed and developed is named: "You have recognized the dialectical structure of the piece" (*P* 13). The speakers are always above all concerned with keeping the spectators entirely aware of their own state of consciousness. This is also the reason that the actors adopt comments and judgments which would normally be used by the audience to describe and criticize events on stage: "You look breathtaking. You look unique. But you don't make an evening. You're not a brilliant idea. You are tiresome. You are not a rewarding subject. You are a theatrical blunder. You are not true to life" (*P* 14). The public present in the theater thus becomes the theme of the play, and, at the same time, anything which might impinge on the audience's consciousness is analyzed. This includes physical responses and attributes, such as sweat, heartbeat, hair length, body odour, saliva, and line of vision. The body and its environment are discussed; dress and seating arrangements in the theater are referred to. In addition, any feelings (such as claustrophobia) which are experienced are investigated.

Finally the story of coming to and leaving the theater is described: not only all the preparations made by the spectators before setting off, but also how they will clap and applaud and how they will make their way out of the theater and go home. When finally every aspect of theatrical reality has been mentioned and any difference between the actors and the spectators, between the stage and the auditorium, has been removed, then the dialectical process has reached its conclusion. It has returned to where it began, albeit on a higher level, as the spectators are now fully conscious of where they are. As a consequence, the previously mentioned idea of unity as an element of classical theater is reinstated:

> Time is not bisected here into played time and play time. Time is not played here. Only real time exists here. Only the time that we, we and you, experience ourselves in our own bodies exists here. Only one time exists here. That signifies the unity of time. All three cited circumstances, taken together, signify the unity of time, place and action. Therefore this piece is classical. (*P* 19)[8]

Offending the Audience continued to create unrest for some time among certain sections of the public who expected traditional theater and took the insults personally. Such false interpretations were not, however, limited to the theater-going public. As late as 2002, leading academics wrote in a drama handbook that Handke had wanted to attack "the complacency of right-wing bourgeois

---

[8]For a critical discussion of this return to classical theater, see Kiermeier-Debre (322-23).

Austrian theatre-audiences" with this play (Lennard and Luckhurst 221). Indeed, Handke eventually felt obliged to ban stage productions of the play for a time (Mixner 28-29). However, whereas some spectators continued for years to feel insulted, others had understood quickly, perhaps too quickly, the actual intention of the theater of speech. As early as the first performance of *Calling for Help*, in the year after the premiere of *Offending the Audience*, the critic Eo Plunien noted in *Die Welt* on 18 October 1962: "Basically nothing new, but the already familiar routine trick of *Offending the Audience*."

*

New Contexts: *Prophecy*, *Self-Accusation* and *Calling for Help*

In October of the same year in which *Offending the Audience* premiered, two other plays by Handke had their first performances. *Prophecy* and *Self-Accusation* were performed together at the Städtische Bühnen in Oberhausen. As both pieces are relatively short, it is not surprising that they have subsequently tended to be put on either together or singly with other plays. Unlike the reception given to *Offending the Audience*, *Self-Accusation* and *Prophecy* do not appear to have provoked the same violent reactions.[9] Both plays, however, continue the same program of language-based theater which had been launched by *Offending the Audience*. *Prophecy* is also a play for four speakers. The material to be spoken consists of single sentences, loosely put together and offering only a vague relationship with one another. Parataxis is the principle by which these statements are joined. Initially, each sentence contains a comparison which functions according to an identical grammatical structure. The subject of the sentence is repeated in a simile: "Blood will be red like blood" or "The wind will be swift like wind" (*RLC* 11). Whereas a metaphor normally brings together two diverse objects in order to make a statement about the subject of the sentence, in Handke's case the comparison refers back to itself. The similes chosen are those frequently and often unconsciously used in everyday speech, including the most hackneyed idioms and clichés.

---

[9]The audience's strong negative reaction to *Self-Accusation* at its premiere seemed to be related to the fact that the actors, though not required by the text, were naked – a definite breaking of taboos in the mid-sixties (Schmidt-Bergmann 664).

A comparison such as "The horse will eat like a horse" (*RLC* 6) clearly amounts to mere tautology. These comparisons, especially when pronounced in a melodramatic tone, take the form of, albeit empty, prophecies. This is, for example, the case with "The Messiah will be longed for like the Messiah" (*RLC* 5). The future is simply the application of the vehicle, the compared object, to itself. There is little literary merit in creating such statements, as the speaker always knows in advance what is going to be said. All objects become identical, so there is no need to discuss them further. A similar process, Handke claims, often takes place in the everyday use of metaphors. The comparison kills what is special in an object by replacing it with something familiar. Handke himself expressed it thus: "Comparisons serve above all to eliminate with one sentence the object compared. Any further effort is superfluous."[10] Anything "incomprehensible, unfamiliar or merely difficult" is easily categorized and neutralized by the comparison: "comparison protects us from any preoccupation with the subject" (*BE* 66). The uniqueness of any object is swept away in the rhetorical flood of comparisons and their predictable pattern glides smoothly over the roughness of reality. The communication machine turns without friction in its circular orbit. Towards the end of the play, Handke abandons the vehicles of comparison: "The ends will stand on end" (*RLC* 15). And as the comparison becomes ever more simple, the tempo of the play accelerates.

In itself the constant repetition of the same grammatical structures echoes the mechanical, unthinking and undifferentiated use of everyday language. For the spectator, or more accurately, as in *Offending the Audience*, the listener, the similes turn into a metaphor of a different order. The comparisons in the play sound just like the worn-out metaphors of daily life. Platitudes and stereotypes are ubiquitous, be it in life or in the theater. But in the theater all these hackneyed and meaningless elements, which otherwise flow along in the stream of daily speech, now become objects of focused attention. The comparison, rendered autonomous, is now observed. When the audience makes an analogy between the comparison

---

[10]Renner (37) points to the adaptation of this elimination process in Handke's *Kaspar* (1967; trans. 1969). For a wider view of the problematic of comparisons, see Thornton (23-24).

made on stage and comparisons made in everyday speech, this also offers them the chance of looking afresh at the metaphors themselves. The audience might ask themselves, for example, how a cad actually behaves after hearing "The bastard will behave like a bastard" (*RLC* 5), or how a poor sinner really stands when the comparison was: "The poor sinner will stand there like a poor sinner" (*RLC* 6). The audience's strongest response will probably be to the comparison: "In the theater you will feel like a theatergoer" (*RLC* 8). This comparison, which is reminiscent of the dramatic situation of *Offending the Audience*, leads back to the audience itself. A production of *Prophecy* will take all this into account and encourage the actors to speak these comparative sentences with an air of reflection and amazement.

The text of *Self-Accusation* is spoken by two actors, a man and a woman, who make use of a microphone and loudspeakers. Handke does not specify who speaks what; nevertheless, the text should be spoken in such a way as to produce "acoustic order" (*P* 34). The stage is empty and the auditorium and stage are both lit, while the curtain is not used at all even at the end of the performance. As in *Offending the Audience*, a situation is created which aims to bridge the gulf between stage and auditorium. The illusion of theater is to be avoided; no play is being performed. In addition, the loudspeakers underline a certain artificiality in the speaking which is intended to evoke a mood of disillusionment. The text itself consists of a long series of sentences, all beginning with the first-person pronoun:

> I became. I was begotten. I originated. I grew. I was born. I was entered in the birth register. I grew older.

> I moved. I moved parts of my body. ... I moved on one and the same spot. I moved from the spot. I moved from one spot to another. I had to move. I was able to move. (*P* 35)

Handke explains this as follows: "The 'I' of *Self-Accusation* is not the narrative 'I' but only the grammatical 'I.' It is not a personal, but rather an impersonal 'I.' ... The story of *Self-Accusation* is not a specific one" (*S* 205). As the 'I' is not involved in any personal story, the theater is able to be immediate, to speak directly to the spectators: "Spectators and listeners are spectators and listeners of themselves. They don't have to join in, as the play is already about them" (*S* 206). The monotonous repetition of the first person singular, along with the use of both hypotaxis and conjunctions exclusively within sentences, erases any impression that a particular story is being told. At the same time, however, the meaning of any single sentence is emphasized by its connection to and relationship with the others.

Initially, each statement represents a learning step or an exhortation to learn; together the sentences reveal the process of growing up. A general process of learning and socialization is thus presented, in which each statement marks a stage or level in the development of becoming a fully responsible member of society. Learning begins with the fact of birth and ends with the final realization: "I became fit for society" (*P* 37). Then follows a short section where the form of the statement changes; now each pair of propositions is linked by a colon. The first shows a competence newly acquired by the individual, while the second links this acquisition with a requirement of society. What Handke wants to emphasize here is that these requirements are a means of purging the individual of natural impulses and instinctive behavior. This can be seen in the way the 'I' already reflects on these instinctive feelings using the language of society: "I became capable of adopting other people's practices: I was supposed to avoid my own malpractices" (*P* 37).

Interestingly, after a while a first step is taken towards individualization. The individual is confronted by society's system of rules, but also acquires some more personal characteristics which, however, never grow into a fully developed story: "With my firm I was entered in the commercial register" (*P* 38). Later, the maturing process is shown to involve becoming integrated into the legal system, and, more generally, into the system of responsibilities which society imposes on individuals. Individuals are subject to the laws of the land and, remarkably, there is no suggestion in the play that they have any rights of their own. The stress is on guilt and repentance and is linked to an earlier reference in the play to "original sin," with which the individual has been "tainted" (*P* 38). A bit later in the play a new grammatical structure takes over. At this point questions begin to be asked: "Which rules of cosmetics did I violate? Which laws of aesthetics did I violate? Which laws of the stronger did I violate? Which commands of piety did I violate" (*P* 39). The issue at stake is to identify which laws, rules and expectations the individual has contravened. As an ironic addition Handke includes the "laws of the theatre" in his catalogue of questions, all of which sound like accusations (*P* 39). The individual has become mature and can now be held responsible for his or her actions.

In order to develop the idea of responsibility further, Handke now begins a large number of sentences with the phrase "I expressed myself": "I expressed myself through ideas" or "I expressed myself by spitting" (*P* 39). An individual gradually becomes discernible with a self capable of accepting responsibility. If every action, every feeling and all knowledge, as well as their absence or omission, can be attributed to a self – however absurd this attribution may be – then the individual can always be held accountable. If, in addition, one takes into account Handke's statement that the 'I' of the play breaks the rules of one form of society, which according to the rules of another form of society, "*should* be broken, and vice versa" (*S* 205), it soon becomes clear that there is no way out for the individual. He or she will become guilty in one way or another, whatever the circumstances, in one or the other system. The question, however, arises as to who is sitting in judgment over the individual. The answer to this is left open, but Handke does state that the play reminds the audience of a Catholic confessional and resembles those public self-accusations which are common in totalitarian regimes (*S* 205). The litany of confession and the ritual of accusation do indeed use similar sentence structures to those used by the 'I.' But if, according to Handke, the litany of confession provides the basic rhythm used in the play, then there is perhaps in his eyes an even closer connection between growing up and self-accusation. One grows up and becomes articulate in order to accuse oneself.

Indeed, the use of the 'I' in Handke's play also suggests that malice and sinfulness are an innate part of the human condition. This is comparable to the all-pervading suspicion under which the individual lives in totalitarian states from childhood onwards. The tendency to be subversive has to be eradicated as early as possible. Since, however, wrongdoing is ubiquitous, the act of self-accusation, as practiced by the play's 'I,' is the surest means to society's disposal of controlling the individual.[11] The courtroom is internal-

---

[11]This interpretation stands in stark contrast to Valentin's view (62) that the 'I' "challenges society" by confessing to the "violent reactions" with which it liberated itself from oppression.

ized as individuals becomes their own prosecutors. The verdict is always 'Guilty' and life is therefore the history of one's own wrong-doings. As a consequence, the individual can only reject his or her own biography. There is no possibility of any positive form of identity based on biography: "I am not what I was. I was not what I should have been" (*P* 49). The grammatical reality of the first-person singular is all that remains.[12]

With *Calling for Help*, Handke introduces a new element into his speech-plays, namely dialogue, or, more precisely, a rudimentary form of dialogue. One party speaks sentences and phrases, the other always answers negatively. This dialogue is therefore not an exchange of opinions or a means of expressing or investigating interests, neither is it a means of manipulation or the acting out of an argument. Instead, the play exploits the same method as the other speech-plays in using the theater to draw attention to a specific use of language. The dialogue is merely an artificial device for showing the spectator how meaning and reality are created through language. The sentences uttered are not to be understood as part of a reality existing outside the theater which is being theatrically represented through mimesis. This situation resembles that of *Offending the Audience*, except that here the theater as an institution is not directly attacked. Rather this play can be seen as an experiment intended to show how the theater generates meaning.

This experiment deserves a closer look. Sentences taken from a wide variety of social contexts, from, for example, a papal encyclical, a news bulletin or police regulations, are recited. These sentences may take the form of, among other things, factual statements, exhortations or orders. In the course of the dialogue the sentences get shorter and shorter, finally consisting of no more than one to three words or even of single words or interjections such as "oh!" or "ah!" With all these utterances the speakers are in fact searching for the word 'help.' At the same time, however, the speakers themselves need help in their search. The title of the play is therefore ambiguous. Not until the word is finally found do they pronounce it,

---

[12]Schmidt-Bergman (644) claims that the 'I' finally develops an identity of its own, but it is difficult to see on what this identity should be based. A visit "to the theatre" and an all-encompassing self-referentiality – "I wrote this piece" (*P* 49) – may, however, become the springboard for a future self-determined identity.

but now without "calling for help." This is because if they are able to call help, then they no longer need to call *for* help (*RLC* 21). At the end of the play the speakers are relieved that they can call help; the word 'help,' however, has lost its meaning as help is not needed any more. The audience will initially refer the meaning of the sentences back to their context outside the theater. With the help of these contexts they will try to construe a semantic connection between the sentences spoken on stage. This attempt will soon prove fruitless. However, the title *Calling for Help*, the intonation, the structure and the development of the dialogue, along with a number of other features, will finally lead the audience to the realization that the usual meaning of the sentences is not intended. The words function like chips in a game: the game itself is autonomous. In other words, the theater constitutes its own world; it does not depict another one. In order to underline the game aspect, Handke also includes analogies with football in his stage directions (*RLC* 22). His comparison with the circus, where the clowning and acrobatics do not have any meaning derived from anything outside the tent, serve the same purpose.

This play makes great demands on the speakers. Not only must their acting produce a radical shift of attitude on the part of the public, but they must also prevent the constant negatives spoken by the answering side from degenerating into monotony. This would risk pervading the whole play and finally engulfing the spectators; indeed it has been criticized for being monotonous (Schultz 40).[13] The play does, however, have its merits. The basic structure provided by the dialogues and the copious performance instructions (more than a fifth of the text) offer Handke the opportunity of realizing his ambition of creating a purely self-referential theater. The play becomes an event or 'happening.' The appeal which the play can still have today might well depend not least on the relief felt by the audience when the burden of this self-inflated world, which tries to dominate, shackle and finally to swallow up our consciousness, is lifted sentence by sentence. The pope, journalists, politicians, policemen, judges and even obtrusive fellow human beings, all are obliged by the play to loosen their hold on language, even if only once.

---

[13]On the question of monotony in *Offending the Audience*, see Behse (356).

In all of Handke's speech-plays the main priority is to challenge established views and to question the existing theater in a provocative way. *Offending the Audience* is a direct attack on the theater of illusion; the following speech-plays continue the attack, even if they no longer name names. However, as with Beckett's early plays, a part of the public seemed to be primarily concerned with the question of how the rejection of traditional theater was to be understood. Paradoxically it was precisely Handke's intention, as expressed most clearly in *Offending the Audience*, of not signifying anything that became the really significant question for some. This situation arose especially with the production of his speech-plays in the United States. An American public that had been brought up over many decades with the naturalistic theater associated with Stanislavsky found themselves confused and anxious to know what it all meant. People left performances in protest, only to wait in the foyer for the end of the play in order to discuss its meaning with the actors and the producer and with those who had stayed (Bauschinger 44-45). This type of response has changed. Today Handke's theater can be seen in its historical perspective. A comparison with other dramatists, as for example Ionesco, shows that he is more strongly rooted in the traditions of modernist theater.[14] Moreover, other contemporary theater groups, such as the *Living Theater*, were also trying to break down the barrier between audience and actors. Happenings and street theater are also relevant in this context (Behse 366-68). Even before Handke, there had been attempts to break away from the theater of illusion, without resorting to the methods of Piscator or Brecht. It would also be interesting to compare Handke's theater of speech with Grotovski's *Poor Theater* and the theater of Tadeusz Kantor, as well as the *Bread and Puppet Theater*.[15]

*

---

[14]For a comparison with Ionesco, see Wendt (67-90).

[15]The latter is of particular interest as Handke himself stated that he was very encouraged by their approach (*BE* 76). The relationship to the avant-garde movement of *Konkrete Poesie* (Concrete Poetry) would also be worth studying (Voris 14-15). For other comparisons, see Behse (349-50).

The Language-Manipulated Individual: *Kaspar*

In 1968, *Kaspar* was first performed simultaneously in Frankfurt am Main and Oberhausen. In it the author goes beyond his previous pieces but remains committed to a theater of language. *Kaspar* is, however, not a speech-play, because plot and gesture are important elements, and the reference to a named individual is also a new feature for Handke. Whereas the public and the institution of the theater, along with a certain, highly circumscribed use of language, were the subject of the first plays, now center stage is occupied by the linguistic development of one figure, and, moreover, one with historical dimensions. *Kaspar* is based on the story of a foundling who, early in the 19th century, showed up out of nowhere in Nuremberg and seemed to be without the power of speech. He appeared to have been excluded from all human society from early childhood and his education from the age of sixteen, when he first appeared, had patently done him in many respects more harm than good. His ultimate fate and possible connection with the high nobility of his time – he even entered the diplomatic arena of Napoleon's far-flung empire – is still today the subject of much political speculation. Anselm von Feuerbach, on whom Handke relies as a source, entitled his report of 1832 *Kaspar Hauser: An Example of a Crime against the Inner Life of Humanity.*[16] The fact that Kaspar was ill-treated gives rise to the notion of "*speech torture*" which Handke mentions in his introduction and then develops in the play itself (*P* 53).

Handke's Kaspar begins his development with a sentence reminiscent of the one which the historical Kaspar Hauser carried with him. Handke, however, generalizes the original statement and transposes it into High German: "I want to be someone like somebody else once was" (*P* 58). Equally, Ernst Jandl's poem about a sixteen-year-old 'lad,' which Handke includes at the beginning of his play (*P* 52), functions as a filter between the historical figure and the theatrical one. Handke makes use of the historical figure, but his aim is not to present him on stage, even though the play contains several references to him: "The play *Kaspar* does not show how *it really is* or *it really was* with Kaspar Hauser. It shows what

---

[16]Handke himself indicates the importance Feuerbach's study had for him (*BE* 25).

is *possible* with someone. It shows how someone can be made to speak through speaking" (*P* 53). What is possible with a human being is to a large extent determined by the language with which he is confronted and which he appropriates. Within this process, however, it should be noted that Handke is primarily interested in two aspects of linguistic development. On the one hand, language makes it possible for Kaspar to relate to his environment and thereby become able to perceive, distinguish, control and communicate. On the other hand, he himself becomes the object of control and manipulation via that same speech process which is intended to make him articulate.

The notion of speech-torture implies that the individual is rendered completely helpless vis-à-vis the powers of language (Malkin 10-17). The language-learning process in the play is a language conditioning in which the trainee is not only taught something but also has something forced out of him. What is forced out of Kaspar is first of all the original sentence expressing the wish "to be someone like somebody else once was." Handke subtly shows how the acquisition of language is at the same time a loss of language. But the process involves even more than only a loss of language. Ultimately, it also involves the complete loss of the ability to live authentically, in harmony with one's own feelings and perceptions. The stages Kaspar reaches on his linguistic journey, however, have only a paradigmatic character. They neither depict the story of a historically identifiable figure nor can they be understood as a psychological study of the various stages since childhood which led to language acquisition.[17] The fact that the play starts with a speaker who can already utter a coherent sentence and who can stand upright should in itself act as a cautionary warning.

In *Kaspar* as in his speech-plays, Handke wants to avoid giving any impression of an illusionist theater. The stage space does not grant the spectator access to another world. On the contrary, "[t]he stage represents the stage," as it is laconically put in the stage directions (*P* 54). It is an open stage without a curtain, which deliberately demolishes the fourth wall facing the auditorium. The objects on stage take on specific functions in Kaspar's linguistic

---

[17]On the relationship with the historical Kaspar Hauser, see Gottschalk (177-226).

education, but they are clearly seen to be props without any further context or suggestion of another world. "None of the props has any particularly unusual characteristic that might puzzle the beholder" (*P* 55). Everything functions theatrically: the spectators must be assured that nothing in the performance is external to the theater. Kaspar himself comes on stage in a mask. He is an everyman who should not be mistaken for a clown or a comedian. Handke himself sees him as comparable to "Frankenstein's monster (or King Kong)" (*P* 53).

The first scenes show Kaspar in an alien world whose objects and dimensions he can apparently no more understand or control than he can his own body. He is obviously helpless and disorientated. But there is astonishment on his part, alongside bewilderment. He shows an interest in the stage and some of its props. Various ways of speaking his single sentence are tried out. It sounds like a misunderstood quotation, but it nevertheless expresses some intention, however vague. Still fully unclear at this stage is how the sentence can teach Kaspar to orientate himself and control his environment. The so-called prompters are heard but not seen as they address Kaspar through loudspeakers (*P* 60). Kaspar is supposed to come to speech via speech, but it is speech which is fully subservient to the prompters' world view and way of thinking. This way of thinking is completely preoccupied with adapting to an ordered, regulated reality. First, the original intention of Kaspar must be overcome as it contains within itself the potential for self-determination. The prompters achieve this by commenting upon Kaspar's original sentence and promising him that its use will bring him all manner of success. They have nothing to say about the meaning of the sentence or about Kaspar's aspirations. Instead, they force on him comparisons which are alien or hostile to his original intention.

> The sentence is more useful to you than a word. You can speak a sentence to the end. You can make yourself comfortable with a sentence. You can occupy yourself with a sentence and have gotten several steps further ahead in the meantime. You can make pauses with the sentence. Play off one word against the other. With the sentence you can compare one word with the other. Only with a sentence, not with a word, can you ask leave to speak. (*P* 61)

The subtle manipulation, to which Kaspar is exposed, develops through various stages. After a while he can no longer pronounce the sentence in its correct word order. He finally admits defeat and the real linguistic conditioning now begins (*P* 69). The prompters subject Kaspar to a systematic discipline in which structured sentences pave the way for a highly structured, rational view of the world. Rule-bound behavior here has its counterpart in the syntax and meaning of the sentences. People and objects follow the same or a similar pattern, as do words. The system dominates and one system is as good as another. Not surprisingly, there is no room for individuality in the world order established by the prompters: "You yourself are normal once you need to tell no more stories about yourself: you are normal once your story is no longer distinguishable from any other story" (*P* 75).

In these set phrases, overworked conceits replace living relationships and thinking is compressed into patterns. However, this approach soon comes up against its own limitations. It becomes increasingly illogical; false conclusions are drawn. Weighty utterances become tautological and strings of sentences end in nonsense. Negative is interpreted as positive, while meaningless definitions become the norm. Arbitrary generalizations are seen as inevitable; analogies are transformed into conditional sentences; the use of metaphor is viewed as the culmination of strictly logical thinking. Finally, Kaspar is initiated by the prompters into the use of the personal pronouns "I" and "You" so that he comes up with the tautology "I am the one I am" (*P* 100). This utterance at least has the effect of bringing him back to himself and, as if vaguely remembering the original sentence which had been exorcised from him, he produces an unusual question which does not fit into the system: "Why are there so many black worms flying about" (*P* 100). But this short-lived breakthrough is soon absorbed into the model-sentence scheme which the prompters have built like an invisible prison around Kaspar. His jailers slam the prison door shut with the words: "You've been cracked open" (*P* 101). The final curtain is down on Kaspar's resistance.

Handke then introduces further Kaspar figures. What initially seem to be mere clones of the original Kaspar subsequently turn out to be an attempt to undermine the closed linguistic order within which Kaspar has installed himself. However, this undermining process does not take place through linguistic means. The other Kaspars totally refuse to communicate through language. They accompany Kaspar's speech or, rather, singsong with unarticulated sounds and body noises, later also with files and other sharp objects which facilitate "all manner of excruciating noises" (P 136). Finally, they are able to make him join them. This process of incorporation ends with infectious laughter. Now the first Kaspar attempts to restore the old order, but he is met again by the other Kaspars using the same methods. Kaspar's speech finally ends in self-knowledge: "Already with my first sentence I was trapped" (P 138). He has discovered a position which allows him to view his own learning process critically instead of merely being its object. The linguistic spell which his educators, the prompters, have cast on him is broken. The seemingly rational universe of language acquisition, the whole system of drill and subjugation, is punctured, not through linguistic arguments, not through political revolutions or psychotherapy, but through the simple refusal to speak and act according to the rules of the prescribed discourse.

The reception of the play was greatly affected by the turn of events that this refusal caused, leading to much long-standing controversy among critics. When the play premiered in 1968, the student movement was at its height. Whereas some critics welcomed the play because it used an individual case to unmask the linguistic and educational system as an instrument of social authoritarianism, others strongly rejected it because the challenge to the system was not presented or acted out on stage in a theatrical manner as a political deed or as an act of enlightened ideological criticism. *Kaspar* provoked a debate of a different nature from the previous speech-plays. In addition, the discussion about the relationship between linguistic philosophy and theater, in particular Wittgenstein's influence on Handke, continued (cf. Hamilton).

*

From the Theater of Speech to the Theater of Narrative: The Later Plays

Offending the Audience and *Prophecy* initiated a theater of language and *Self-Accusation* introduced the idea of the development of a de-individualized self through language. *Kaspar* took this approach one step further and presented the process by which the adoption of social roles is transformed into a history of self-alienation, leaving the protagonist trapped in a web of language and actions. Still, the prompters of society do not have the last word. In fact, the end of the play prevents the spectator from seeing one or the other side as victorious. The quotation from Shakespeare's *Othello*, "goats and monkeys" (*P* 140-41), with which it ends, certainly gives Kaspar and not the prompters the last word, but this word is artificial and alienated in that it has lost any connection with his original search for identity, his wish to "become like somebody else" (Bekes 111).[18] The quotation does, however, draw attention to its own context as fictional theatrical reality and, as the end of the play can hardly be read as the successful completion of the process of language acquisition, at least not in the way the prompters intended, the process itself is thus foregrounded and made recognizable as a piece of theater. In spite of differences to the earlier plays, *Kaspar* shows clearly that Handke is still loyal to his original project of a Theater of the Here and Now that dispenses with individual storytelling (*P* 309).

It then seems like a confirmation of this program when *Das Mündel will Vormund sein* (1969; *My Foot My Tutor*, 1976) ends in the same way. Here too there is no conclusion bringing a plot and thus a narrative to a meaningful end. Instead, the spectator is repeatedly presented with a certain action, namely the dropping of sand into a basin of water. Once again this end can be understood as meta-theater. The closing scene is not the continuation of and conclusion to a previous chain of actions but the representation of what the play is about, namely the exact observation of an action as action. The appeal of the play lies in the way the spectator shares the task of precise observation with the play's protagonist, a ward. And if spectators initially fail to understand the play, then they share this with the protagonist, who does not grasp the instructions of his guardian. The ward, however, has set himself the goal of becoming a guardian, and he can only achieve this if he observes the guardian exactly and fully adapts himself to him. The ward knows of no story which is to be narrated, nor of any framework

---

[18]For a discussion of different interpretations of the end of the play, see Linstead (64-65). Incidentally, the Shakespeare quotation is also used by Aldous Huxley in chapter 16 of his *Brave New World* (1932). Like Kaspar, Huxley's protagonist uses the quotation to criticize the linguistic restrictions that have been imposed on him.

into which his actions have to fit. What is relevant, though, is his immediate observation of and response to the guardian's actions.

Here too it seems like a continuation of *Kaspar* when Handke uses a Shakespeare quotation. In this case the title of the play *My Foot My Tutor* is taken from Shakespeare's *The Tempest*, although the play, which had its premiere at the Theater am Turm in Frankfurt in 1969, is not a response to Shakespeare's theater. The title points only in general terms to the fact that we are dealing with theater. It is rather a game with relationships and expectations and does not involve the presentation of particular historical or contemporary characters or events. It takes the form of a series of actions which are to be interpreted in the light of the ward's intention to become a guardian. In other words, it is not a biography, with his intention as its constituent part, that is told on stage as a coherent, developing story. Each scene is to be looked at on its own and the title of the play is to be understood merely as a guideline for the audience: this is what the ward is supposed to intend. With this quotation Handke is therefore continuing the approach he had already adopted with the choice of title for *Self-Accusation*. The play's title should prevent the spectator from expecting to be presented with "something special, unique," the story of what once happened to a particular individual (*S* 205).

In a way the title echoes Kaspar's intention to become like somebody else, which is, of course, simply presented as a fact to the audience. However, unlike Kaspar, the ward is not diverted from his original intention. He is directly confronted both with the role and with the person who represents his goal; there are no prompters. Kaspar's wish remains vague because he lacks a concrete role model. This lack offers the prompters a subtle pathway into the unprotected mind of the adolescent. By contrast, throughout *My Foot My Tutor*, the ward is fighting both for his independence and in order to extend his sphere of influence. The conflict takes place without any spoken language, but involves instead a whole range of actions, gestures and bodily movements by the ward, all of which either emulate the guardian or represent resistance to him. Handke is always interested in showing how people attempt to gain power and influence. The actual actions, be they those of the ward or of the guardian, stand at the center of everything, but do not constitute a coherent story. The search for such a story would only distract the spectator from observing what is really happening (*BE* 76). In order to prevent and undermine this search, Handke sometimes repeats the same action several times, does not show the effect of an action or interrupts an action and allows it to fizzle out. In addition, the typical cause-and-effect relationship, often used in everyday life to interpret the connection between a series of actions or events, is sometimes ruptured and thus serves the same purpose.

The play *Quodlibet* (1969; trans. 1976), on the other hand, which had its first performance in Basel in 1970, appears at first more conventional. The author here includes traditional roles from world theater: a general in uniform, a bishop in robes, a Chicago gangster with a hat and double-breasted suit, along with other characters who are easily recognizable as stock figures. Nonetheless, appearances are deceptive. Handke is not returning here to the old theater of illusion. There is no relationship between characters' words and actions and how they appear on stage. The roles no longer determine the language used. This mismatch is the consequence of a language that has rigidified into cliché and convention but still has the power to create reality. The reality created is that of gossip, rumour, half-digested news bits, half-understood explanations and statements, generalizations, misunderstandings, prejudices and other elements, all thrown together into a hotchpotch. It is the kind of reality produced by flicking between several TV or radio channels, by skimming quickly through newspapers or – the contemporary equivalent – by surfing fast from website to website. It is reminiscent of moving between groups of people at parties or busy receptions or of several talk shows blending into one another. As Handke had already shown in *Offending the Audience*, his concern is with presenting language as a force for shaping a world. It is only in this sense that *Quodlibet* is world theater.

Handke only laid down the speaking parts for these typical characters, but he left it open how the spoken language with its "figures of speech" and corresponding situations were to be complemented on stage by movements and gestures. Actors and producers are meant to work this out for themselves through their own experiences and experiments (*S 2* 157-58). The objective was to give the action on stage a certain ornamental quality which only comes to the fore and thus becomes noticeable by contrast with the visual reality outside the theater. Handke certainly did not wish to create a "play of sketches" in which one social role after another is presented. He speaks explicitly of an "organic ... sequence of language and movement" (*S 2* 158). The cliché-ridden speeches of the characters are intended to produce a whole that is a moving, entirely interlinked system which in itself, however, is purely decorative. This system is also meant to include all forms of political discourse, along with all dissonant and critical voices which question society. Auschwitz, political persecution and murder, racial prejudice, ideological convictions – all of these are mentioned or invoked as a point of reference and are integrated into the constantly changing language game called society. They are thus robbed of their critical and provocative potential.

Nonetheless Handke did not want the audience to lose sight of the characters who are trapped in a prison of small talk and conventional chit-chat. He mentions tenderness and rage as desired reactions of the audience to the characters, but also, in the tradition of classical tragedy, fear and pity (*S 2* 159). A new sympathy with the characters now complements the audience's critical observation of the language game. *Quodlibet* thus develops the approach introduced with *Kaspar*, namely the presentation of more clearly defined roles and characters within the context of a specific system of language and action.

The following play, *Der Ritt über den Bodensee* (1970; *The Ride Across Lake Constance*, 1975), premiered in 1971 at the Schaubühne am Halleschen Ufer in Berlin and also works with clearly delineated roles along with, for the first time, dialogues and plenty of scenery. Still, the roles, consisting of famous actors from the history of German theater, only exist for form's sake. In a later interview Handke stated that the names of these actors just symbolized different forms of behavior (*André Müller* 18). In the text as performed on stage the names are replaced by the actors playing the parts on that occasion. In other words, the actors play themselves (*P* 166; *RLC* 69).[19] Again, the emphasis is on the artificiality of the world of the theater and, more specifically, on the artificiality of the world being presented (Mixner 105). Handke underlines the idea of artificiality, the idea of theatrical reality being

---

[19]This situation seems to have contributed to the profound perplexity and confusion that the premiere of this play in the United States (1972) caused among critics and spectators (Bauschinger 42-45).

different from everyday life, with the motto for his play, "Are You Dreaming or Are You Speaking?" (*P* 163; *RLC* 71), and with repeated references to dream sequences in the play itself. Moreover, statements in the play can easily be misunderstood by the audience. This is not only because it is not always made clear that a dream is being referred to but also because the play itself has characteristics of a dream sequence as principles of causality no longer apply. Equally, the actions do not appear to be organized for any specific final purpose. Each individual, action and statement is valid only for as long as it is presented. As the play advances mainly through dialogues, each participant is in danger of losing the point of reference normally provided both by language and by the significance of routine everyday actions. What was assumed to be reliable turns out to be extremely fragile. The characters share the same fate as the farmer who, according to legend, once rode over the frozen Lake Constance thinking that he had *terra firma* under his feet. The characters' various attempts to influence and manipulate each other show how risky one's relationship with reality can be. A subtle game of power and deceit unfolds, ending for many in dependence and the breaking of the Lake Constance ice of false securities.

In the play *Die Unvernünftigen sterben aus* (1973; *They Are Dying Out*, 1975) Handke continues this power game with language. Whereas his previous play had dealt with social situations of a more general nature, *They Are Dying Out* is set in the world of the capitalist entrepreneur. Premiered in Zurich in 1974, it shows how the life of Hermann Quitt, the play's protagonist, is entirely oriented towards increasing economic power. Gaining power is experienced by him as a liberation of personality and an increase of his sense of self. At the same time his self becomes a "means of production." Self-discovery – "I haven't had anything of myself as yet" (*P* 270; *RLC* 211) – is in fact the driving force in the competitive struggle in which he is involved. When all his opponents have been finally quashed, however, it turns out that the self has not been liberated, but rather that the role of the capitalist entrepreneur, as prescribed by the system, has been perfectly executed. The liberation of the self cannot be realized by performing the entrepreneurial role, but only by breaking out of this role. Quitt should have become, as the German title states, *unvernünftig* (unreasonable or irrational), but even an attempt to risk such an escape by means of art is doomed to failure. The reading from Adalbert Stifter's story *Der Hagestolz* (1844; *The Recluse*, 1968), which is performed on stage, reminds Quitt of his own experiences; it does not, however, provide a solution. Quitt is a captive in his role, and his alienated language does not permit him to narrate his own biography. All that is left for him is suicide which, in turn, also confirms the play's title.[20]

With this play Handke has kept faith with his original conception of theater in so far as an individual biography is not narrated, but rather a social role is presented which is created and bound by a language that typecasts and pigeonholes. The characters play roles which consume them, the perfect role ending with the dissolution of the individual. Still, the roles are recognizable, clearly differentiated and firmly tied to individual protagonists within a fixed social framework. Handke's theater, however self-referential it remains (as in the early plays), nevertheless also now refers more explicitly to the outside world. Moreover, the reading from Stifter, through its very failure, puts the utopia of a successful life more clearly into the spotlight. It can be seen that this utopia is tied to narrative, to the ability to tell stories about oneself in a way which does justice to one's individual experience. With *They Are Dying Out*, Handke has taken his theater so much further that it is now hardly any longer possible to talk of a theater of speech.

At the same time, in all his later plays Handke remains faithful to important elements of his previous work, and, above all, to the idea that the stage does not depict social reality as it exists outside the theater, but rather produces its own reality. The monumental and daring experiment of *Offending the Audience*, which forced spectators and actors alike to abandon the idea of representational theater, remains representative. It would therefore be wrong to speak of a caesura within his dramatic œuvre. It is true, though, that new elements are gradually introduced as Handke's career progresses. There is an eight-year gap between *They Are Dying Out* and Handke's next play,[21] the dramatic poem *Über die Dörfer* (1981; *Walk About the Villages*, 1996) that premiered during the 1981 Salzburg

---

[20]The end bears a certain similarity to the end of *Kaspar* ("Goats and monkeys") in that repetition (of a melody) and images break into the (so-called) rational discourse (Dying 62-63).

[21]As for some changes between Handke's theater of the seventies and the eighties, see Kathrein (157-58) and Roelcke (146).

Festival with the film director Wim Wenders as producer. Here for the first time Handke presents characters who, in contrast not only to Quitt but also to his predecessors, have their own biographies, even if these are all marked by failure. Surely these failures have severely limited any process of individuation, yet at the same time they have brought the characters of the play closer together, albeit also into conflict. Whereas Quitt, by trying to aggrandize his own self, had failed to realize this self, with his suicide at the end of the play underlining this quintessential failure, the characters in *Walk About the Villages* seek first conflict and then repeatedly reconciliation with their counterparts. As they partly suspect and partly clearly know, their personal biographies are inseparably linked with each other, even when they are far apart. How they continue and whether they succeed depends on the others, as does whether they are distorted and destroyed in the process. From now on Handke will show how characters' biographies could continue.[22] Alongside the analysis of the destruction of individuality, as presented in *Kaspar*, *Self-Accusation* and *They Are Dying Out*, creative forces now appear. The characters begin to demonstrate imagination and the ability to create artistic form. These new forces are intended by Handke to prevent the biographies from being lost and destroyed in the kind of an all-out struggle between the protagonists that is hinted at as an extreme possibility in the cemetery scene in *Walk About the Villages* (*WV* 99-110).

Nevertheless, the characters' biographies are threatened not only from outside, by fossilized and limiting social conditions, by relationships between individuals which have atrophied into empty routine and compulsive rituals, but also by the penury within themselves, by hatred of others and self-hatred, by the forces of denial, self-frustration and failure which dominate the psyche. Where this threat appears in Handke's plays one finds dark, almost inscrutable figures, with their devastating machinations and manipulations, who also always stand for patterns of behavior and attitudes which are, to some extent at least, universal and thus familiar. The siblings in *Walk About the Villages*, trapped within family history, who be-

---

[22]The play illustrates forces and conditions which, if developed, might lead to biographical identity. Frietsch's claim (207) that it shows all stages of a process of individuation thus needs to be considered with caution. For a closer look at *Walk About the Villages*, see the essay by Karl Wagner in this book.

come increasingly caught up in resentment and hatred, come into this category (Kurzenberger 54-58). The same is true of Spoilsport and his counterpart Wide Eyes in *Das Spiel vom Fragen oder die Reise zum sonoren Land (1989; Voyage to the Sonorous Land, or The Art of Asking*, 1996), premiered in 1990 at the Burgtheater in Vienna, with their seemingly intelligent but ultimately sterile language games which in the end are nothing more than a hopeless attempt to lay snares and to escape the snares laid by the other.[23] The same can be said of the space coercion gang in *Zurüstungen für die Unsterblichkeit* (1997; Harnessing for Immortality), premiered at the Burgtheater in 1997, who not only want to make every place on earth the same and force the individual out of his or her own natural and autonomous space, but also want to bring about the self-destruction of the mind's internal space through suggestion and manipulation. And finally, also of the same ilk, there is the wild man from *Untertagblues* (2003; Underground Blues), one of Handke's most recent plays, which was first performed at the Theater am Schiffbauerdamm in 2004. This man is the critical contemporary who sees deception and deficiencies everywhere, who has a gift for sniffing out failure and loss and a special gift for detecting ugliness in every aspect of human life. Yet at the same time he is the self-inflated individual who, lacking pity and sympathy, is incapable of communing with others.

These characters, who represent just a few examples from among many others in the plays discussed above, are living images of a mental and intellectual failure: a failure which in *Voyage to the Sonorous Land* culminates in the inability to ask correct questions, in other words, the inability to react to the world with amazement, openness and lively interest. These images reflect the loss of civilization and humanity in the present time and point to the dangerous mixture of political exploitation, alienation through the manipulation of language and bedazzlement caused by the media, along with other manifestations of modern culture. They also show the doomed attempts made by characters to escape from this misery and to avoid personal catastrophes. These attempts include renunciation of civilization, otherworldly idealism, the search for idylls and heroic

---

[23]For the relationship between *Walk About the Villages* and this play, including discussion of these two characters, see Wagner ("Volkstheater" 210-16; "Ohne Warum" 203-11).

scorn for the world and its culture, a scorn which is underpinned with arguments from both left- and right-wing cultural criticism. The apocalyptic mood of *Walk About the Villages* must be mentioned here, along with the characters' general negation of life and the future. Pessimism and playing with a sense of entrapment, to which so many of Handke's characters are attracted, often only barely conceal arrogance and self-delusion. The prophetic character of Nova in *Walk About the Villages* insistently warns against these, and her admonitions are accompanied by a child hitting the ground with a stick. The child as a living symbol of the future, of play and the imagination, serves as a warning to the adults.[24] There are warning figures in other plays as well, such as the storyteller in *Zurüstungen für die Unsterblichkeit*, the Fur-Woman in *Die Fahrt im Einbaum oder Das Stück zum Film vom Krieg* (1999; Voyage by Dugout, or The Play of the Film of the War) and the Wild Woman in *Untertagblues*. They all give advice and direction, they encourage and awaken, but they also reveal and unmask. The child too appears elsewhere: in the play *Die Stunde da wir nichts voneinander wußten* (1992; *The Hour We Knew Nothing of Each Other*, 1996), which premiered at the Theater an der Wien in Vienna in 1992, it is laid as a newborn baby in the arms of an old man who is about to deliver a sermon but then instead breaks out into cheering and rejoicing.

Handke's intentions are most clearly expressed in these warning characters, but it is important to note that they should not be seen exclusively as his mouthpieces. Indeed, the characters themselves can come into conflict with their own aspirations, at times falling victim to the same absolutism which they criticize in others, as is the case with the wild woman at the end of *Untertagblues*. Even the narrator from *Zurüstungen für die Unsterblichkeit*, who articulates more clearly than in almost any other of Handke's plays the artistic principle which links the late plays as their secret driving force or task, is not without this authoritarian and schoolmasterly tone (*ZU* 134).

---

[24]Like other positive characters in Handke's work the figure of the child is not entirely unproblematic (see Kurzenberger 78-79). For a very critical view of Nora, see Schuller (14-16); for an interpretation of both characters that comes probably closest to Handke's intentions, see Bohn (276-77).

It is reasonable to suppose that this tone is consciously chosen in order both to provoke reactions and to underline the seriousness of what is being said. And the seriousness of the issue for the narrator of *Zurüstungen für die Unsterblichkeit* is shown by the narrative principle she represents which can also largely be seen as the categorical imperative of narrative for Handke himself (Lüdke 90; Heyer 139-75): "Imagine what you do or do not do as narrative. Is that possible? Yes. Then it is right. Is it impossible? Then it is wrong" (*ZU* 123).[25] Handke himself uses the imperative in his theater of narrative in order to recount or hint at a story by using theatrical images, which at the same time is very often thrown into question.[26] Alongside this imperative Handke uses a plethora of proposals, examples and references which all serve to prevent the paralysis and hardening of one's life and thus of relationships with other people, as well as of the relationship with history and landscape. This aspect can only be referred to briefly here. Thus the character Nora draws attention to the significance of the after-image which does not simply copy, but in fact represents the creative processing of a sensual experience. It places the individual in a relationship with the object experienced and to this extent has an artistic significance. In his translations of dramas Handke has employed a similar principle (*Zw* 195-97), wanting to share feelings (*mitempfinden*), not to imitate them (*nachempfinden*). The latter would just be the recreation of the original sentiment, whereas the sharing of feeling underlines the active component in watching and appropriating the experience.

Handke's concern in his drama is always to overcome fragmentation as it affects conditions of life and their representation. His plays are attempts to search for and create coherence, but this coherence must not be arbitrary either. Handke talks here of freeing oneself through imagination (*freiphantasieren*) as the activity that produces such coherence (*Zw* 67). In the close scrutiny of history and experience, coherence is discovered or, as it were, set free by

---

[25]For a critical view of this imperative, see Fuß (136).
[26]See Heyer (29-34) who uses the term 'narrative theater.' The term 'theater of narrative' is preferred here in order to stress that Handke not only tells stories with his plays but also thematizes storytelling. The term also avoids any association with Brecht's epic or narrative theater (see Wefelmeyer, "Theater" 207-09).

the powers of imagination. Achieving coherence is thus not merely
a case of simple discovery (*finden*), but of rediscovery (*wieder-
finden*).[27] Imagination, attention and reflection place things and experiences in their appropriate location; we find them now in the
correct context and thus find them once again (*PhW* 93). With this
in mind, Handke has examined in *Voyage to the Sonorous Land* the
major role the right kind of questioning can play in understanding
both oneself and others. Here he presents the imagination of questioning in constantly new and different situations and thus shows
the possibilities of openness to a life yet to be discovered (*V* 73-74).
Through the right questions a key to understanding reality can be
found. But reality can also remain dead if it is confronted unques-
tioningly. Those of Handke's characters who do not question, who
are unwilling to do so or whose questioning has ceased (and there
are many of them) provide a warning lesson on stage. In *Voyage to
the Sonorous Land, or The Art of Asking* Handke could be said to
celebrate a new literary anthropology or poetics of questioning.[28]

*

Theater as Search for Form: *Die Fahrt im Einbaum oder Das Stück zum Film vom Krieg*

Die Fahrt im Einbaum oder Das Stück zum Film vom Krieg may
be seen as a representative example of Handke's later theater productions. Its author's answer to the war in Kosovo and the bombardment of Serbia by NATO in 1999, it had its first performance at
the Burgtheater in Vienna the same year. As in his prose works
dealing with the human and political situation and the war in
Yugoslavia, Handke wanted to seek out the forces at work in this

---

[27]This distinction goes back to Handke's earliest writings on theater (*BE* 28)
and must be seen in the context of two similar distinctions: *nachempfinden* and
mitempfinden, as mentioned above, and *holen* (to get) and *wiederholen* (to
repeat); see Handke (*PhW* 42 and 75; cf. also Wefelmeyer, "Postmodernism"
53).

[28]Grieshop (180) offers an alternative to such anthropology: the idea of a
rhetoric of 'Augenblick.' Weiss (677) speaks of a "poetics of questioning" in
connection with a study of religious images. Whether, however, such a poetics
sits comfortably with postmodernism is too complex a question to be discussed
here. For more on this, see the study by Pascu.

regional trouble spot.[29] However, for him this meant not only investigating political interests, historical influences and cultural conditions, but also looking for a form by means of which these might be presented. At the same time, this search for an appropriate form is in many respects identical to the attempt to create peace. As in earlier works, Handke puts his faith in the ability of art and the creation of form to bring healing and order into the chaos of the real world which affects individuals as much as communities (Janke 153-73).[30] In this process the search for form counters the gradual loss of certain kinds of activity, as in everyday public behavior where forms of social intercourse have to be creatively maintained. In short, art demands a radical effort of a type which people in modern societies are no longer always willing to make. The consequence of this loss of form is the dissolution of society, since the individual self can no longer be reconciled with the self and the intentions of others. This play provides an example from the everyday world of interaction between people on the street. People, a character in the play claims, don't seem to be able to "make way gracefully" for each other any more: "They've lost their sense of direction. They keep banging into each other, and not even deliberately: they have forgotten what it means to stand up for oneself while allowing the other a place to stand" (*FE* 123-24). Handke associates this effort to achieve a social form with the aesthetics of beauty,[31] in so far as a sense of proportion and balance are appealed to here and linked to sensory perception. If society is to be restored, then the task for the individual is to strengthen and refine this aesthetic sense.

However, a loss of form also precedes those violent hostilities with which Handke's play deals. Other people are no longer perceived as individuals. The forces that give form fail and perception disintegrates: "Now, even when I have someone clearly in front of

---

[29]Of particular relevance here are *Unter Tränen fragend* (2000; Questioning While Weeping), *Eine winterliche Reise zu den Flüssen Donau, Morawa und Drina oder Gerechtigkeit für Serbien* (1996; *A Journey to the Rivers: Justice for Serbia*, 1997) and *Sommerlicher Nachtrag zu einer winterlichen Reise* (1996; A Summerly Postscript to a Winter's Journey).

[30]Janke (154) also points out the ability of form to preserve and to create distance.

[31]The German original "schönes Ausweichen" (making way gracefully) perhaps conveys this aesthetics of beauty more forcefully.

me, eyes, nose, mouth, I can't see a face any more. And what an
event a face used to be! I have lost the other's face. It had lost its
form, long before I trampled it to mush" (*FE* 30). Once this loss of
form has degenerated into war, then there seems to be no effective
way of ending the violence – unless some means could be found to
restimulate the form-giving forces among the people involved. In
Handke's view, this way exists in art which represents an analogous
situation: just as there can be no lasting political peace without
people coming together to create a new form, in the same way no
work of art can exist without some kind of formal coherence. This
coherence must, however, be produced by the spectators themselves. In their activity lies the justification for art as a training
ground for those operating in the political sphere, since the latter,
too, is searching for a new form. This means that in this kind of art
there can be no question of presenting a finished product to the
spectators. It is rather a question of creating a work which both
provides them with the necessary materials and encourages them to
make appropriate use of these materials in order to create form.

Part of the play's very title hints at the originality of its genre.
"The Play of the Film of the War" places two artistic genres in
relation to one another: theater and film. The play then goes on to
show that the medium of film is a constant point of reference for
what is happening on stage. What happens there relates to a film
that is to be made. Everything is material which may or may not be
used for the film. This material is viewed by two directors in a
hotel, located in an almost deserted area "in the depths of the
Balkans, far from any sea, far from any palm tree, far from the
Euro-American world" (*FE* 11). It is in this setting that the two
directors want to make a film about a war which took place in this
region nine years earlier. The directors have only just arrived, but
all preparations have already been made for casting the individual
roles in the film and for obtaining a picture of the situation during
and before the war. An announcer, acting like a master of cere-
monies, supervises a parade of figures and images, from which the
directors intend to create their version of history. Among these
figures are a tourist guide, a chronicler and a historian. Later they
are joined by three journalists, characters from an earlier film about
the war, and many others. The announcer immediately points out to
the directors that both the sequence in which the figures appear, as

well as the scenes that are acted out, do not necessarily have to be incorporated into the later film. They are rather intended to put the directors in the right mood for making their film.

The arrangement Handke has made thus allows the spectator to judge the events on stage according to guidelines prescribed by its form. The material presented is to be synthesized into a film. In order to produce this synthesis, the audience is provided with explanations about filmmaking, insights into the genres of social drama and western and examples of classic film castings (for example, Henry Fonda and Richard Widmark). In addition, statements are made about American and European preferences and characteristics in filmmaking. The question for the spectator is how what has been presented by the announcer can be turned into a film. The audience may not always be fully aware of this question; nevertheless, they form the essential cognitive framework within which each objection, comment or rejection on the part of the directors must be understood. Only those in the audience who keep in mind the idea of a film can judge the behavior of the directors. This arrangement is an example of an artistic sleight of hand which might be called didactic; yet it does not turn the whole play into a series of filmmaking instructions, but rather serves to stimulate the spectators' artistic imagination.

Having determined the framework for the continuation of the play using the directors' plan, the idea of a parade and the film narrative, Handke develops a series of scenes and characters which lead quickly into the history and prehistory of the war. Most characters who appear at this point have been involved in the war. Only later on does a further character, the already mentioned fur-woman, appear, who was not involved in the war or whose involvement remains unclear.[32] What is striking is that all those involved give an interpretation of the war. Though each person has a different version, all versions contain the germ of an attempt to give meaning to what has happened. Everyone presents a certain view or history of the war, even if only implicitly, and everyone claims that their view is the right one. Instead of only projecting roles or giving expert knowledge, characters compete with one another to provide

---

[32]It is not only the woman's clothing which is reminiscent of John the Baptist (cf. Wefelmeyer, "Postmodernism" 45-46). Like him, she is preparing the way for something new, to whose arrival she wants to alert her contemporaries.

the only legitimate version of the war, the single correct point of view from which this war can be described and understood. From the very beginning, the first three characters to appear, the tourist guide, the chronicler and the historian, are engaged in this competitive struggle.

Having drawn the audience's attention to the question of different viewpoints, Handke introduces *en passant* a number of other elements which are essential to the making of a film, including plot and screenplay. The role of a screen hero is discussed and a reference to the twenty-seven previous films about this war makes the audience aware of further elements that might play a role in the aesthetic construction of reality: the genre of war films and the specific history of interpretations created by these films. In addition, the announcer gives examples of how emotions are stirred by certain scenes and images. Film reception and techniques of film narrative are also topics within the play about the war. After introducing the spectator to a whole series of narrative and other elements which are needed in order to construct a history of the war, Handke presents a further element, namely the language in which this war can be narrated. Here war journalism and its failure to do justice to the country where the war is taking place serve as a point of orientation.

Three journalists, appearing as mountain bikers, embody important aspects of this failure. Their activity suggests something about their approach to the war. They are not interested in the comparatively slow process of scouring the landscape on foot, acquainting themselves with its geology, flora and fauna, the people and their living conditions, but rather in speed and mobility, the ability to overcome physical barriers through both technology and the skilled use of their muscles.[33] The mountains represent to these bikers a challenge against which it is necessary to measure oneself. For them it is not a case of familiarizing themselves with something unique, but rather of using knowledge of the conditions encountered en route in order to accomplish a task. Thus all three journalists now no longer recognize the countryside from which they once reported. At that time they knew only war: "mere war zone, terrain, front line, escape tunnel, massacre site, parachute drop zone" (*FE* 57).

---

[33]On the importance of exploration on foot, see Barth (76-100).

Features of the landscape were only perceived as places of possible terrorist or military operations. One of the journalists had nothing more than a template into which interpreters and those with local knowledge could put the names of relevant rivers, villages and landscapes. In a grotesquely one-sided view of the political situation, the journalists now interpret even the natural conditions of life in Yugoslavia's former war zone as an expression of inferiority. The war itself is seen as a step backwards in the process of civilization, as regression into an evil pre-Enlightenment era. According to the journalists, even the natural world confirms the lack of civilized progress: the rivers flow in self-contained circles (*FE* 58).

It would nevertheless mean to misunderstand the play to interpret it as Handke settling scores with the various parties involved in the war in former Yugoslavia. It is certainly not a case of a covert trial, perhaps an adjunct to the international trial in The Hague which Handke subsequently described in the prose text *Rund um das Große Tribunal* (2003; All Around the Mighty Tribunal) and in which individual figures from this play also appear.[34] Even the claim that Handke is excoriating the marketing of the war by the media does not hit the nail on the head (Kienzle 327). Rather, Handke is showing, in a way that is entirely in keeping with his early speech-plays, how, through certain forms and predispositions, as well as through patterns, narrative techniques and points of view, reality is not simply reflected but also produced. The main issue therefore is the nature of the artistic forms that can be used in order to create a particular image of the war. Will these forms contribute to the making of peace or will they subtly maintain the status quo of hate and aggression?

The directors finally break off their project. Accordingly, the play does not give any answer to the question of how the war might be appropriately turned into a film narrative. However, it presents important material as well as viewpoints and artistic forms which could one day be picked up again and developed by a narrator, maybe even by a member of the audience. If the grand narrative is still to come, then Handke's play has at least provided its prologue. The fur-woman, who, with her prophetic vision, stands apart from

---

[34]For a study of the play's imagery, this and the works cited in note 29 are particularly relevant; see also Meyer-Gosau's article.

the other characters in the play, insistently invokes and appeals to the spectators' power of imagination. This power represents the only possible help now, because it is creative imagination which can give form and thus do justice to our humanity.

Works Cited

André Müller im Gespräch mit Peter Handke. Ed. Richard Pils. Weitra: Bibliothek der Provinz, 1993.

Au, Alexander. *Programmatische Gegenwelt. Eine Untersuchung zur Poetik Peter Handkes am Beispiel seines dramatischen Gedichts 'Über die Dörfer.'* Frankfurt am Main: Peter Lang, 2001.

Barth, Markus. *Lebenskunst im Alltag. Analyse der Werke von Peter Handke, Thomas Bernhard und Brigitte Kronauer.* Wiesbaden: Deutscher Universitätsverlag, 1998.

Bauschinger, Sigrid. "Sprechtheater und Theaterbild. Peter Handke auf der amerikanischen Bühne." *Vom Wort zum Bild. Das neue Theater in Deutschland und den USA.* 16. Amherster Kolloquium zur Deutschen Literatur. Ed. Sigrid Bauschinger and Susan L. Cocalis. Bern: Francke, 1992. 39-58.

Behse, Georg. "Über Peter Handkes Erfolgsstück *Publikumsbeschimpfung.*" *Wege der Literaturwissenschaft.* Ed. Jutta Kolkenbrock-Netz, Gerhard Plumpe, and Hans Joachim Schrimpf. Bonn: Bouvier, 1985. 345-71.

Bekes, Peter. *Peter Handke, Kaspar, Sprache als Folter. Entstehung – Struktur – Rezeption – Didaktik.* Paderborn: Schöningh, 1984.

Bohn, Volker. "Unter dem Wind und über die Dörfer. Zu Peter Handkes Dramatischem Gedicht." *Spectaculum 36. Sechs moderne Theaterstücke. Samuel Beckett. Christopher Hampton. Peter Handke. Gerlind Reinshagen. Botho Strauß. Anton Tschechow.* Frankfurt am Main: Suhrkamp, 1982.

Bubner, Rüdiger. "Sprachfindung." *Suhrkamp Literatur Zeitung* 3 (3. Programm: Peter Handke. *Kaspar*) 1976. 1-2.

Frietsch, Wolfram. *Peter Handke – C. G. Jung. Selbstsuche – Selbstfindung – Selbstwerdung: Der Individuationsprozess in der modernen Literatur am Beispiel von Peter Handkes Texten.* Gaggenau: Verlag Neue Wissenschaft: 2002.

Fuß, Dorothee. *"Bedürfnis nach Heil"*: *zu den ästhetischen Projekten von Peter Handke und Botho Strauss.* Bielefeld: Aisthesis, 2001.

Gottschalk, Birgit. *Das Kind von Europa. Zur Rezeption des Kaspar-Hauser-Stoffes in der Literatur.* Wiesbaden: Deutscher Universitätsverlag, 1995.

Grieshop, Herbert. *Rhetorik des Augenblicks. Studien zu Thomas Bernhard, Heiner Müller, Peter Handke und Botho Strauß.* Würzburg: Königshausen & Neumann, 1988.

Hamilton, James R. "Handke's 'Kaspar,' Wittgenstein's 'Tractatus' and the Successful Representation of Alienation." *Journal of Dramatic Theory and Criticism* 2 (1995) 3-26.

Hern, Nicholas, *Peter Handke. Theatre and Anti-Theatre.* London: Oswald Wolff, 1971.

Heyer, Petra. *Von Verklärern und Spielverderbern. Eine vergleichende Untersuchung neuerer Theaterstücke Peter Handkes und Elfriede Jelineks.* Frankfurt am Main: Peter Lang. 2001.

Janke, Pia. *Der schöne Schein. Peter Handke und Botho Strauß.* Vienna: Holzhausen, 1993.

Joseph, Arthur. *Theater unter vier Augen. Gespräche mit Prominenten.* Cologne: Kiepenheuer & Witsch, 1969.

Kathrein, Karin. "'Die herbe Lust, kein Wiederholungstäter zu sein.' Einige Überlegungen zur Rezeption von Peter Handkes Bühnenwerken der achtziger Jahre." *Peter Handke. Die Langsamkeit der* Welt. Ed. Gerhard Fuchs and Gehard Melzer. Vienna: Droschl, 1993. 155-64.

Kienzle, Siegfried. *Schauspielführer der Gegenwart.* Stuttgart: Alfred Kröner, 1999.

Kiermeier-Debre, Joseph. *Eine Komödie und auch keine. Theater als Stoff und Thema des Theaters von Harsdörffer bis Handke.* Wiesbaden: Steiner-Verlag, 1989.

Kurzenberger, Hajo. "Peter Handke: *Über die Dörfer.* Ein Werk der Liebe, des Hasses, der Erlösung?" *Deutsche Gegenwartsdramatik.* Ed. Lothar Pikulik. Göttingen: Vandenhoeck & Ruprecht, 1987. 35-85.

Lennard, John, and Mary Luckhurst. *The Drama Handbook. A Guide to Reading Plays.* Oxford: Oxford UP, 2002.

Linstead, Michael. *Outer World and Inner World. Socialisation and Emancipation in the Works of Peter Handke, 1964-1981.* Frankfurt am Main: Peter Lang, 1988.

Lorenz, Otto. *Die Öffentlichkeit der Literatur. Fallstudien zu Produktionskontexten und Publikationsstrategien. Wolfgang Koeppen. Peter Handke. Horst-Eberhard Richter.* Tübingen: Niemeyer, 1998.

Lüdke, W. Martin. "'Am Ursprung liegt das Ziel.' Über die Echternacher Springprozession, das Glück, die Moderne, Handke und Heraklit." *Peter Handke. Die Arbeit am Glück.* Ed. Gerhard Melzer and Jale Tükel. Königstein: Athenäum, 1985. 82-96.

Malkin, Jeanette R. *Verbal Violence in Contemporary Drama. From Handke to Shepard.* Cambridge: Cambridge UP, 1992.

Meyer-Gosau, Frauke. "Kinderland ist abgebrannt. Vom Krieg der Bilder in Peter Handkes Schriften zum jugoslawischen Krieg." *Text und Kritik* 24. Ed. Heinz Ludwig Arnold. 6th ed. Munich: edition text + kritik, 1999. 3-20.

Mixner, Manfred. *Peter Handke.* Kronberg: Athenäum, 1977.

Pascu, Eleonora. *Unterwegs zum Ungesagten. Zu Peter Handkes Theaterstücken 'Das Spiel vom Fragen' und 'Die Stunde da wir nichts voneinander wußten' mit Blick auf die Postmoderne.* Frankfurt am Main: Suhrkamp, 1998.

Pfister, Manfred. *The Theory and Analysis of Drama.* Cambridge: Cambridge UP, 1988.

Renner, Rolf Günter. *Peter Handke.* Stuttgart: Metzler, 1985.

Roelcke, Thorsten. *Dramatische Kommunikation. Modell und Reflexion bei Dürrenmatt, Handke, Weiss.* Berlin: de Gruyter, 1994.

Sauerland, Karol. "Brecht, Handke und das Publikum als Konvention." *Soziale und theatralische Konventionen als Problem der Dramenübersetzung.* Ed. Erika Fischer-Lichte. Tübingen: Narr, 1988. 145-52.

Schmidt-Bergmann, Hansgeorg. "Peter Handke." *Deutsche Dramatiker des 20.Jahrhunderts.* Ed. Alo Allkemper, Norbert Otto Eke. Berlin: Erich Schmidt, 2002. 660-82.

Schmidt-Dengler, Wendelin. "'Wittgenstein, komm wieder!' Zur Wittgenstein-Rezeption bei Peter Handke." *Wittgenstein und Philosophie ↔ Literatur.* Ed. Wendelin Schmidt-Dengler, Martin Huber, Michael Huter. Vienna: Österreichische Staatsdruckerei, 1990. 181-91.

Schuller, Marianne. "Die Lust am Aufschwung. Zu Peter Handkes *Über die Dörfer*. *Ein dramatisches Gedicht* – Ein Essay." *Literatur der siebziger Jahre*. Ed. Gert Mattenklott and Gerhart Pickerodt. Berlin: Argument-Verlag. 1985. 10-19.

Schultz, Uwe. *Peter Handke*. Velber bei Hannover: Friedrich, 1973.

Thornton, Thomas S. *Die Thematik der Selbstauslöschung und Selbstbewahrung in den Werken von Peter Handke*. Frankfurt am Main: Peter Lang, 1983.

Valentin, Jean-Marie. "Reine Theatralität und dramatische Sprache." *Peter Handke*. Ed. Raimund Fellinger. Frankfurt am Main: Suhrkamp, 1985. 51-74.

Voris, Renate. *Peter Handke: Kaspar*. Frankfurt am Main: Diesterweg, 1984.

Wagner, Karl. "Das große Salzburger Volkstheater. Zu Peter Handke." *Das zeitgenössische deutschsprachige Volksstück. Akten des internationalen Symposions, University College Dublin, 28. Februar – 2. März 1991*. Ed. Ursula Hassel and Herbert Herzmann. Tübingen: Stauffenburg,1992. 207-16.

–. "Ohne Warum. Peter Handkes *Spiel vom Fragen*." *Peter Handke. Die Langsamkeit der Welt*. Ed. Gerhard Fuchs and Gehard Melzer. Vienna: Droschl, 1993. 201-14.

Wefelmeyer, Fritz. "Beyond Postmodernism. The Late Works of Peter Handke." *From High Priests to Desecrators. Contemporary Austrian Writers*. Ed. Ricarda Schmidt and Moray McGowan. Sheffield: Sheffield Academic Press, 1993. 45-62.

–. "Das Theater der verlichteten Erzählung bei Peter Handke und Wim Wenders." *Centre Stage. Contemporary Drama in Austria*. Ed. Frank Finlay and Ralf Jeutter. Amsterdam: Rodopi, 1999. 205-22.

Weiss, Walter. "Peter Handkes *Spiel vom Fragen*." *Welttheater, Mysterienspiel, Rituelles Theater. "Vom Himmel durch die Welt zur Hölle." Gesammelte Vorträge des Salzburger Symposions 1991*. Ed. Peter Csobádia, et al. Salzburg: Ursula Müller-Speiser, 1992. 675-82.

Wendt, Ernst. *Moderne Dramaturgie. Bond und Genet. Beckett und Heiner Müller. Ionesco und Handke. Pinter und Kroetz. Weiss und Gatti*. Frankfurt am Main: Suhrkamp, 1974.

Between Violence and Transcendence: Handke's Poetry

Christiane Weller

THE POETRY OF PETER HANDKE can be seen as tracing a journey from a critique of language to an affirmation of the transcendental power of language (Dronske 85), from deconstruction to reconstruction. This passage is no more evident than in a certain marked tension between concepts of objectivity and subjectivity and hence in Handke's representation of the communicative process itself. No serious interpretation of this part of Handke's output can avoid engaging with the language-critical dimension, as it is played out in Handke's poetic reworking of such luminaries as Husserl, Heidegger, Wittgenstein and Whorf. Numerous critics do not seem to get much beyond accusing Handke of a careless and superficial understanding of his favorite theorists (Hamm 304-14; Durzak 20-25).

Studies of Handke's critique of language take their bearings almost exclusively from his early work. Much critical attention is paid to the poetic subject as someone delivering himself up to language, or to the question whether that subject is effectively extinguished by the violence of language, or again how the subject finds itself in the grip of restrictive linguistic paradigms (Dronske 87). According to Durzak, the early Handke is essentially making a simple-minded plea for a more precise use of language on the basis of a shallow reading of Wittgenstein. Handke's view is supposedly that reality – thoroughly misrecognised prior to the poetic act – becomes amenable to closer and livelier inspection as a result of that act; though apparently Handke pursues this program so naïvely that he goes on to thoroughly problematize language anyway (Durzak 25). In his discussion of *Die Innenwelt der Außenwelt der Innenwelt* (1969; *The Innerworld of the Outerworld of the Innerworld*, 1974), Mixner speaks of a memory which suddenly penetrates consciousness, of "terror in the face of the distance between the subjectivity of individual consciousness and the objective meaning/meaninglessness of the poem as 'linguistic artefact'" (80), and of the attempt made in Handke's poetry to "blaze a path through pre-emptive formulaic pronouncements about reality" (Mixner 88).[1]

Bohrer's diagnosis is that Handke's work is the expression of the ambivalence on the part of a self-righteous individual who strings together clichés in order to throw light on the process of cliché formation but is nonetheless forced to hold on to "an antiquated picture of subjectivity" (54). The ambivalence between these two aspects of Handke's work, according to Bohrer, stems from Handke's "extreme sensitivity" or, alternatively, from his "experience of terror." Handke's basic experience is one of fright, not in the face of words or word-meanings, but rather the world of objects, the material world to which those words refer (Bohrer 54). This assessment contrasts dramatically with Laemmle's reading of Handke as a "literary technocrat," one who suppresses any sorrowful or affective dimension of human experience in such a way that only the surfaces of material objects remain to be tentatively explored. Handke's true domain is not that of a "new interiority" but that of "externality made absolute" (Laemmle 203). Drews reproaches Handke for conjuring up a sterile poetic world and artificially formalizing what has been said, and said better, by others (50), while for Dronske the language of the early poems is to be understood as strictly hermetic, as a language which foists its logic on the poetic subject (87). If this poetry has any claim to radical status or shows any sign of political influence, then it does so at the level of language and form.

The subject in its relation to language is the main theme of a large part of Handke scholarship, at least as far as the author's poetic output is concerned. In Handke's earlier poetry the position

---

[1]Some of Handke's poetry has been translated. For the English version of *Innenwelt*, Michael Roloff's translation (*The Innerworld of the Outerworld of the Innerworld*) of 1974 was used. The three poems from *Als das Wünschen noch geholfen hat* (1974; When Wishing Still Helped) and the title poem of *Das Ende des Flanierens* (1976; The End of Idling) have also been translated by Roloff in *Nonsense and Happiness* (1976). Both volumes, however, omit several texts contained in the German collections. All German primary and secondary sources that are not available in English translation have been translated by Cameron Shingleton and the author of this chapter. In some isolated cases where the published translation was deemed insufficient the passage was translated by this author with reference to the German original.

of the subject is viewed as precarious, as unstable, as caught up in ungovernable anxiety. Language, as it were, casts a spell over the subject, it inscribes itself into the subject and is productive of structures and paradigms which the subject can only escape at the cost of its own annihilation.

Handke's understanding of language is generally seen as undergoing marked changes from the early to mid-70s. What is at issue, as Wesche puts it, is no longer "the pathology of semiotics but the overcoming of that pathology" (62). Language is increasingly seen as harnessed to experience, the breach between word and world is negotiated, with special emphasis on delicate moments where feelings run up against each other, what Wesche terms "threshold experiences." Handke, according to Wesche, begins to conceive of writing as an imparting of the object of experience, and this entails a turn in the direction of an interior world, accompanied by a new choice of metaphors (63). Bartmann sees Handke moving beyond the disruption of context inherent in the early work, something which is achieved by means of an "implicit poetics" the crux of which is a new sense of connectedness. The subject becomes the poetic locus in a surprising new way; the "imaginative process" (1) becomes the key factor in deciding whether the world can be experienced as a continuous, connected whole.

Bartmann sees in *Der Kurze Brief zum langen Abschied* (1972; *Short Letter, Long Farewell,* 1974) not so much a shift of emphasis *towards* the subject but a shifting *of* the subject, the terror felt by the subject in the face of the world around him occasionally giving way to moments of (relative) contentment (102). Durzak too notes a discernable return to the subject, but now as a "manic fixation," an all-consuming preoccupation with the self (7). Reviewers and interpreters recur time and again to Handke's inveterate narcissism and, in doing so, regularly conflate the subject of the text with the author. Horn (61) reads Handke's apparent attempt to make himself the sole topic of his writing in brutally negative terms, reproaching him for a species of literary exhibitionism which in turn reduces readers to little more than facile voyeurs. In theoretical terms, this interpretation of the new conceptualization of the subject in Handke's later texts is thus a return to an imaginary order preceding any linguistic-symbolic order. In narcissism the other can only be understood in reference to the self, unity only attained at the expense of otherness.

In a surprising twist to what appears a slightly superficial debate, Handke himself claims to have seen through what he terms a "modern kind of narcissism," debunking it as a hysterical staring/ gazing at the other which claims to be compassionate. He then purports to reclaim the narcissism myth for himself as a "long, inquiring contemplation of one's own mirror image" (*WW* 178), which in turn makes contemplation of the other possible. The shift from 'gaze' (*Anstarren*) to 'contemplation' (*Anschauen*) marks the transition from exclusion of otherness to incorporation, as can be seen in the late *Gedicht an die Dauer* (1986; Ode to Permanence). The subject's fixation within an imaginary, narcissistic dynamic creates a context in which the other's connection to the self can be reestablished. Narcissism, as dynamic identification with the other in the realm of the imaginary, also opens up the possibility of an epiphanic experience for the subject. In such moments of epiphany, the subject-object distinction is set aside and a linear conception of time abolished (Frietsch 17). Handke the new mythologist sets before us the myth of an integrated self (Horn 53), while the immediacy of experience can also be seen as a key topos in Handke's later poetic output. At issue is the resurrection of a mythological style of 'saying' or 'naming,' which at least one critic sees as proof of Handke's rudimentary faith in the correlation between the sign and its signified (Marschall 66-68).

The process by which the Handkean subject is contaminated by language, then reconstituted and healed by it in a sort of countermovement, supplies the basic schema according to which interpreters have charted his poetic trajectory. This chapter looks at the same process from the standpoint of the object. From the period of Handke's *Deutsche Gedichte* (1969; German Poems),[2] the collection *Die Innenwelt der Außenwelt der Innenwelt* (1969; *The Innerworld of the Outerworld of the Innerworld*, 1974) and *Als das Wünschen noch geholfen hat*, through to *Das Ende des Flanierens* and *Gedicht an die Dauer* the object in Handke's texts has taken center stage both thematically and at the level of form. Locating the inanimate object, as it is bodied forth verbally at the moment of visual recognition by the subject makes it possible to reconstruct the

---

[2]These were originally published as an unpaginated collection of envelopes containing the 'poems' on slips.

development of Handke's conception of the object from that of the earlier *objet trouvé* to the object as thing in *Gedicht an die Dauer*.

In ready-mades from *Deutsche Gedichte* such as "Witz des Tages" (The Joke of the Day) and "Prominente Kritiker empfehlen neue Bücher" (Famous Critics Recommend New Books), as well as texts such as "Bei uns zu Gast" (*IA* 39; Visiting Us), "Die Aufstellung des 1. FC Nürnberg vom 27. 1. 1968" (*IA* 59; The Line-Up of 1. FC Nuremberg on Jan. 27, 1968), "Die Japanische Hitparade vom 25. Mai 1968" (*IA* 78-80; "The Japanese Hit Parade of May 25, 1968"; *IO* 95-99), "Das Rätsel vom 17. August 1968" (*IA* 98; The Crossword Puzzle of Aug. 17, 1968), "Warner Brothers and Seven Arts zeigen:" (*IA* 119-21; Warner Brothers and Seven Arts Present:), the collage "Legenden" (*IA* 81-86; Legends) and the untitled text number 39 (*IA* 133), the *objet trouvé* highlights the formulism of the prefabricated texts, the inundation of social reality by communicative patterns which have degenerated into stereotypes and which reinforce the gulf between the subject's individual experience and a reality thoroughly cheapened by cliché. Although the ready-mades – these quotations of reality – emphasize the factual in favour of the fictional, the reception of Handke's work has laid stress on the literariness of this particular form (Dronske 90). The much anticipated 'end of art' and the 'death of literature' (see Bohn, "Tod") cited in these *objets trouvés* is undermined by the fact that the documentary scraps are placed in the context of poetry.

Handke's ready-mades do not conform to the late-60s' dictum that the social and historical subject should find its voice as the subject of art. Everyday material objects, as they appear in Handke's ready-mades, were seen as provocative in the intellectual atmosphere of the late sixties and early seventies precisely because they did not give voice to the politically or socially disenfranchised – in other words because they were markedly devoid of emancipatory idealism (Bohn, "Aufstellung" 105). Handke prefaces his *Deutsche Gedichte* with the by-line: "Some will say: 1. These are not poems. 2. I can do that too! One could add here," with the last clause left deliberately incomplete, apparently with a view to opening up space for dissent in the very discourse about the 'poems' which are to follow. And yet the controversy surrounding literary innovation in line with Marxist literary theory nonetheless fails to resonate down the decades. The by now well-known justification of the ready-made along the lines that "whatever has been published as a poem is a poem" (Bartmann 93) falls somewhat flat. If this aesthetic moment was one in which the system of public opinion-making or the place of literature in society might have been subject to scrutiny, the opportunity has certainly been missed.

Since the ready-mades have often been the main focus of interpretations of Handke's poetry, the emphasis here will not be on Handke's conception of the formal poetic object as *objet trouvé* but on object conceptions articulated at the level of content in the collections *The Innerworld of the Outerworld of the Innerworld*, *Als das Wünschen noch geholfen hat*, *Das Ende des Flanierens* and, finally, in the lengthy *Gedicht an die Dauer*. In these texts a multitude of singular objects are strung together by means of sentence structure, then brought into a variety of disjunctive relations with one another. Bossinade sees here a process by which the domains of individual words are extended so as to become "complete prototypes of perception" (138). Handke's early criticism is directed against all literature which clings naïvely to the identity of word and object. He speaks of deep linguistic "sources of error" (*BE* 30), which poets and language users fall victim to when using language unself-consciously, a viewpoint which will be seen to have some relevance to Handke's practice as a poet as well. A world of objects is unattainable by the simple use of words, and Handke sharply criticizes Sartre for suggesting that words could be in any way as transparent as glass (*BE* 42): "Just as things lose their so-called innocence in being named, words lose their innocence in literary citation; to our astonishment they no longer point us to a world of objects, but to themselves: what they show us is – themselves" (*BE* 47).

Objects in "The Inverted World" oust the subject from the realm of action and of agency. Actions are not directed by the subject at the object, but vice versa. In Handke's striking formulation, "I don't look at the objects, and the objects look at me" (*IO* 41). In Sartre's view, the look of the other confirms the subjectivity of the subject, while at the same time confirming (or failing to confirm) the object as a subject standing on equal existential footing. To cite Sartre, "my fundamental connection with the Other-as-subject must be able to be referred back to my permanent possibility of *being seen* by the Other. It is in and through the revelation of my being-as-object for the Other that I must be able to apprehend the presence of his being-as-subject" (256). The look of the Other gives rise in Sartre to shame on the part of the subject looked upon – a difficult movement of feeling which Handke attempts to bring to literary expression.

In Handke's texts, subject and object do not give confirmation or any sort of mutual support to each other. What takes place between the subject who alternately looks and averts its gaze and the object (other) whose gaze remains fixed is a deep, quasi-metaphysical rupture. The potentialities of the look or gaze appear almost to have migrated to the side of the object, which in turn fixes the subject from a perspective which is bound to escape that subject. The self, represented by the first-person agency of the poem, only finds itself positioned in the world once the gaze of the object, or Other, has pinned it down. Language too overtakes the subject from the place of the Other, or as Handke puts it, "I don't pronounce words, and words pronounce me" (*IO* 41). A reversal of subject and object as bearers of action takes place in Handke and is systematically intensified, resulting in a cacophony of action: "and listen! The watch ticks outside itself! / And look! The guttering candles are growing! / and listen! The scream is whispered! / And look! The wind petrifies the grass!" (*IO* 45-47). The experience Handke attempts to evoke is one in which the senses of the perceptive consciousness at the center of the poem are almost under attack by the object-world of which it is part.

In "Verwechslungen" (*IA* 65-68; Mix-Ups), the "open entry hatch of a plane" is mistaken for "the wide-open mouth of a shark," "rotten apples" for "a pile of hand grenades" and "a ladder in a pair of stockings" for "corrosive acid" (*IA* 65). Trains of association lead in the direction of imaginary objects which unleash inexplicable acts of violence. "I mistake the creaking sound of the cupboard for the release of the pistol's safety catch. / The cold doorhandle I mistake for a punch in the neck" (*IA* 66). In *Ich bin ein Bewohner des Elfenbeinturms* (1972; I Am an Inhabitant of the Ivory Tower), a kind of a programmatic statement of Handke's, he puts forward the view that terms like Auschwitz, napalm, or Berlin are overladen with meaning and too political to be used in literature except with the utmost circumspection (*BE* 25). His purported concern is with "methods" as opposed to "themes"; the one and only true topic is that of gaining self-understanding (*BE* 26).

In "Verwechslungen," objects not only become visible *qua* objects, in their objectivity, the internal state of the subject is equated with the realm of objective process. "'I feel like a phone put back on the hook' / – 'You are just exhausted.' / 'At the moment I'd like to be at a country wedding.' / – 'You are bloodthirsty and nothing else'" (*IA* 67). Or, even more directly: "Unease is a coat laid across knees at the movies" (*IA* 68). It is only in the last lines of the poem that the emotional world of the subject and the object-world of the poem are brought to cohere in a meaningful way. "Only one arm has been raised in the classroom – yes, that is shame – yes, I'm the only one raising his arm in the classroom – yes, I am ashamed" (*IA* 68). The act is again attributable to a subject, the raised arm is the arm of the subject whose consciousness centers the poem. The depersonalized feeling of shame – and here one is again reminded of Sartre – comes into focus as the feeling of shame of this particular subject.

"The Innerworld of the Outerworld of the Innerworld" sheds new light on the overinflated importance Handke's object-world can take on vis-à-vis the interior life of the poetic subject. Here the narrating persona finds himself in a department store where the stationary escalator "on which we are walking up / transforms itself into our breath / which we are holding" (*IO* 65). A singular connection is established between worryingly arbitrary elements of the object-world and the emotional state of the subject: "So let us agree to call innocence / shoe nails / perplexity / hotel room / inescapability / nine o'clock / indecisiveness / a stationary escalator … or vice versa / or vice versa –" (*IO* 69-71). Heintz describes this process in very formal terms as "a sort of intermixture of energy from the side of the subject and an urge to let oneself be led along by stimuli impinging from the external environment" (18). It is a process whereby the subject forgets himself, allowing himself to be assimilated by his surroundings (Heintz 80).

Lex (60) also sees here a certain subjectification of external reality. The proliferation of insignificant objects initiates a sort of self-forgetting on the part of the subject: "Someone sees so many objects / he becomes indifferent to them – / someone sees so many indifferent objects / he gradually loses himself out of his consciousness –" (*IO* 71). The subject is only reawoken to consciousness when objects give rise to recognizable emotion-laden reactions, those of "curiosity, desire, reluctance" (*IA* 132). If the object-world is initially experienced as a threat, the sense of threat is brought to an end once something of it can be incorporated into the subjective web of desire. The act of desiring presents the subject with the possibility of distancing himself from a realm of terrifying externality, re-initiating him into the experience of self-consciousness.

In "Fright," too, contact with a deeply extraneous object-world provokes the subject to strong feeling, but in this case the reaction is uniformly one of sheer terror. The world of objects represents a world standing under the spell of something ominous yet to happen: "'This border has not been mined yet!' / 'This head has no nylon stocking over it yet!' / 'This telephone booth hasn't been burnt yet!' / … What a fright! / What a fright! –" (*IO* 145). Terror here is not unleashed by violence – the destructive reduction of the object-world – but by what is apparently normal, the sheer fact of expectation met or disappointed:

> … to be frightened by something which one anticipates, and to be frightened by something which one does not anticipate because one anticipates being frightened by something *else*, and to be startled by *nothing* because one anticipated being frightened by *something*: (*IO* 139)

If terror is understood, in accordance with the Freudian conception of trauma, as a reaction to an external force unexpectedly impinging upon the boundaries established by the ego or subject, a useful distinction can be made here between terror and fear. In Freudian terms, shock or terror denotes an emotional condition into which the subject is plunged by unexpected danger, with the emphasis on the element of surprise, while fear or anxiety are characterized by the expectation of and consequent defense against consciously apprehended danger. Handke, however, circumvents this distinction by regularly placing terror and shock in temporal contexts and by linking it strongly to the object-world. In "Fright," the distinction is made between "[t]he fright which does *not* set in, and the fright which has not *yet* set in, and the fright which *has* set in and *will* set in again" (*IO* 143). For the Handkean subject, shock arises first and foremost in the face of all worlds which are found to be intact – in other words, in the face of the order of things the destruction of which is assured by the inherently destructible nature of objects: "'This jeweler's window has not been smashed in yet!'"

'This car has not been turned over yet!' 'This paving stone has not been dug out yet!'" (*IO* 143). Proceeding beyond Freud, it seems possible to say that trauma – understood as manifesting itself retrospectively through the verbalization of a deeply unsettling event – for Handke becomes something of a compulsively repeated pattern in which anticipation, act and memory collapse into one another. In a byword about anxiety (*Wü* 102), Handke makes reference to anxiety without so-called cause, to panic sparked by external particularities. In effect, it is fundamentally impossible for the subject of Handke's poetry to escape from the panic called forth by the object.

In "Unused Opportunities," everyday objects, gazed upon or desired, bring the subject regularly to the verge of a fatal abyss; potential causes of death which are then denied the subject, or denied by the subject, appear from all sides: "When I'm in the butcher shop the hacking blows of the meat cleaver are not meant for me. / When I touch the high tension wire I wear shoes with rubber soles. / When I bend out of the window the window sill is much too high" (*IO* 113). The place of the subject, *his* place ("I stand right here, on *my* spot"; *IO* 117) remains at too great a remove from the causes of death that encompass him. Longing for death dissolves into paradoxical nuances bordering on self-mockery: "Making a bet with myself, I take a blind step into the elevator shaft – but the elevator is there: did I lose the bet?" (*IO* 113). The subject undermines any and all desire it has already expressed by its physical inertia. As "Unused Opportunities" has it: "and [I] don't inhale / and don't exhale / and don't move from the spot." (*IO* 119).

And yet the object is always conceptually articulated, always already word designating difference. In his poem "Distinctions," Handke puts it as follows:

> Scarcely have I begun to speak – already I am camouflaged and no longer distinguishable from my surroundings....
>
> Scarcely have I become one with my surroundings – already I begin to speak again and am different....
>
> Scarcely have I stopped hearing anyone speak – already I am secretly translating objects I perceive into words, and scarcely have I finished translating the objects – already I have a concept of them. (*IO* 129-35)

In these stages of transition, the notion of difference can arise. In speech, distinction as well as identity are manifested. Conceptuali-

zation is achieved via the translation of things into words. Where
what is perceived resists verbalization, the subject comes up fast
against a realm of "outlandish outlandishness" (*IO* 137). The
moment speech resumes, "already each sentence seems like a dream
of what I perceive" (*IO* 137).

In "Changes during the Course of the Day," the subject of perception is transformed – through action – into an object of perception when the first-person persona changes to the third person. The
shift from an internal to an external viewpoint is marked by the use
of phrase doubles. The poem depicts a progression from a state of
solitude, that of the subject standing alone – "As long as I am still
alone, I am still alone" (*IO* 101) – via a series of action-driven
engagements with an object-world – "As soon as I am asked how
one gets to BLACK ROAD – I become someone who knows his way
around town.... As soon as I enter the church – I become a layman"
(*IO* 103) – back to the isolated subject. The subject then moves
beyond this solitary state by relating to another, and finally to the
subject *as* other: "Then, finally, I sit down next to someone in the
grass – and am finally someone else" ("ein anderer"; *IO* 107).

Heintz stresses the political dimension of the process underway
here, the reduction of the subject to function, and the fact that the
subject seems to be stepping beyond the sense of "personal uniqueness" (14) encapsulated by the first part of each of these dual
clauses. He goes on to note that the language of the poem points in
the direction of specifically ideological forms of communication.
Yet, above and beyond any self-attribution of socially recognizable
roles, the subject's mounting alienation leads to an even deeper
acknowledgement of a split inherent in subjectivity itself. The
poem's last line echoes Rimbaud's dictum that the 'I' is other to
itself, fixing the subject's alienation vis-à-vis itself and the world in
the most clear-cut of ways.

Handke's "Die Reizwörter" (*IA* 87-91; Word-Signals or Trigger
words) opens with the interrogation of an alleged criminal. The
verbal snippets thrown at the interviewee by his interrogators
function paradoxically as provocations, becoming ever more highly
charged the more indifferently the interviewee reacts to them. The
emotive words here are those that evoke a sense of guilt, which in
turn is measurable by the lack of response of the individual under
interrogation. As "dream words," "words of shame," "words of dis-

grace," and "ghost train words" (*IA* 87), they refer to something which compels forgetting, either a crime the purported criminal wills himself to forget or a crime which his interrogators have foisted on him but which cannot be conjured into existence except by means of word-signals. That stimulus is in short something that evokes a reaction, or fails to evoke a reaction, in accordance with the logic of the interrogators alone. The poem's center is constituted by an absence, that which the interviewee's statement cannot contain. This is the only point of reference for the imaginary history of the crime as fabricated by the interviewers. Handke's strategy is to insinuate, or attempt to insinuate, a startling connection between the emotive words and a series of actions on the part of miscellaneous subjects.

> someone in despair takes his own life
> after hearing the word
> GOLDEN HAMSTER ...
> And someone
> who frequently longs to creep away
> gives a guilty start
> when he hears
> the word
> VIP AIRPORT
> the word
> APPLAUSE MID-SCENE
> the word HUNTING ROOM – (*IA* 88-89)

The very arbitrariness of the word-signal appears to trigger particular reactions, such as suicide or pangs of conscience, depending on the context in which it appears. The memory that the word recalls to consciousness remains hidden from view, leaving readers to imaginatively reconstruct the specific power of the word or the power of the situation or object it refers to. In spite of this, the word-signals do not merely spark memories of individual events. Handke also tries to cast them out across the social world, a world of social roles and functions: "the word-signal of the traffic police on patrol is / RICOCHET / the word-signal of the defender in football is / OWN GOAL / the word-signal of the dying is / QUIET" (*IA* 90). Removed from its functional context, the word-signal determines at the same time the limits of this context, namely that which is charged with anxiety and aversion. Remaining unconstrained by any network of functionality, the first person of the poem comes to experience every verbal utterance as provocation: "*my* word-signal is / every word / every word / is a word-signal" (*IA* 90). This is tantamount to saying that every word demands to be powerfully reacted to, as it assaults, demarcates and forces the subject towards what looked to have been successfully negotiated and hence forgotten. Language, in the pathological world of Handke's poem, tends to lose its function as mediator between subject and object or subject and situation, collapsing, as it were, into an endless succession of empty metaphorical associations. To put it in Freudian terms, the *Reizwort* signals the return of the repressed. In the related forms of the "dream word" and "word of shame," the full ambivalence of the psychological complex becomes evident, illustrating the full force of the latent/manifest and conscious/unconscious aspects of language use. The subject, finding itself under constant bombardment by emotionally overcharged signifiers, operates in a continuous state of tension and anxiety.

A similar point can be made about the three poems that are included in the collection *Als das Wünschen noch geholfen hat*, which effectively sets out alternating reflections about the meaning and meaninglessness of linguistic utterance, the integration and alienation of the subject, the proximity and distance of the object-world. Handke's subjects here take on an increasingly autobiographical coloring, and the form of the poem, too, has changed dramatically. The narrative element is foregrounded in place of reliance upon forms of concrete poetry, such as the variation of grammatical structures or the playful use of visual and lexical elements. In "Life Without Poetry," the subject is struck by the standstill at which it finds itself. It comprehends its condition as an uninterpretable symptom that prevents it from knowing what it wants. Demands by literary critics for more rigorous use of words and concepts push the subject into an ever more profound speechlessness: "The novels ought to be 'violent' and poems 'actions' / Mercenaries had strayed / into the language and occupied / every word / blackmailed each other / by using / concepts as passwords / and I became more and more speechless" (*NH* 15). The subject's autumnal surroundings obstruct any detailed view out onto the world, making writing impossible: "Before the external magnificence of nature / there was no imagining anything anymore / and within the monotony of the sum total of daily impressions / nothing particular moved me" (*NH* 21).

In analogous fashion, the beauty of a woman sitting in front of him vanishes as soon as he approaches; it is only the occasional phrase, picked up in passing, which affords as much as the most fleeting pleasure. Roller-skating children temporarily delight the subject in announcing that their mother "went to the supermarket" (*NH* 23), and the string of observations of the material world which follows – of breadcrumbs on the carpet, a garden hose in the grass, an overturned glass of aquavit, a "consolingly yellow" neon shop sign – culminate in the image of a bunch of herbs tied with a rubber band which moves the subject "to tears" (*NH* 25). Plagued by the thought that he can no longer write, that he is virtually condemned to break off all attempts to write before even beginning, a turning point is finally reached in an "insolent" or shameless moment of putting pen to paper, which annuls all preconceived ideas and renews the subject's sense of connection with his world: "and really with one jolt / I again knew what I wanted / and I felt eager for the world" (*NH* 27). The act of writing turns out to be the sole path on which to reestablish "poetic desire for the world" (*NH* 29). The natural world, formerly viewed in its unmitigated externality, undergoes a sort of revivification, and is now associated with the internal, the human and the musical realms.

In "Blue Poem," the outbreak of nonsense due to domineering external powers again becomes thematically important. The singing of birds, degenerating into noise, paralyzes the subject with fear – "illiterate from the horror outside me" (*NH* 35) –, erasing memory and all thoughts of the future. The fear of death, experienced on a nightly basis, becomes the occasion for a change of place, an exchange of the known for the unknown. The gaze which lights only upon the unfamiliar leads not to inarticulateness but to understanding:

But I could look and look
without becoming speechless!
I let everyone count
and understood him –
since all were strange to me.
I could even have hit it off
with my murderer
He was my likeness (*NH* 39)

In this moment of pure experience, the subject is "THE OBJECTIVELY LIVING THING" (*NH* 41), selfless and self-confident, it becomes "inspired machine" (*NH* 41). "I lived / as it came / no longer HESITATED / reacted IMMEDIATELY / experienced nothing SPECIAL" (*NH* 43). Tedious uniformity of waking life is now circumvented in dreams. Becoming dispirited, the subject gives up and moves on again, and in the next unfamiliar, symbolically overcharged city a none too highbrow conversation about sex brings with it a sense of release. "The indescribable particulars / of the grim new age / found the order of their lost connection / in the dirty stories / Hello / meaning is back!" (*NH* 49). Smutty chatter without much of a true sense of desire finds itself transformed into the earnestness of longing. Anonymous "fucking" becomes "sleep[ing] with you"; while that which is "most unsuspected" (*NH* 51) was a metaphor for the sexual act earlier in the poem, when lived out, the act becomes a metaphor itself. "'Real' pictures" prepare the ground for "'other' pictures"; however, the latter are "not allegories / but moments / from the past / set free by the good feeling" (*NH* 53). The particulars of the subject's existence are reconfigured into a whole and the significance of existence itself again becomes obvious.

In "Nonsense and Happiness" Handke's theme is again the subtle dissipation of meaning, this time on a supposedly "indescribable day," one which is neither bright nor gloomy, without "When and But" and without a sense of "Earlier" or "Then" (*NH* 57). The absence of meaning triggers in the subject a desperate thirst for violence and yet the "mysterious JOLT" that will be the spur to violent action, this jolt "with which love set in at one time" (*NH* 59), fails to materialize. The world is experienced as fundamentally fragmentary, objects that make up material reality viewed as if in a half-finished state, "and no hope of completing them" (*NH* 59). The beholder of such a world has a hefty quantity of disgust to endure, and in the face of such "TIMELESS," "SPEECHLESS" and "SENSELESS HUMBUG" (*NH* 61) he remains in a permanently uneasy state of wakefulness. French fries left in the street become "homeless remnants / from that already unimaginable time / when every object still hugged its meaning" (*NH* 61).

Pushed back into its own empty sentimentality for a childhood in which almost everything was seriously out of joint anyway, the subject confronts not a case of meaning going astray but of meaninglessness regained. In such a condition, one's own body is experienced as "a revolting outer world / where everything separates into things / that repel each other" (*NH* 63). There is nothing here that does not partake of the quality of an "abrasive outer world" (*NH* 65) the main mark of which is inexpressiveness. Because the view out into the splintered world around it produces nothing more than "dyed-in-the-wool HUMBUG" (*NH* 73), the subject is left with no choice but to keep its gaze fixed to the ground, and it is here that "[you] finally discovered, / BECAUSE you had no choice / SOMETHING NEW" (*NH* 73). The sense of novelty turns out to extend no further than the green carpet in a cinema foyer, but provides the spur nonetheless to a "new intimacy" (*NH* 75). The downcast gaze is described by Handke in an article entitled "Die offenen Geheimnisse der Technokratie" (*Wü* 31-38; The Open Secrets of Technocracy) as a reflexive response to overwhelming experiences of "monumental strangeness" (*Wü* 31) poetically encoded in miscellaneous objects lying on the floor.

In "Nonsense and Happiness," the same downward look functions as a significant defensive posture which comes to an end once the gaze can be raised again. A woman with a noteworthy expression (as opposed to none at all) puts an end to a state of inarticulateness, making an "indescribable day" "describable" again (*NH* 77). Nonsense has relented but this, together with a new feeling of trust, is nonetheless experienced as pain. A return to a world of stable meanings and to a time of reason is marked by dreams which are their own fulfilments and which start the subject hoping that it will live on to grow old.

The collection *Das Ende des Flanierens* includes largely, though not exclusively, poems of no more than a few lines, two of which Handke titles "Gelegenheitsgedicht" (*EF* 60; 106; Pastime Poem). "Die Verlassenheit" (*EF* 120; Forlornness), takes up the twin motifs of the above-mentioned mysterious jolt and downcast look. In this case, the face of a madman is attributed to the first person of the poem and the objects in his vicinity find themselves metaphorically transformed into torn-up cobblestones. Not even an act of unmitigated and gratuitous violence, a knife thrust into a cat, can restore contact between internal and external worlds. While "The End of Idling" had made a metaphorical equation of cats springing between graves in Montparnasse cemetery and the "moments of life" (*NH*

91), in "Die Verlassenheit," the external world remains closed to the subject "up to eye level and beyond" (*EF* 120) in spite of his despairing act of cruelty.

In "Abschied in der Basilika" (*EF* 146; Farewell in the Basilica), a face which threatens to dwindle into a sort of mask can be fixed in the mind through contemplation of the stone floor. Absorption in the mosaic world he finds at his feet reestablishes the link between first and second person, just as the latter is on the verge of disappearance. Bartmann reads the downcast look, at least that of the subject of *Die Hornissen* (1966; The Hornets), as a reaction of a son-figure to a powerfully dominant father. Only when a synoptic view out into the landscape has displaced the previous shame-filled perspective can the subject be freed from childhood trauma (cf. Bartmann 67-72). However, the downcast gaze denotes not merely departure from reality but also a renewed attention to detail, an itinerant descriptive scouring of the world of objects determined by a metonymic principle (Bartmann 71). This process of metonymy, in Jakobson's and Lacan's sense of the term, arranges signifiers along a diachronic combinatorial axis and thereby creates meaningful connections.

In the collections *Die Innenwelt der Außenwelt der Innenwelt*, *Als das Wünschen noch geholfen hat* and *Das Ende des Flanierens*, alienation plays a key part in determining the subject's standpoint, vis-à-vis both the object and itself. Insofar as it seeks to identify himself with an external object, the subject is always already a split subject. Dividing lines can be located between inner and outer worlds on the one hand and within the internal world on the other. In general terms, the subject can never be said to be whole because it only comes into existence in relation to an object. Definitionally incapable of grasping a sense of its own prior existence, incompleteness and lack are inscribed into it from the outset. In the downcast look and the ensuing sense of proximity to objects the subject is able to imagine itself as whole. On the one hand, the metonymic connection between signifiers is no longer entirely opaque, on the other, the objects on the floor can be understood as *pars pro toto* figures, as components of the overwhelming external world as experienced by the subject, and as such bound (metaphorically) to this external world by means of the substitutive process. Vis-à-vis the subject, the object or word denoting it appears to function ambivalently, undermining the subject as an entity, while at the same time positioning it in relation to the external world, or, more particularly, in relation to language.

In Handke's extended *Gedicht an die Dauer*, however, the structural position of the object undergoes a significant shift. The object-world of the Turkish resort that provides the poem's backdrop, its wild sage, almond trees, grapes, figs, pomegranates and Byzantine ruins, the tapered figures of hornets, the babbling of fountains, overwhelm the viewer precisely with their tangibility. The object here is initially anchored firmly in the empirical world. The central figure feels himself deeply moved by objects but also the victim of an onslaught on the part of objects. This onslaught provokes an ecstatic lust for self-destruction, the desire to plunge headfirst into a ship's propeller. Objects here seem capable of carrying the subject beyond the bounds of the world itself, hence of banishing temporality. When bound up with particular experiences, objects tend to locate the subject in the position of the permanent outsider and are the source of pain or displeasure. It is only in the later stages of the poem that the subject is held within the orbit of the object or thing.

Kolleritsch goes so far as to speak in Handke's case of a Heideggerian-style turn on the phenomenological pathway. In consequence of the supposed turn, perception itself, the very basis of all engagement with the world, receives its directives from pure appearance rather than from the subject (117). Handke's poetics cannot be rightly described as one of interiority because, in this view, there is no referential move back in the direction of the subject or the artist, Handke himself. The process of perception bodied forth by the poem takes its bearings from the external world emerging through the poem, rather than from any interior world. The subject in *Gedicht an die Dauer* can be seen as making an approach to objects via a series of key terms, "spring, new snow, sparrows" (*GD* 23). Any material thing, even if small or tarnished by use, can be poetically preconfigured to form the 'center of the world' (*GD* 25) – a notion which is clearly reminiscent of Wittgenstein's view that "objects form the substance of the world" (*Tractatus* 2.021) and that "substance is what exists independently of what is the case" (*Tractatus* 2.024). Duration is only possible to the extent that one "keeps to the point," namely one's own point (*GD* 24). The knotting of thing and duration, of object and temporality, is brought about by love.

The thing here is no longer a purely empirical object; it is comparable to what is denoted as *Ding* by Lacan, who in turn takes his bearings from Kant. In the work of the latter, the *Ding* (in the sense of the thing-in-itself) can be contemplated as removed from the realm of sensory intuition from a noumenal world-perspective, though it can be said to belong to the noumenal realm only in a negative sense. Regarded positively, however, the thing-in-itself is also the ground of the possibility of all appearance. Thus, on the one hand, it plays the part of an unknowable remainder, which cannot but disappear into the prehistory of individual thought and experience, while on the other hand fulfilling an ongoing conditioning function. By the very fact that it is unattainable, every perceptible, conceptually determined object is marked, as it were, by an absence or lack. No empirical object can have attributed a single identifiable quality to a thing thus belonging to the quasi-mythical prehistory of the subject of experience. As Widmer puts it (11-12), things remain uncertain points of reference for a subject in search of satisfying experiences, the site of an impossible identification of subject and object-world. The mythic qualities of the object or of duration do indeed seem to find expression in a verb like "bestirnen" (to shine protectively; *GD* 31), which refers obscurely to an object that only makes an appearance in relation to the prehistory of the poetic 'I' – an object which must remain at a distance from this poetic 'I,' yet is understood to be intrinsically connected to it.

The ambiguous status of the thing in question is made obvious at the level of language. First and foremost, it is barred from language, removed from the sphere of conceptually mediated knowledge. By identifying itself with language, the subject is decoupled from the core of being; upon entering into the linguistic order it cannot but experience its being in terms of a lack. In language the subject finds itself in an alienated state. Compelled to live out its life in terms of metaphor, it appears to circle around something eternally absent, something which does not allow positive expression in language: the thing. Since language is constituted by absence, it is quintessentially a positioning of the speaker in relation to what he lacks. As Lacan puts it, "the Thing only presents itself to the extent that it becomes word" (*Ethics* 55). Or, in Heideggerian terms: "There is no thing where the word is missing" (164). What the thing contains is a referential gesture (Bossinade 142). In Lacanian terms, the subject as a being directed towards objects is always already in a castrated condition at the symbolic level due to the unbridgeable divide between (empirical) object and (transcendental) thing. As an entity beyond (the forms of) space and time, the thing belongs to the psychological realm of the Lacanian real (Widmer 13-14).

In Handke's later poetry, duration can be understood as thing, and this is to be pinned down precisely through love or desire. In *Gedicht an die Dauer* it is sex ("Geschlechterliebe"; *GD* 29) that gives durability, though the purpose is apparently best served by juxtaposition of a variety of sexual experiences. The effect of this is transformatory: "Your straight hair began to curl, / your bright eyes darkened, / your large teeth became small" (*GD* 28). The sensation of durability, to the extent that it is not exclusively bound up with sex, arises in the presence of "many a small thing, / the more touching the more improbable" (*GD* 32), though it is also spurred by thoughts of the subject's own child, or the child he once was himself. Special emphasis is often placed on unremarkable locations which conjure up a sense of the enduring, the now silted up Lake Griffen or Lake Doberdob: "In the stillness by these lakes / I know what I am doing, / I learn who I am" (*GD* 38). Together with these two loci of childhood memory we find two further places, both Parisian: the Porte d'Auteuil, a "secular place of pilgrimage," where the subject feels "as if I might have spent my youth there, and were still spending it there" (*GD* 42), and the Fontaine Sainte-Marie, which the subject calls the "center of my world" (*GD* 43). At this, and only this fountain in the midst of one of the great world cities, thought itself becomes something more rarefied, a "pure contempla-tion of the world" (*GD* 44). Or, as Handke puts it at his most ebullient:

In place of the chatter within me,
the agony of many voices,
there springs reflection,
a kind of redeeming silence,
out of which my highest thought,
a clear thought, rises up as I arrive at the place:
O rescue, rescue, rescue!
With a jolt as gentle as it is powerful
my eyes become round,
there is a crackling in my auditory canals,
and in the clearing I celebrate

the thanksgiving of the presence. (*GD* 45)

The space around the fountain – or perhaps even just uttering the fountain's name – conjures up something noumenal. In a moment of quasi-religious devotion, the many voices within him, primarily those of others, merge into one. As he waits for the promise of salvation to be fulfilled, his thoughts are focused ever more precisely on a single point represented by the thrice-uttered cry of "rescue." The transformatory act that appears to be underway here, at once delicate and wrenching, takes effect primarily in the world of sensory experience. Taking his cue from Heidegger, Handke reconfigures the space before him as the clearing where a kernel of much sought-after meaningfulness can reveal itself. If, in *Gedicht an die Dauer*, such a quasi-mystical experience of temporality is initially bound up with a particular geographical location, once grasped it can be re-called, given a name and reactivated in any number of places or at any point in the future:

> By now I need no more trips around the world
> to the sites of duration.
> In their absence too,
> when I take my time,
> calmly tightening a
> light bulb,
> weighing a stone in my hand,
> taking something cautiously in my hand,
> I am perhaps
> overwhelmed by the murmuring silence of Lake Griffen,
> the *Residenzplatz* resounding
> of hackney cabs
> passes over into the turmoil and surging of the Porte d'Auteuil,
> I straighten up, ageless,
> at the Fontaine Sainte-Marie's triangular surrounds.
> I have trained myself
> to await the duration;
> the extravagance of pilgrimages is no more. (*GD* 48-49)

Again it is the least likely of objects or situations, trivial but carefully executed daily chores, which open the subject to the experience of duration. What in the early poetry is more often than not a compulsive downward glance is here finally transformed into appreciation of detail. Everything metonymic is viewed from the perspective of a sense of belonging, although in coming to apprehend duration, the subject is also aware of itself in its separateness, for "duration is not a communal experience" (*GD* 51). The experiential possibility opened up is of a well-balanced sense of distinctness which does not exclude simultaneous acceptance of connectedness with all others, including past and future generations:

> Kindled by duration,
> I am also each and every other,
> who stood before my time at Lake Griffen,
> who, after me, will circle the Porte d'Auteuil,
> with whom I will have gone
> to the Fontaine Sainte-Marie.
> Borne up by duration,
> I, the man of a single day, carry
> my predecessors and my successors
> on my shoulders,
> an elevating burden. (*GD* 51-52)

Temporality, as a condition underpinning the life of the individual, has been annulled; past, present and future have been melded into a unity, into a single temporal frame where duration is what is awaited and simultaneously dissolved into an ecstatic "will have gone," a state of perfect futurity which is closed off even as it is anticipated. One is reminded of St. Augustine's three temporal modes, in none of which either future or past can be said to exist – a conceptual scheme which seems to have supplied Handke with something of a model:

> It might be correct to say that there are three times, a present of past things, a present of present things, and a present of future things. Some such different times do exist in the mind, but nowhere else that I can see. The present of past things is the memory; the present of present things is direct perception; and the present of future things is expectation. (St. Augustine 269)

For St. Augustine, time is nothing less than a dilation of the soul, a departure from sensory perception that looks to memory, or, in other words, an "entering into oneself" that marks a relation to God or eternity (Lloyd 20). Time itself is structured analogously to the word or speech. Speech, too, is said to situate itself between memory and expectation, and the present time which provides speech with its context is located in a wider sense in all that is past and all that is to come. As such, time is always already inherent in consciousness. In relation to time, the self can thus only be understood by means of an inward gaze, aimed in the final analysis at God and eternity:

"The spoken word is the metaphor through which this crucial relation between time as the stretching out of consciousness and God's
eternal now is to be grasped" (Lloyd 37). In the cry "Rescue, rescue,
rescue" (*GD* 45), the invocation of the noumenal crystallizes into a
moment of pure present time, allowing all that is past and all that is
to come, all memory and expectation, to fuse into a single word.
The unification of time and the subject is brought about forcibly by
means of the thrice-repeated word.

As for St. Augustine, it is only in the absence of past and future
that Handke's eternal present, that of duration, can shine through.
Duration is hence what might be called 'lived time' or *temps duré*
as understood by Bergson, whom Handke brings into play in his
postscript to the poem. Bergson, too, is apt to let past and present
merge in the sense that he conceives them as coexisting, the past
effectively constituted *as* past in being present. As Deleuze referring to Bergson puts it: "Duration is indeed real succession, but it is
so only because, more profoundly, it is *virtual coexistence*" (60).
Bonn gives the impression that Handke takes up such philosophical
threads in a spirit of thorough-going eclecticism but fails to give
them any poetic resonance. He also sees Handke as referring back
to Taoism, while in general terms "Handke's concept of duration
has to be positioned within the context of mythical-religious thought
and most likely represents a highly developed variation of the theme
of the wondrous moment, which in this case finds its manifestation
in writing" (Bonn 163). Lacan similarly locates the subject in a
present in which past meanings are constantly restructured but never
left behind and future meanings restructured but never actualized:
"What is realized in my history is not the past definite of what was,
since it is no more, or even the present perfect of what has been in
what I am, but the future anterior of what I shall have been for what
I am in the process of becoming" (*Écrits* 94). The therapeutic effect,
or, in Handke's case, the promise of redemption, is enacted in a sort
of anticipatory gesture which makes possible that part of the past we
care to discover anew in speech (Bowie 39).

It seems possible to argue, contrary to Bonn, that one aspect of
Bergson's agenda has been successfully brought to poetic life by
Handke, namely the internal division of memory and the interaction
of respective parts of the division. Bergson speaks of a so-called
"motor mechanism" and of "independent recollection" (87), of a

physical reaction based on past experiences which does not require any calling to mind of specific memory images on the one hand, and of a faculty of memory that is based on particular conscious images on the other. The former memory is linked by Bergson with activity in the present, the latter with dream life, just as in Freudian dream theory the optative dream thought is understood as present from the outset. For Bergson both types of memory capacity are necessary for meaningful activity in the present. Dreams negate the future insofar as they enact what is wished for in the present (Bowie 18). In *Gedicht an die Dauer*, specific images are inscribed in what Bergson calls motoric or habit memory, giving the appearance that they could henceforth be continually recalled to consciousness. Tightening a light bulb, weighing a stone in one's hand, a careful movement or chore revive images of lake Griffen, the Porte d'Auteuil or the Fontaine Sainte-Marie (*GD* 48-49), a process which is essentially metaphorical because it is substitutive in nature.

At this point in Handke's poetry what is sought is identity with the thing, a sort of devotional merging with duration which brings the memory trace to the fore and in doing so collapses past, present and future. A kernel of the Lacanian Real lies at the bottom of this imagined object, this state of permanence. However, the real can never be grasped. It remains elusive despite drawing the subject into the maelstrom of continual anticipation. As Boothby has it, "*das Ding* designates an unencompassable aspect of every representation, a kind of ungraspable centre of gravity that lends coherence to the various manifestations of an object while remaining itself ineluctably out of reach" (204). The homogeneity of an image, of the durability of a childhood memory of Lake Griffen, for example, occludes the complexity of the original experience, promising the rediscovery of an object that has never been the possession of the subject in any unitary sense. Desire arises from this chasm between object and thing. It can never reach its proper place, if that place is to be understood as the preconceived object of desire. Fundamentally it will always aim at an eternally elusive reminder.[3] The thing is

---

[3]The thing only presents itself in a void opened up by the signifier. As Lacan puts it, the thing is the "beyond-of-the-signified" (*Seminar* 54). Signifiers are characterized by deferred action, a retrospective structuring of images or memory traces. The product of this relation between image and word is the

placed in connection with the subject by way of the signifier. The signifier however also serves to maintain an unbridgeable gulf between thing and subject.

Handke nonetheless pictures this process as having been brought to completion. Though once believed lost, the object can be recuperated by way of a mystical fusion of subject and world. The experience of castration – in plainer terms: the experience of being wounded – will only be apprehended in a moment of healing, which is to say at the moment when castration is overcome: "With the healing touch of duration / the wound closes / which I only become aware of as it closes over" (*GD* 53). The search for connection leads to an inflation of the ego, an appropriation of the thing contained in the real. In recurring to permanence, the subject is returned to mythical territory: to a world which precedes all difference, all differentiation between subject and object.

"The impetus of duration is / what I was missing. / He who has never experienced duration / has not lived. / Duration does not enrapture, / it sets me in alignment" (*GD* 53-54). In taking up for a second time the motif of the mystical jolt "with which love once began," Handke comes full circle. The force of this jolt, the jolt of duration, does not shift the subject towards the "enraptured" position of the object, but in the opposite direction. What was formerly an obstacle is now to be transferred into poetic language, and thereby shaped into a new order. "Jolts of duration: / you are now brought to convergence / as poetry" (*GD* 55). In a word, desire and the thing, the imaginary and the real are seamlessly enmeshed in the symbolic order. At this moment, the simultaneously mystic and psychotic vision of identity with the world evoked so desperately by the subject is at last made manifest.

Lacanian 'objet a,' that which remains of the thing after its subjection to the process of symbolization.

Works Cited

Bartmann, Christoph. *Suche nach Zusammenhang. Handkes Werk als Prozeß.* Vienna: Braumüller, 1984.

Bergson, Henri. *Matter and Memory.* Trans. Nancy M. Paul and W. Scott Palmer. London: George Allen, 1913.

Bohn, Volker. Bohn, Volker. "Die Aufstellung des 1. FC Nürnberg vom 27. 1. 1968. Methodische Vorüberlegungen zu einer Interpretation." *Peter Handke.* Ed. Raimund Fellinger. Frankfurt am Main: Suhrkamp, 1985. 92-113.

–. "Zum Hinscheiden der These vom Tod der Literatur." *Nach dem Protest. Literatur im Umbruch.* Ed. Martin Lüdke. Frankfurt am Main: Fischer, 1979. 241-68.

Bohrer, Karl Heinz. "Die Liebe auf den ersten Blick." Ed. Michael Scharang. *Über Peter Handke.* Frankfurt am Main: Suhrkamp, 1972. 52-56.

Bonn, Klaus. *Die Idee der Wiederholung in Peter Handkes Schriften.* Würzburg: Königshausen & Neumann, 1994.

Boothby, Richard. *Freud as Philosopher. Metapsychology after Lacan.* New York, London: Routledge, 2001.

Bossinade, Johanna. *Moderne Textpoetik. Entfaltung eines Verfahrens. Mit dem Beispiel Peter Handke.* Würzburg: Königshausen & Neumann, 1999.

Bowie, Malcolm. *Psychoanalysis and the Future of Theory.* Oxford (UK) and Cambridge (US): Blackwell, 1993.

Deleuze, Gilles. *Bergsonism.* Trans. Hugh Tomlinson and Barbara Habberjam. New York: Zone Books, 1988.

Drews, Jörg. "Sterile Exerzitien." *Text und Kritik.* 24/24a. Ed. Heinz Ludwig Arnold. 1st ed. Munich: edition text + kritik, 1969. 50-55.

Dronske, Ulrich. "Dichten und Dauern: Peter Handke als Lyriker." *Zagreber Germanistische Beiträge* 3 (1996) 85-95.

Durzak, Manfred. *Peter Handke und die deutsche Gegenwartsliteratur. Narziß auf Abwegen.* Stuttgart, Berlin, Cologne, Mainz: Kohlhammer, 1982.

Freud, Sigmund. "Jenseits des Lustprinzips." *Gesammelte Werke.* Frankfurt am Main: Fischer, 1999. 2-69.

Frietsch, Wolfram. *Die Symbolik der Epiphanien in Peter Handkes Texten. Strukturmomente eines neuen Zusammenhanges.* Sinzheim: Pro Universitate, 1995.

Hamm, Peter. "Der neueste Fall von deutscher Innerlichkeit: Peter Handke." *Über Peter Handke.* Ed. Michael Scharang. Frankfurt am Main: Suhrkamp, 1972. 304-14.

Heidegger, Martin. *Unterwegs zur Sprache (1950-1959).* Pfullingen: Neske, 1992.

Heintz, Günter. *Peter Handke.* Stuttgart: Klett, 1971.

Horn, Peter. "Die Sprache der Vernünftigen und die Sprache der Unvernünftigen." *Handke. Ansätze – Analysen – Anmerkungen.* Ed. Manfred Jurgensen. Queensland Studies in German Language and Literature 7. Bern: Francke, 1979. 45-64.

Kolleritsch, Alfred. "Die Welt, die sich öffnet. Einige Bemerkungen zu Handke und Heidegger." *Peter Handke. Die Arbeit am Glück.* Ed. Gerhard Melzer and Jale Tükel. Königstein/Ts.: Athenäum, 1985. 111-25.

Lacan, Jacques. "Function and field of speech and language." *Écrits: A Selection.* Trans. Alan Sheridan. London, New York,: Routledge, 2001. 33-125.

–. *The Seminar of Jacques Lacan. Book VII. The Ethics of Psychoanalysis 1959-1969.* Ed. Jacques-Alain Miller. Trans. Alan Sheridan. New York, London: Norton & Company, 1992.

Laemmle, Peter. "Literarischer Positivismus: Die verdinglichte Außenwelt." *Über Peter Handke.* Ed. Michael Scharang. Frankfurt am Main: Suhrkamp, 1972. 195-204.

Lex, Egila. *Peter Handke und die Unschuld des Sehens.* Zurich: Paeda Media, 1985.

Lloyd, Genevieve. *Being in Time. Selves and Narrators in Philosophy and Literature.* London, New York: Routledge, 1993.

Marschall, Susanne. *Mythen der Metamorphose – Metamorphose des Mythos bei Peter Handke und Botho Strauß.* Mainz: Gardez!, 1993.

Mixner, Manfred. *Peter Handke.* Kronberg: Athenäum, 1977.

Sartre, Jean Paul. *Being and Nothingness: An Essay on Phenomenological Ontology.* Trans. Hazel E. Barnes. London: Routledge, 1993.

Saint Augustine. *Confessions.* Trans. R.S. Pine-Coffin. Harmondsworth: Penguin, 1961.

Wesche, Ulrich. "Metaphorik bei Peter Handke." *Monatshefte* 89.1 (1997) 59-67.

Widmer, Peter. "Einleitung." *Ethik und Psychoanalyse. Vom kategorischen Imperativ zum Gesetz des Begehrens: Kant und Lacan.* Ed. Hans Dieter Gondek and Peter Widmer. Frankfurt am Main: Fischer, 1994. 7-23.

Wittgenstein, Ludwig. *Tractatus Logico-Philosophicus.* 1921. London, New York: Routledge, 1974.

Handke as Director: *The Absence*

John E. Davidson

PETER HANDKE IS A WRITER for whom narration has always taken precedence over narrative. Having spent years developing a descriptive style in nearly all literary genres that avoids symbols where possible, it should come as no surprise that Handke perceives film to correspond to his fondness for brevity in expression even better than books: "To me at least," he remarks in a conversation with Wim Wenders, "it seemed that I can attain a level of laconic expression in pictures that I can no longer reach through language. With language I must, and now I use this vague word intentionally, baroquicize ["barockisieren"] a great deal more" (*A* 154*)*. And yet, even with four films to his credit, Handke remains a cinema-loving author who at times makes movies. Rather than a director, he is best known in cinema as the writer and screen writer for a number of Wenders' productions, especially for *Die Angst des Tormanns beim Elfmeter* (1971; *The Goalie's Anxiety at the Penalty Kick*), *Falsche Bewegung* (1974; *False Move*), and *Der Himmel über Berlin* (1987; *Wings of Desire*).[1]

Furthermore, since his best known solo effort in film, *Die linkshändige Frau* (1977; *The Left-Handed Woman*), was made from his own novel, it has been all the more tempting to allow perceptions about Handke the writer to determine the perception of his films. Many discussants rightly borrow terms associated with his literary work to describe his cinema. The "cult of interiority" attending the New Subjectivity of the 1970s (Hake 163) is found reflected in his film writing and movies (especially *The Goalie's Anxiety at the Penalty Kick* and *The Left-Handed Woman*). The protagonist script-

---

[1]To be sure, Handke's love of the cinema is universally recognized, and his frequent commentary on films and film genre find wide reception. In the massive *Geschichte des deutschen Films*, for example, the relevant contributors mention Handke in connection with Wenders and cite several passages that he writes about film but do not consider him as a director or his movies as contributions to German cinema in their own right (Jacobsen, Kaes, Prinzler).

ed for Wenders' *False Move* is driven by his "introspective side" (Elsaesser, *Cinema* 288; *Film* 383) to search for an identity, a wrong move that "fails ... because the hero only undergoes outer rather than inner change" (Pflaum and Prinzler 40). The "clear validation of psychological reflection over political reaction" (Hake 162) does seem to be a component here, for the main character in *The Left-Handed Woman* follows the pattern of the "footloose adventurer" (Elsaesser, *Cinema* 288) driven by *Erfahrungshunger* (a hunger for experience; see Rentschler 172) and a "politics of the self" (Mc-Cormick).[2]

Handke's films certainly have a reflective quality and a psychological level; however, the question of how one gets to that level is vital, that is, the question that pursues the narration rather than the psychological narrative. The author himself writes of the opening envisioned for one of his films, which includes a distinct proscription: "no psychologizing takes place, neither with words nor with looks. Only a clear, strong, precise impression (*Inbild*) should be conveyed, slow, laconic, monumental" (*A* 13). What, then, is the slow path from monumental presentation to psychological reflection? The following reading of *Die Abwesenheit* (1992; *The Absence*) suggests that a tension exists between the author's sense of the laconic and the director's actual presentation of images in the

---

[2]Handke's early literary works had, of course, come under a great deal of fire launched in salvos from the committed left, and much of that criticism would attend his films as well. As with many of the controversial artists in the Federal Republic at the time, a problem arose in squaring the political demands of critics with the aesthetic power of the works. As Eric Rentschler insightfully put it: "However easy it might be to invoke the epithets so commonly found in leftist diatribes against Handke – narcissism, isolationism, objectless subjectivism, negative romanticism – one is struck by the virulent nature of Handke's image-making, aware of an atmosphere of refusal and a shock character beneath the surface placidity of *The Left-Handed Woman*, for all its slow pacing, long static takes, visual austerity, and dramatic minimalism" (170). Along with Rentschler's treatment of the filmmaker, Gerd Gemünden's comments on film and popular culture as components of "the specular America of Peter Handke" remain the most fruitful in this regard, as he argues for the historical anchoring of even Handke's seemingly most decontextualized realism. Many other works, among them most recently Christopher Parry's fascinating discussion of "landscapes of discourse," concentrate on the visual as a vital aspect in Handke's letters, but do not find it necessary to buttress the argument with consideration of his actual practice in a visual (and aural) medium.

filmic medium that might help us understand his vague notion of "baroquicizing."[3] Handke's laconic use of what one practitioner has termed the "grammar of the film language" (Arijon), on the one hand, minimizes the predetermination of meaning for the viewer but, on the other hand, weakens the sense of essential narration in film that Handke ostensibly wants to convey.[4] While largely effective against an overt infusion of pop psychologizing on the viewer's part in regard to the film's characters, Handke's method at times increases the film's reliance on speech and on symbol to the detriment of cinematic power.

To describe the plot of *The Absence* is to fall quickly into a description of the players rather than of the actions. The film introduces and relates the movements of five characters, only two of whom initially know one another well. It begins in an unidentified European town, where a Writer (Eustaquio Barjau – variously referred to as the old man, the pilgrim, and the scribe) takes leave of his Wife (Jeanne Moreau) in order to discover if there is quiet authenticity left in this world of noise-makers. He considers himself to be the last writer, but we hear from a bystander (a cameo by Handke himself) that the Writer has been reduced to copying texts from Greek and Latin antiquity.[5] On the way he meets and becomes

---

[3]While the title *Die Abwesenheit* first appears on Handke's short novel of 1987 (*Absence*, 1990), the goal here is less to compare the motion picture with its literary forbear than to analyze the film with the help (often through contrasts) of the texts generated specifically in association with making it a cinematic work (primarily the film treatment [*A*]). When not otherwise noted, dialogue is quoted from the film itself.

[4]Wenders and Handke seem to take the parallel of film and written language seriously. Handke: "… that one pan, I find it false." Wenders: "It's almost as if a period could have been used there rather than a comma...." Handke: "The pan is more like a parenthesis" (*A* 158).

[5]Handke appears briefly as the Writer leaves his home and sets out. He speaks to another "Older Man" played by Luc Bondy, the award-winning theater and opera director who had recently put on one of Handke's plays at the Schaubühne in Berlin (*Die Stunde da wir nichts voneinander wußten*, 1992; *The Hour We Knew Nothing of Each Other*, 1996). It seems significant that these stars of literature and theater appear as laymen here, and that Barjau is the only layman among the otherwise very renowned actors playing the principals. The "natural" presentation of the non-actors adds an interesting stylization to the figures of artists here that reflects their quality of being out of step with the modern world.

the guide for a Soldier (Alex Descas), a Woman (Sophie Semin), and a Gambler (Bruno Ganz). Each of these characters has emerged from circumstances in the town both mundane and peculiar, embarking on a journey of discovery almost without knowing it. The Soldier, a French-speaking black man, begins the film's action by bidding his parents farewell at a train-station café, then a short time later leaving his post and uniform to walk out of town, alternately reading a book and reciting the names of four Chinese dissidents executed by their regime. The Woman also speaks French and spends most of her time waiting in her apartment. She waits and then receives a call, presumably from a lover asking her to travel spontaneously with him. She says she has time, then goes to the airport, slaps a man, and then, too, leaves town. The German-speaking Gambler goes straight from an all-night poker game into the woods, as he fears that he has become soulless: he knows nothing of seeking, he says later, for as a gambler he only has a feeling for what is in immediate proximity to him. At a crossing of paths in a clearing these three meet the Writer, who immediately begins leading them as if on a mythic quest. On occasion the film cuts back to the Writer's wife, implying that she is in some sense sharing their journey or, as she puts it at her husband's departure, that she will know each step of his journey as well as he will.

What links the four figures here is that they have been in a state of waiting in particular spaces from which they now break free: the Soldier from his post, the Gambler from the smoky back rooms of proximity, the Woman from her apartment, the Writer from his lectern.[6] They now travel primarily by walking, although they occasionally drive a bus, with which they pick up and deliver passengers seemingly at random along the way. They traverse a serene landscape of woods, hills, and valleys, infrequently passing through a town. They make their way to a cave where they share a ritual feast, and the Writer recites an elegy to "silence." The four begin the night shoulder to shoulder on a mattress under one blanket, but the communal solemnity is broken as the Woman begins a speech in which she unmasks the project of the Writer: all

---

[6]For all their similarities, one could argue that this attitude in regard to the possibilities open to "those who wait" marks a significant difference that has developed between Handke and Wenders over the last decade (see Davidson).

his tokens of antiquity are modern items or fakes left over from a film shoot. As she speaks with her eyes closed, the Writer arises and disappears from the cave and the film. At that moment the film cuts back to his house, where a thin white shawl flies through a window into his Wife's arms. As the periodic cross-cutting has shown, she has been the last "waiter" and now will strike out as well.[7]

The rest of *The Absence* is spent with the three remaining travelers going separate ways to seek the Writer, with his Wife joining the search as well. They do not turn him up, and toward the end the new foursome (re)unites to take part in a "Celebration of Absence." At a somber boardwalk café near the seashore, they sit near but not with one another, and the old woman speaks to her husband in his absence, recounting in not very kind terms the difficulties his sense of calling has caused her throughout her life.[8] In her account, the narration is again a description of personal experience, bare and yet somehow fundamental because it reflects inner feeling in the form of outward events: "oh what a light that was," is her entranced murmur. Ironically, her overall invective condemning his quests has the effect of revalidating the Writer's ideals about approaching authenticity even at the moment of refuting them. In failing to find his "center point," or even to have convinced the others that it is real, he has inaugurated a process in which the yearning is rekindled for the possibility of such a central ground of authenticity where presence and absence meet.

---

[7]The shawl is the same article that one Older Man (Bondy) is folding as the Writer leaves on his quest. Even if the viewer remembers that the Older Man was holding it, the angle of the shawl's entry through the window leaves the impression of it from high off the ground and makes this incident the film's one overt bow to the "Fairy Tale" that gives the original novel its subtitle, an impression made stronger because the scene is visually reminiscent of Murnau's *Nosferatu* (1922). The Wife's being set in motion by this inexplicable sign, along with the long monologue she holds at the end of the film, induced Wenders to posit that she was the "real" narrator of this film (*A* 144).

[8]At the ceremonial dinner in the cave the Gambler relates a dream about feeling his mother's presence, and the Soldier speaks in apostrophe to his father, ending with a forcefully repeated demand that he "appear." This scene, filmed as a kind of Last Supper and occurring near the film's temporal and thematic center, might well be thought of as a festival celebrating or yearning for presence, which would then form a counterpoint to the final "festival of absence."

In the case of *The Absence*, essential narration has something to do with Handke's sense of authenticity as well, with his intimate knowledge of a locality, a knowledge gathered both through his own cultural background and his repeated journeys on foot. Three treatments for this film exist, developed over a number of years: a sketch, which centers on a family from the Carthusian mountains; a film treatment, which introduces the main characters we see in the film; and the film itself, which is similar to, but not identical with, the written film treatment. The movie was initially to be shot in Yugoslavia, in areas the author knows intimately from his wanderings throughout his life.[9] However, this region became inaccessible at the time of production because of the war in the Balkans, so the project was moved to the Spanish Pyrenees regions north of Barcelona, which Handke also knows well. At Wenders' suggestion that the film was experienced, or "strolled through" ("ergangen"), by the crew as much as it was made, the director retorted: "Well, the one who 'experienced' the film was I, in as much as I looked at every corner of that area, and the surrounding vicinity in the months before this undertaking both threatened and beckoned to me. In a sense I had earned that film already because I didn't go looking for locations, the way one does for a film, but rather had actually already experienced every site. Over the course of years I experienced these places."[10]

What threatened and beckoned Handke were the need and the opportunity to tell this story on film. Of interest here is the role that internalizing a geographical area by means of traversing and viewing it plays in Handke's description, for it is precisely that

---

[9]The term *Heimat* certainly comes to mind when reading about the feeling of familiarity Handke seeks in the setting of this film: "Originally I wanted to shoot the film in the Yugoslavian area of the Karst, because that landscape is so much more familiar, and naturally at the same time also strange to me" (*A* 147).
[10]The Writer in the film treatment opens by speaking of the "true word: experience (for) oneself [sich ergehen]. But look, no one out there does that ... snorting and trampling.... Now silence only means: the monstrosity dozes now, the tumult will break out again at any moment" (*A* 33). No wonder that Handke reacts so strongly to Wenders' suggestion, for though "no one out there" can do this ("sich ergehen"), he can. The egotism that shines through Handke's words are reminiscent of Nietzsche, who also insisted on the importance of going in order to allow ideas to pass out of him and be captured on tiny slips of paper during walks, which were to be incorporated in the body of his work later.

accumulation of familiarity by moving through a place looking – he terms it *Erlebnis* – that is denied the viewer because of the author's directorial style. Reference back to the structure of myths and epic tales, which often embody journeys but show only the various stages and tales along the way, is useful here, as is the notion of the station drama, which eschews the exposition of a narrative journey as a whole in favor of presenting a series of individual episodes often circling around moral questions. The film-takes tend to be quite long, linked by editing in which conventions of continuity play little role, although it would go too far to say that they are actively frustrated, for, at least as Handke understands it, the montage of these images creates a continuity through rhythm that is an indispensable part of this film (*A* 145).

The simple attention paid to it by the camera allows the landscape to become in some ways more than it is, and yet many shots seem haphazard rather that carefully composed. The static nature of the individual images is augmented on rare occasions by pans and, even less frequently, by associative montages and point-of-view shots. The immobile camera work and minimal editing potentially undermine the "laconical" presentation Handke desires. First, it raises the role that words have in infusing meaning into the images and, second, in images that do seem carefully composed, it invests many with an allegorical quality: the Writer at his lectern in the background set against his Wife engaged in domestic work in the foreground; the Gambler sitting by a fallen log watching a hawk perched in the trees; the Soldier looking at his hand, which bears the names of those killed by other soldiers; the Woman alone at her breakfast table holds a roll to her ear as if it were a telephone; a point-of-view shot looking down on a snake slithering around a hedgehog; a similar angle depicting an empty boot next to a circle of dust on a street corner, which an eyeline match has indicated to be the subject that a blind man has just photographed.[11] The duration of these takes and their lack of filmic vibrancy suggest over-determined still-life images and invite an attitude on the viewer's part that might come close to what Handke means by

---

[11]Eyeline-match editing is a convention whereby a shot of a person looking is followed by one of an object from an angle that the viewer identifies as the direction of the look. This convention implies both a durational continuity and that this is the object the person is observing.

"baroquicizing," that is, of seeing these images as ornate and allego-rical. Handke does not use the cinematic techniques to interrupt the invitation to the viewer to read these images symbolically, and this lack of intervention runs counter to his stated desire in using the medium of film. It is a literary, rather than cinematic, use of film.

Where one might usefully talk about an active attempt to chal-lenge viewer expectations would be in the tension often arising between sound and vision. No music punctuates the film, and most of the sound consists of diegetic material, such as voices and foot-steps, sometimes posited as being off camera to fill out the world of the film. But quite often the footsteps imply a much closer proximi-ty to the walkers than that offered by the camera, and in many instances the viewers become acutely aware that the footsteps they are hearing are indeed not diegetic but rather dubbed in from a different source. Mechanical noises are also frequently present, even when no machinery can be discerned, breaking the solemnity with a steady roar that questions the very possibility of the kind of idyllic setting the Writer seems to seek. On the one hand, while the aural track is in many ways naturalistic, it very often exhibits a kind of hyper-naturalism that undermines any sense of immediacy by evoking, in the case of the footsteps, the echoes of other journeys. On the other hand, the sound track at times quite simply does not fit the visuals. The first moments of the film are the most explicit examples of this: as the opening credits appear on a dark screen, the sound of running water evokes a stream close to one's ear, but when the darkness gives way no stream can be seen. Soon the water fades into the sound of feet running down an echoing stairwell, perhaps on metal steps, but the montage of images, primarily of different landscapes that have neither streams nor stairs, shows nothing that could cause or even be near this noise. Indeed, one shot up a set of stone steps in an old building immediately makes the viewer aware that this could not be the source of the sounds being heard.

Different modes of "absence" are enunciated by the tensions between sound and vision: the absence of the past for the present; the absence of the bodies (human, natural, or artificial) making the sounds; the absence of the human being in the initial images of nature the viewer sees; the absence of silence. The subsequent and more important point, however, is that this invocation of absence only evokes a sense of presence more strongly than if the illusion of presence offered by the cinematic medium were left unchallenged. Hence, Handke's insistence on authentic experience of the land as a basis for this film translates to the filmmaking, despite the fact that the viewer's experience of the landscape as one who walks through it is broken: "I had the sense that the pictures could not be allowed to stand still in the way that a walker ideally experiences them, but rather that they all needed to be disrupted, that all pictures are to be disrupted, so that later these images could really be seen afresh...." (*A* 146).[12] Since no filmic techniques are deployed to make the scenery mobile, what disturbs the stationary effect of the images of the land is the presence of the humans within the frame, who, paradoxically, bring with them the burden of absence that has transformative power.

At other points the bucolic settings, industrial sites, roads, and railways depicted by the camera do not gain meaning in themselves, but only serve as reminders of difference – and it becomes clear that absence is intimately connected with the human world. The absence of people from the creations of progress (shots from empty trains driving themselves, for example) is just as palpable as their visual absence in nature when we hear those opening footsteps. Twice this reminder of absence has to do with artists. First, the Soldier approaches a painter, who is shown at an easel facing an open landscape. The film cuts to a view over the painter's shoulder (an approximate point-of-view shot from the Soldier's perspective) to see that what he paints, a naturalistic country scene, does not correspond to the landscape we see before him. At another point the four travelers stop at the crest of a rise and look out at the green, rolling hills that stretch before them. A cut again places the viewer in a vantage point similar to that of the wanderers, followed by a cut to a close up of the charcoal sketch made by the Soldier's father in one of the film's early sequences. This montage allows the similarity of the sketch, shown earlier being made in a café, to the open landscape glimpsed a moment before to occur to the viewer

---

[12]This description is interestingly reminiscent of Handke's description of his critical project in his first (TV) film, *Chronik der laufenden Ereignisse* (1971; Chronicle of Ongoing Events), in which he finds that television distances images in order to make them familiar and empty rather than truly experienced anew: "Images are to be seen there that one feels one has seen before some place, but that also look strange and different..." (cited in Netenjakob 162).

immediately. These two moments strengthen the theme of art and its relation to the contemporary world, which seems to have banished all of the traditional sources of art: solitude, silence, quiet reflection, reverence.

The expression of this potentially transformative experience of those absences is art, and the film's first words bring the two together. Directly following the montage of images and sounds that open the film, Handke cuts to a panning shot of the Soldier crossing the street with his parents to sit in a café before bidding them farewell. The movement is from screen left to right, which is the direction of most of the film's handful of pans. In them, the camera almost invariably tracks figures as they move through space, and they tend to indicate that a new stage of the film is being reached. They (re-)introduce a forward-moving, contextualized temporality that will then be immediately suspended in the ensuing tale-telling. For example, after this trio crosses the street, the film cuts to them seated in the interior, where the mother addresses a long monologue to the son during which the men sit silent with eyes averted, the father working on his charcoal drawing and the son reading. She explains that there are different types of absence and that the son has always had a quality of being absent or leaving no mark. None of his school friends can remember him and neither could the soldiers she asked at his barracks. Even when present he was often absent as a child, just as he has been distant during the entire time spent with his parents: "There are absences that spread peace, and those that disturb: if I only knew which kind yours are, my child."[13] She worries that her son will become like her husband, who finds the world horrible and yet does nothing about it except to "shut himself into his absence, his art."

This explicit connection between absence and art is fused into place by the Father's silence throughout the episode, adding the notion of "silence" to the picture. Even after the Soldier responds to his Mother, thanking her for her "presence," the Father and his son

---

[13]In the German film treatment the terms are slightly different, expressing more forcefully a sense of uniting and dividing: "There are absences that unite and spread peace, and there are absences that make uneasy and divide. If only I could say to which kind your absences belong, dear child" (*A* 25-26). The reduction to "spreading peace" and "making uneasy" parallels closely Handke's sense of his own project as something that both beckons and threatens him.

take leave of one another, warmly but wordlessly. Coming very near the outset, this verbal conjoining of absence and art, and the further link to silence (the absence of [the Mother's] words) introduces the central themes of the film and is underscored by the camerawork. During the speech, the camera motionlessly frames all three characters with the Mother occupying most of center screen and the two men along the right edge of the image. Three sets of cuts give the audience a chance to see the Father's sketch-in-progress, the charcoal marks lightly drawn and then smudged into the outline of a hilly landscape which fills the screen, and then return to the view of all three figures.

Visually, *The Absence* is presented as a series of images, moments along the way, rather than as a continuous, flowing journey. A static camera predominates, and what motion occurs within individual shots is generated almost exclusively by the characters.[14] The effect, then, is one of stations: the viewer is presented with points along the journey that are given particular weight in two ways. First, events take place that turn ordinary shots into something loaded with meaning. For example, early in the film a high angle long shot through trees depicts four paths coming together in an overgrown meadow below a hill. After several seconds, the four main figures (introduced only individually to this point) begin to come into view on the different paths, transforming the site in the shot into the crossroads of meeting from myths and legends, representing the place where these travelers find their comrades and depart on their quest. Later on, another shot from a peak points down and across a hillside to a valley and a hill beyond. One after

---

[14]One notable exception is a pan moving left to right that breaks the trends of tracking the characters. It opens with a full shot from a middle distance of the four figures standing at the edge of a lake with their backs to the camera. After several seconds, the camera slowly pans left to discover a couple embracing only a few feet away from its position. In their discussion, Wenders notes his pleasant surprise at this shot while Handke hates it because it is "false" and does not fit with the film. He sees it only as a bad joke (one member of the kissing couple holds the penal code) and claims to have left it in only because the editor (the vastly experienced Peter Pryzgodda) insisted upon it (*A* 154). One might find here evidence that Handke is ultimately bent on evoking a notion of absence that is largely metaphorical and is not really concerned with film as a medium, whereas this shot challenges the viewer to think about absence in regard to the film world in a way unique within the context of this work.

the other the figures begin to come into the image at different depths, each entering screen left to walk out onto a subsequent finger of the ridge line. Their appearance suddenly restructures the visual field into a highly differentiated and more exactly known landscape on the basis of the insertion of human figures as points of reference, a landscape which by the same token looms larger than the quest they have undertaken.[15]

The second way in which stations become meaningful is through the stories told by those stopping there. For example, while only the Writer and his Wife have a level of intimacy at first, the Gambler and the Woman also have a history. In one of the film's many interludes in which personal stories are told, the viewers learn that she was presented as a case study for students in a psychology class that the Gambler had once attended. As a child she had often wandered aimlessly from her parents' house without apparent reason, a kind of sleepwalking in broad daylight. At times she had been gone for days, without eating or drinking, and in most cases she had been found at the end point of a rail or bus line. The officers who had found her treated her with care, for she was not "picked up" but rather carefully attended: "They understood nothing about my wandering and yet understood everything." In the lecture hall, the laughter that greeted the other "crazies" would die down at her entrance, and even the professor was silent. The Gambler replies that it was the "stillness of her beauty" that made her seem less like the next patient and more like "the first human." She responds that the tale she related furthered this reception: "As I told my story, I felt the silence become deeper. The listeners allowed themselves to be torn from their secure places.... They envied me in the end, wished my illness upon themselves." The Gambler understands, but remembers it differently: it was not the report of an illness that they had heard, "but the tale ... of a wholly unique expedition. An expedition that had far more to do with our inner life than any other expedition ever. No, I didn't envy you your wandering in the emptiness, I worshipped you." She responds that if he had thought her

---

[15]This process works in reverse as well, however. Tranquil scenery, often including our travelers at rest, will suddenly be interrupted by bicyclists racing through and crowding them on the path, or even motocross racers, who disrupt the visual and aural serenity.

illness a holy one, she has been cured of it, for the only place she wants to be is her apartment.

They exchange these thoughts seated under a tree by a pond, filmed in an idyllic two-shot with a breeze playing gently in the branches and on the water. Compositionally, this conversation is introduced through a shot from across the water showing two of their companions on a dock, then cuts to a close-up of the Gambler and then a reverse angle close-up of the Woman seated on the bank opposite the spot from which the previous view might be had. Each close-up lasts a few seconds, and after that the camera is placed at a medium distance from the pair looking out at the water. The extreme duration of the two-shot is broken only twice, once by a return to the opening shot of their companions getting up and leaving the dock, and later by a two-second cutaway to a tree's green leaves. It is evident that this sequence is relatively conventional in its technique, setting the scene and leaving the spectator in no doubt about the physical space in which the conversation takes place. While Handke avoids the illusionist convention of shot-reverse-shot editing to make the viewers feel part of the verbal exchange, nothing breaks the sense of being an intimate observer or detracts attention from the stories being told.[16] In fact, the Woman switches from French to German for her final lines, so that the initial (German-speaking) audience will understand the words of the narrative without even the visual disturbance of subtitles to distract them. Though not Hollywood-esque, the filming here is conventional in the sense that it posits a sense of presence and immediacy in regard to a diegetically rounded space in which an unbroken communion through memory unfolds. The convention here may come as much from the influence of Ozu as anyone else,[17] but rather than break the

---

[16]Alice Kuzniar borrows the concept of "suture," often associated in film theory with shot-reverse-shot editing, to approach Handke's literary work, claiming that "Handke's writing not only describes the gaze but enacts it" (204). A double movement is implied here that allows and subsequently negates the specularity of secondary identification (with characters) and primary identification (with the camera). The film under discussion here, however, while obviously conscious of visual representation, eschews any emphasis on suture – affirmative or subversive – throughout.

[17]The inserted image of the tree represents a so-called pillow-shot, a term developed in reference to the Japanese filmmaker Yasujiro Ozu, who is a clear influence on Handke. It has to do with shots of nature inserted in his work in a

anthropocentrism inherent in human narratives, the use of that set of presentations here serves to imply the presence of the humans even in their (visual) absence.

Much of the camerawork here remains consistent with the notion of "specular representation" that Rentschler set forth in regard to *The Left-Handed Woman* (170) and Gemünden and others have subsequently expanded upon. While Rentschler uses Adorno to understand this presentation of the real as a reflection of the "*bourgeois intérieur's*" combat against the outside world, Gemünden argues that since Handke does not share Adorno's distrust of popular media he still holds out the possibility that stylistic conventions, such as those used to film the conversation of the Gambler and Woman, remain potential vehicles of real experience (140-44). But in this picture a contradiction seems to arise: while slow, the film-making here is neither laconic nor monumental. It is sparing in its use of film language, but this only subordinates the cinematic to the spoken word, for the narration of cinema here disappears into a mere site for oral storytelling, and the spectator's experience is reduced to the sense of hearing a story that is like one that has been heard before. Furthermore, the words of the story themselves become "baroque" as they unavoidably seem to have immediate allegorical significance for the film as a whole. The child's illness seems directly parallel to the Writer's desire, in that both traits seem connected to an essential human drive, encumbered only by the context of coming of age in the modern world. Although her own expeditions left her bewildered and lost (she often became hysterical at coming to consciousness in completely unfamiliar surroundings), relating those stories to others had the effect of awakening in them the desirability of such expeditions, such searches. The yearning for the presence of silence, then, was created through the situation of oral storytelling and is reproduced in the present of the film in the space between the speaker, the listener, and the viewer. Having been cured in the modern world, she now steps out to try to get some of her illness back. This is an impossibility since the innocence of that illness has been lost, but, like the effect of the

---

manner that does nothing to further the plot or atmosphere. On Handke's relation to Ozu see Rentschler (172-74).

278 John E. Davidson

Writer's failure and disappearance, her disappointment leads to a re-awakened sense of what the absence of that fulfillment means.

There is an undeniably neo-romantic undertone to much of *The Absence* generated by a number of tropes. The two most striking are the artist's connection to alienation and (mental) illness, and the insistence upon the impossibility of art in the contemporary world stated in such a way as to maintain a continued projection of the aesthetic sphere. In this film, however, the aim is to use the cinema to recuperate the oral transmission of storytelling as an authentic experience of presence and absence – a long-standing concern in Handke's literature, but one impossible to attain in writing.[18] The much remarked emphasis on seeing, the gaze, and visuality in Handke's work overall is absent here. The lack of stress on the look both within and between frames noted in the conversation between the Soldier and his parents and in that of the Gambler and the Woman, attend all of the subsequent episodes during which the figures "tell one another (things)." Similar patterns hold when the Writer speaks almost liturgically of "silencio," when the Gambler speaks of how on this day's journey it was as if his mother went beside him, and when the soldier tells of his father the painter. Handke feels these to be the best moments: "I only wanted to say that these four are not 'isolated.' I don't see them as isolated, but rather that they open each other up by telling each other [stories]. There is no more beautiful communication than to tell one another stories" (*A* 167). One might say that the explicitly anti-psychological content of the Young Woman's story and of Handke's approach to the film itself ("no psychologizing ...") are targeted at dissolving the isolation inherent in individualized notions of the psyche in order to generate the possibility of real psychological communion. The vehicle for this in Handke's filmmaking is the oral story within a visual presentation that evokes presence in a manner that does not require identical experience.

In Handke's conception this communication is not limited to the world of the characters: "The pictures don't stand for themselves. The most important thing is the way they tell each other('s) stories" (*A* 150). There is a sense in which the film itself is meant to tell a

---

[18]See, for example, the last passages of *Die Wiederholung* (1986; *Repetition*, 1988).

history of images that is both familiar and yet strange, communal and yet particular, present and yet absent. The argument presented here has been that this twofold projection of "telling each other" does not, and cannot, have a harmonic cohesion within the film. As a director, Handke's manner of presenting the communal narration between people within the film and to the audience watching the screen reduces the cinematic aspects of narration to narrative, in that the images are ultimately subordinated to their function as places where things happen. This is a reduction that causes words and symbols to clearly overshadow sounds and images; however, *The Absence* ends with two sequences which potentially tell a different story by recalling and recasting what has come before.

The final festival of absence is dominated by the Wife's monologue, delivered as a kind of eulogy for the Writer that hardly immortalizes him as a saint. In its duration it evokes the speech of the Soldier's Mother at the beginning, and in content it reminds the viewer of the Young Woman's uncomplimentary lines in the cave. But these comments are filmed differently, in that they are presented in a medium close-up with the Wife addressing the camera directly, with the shore and ocean visible behind her torso. She speaks in the third person, remembering how he claimed to want to find a path for both of them but really wanted to go alone; how he yearned for "adventures of silence" while she yearned for "those of tumult"; how he felt that only his dream was the real one. But in the midst of these memories she remembers other things, moments that were made possible by the Old Man despite himself, like the experience of the light on an evening after a rain. Then, seemingly overcome with mirth, she switches to the second person: "You Idiot! What could I have become without you: physicist, ballerina, deep sea diver...." As she ends her lines she closes her eyes and the sound of helicopters, which has been building steadily for half of her monologue, grows to an excessive level. Here, one could argue, the difference between the exploits of silence and noise is to be made palpable, but the Wife in this moment of remembering and telling – even in remembering and telling all that was wrong in their life together – has now finally begun to share the Writer's

adventure.[19] Similarly, the spectators have become part of the
narration in a manner different than anything felt to this point in the
film: we take the place of the Writer addressed in apostrophe and
our position in this situation of "telling each other" makes us the
idiots who both prevent her full becoming and share her sense of
unfulfilled desire.

The final shots of *The Absence* similarly recall and recast the
opening, this time changing the way the images tell each other
things. After a glimpse of a man playing with a boy on his back
(who is learning what verbs go with what nouns) and another of a
child standing in the water by a pier counting for hide-and-seek
(that prototypical game of searching for people who are there and
not there), a shot from a human perspective looks straight down on
a pair of footprints in the sand filled with water. Absence is evoked
from every angle here. Nothing has established a specific point-of-
view referent for this perspective, nor have we seen a character who
could have left these marks. They are close enough to be "ours," yet
"we" have not made them. They are filled with water, but we see no
evidence of the surf that has done so. In fact, we see no trace of
motion beyond a faint flutter from the breeze on the surface of the
water. In addition to these questions about what is lacking in our
ability to place this image, something else haunts the viewer here
with its absence: the sounds of running water and running feet from
the film's opening minutes. This final image and its corresponding
impossibilities, lasting just a few quick seconds before the screen
goes to black and the credits roll, may in the right framework
catalyze a retracing of the viewer's sojourn through the film and,
perhaps, initiate a process in which "later these images could really
be seen afresh." It is there, absent the film, that the moment of
psychological reflection begins.

Handke's style as a director as exemplified in this film uses this
medium to liberate oral storytelling, which becomes a site of com-

---

[19]As if to make this unmistakable, the sequence immediately following her
monologue cuts to a table of three guests and continues with the sounds of war
machines, which slowly give way to a waiter telling them to get out, disappear,
that the war is coming, and "I know I am a dead man." If the film had been
made in English, one would be tempted to see a return to the notion of the
doomed or trapped status of waiters – those who wait – in general, which
formed the point of departure for the characters at the outset of the film.

munion in and with the movie. Despite *The Absence*'s similarity to the station drama in its presentation, it is not really concerned with morality in the conventional sense; rather, it pursues the place of art in the modern world. Film offers a particularly useful vehicle for that concern, although the art of the cinema itself takes a backseat to the word often enough. Sought-after are myths with explanatory powers, journeys designed to find home, discoveries to satisfy desires, and, hence, what is unattainable in this life: stillness. In some ways the drive for such journeying remains unchanged from its roots in antiquity that the Writer quotes and transcribes. In other ways, it is a complete impossibility in the modern world, which takes the existential quandary of the destruction of silence through our expression of desire for it and makes it physical. For Handke, much like his Writer, the modern world is composed of noise-makers, and neither a pilgrim's journey nor any attempt to inscribe the noisemakers' by-products in the explanatory power of myth is a match for them. But film direction offers him one advantage over his Writer, and perhaps over Handke the author. He does not have to depict the pursuit of his personal desire as an epic task in this film nor have it unmasked as delusion; he can remain at a distance throughout. In a sense, it is not until the final picture fades that Handke's real cinematic project begins, at which point the viewer and the memories of those images "tell one another" again, a narration that is indeed slow, laconic, and monumental.

Works Cited

Arijon, Daniel. *Grammar of the Film Language*. Hollywood: Silman-James Press, 1976.

Davidson, John E. "'Against Rushing through Places that Ought to be Dwelt in': Kracauer, Wenders, and the post-Turnerian Impulse." *Studies in European Cinema* 1 (2004) 117-28.

Elsaesser, Thomas. *Der neue deutsche Film. Von den Anfängen bis zu den neunziger Jahren*. Munich: Heyne, 1994.

–. *New German Cinema: A History*. New Brunswick: Routledge, 1989.

Gemünden, Gerd. *Framed Visions: Popular Culture, Americanization, and the Contemporary German and Austrian Imagination.* Ann Arbor: U of Michigan P, 1998.

Hake, Sabine. *German National Cinema.* London, New York: Routledge, 2003.

Jacobsen, Wolfgang, Anton Kaes, and Hans Helmut Prinzler, ed. *Geschichte des deutschen Films.* Stuttgart: Metzler, 1993.

Kuzniar, Alice. "Suture in/Suturing Literature and Film." *Intertextuality: German Literature and Visual Art from the Renaissance to the Twentieth Century.* Ed. Ingeborg Hoesterey and Ulrich Weisstein. Columbia, SC: Camden House, 1993. 201-17.

McCormick, Richard. *The Politics of the Self: Feminism and the Postmodern In West German Literature and Film.* Princeton: Princeton UP, 1991.

Netenjakob, Egon. *TV-Filmlexikon. Regisseure, Autoren, Dramaturgen 1952-92.* Frankfurt am Main: Fischer, 1994.

Parry, Christopher. *Peter Handke's Landscapes of Discourse.* Riverside: Ariadne, 2003.

Pflaum, Hans Günther, and Hans Helmut Prinzler. *Cinema in the Federal Republic of Germany.* Bonn: InterNationes, 1993.

Rentschler, Eric. *West German Film in the Course of Time: Reflections on the Twenty Years since Oberhausen.* Bedford Hills: Redgrave, 1984.

Text as Life/Life as Text:
Handke's Non-Fiction

Thomas F. Barry

IN ADDITION TO HIS CONSIDERABLE output in all fiction genres including cinematic writing and numerous literary translations, Handke has also produced a number of non-fiction volumes, specifically various essays and essay collections, four journal compilations, numerous published interviews, and a memoir of his mother who committed suicide in November 1971. He has also published several books of travel writings, namely on trips to Yugoslavia and to various other countries. His non-fiction includes the collection of twenty-five essays and book and film reviews entitled *Ich bin ein Bewohner des Elfenbeinturms* (1972; I am an Inhabitant of the Ivory Tower) and another collection of essays and poetry called *Als das Wünschen noch geholfen hat* (1974; When Wishing Still Helped). He has further published two collection of speeches and brief reviews of books, paintings, and films entitled *Langsam im Schatten. Gesammelte Verzettelungen 1980-1992* (1992; Slowly in the Shadow. Collected Notes 1980-1992) and *Mündliches und Schriftliches. Zu Büchern, Bildern und Filmen* (2002; Oral and Written. On Books, Paintings and Films). He has also produced a series of journals *Das Gewicht der Welt* (1977; *The Weight of the World*, 1979), *Die Geschichte des Bleistifts* (1982; The Pencil's Story), *Phantasien der Wiederholung* (1983; Phantasies of Repetition), and *Am Felsfenster morgens* (1988; Mornings at the Natural Arch).

These texts have constituted a creative continuation of the innovative thematic and stylistic project of his fictional writings. The formal and critical thrust of Handke's early work is based on the difference between objective reality (what is real outside consciousness) and phenomenological reality (what is experienced by consciousness as being real) (Mixner 149). The goal of his early writings has been to demonstrate the ways in which language formulates – in both positive and negative ways – the individual's experience of reality; or, in a Nietzschean sense, to deconstruct what are held to be truths made from a discourse or language that has become confused with objective reality. He explores both the fictional realities presented in literary texts and the ideological texts perceived as realities in (real-life) social, cultural, and political contexts.

The psychological and autobiographical impetus of his writings has consistently underpinned these formal themes of language and perception from the beginning of his career. It has revolved around personal issues of existential orientation: questions of psychological trauma, loss, and healing, of self-estrangement and transcendence, and of childhood memories and the act of remembering (especially in narrative) as a healing repetition and revision of the past. The assertion that Handke's early works revolve around "the psyche and its inability to come to terms with its existential context" (Perram 30) applies to all of this writer's creative works.[1]

Handke's efforts towards the existential orientation of consciousness through aesthetic acts of imaginative self-determination have been present in his texts since the beginning of his career. But they have emerged, most clearly in writings since the mid-1970s such as *The Weight of the World* and the *Langsame Heimkehr* tetralogy (1979-81; *Slow Homecoming*, 1985; 1996), as being central to his creative project. These efforts involve what might be called the anagogic use of language and the activity of narration as a quasi-spiritualized act which (re)connects the self to the world in a mystical vision of totality.[2] Coury suggests that the narrative

---

[1]Linstead's characterization of Handke's themes also provides an excellent summary of the modernist existential concerns that inform his writing: "the split between the self and the world, the consequent feelings of dislocation, disorientation and alienation of the individual, the fall back into the self as the only source of anything approaching reliable information about the world, the sense of no 'connection,' of no overall structure of coherence which is absolute or even generally valid, the mistrust of language both as a vehicle of experience and expression" (193).

[2]The anagogic refers to the spiritualized or mystical use of words and has its roots in Biblical hermeneutics (Old Testament writings interpreted as foreshadowings of New Testament texts). It also has a meaning in psychoanalysis in which it indicates the strivings of the psyche towards progressive states of awareness. Handke's supposed turn in the mid-seventies from more formal/experimental concerns with language/reality to a quasi-mystical experience of language/reality is really an evolution of the themes and concerns of his earlier

impetus in his more recent works seeks "to establish human contact and a sense of community" (64). Storytelling establishes for him a sense of "world harmony" (Schlueter 176). Handke's works of the New Subjectivity during the seventies portray "a state of mystical union and peaceful existence freed from societal functionality and prejudice" (DeMeritt 141), a "utopian union" that "is bonded by an acute awareness of others and of oneself based upon the feeling of shared existence" (DeMeritt 151-52). He simultaneously reflects, at times ironically and self-critically, upon the linguistic conditions of the creation of his writing and his spiritual-existential quest. The experience of objective reality presented in Handke's writings is a mediated one, a reality of subjective experience that is both preserved in and transcended through language in what can be described as a creative and therapeutic dialectic of life and (literary) text.

Handke's awareness of this mediated existence suggests the conviction that objective reality exists only in the eternal present, the *nunc stans*, and that the perceived modalities of past and future are essentially imaginative linguistic constructions. This leads to the insight that the psyche is itself a construct of language. His literary

---

work. Paul Ricouer once reportedly remarked at a Harvard Divinity School colloquium that the deconstructive enterprise is fundamentally a "religious" one (Klein 51), a questioning of and search for the divine *logos* as it were. While the Latin origins of the word "religion" are unclear, some sources indicate the verb *religare*, to tie or join together (the mystical union of the individual soul with the divinity). Others suggest *relegere*, to read a text over again. Both meanings would seem to resonate in the context of Handke's work. Elsewhere I have referred to the project of Handke's writings as an "existential aestheticism," where aesthetic experience provides a mode of transcendence for the estranged self in acts of imaginative self-determination (Barry, "Sehnsucht"). This essentially spiritual project involves to a great extent the revitalization of (aesthetic) language, restoring to metaphor its sensuous and mystical power to reconnect "the world of writing" to "the world of things that a person can touch" (*Zw* 183), to realign consciousness with the world and to thereby transcend, at least for a moment, its alienation from that world of things. The meanings of the postwar philosophy called existentialism are reviewed in the first chapter of Cooper's book. The word 'ex-istence,' as used in Heidegger, is etymologically related to the mystical 'ecstasy' or transcendence that hovers beyond Handke's texts. Existential questioning and the spiritual impulse are not opposites but closely related activities. For a discussion of Handke and Heidegger, see the essay by Kolleritsch. The monograph by Strasser also discusses Handke in the context of Heideggerian philosophy.

efforts have been accompanied by a psychological attitude that the author has called an "illumination of slowness," a meditative stance of practiced attentiveness to the external world and his linguistic experience and poetic transformation of it: "When I was 36 years old, I had the illumination of slowness. Slowness has been since this time a principle for my life and my writing.... Perhaps instead of slowness one could speak more exactly of a deliberateness. Never, never become fast, never suggest, always keep a distance to things and be cautious."[3] The great achievement of Handke's writing is this singular linking of poststructuralist issues of language, perception, and ideology with personal existential and spiritual themes, issues that lie at the interstices of art and religion. Virtually all of Handke criticism – when not attacking the writer personally – has focused either on such formal issues of language and perception or on psychobiographical and existential themes. There has also been an ongoing debate on the question of whether the author is to be classified as a modernist, a postmodernist, or even, in the wake of his writings on Yugoslavia, as a conservative neo-romantic and neo-fascist.

*

The early non-fiction collection *Ich bin ein Bewohner des Elfen-beinturms* is essential as it contains several essays from the mid-sixties in which Handke, in the wake of his controversial speech at Princeton in April 1966, seeks to define his views of writing and literature: "Ich bin ein Bewohner des Elfenbeiturms" (1967; I am an Inhabitant of the Ivory Tower), "Zur Tagung der Gruppe 47 in den USA" (1966; On the Group 47 Meeting in the USA), and "Die Literatur ist romantisch" (1966; Literature is Romantic). The intellectual spirit behind many of these pieces owes much to Roland Barthes, especially the ideological criticism present in his essays on popular culture in *Mythologies*.[4] The title of the collection, express-

---

[3]The quote is taken from the rear cover of the essay collection edited by Fuchs and Melzer. The ellipsis is mine. The author figure in *Nachmittag eines Schriftstellers* (1987; *The Afternoon of a Writer*, 1989) also mentions this enlightenment: "You know of course slowness is the only illumination I have ever had" (*AW* 53).

[4]Handke's early texts, along with his initial literary theories in general, have been discussed extensively in the secondary literature in terms of one or more of the following critical rubrics: metafiction, Barthes and Robbe-Grillet, Rus-

ly rejecting any notion of a politically engaged literature, stands as a deliberate provocation to the social activism of many writers and critics in the late 1960s. The existential and introspective nature of his enterprise has earned Handke the ire of politically engaged critics like Manfred Durzak, who proclaimed Handke to be a neurotic narcissist with the critical implication that his literary work is trivial.[5] The often highly negative reception Handke's work has received in the German-language critical establishment suggests both the politicized climate of literary criticism and a source of the author's hostile stance to the media. The reception of his translated writings in the United States has been mostly positive.

The first section of the *Elfenbeinturm* collection contains only one text (composed in 1967) with the simple title "1957." It presents the reflections of the then twenty-five-year-old Handke upon his worldview at the age of fifteen when he was a student in the Catholic seminary Marianum near Klagenfurt (from 1954-1959). The adolescent student was known to escape to an unused tower of the seminary (hence the title of Handke's essay collection) where he

---

sian Formalism and French structuralism, the *nouveau roman*, Derrida, post-structuralism, and postmodernism. DeMeritt stresses Handke's radical assertion of his subjectivity and his rejection of any literature of social or political commitment (142-47). Perram asserts that Handke's poetics at this time grew out of his defense against the numerous and highly critical attacks on his first two novels (248).

[5]Durzak's accusation (*Narziß* 26-31, et passim) is meant to be understood in terms of secondary narcissism, a self-absorbed isolation from the world. The critic's diagnosis is perhaps true when one views Handke in terms of the social history of western cultures, that is, the development of European bourgeois subjectivity in the late twentieth century. Yet it is mean-spirited and more reflective of Durzak's ideological rejection of any literature that deals with psychological, existential, and spiritual themes as well as an obvious personal antipathy towards Handke evident in their interviews. Durzak also seems to miss the alternative and radical political viewpoint that any true social revolution must begin from within the individual. The Freudian notion of primary narcissism, however, the "oceanic feeling" of the merging of the self with the universe/mother, may also be appropriate to understanding in psychological terms the narcissism and the virtually mystical elements in Handke's more recent writings. The reader is referred to Marcuse's discussion of images of Orpheus and Narcissus in his *Eros and Civilization* (144-56) and to Alcorn's work on narcissism and literature. For a brief discussion of narcissism in Handke, see Thornton (12-14).

would read, daydream, and work on his writing. This first essay in the collection is significant in that it illuminates some of the early psychological and existential dimensions of Handke's writings but has received scant attention in the secondary literature.[6]

The final subsection of this piece, "Der Ernst des Lebens" (The Seriousness of Life), begins with the sentence: "I was often ashamed of myself" (*BE* 15). The theme of shame and the existential-psychological estrangement from self and others that it entails has remained a major, if not the most important, issue throughout Handke's work and is a theme which links him closely to the writings of Kafka. The shamed self and the adult narcissistic personality structure that often accompanies it is most certainly a result of the traumatic childhood Handke experienced growing up in a dysfunctional family in which alcoholism and physical abuse occurred with some frequency. The adult narcissistic personality suffers from severely damaged self-esteem and a feeling of being unheard or voiceless in the world and hence becomes obsessed with self and self-assertion. The theme of a kind of autistic speechlessness in Handke's life and texts is directly related to his childhood trauma and to his vocation as a writer and the conviction that it is only in the voice found in the therapy of writing that he finds and grounds himself.[7]

Towards the end of this section, Handke discusses shame and his liberation from it in poststructuralist terms, that is, in terms of the oppressive regulations of the sheltered seminary life. He makes a statement which stands as a remarkably terse and accurate description of both the critical and psychological project of his writing career as an existential dialectic of life and text: "The apparently EXTERNAL WORLD in which I lived, the seminary, was actually an INTERNAL one, an INTERNAL WORLD applied externally, and my internal world was the only way to reach the EXTERNAL WORLD" (*BE* 16). In hindsight, the young Handke reaches here his (post-

---

[6]One exception is the article by Michael Springer, who links Handke's essay to Austrian turn-of-the-century preoccupations with adolescence and to Musil and Kafka.

[7]In his interview with Gamper, Handke speaks of such states as a kind of autism and identifies them as the source for his impulse to narrate as a means to transcend this experience of estrangement and absolute otherness (*Zw* 181 *et passim*).

structuralist informed) insight that the world of the Catholic seminary, which declared all of his natural impulses to be unnatural and
shameful and which presented itself as natural and a matter of fact,
was in truth itself only a text. It was an elaborate construct of
consciousness, an ideological formulation or fiction, not of natural
or divine design, as the priests – like the many father figures who
hover like ghosts in his texts – would argue, but of solely human
invention.[8] Handke echoes here the fundamental poststructuralist
assertion found in the preface to Barthes' *Mythologies* (a text with
which he was well familiar), namely that much of what passes today
for reality, in all its multifaceted political, social, and cultural
dimensions, is based upon a logocentric confusion of history and
nature, of signifier and signified. In the author's existential dialectic, his own inner world became his only alternative mode of access
or escape to any possibly 'real' world that might serve as an orientation to his estranged and shamed consciousness. [9]

The critical emphasis of "1957" is both on the power of ideological texts to distort and pervert reality and on the healing power
of texts, the alterity of the experience of literature, the vision of
another possible kind of existence. Handke's vision of his project is
not new by any means; the power of literature (and art) to make us
see ourselves and the world in a new light is a traditional, even
conventional view. The productive otherness of the experience of
literature in acts of reading and writing is, as Handke phrased it in
his acceptance speech for the Büchner Prize, "Die Geborgenheit
unter der Schädeldecke" (The Sanctuary Beneath the Cranium), in
1973, "nothing other than poetic thinking that is all about hope, that
allows the world to begin anew again and again whenever I, in my
obstinacy, have already considered it predetermined, and it is also
the basis of the self-awareness with which I write" (*Wü* 80). The
"therapeutic effect" (Perram 42) in Handke's personal view of
literature is unquestionable. Literature is a political act of both
ideological and psychological liberation, escapist and utopian in the

---

[8]Handke's charge of "descriptive impotence" ("Tagung" 29) leveled at the
patriarchs of post-war German literature during the 1966 Group 47 meeting, is
not without its intentional (and unintentional) Oedipal associations.

[9]His early reading of literary texts was essential to Handke, especially those
forbidden to the seminary students, such as Graham Greene. Reading in his
ivory tower was a revolutionary act for him.

best sense of these terms and it is, above all, healthful (in the positive sense of Nietzsche's assertion that life is only justified, legitimized, and made ultimately bearable as an aesthetic illusion). In *Langsame Heimkehr* (1979; *The Long Way Around*, 1985), Sorger proclaims in Zarathustra-like fashion the aesthetic illusion of the union of life and text, consciousness and world to be a therapeutic distortion of reality: "'Falsification!' But this idea was no longer an accusation; rather, it was a salutary idea: he, Sorger, would write the Gospel of Falsification; and he triumphed in the thought of being a falsifier among falsifiers" (*LWA* 130). The "Gospel" Sorger will write becomes eventually *Die Lehre der Sainte-Victoire* (1980; *The Lesson of Mont Sainte-Victoire*, 1985) and Cézanne's teaching of 'realization,' the transformation of mute and indifferent reality into the liberated domain of human consciousness through the magic of art.

It must be mentioned, however, that there is a dimension of Handke's dialectic of life and text that guarantees its own failure, an underlying tension that would seem to undermine his texts and condemn them to endless repetition because the magic of the metaphor is ephemeral. The existential transcendence of estrangement is a short-lived occurrence and must be repeated – with all due echoes of Kierkegaard here – moment by moment. In a sense, one might argue that Handke remains addicted to literary experience, its mystical-literary transformations of mute reality, and is constantly in need of the 'fix' that reading and writing supplies. For Handke, the cultivation of alienation has reached the level of an "aesthetic condition" (Thornton 29). Neurosis has been transformed, as it has with numerous artists, into an art form, a life style.[10] His project as writer seems to be governed by an imperative of narration, a tactic in order to ward off the silence and the speechlessness that threaten him and ultimately the death that they imply. It is an issue, however, of which Handke is well aware and which makes up both the ironic and the spiritual-existential dimensions and tensions of all his writing. The invocation of totality that permeates his texts is for him a process of radical immanence, a joyful construct of the imagination and an ecstatic celebration of subjectivity in the acts of reading and

---

[10]In *The Weight of the World*, Handke notes that he habitually lacks a sense of himself and that his personal difficulties or "calamities" are (presumably) something he needs in order to feel that he exists (*WW* 148).

writing, the magic of metaphor. Perhaps more than any other writer of his generation (and much to the anger of those critics of an engaged and politically correct literature), Handke has made a radical vision and assertion of human subjectivity, both private and public, in all its existential, literary-linguistic, social, and political implications, a central theme of his writings. He seeks to make the narcissistic exploration of his own subjectivity paradoxically into an objective statement that claims a universality, as he does in his journal writing (Wagner 231). The sphere of private, autobiographical writing is, in Handke's recent texts, pushed to its limits in such a way that it becomes a public document of everyone's subjectivity.

The important essay "Ich bin ein Bewohner des Elfenbeinturms" also takes up the themes of the shamed childhood self and the healing and salutary effects of literature on a debilitated sense of self-esteem. Handke discusses his experience of himself in terms that suggest a psychologically dissociated sense of identity, the self as being monstrously unique and somehow diseased:

> Without literature this self-consciousness, so to speak, would have overcome me. It was something horrible, shaming, obscene; natural processes appeared to me as some kind of intellectual confusion, as a disgrace, as a cause for shame because I seemed to be alone with it. It was literature that first created my awareness of this self-consciousness; it enlightened me in that it showed me that I was not a unique case that others went through similar experiences. (*BE* 19)

The experience of the shamed self as being horribly and utterly unique, as an obscene monstrosity, is central to numerous Handke texts and forms the starting point for the existential quest of many of his fictional characters. Like Kafka, he manifests a strong sense of physical self-awareness, a dissociated body ego. In *Die Angst des Tormanns beim Elfmeter* (1970; *The Goalie's Anxiety at the Penalty Kick*, 1972), the former soccer goalie Josef Bloch undergoes a schizophrenic breakdown and during one of his more extreme episodes, he perceives himself in grotesquely physical terms similar to those Handke uses to talk about himself:

> For a moment, it seemed as if he had fallen out of himself.... A cancer. He became aware of himself as if he had suddenly degenerated.... He thought he was touching himself unpleasantly but realized that his awareness of himself was so intense that

he felt it like a sense of touch all over his body; as though his
consciousness, as though his thoughts, had become palpable,
aggressive, abusive toward himself.... Nauseatingly his insides
turned out; not alien, only repulsively different. It had been a
jolt, and with one jolt he had become unnatural, had been torn
out of context. He lay there, as impossible as he was real; no
comparisons now. His awareness of himself was so strong that
he was scared to death. (*GA* 80-81)[11]

The narrative *Stunde der wahren Empfindung* (1975; *A Moment of
True Feeling*, 1977) deals with a similar psychological crisis in the
character of Gregor Keuschnig. At the beginning of his breakdown,
he is depicted in images that recall both Bloch in *The Goalie's
Anxiety*, the mother in *Wunschloses Unglück* (1972; *A Sorrow
Beyond Dreams*, 1976) and the "Elfenbeinturm" essay. Keuschnig
sees himself as a bizarre other, as "something BLOODCURDLINGLY
strange, yet known to all – a creature exhibited in a nest and
mortally ashamed, IMMORTALLY DISGRACED, washed out of the
matrix in mid-gestation, and now for all time a monstrous,
unfinished bag of skin, a freak of nature, a MONSTROSITY, that
people would point at" (*M* 78). The perception of the self as shame-
fully and uniquely other – a pervasive sense of unreality often initiated by the experience of a jolt or shock to consciousness – implies
a moment of speechlessness. It is a state of being – the author's self-
proclaimed "autism" (*Zw* 181 *et passim*) – which represents the
absolute nadir of existence for the figures in Handke's texts: silence
is equated with death.[12] Here the individual transcends all linguistic
formulations. There are literally no words that can describe this
monstrous consciousness or establish its connection to external
reality; the self becomes formless and virtually paralyzed, unique.[13]
In his novel *Mein Jahr in der Niemandsbucht* (1994; *My Year in the
No-Man's-Bay*, 1998) he describes this state (with appropriate refer-

---

[11]Similar imagery recurs in *A Sorrow Beyond Dreams* in the description of the
mother: "It was a torment to see how shamelessly she had turned herself inside
out; everything about her was dislocated, split, open, inflamed, a tangle of
entrails" (*SBD 52*).

[12]Michaelis suggests that death is a central theme in Handke and links him to
the Austrian tradition of melancholic speculation on ephemerality (58).

[13]The parallels to Kafka's characters of Joseph K. in *Der Process* (1935; *The
Trial*, 1968) and Gregor Samsa in *Die Verwandlung* (1915; *The Metamorphosis*, 1972) are again playfully acknowledged by Handke in his character names.
Handke, as notations in his journals indicate, is an avid reader of Kafka. The
texts of both writers have their existential source point in the experience of the
shamed self.

ence to Kafka) in the first few sentences about the lawyer who experiences a breakdown and abandons his profession:

> There was one time in my life when I experienced metamorpho-
> sis. Up to that point, it had only been a word to me, and when it
> began, not gradually but abruptly, I thought at first it meant the
> end of me. It seemed to be a death sentence. Suddenly the place
> where I had been was occupied not by a human being but by
> some kind of scum, for which, unlike in the well-known gro-
> tesque tale from old Prague, not even an escape into images,
> however terrifying, was possible. This metamorphosis came
> over me without a single image, in the form of sheer gagging.
> (*MY* 3)

The inability to find even a single image through which he might orient himself to some kind of objective reality leaves the self adrift in a vacuum of absolute nothingness.

The experience of the dislocated and shamed self prompts the author to generate metaphor/sign (at the most simple level in characters such as Bloch and Keuschnig) and to compose his own narrative texts of remembering as a poetic/textual relocation of the self, as a bridge back to a sense of community, of a connectedness with others and the outside world. Reading Kleist, Flaubert, Dostoyevsky, Kafka, Faulkner, and Robbe-Grillet fundamentally changed his awareness of himself and thereby of the world: "Since the time that I recognized that I had been able to change myself through literature, that literature had made me a different person, I expect of literature again and again a new possibility to change myself because I do not regard myself as having been finalized" (*BE* 20).

Criticism that in his early views on the role of literature in society Handke retreats to an ivory tower formalism that is highly subjective and focused on abstract theories of language devoid of social relevance, misses the explicit element of ideological criticism that is present in this essay: "The reality of literature made me attentive to and critical of actual reality. It enlightened me about myself and about that which was happening around me" (*BE* 19). From this individual, existential experience with reading in the privacy of his ivory tower, Handke makes the leap to a critique of ideology in the public domain with this often quoted sentence: "I expect of literature a shattering of all images of the world that make it seem finalized" (*BE* 20). The experience of reading literature – the imagination – is the destroyer of the hegemony that is and supports all ideologies, be they social, political, racial, religious, gender-based, or even aesthetic. Here he takes up his attack – begun at the Group 47 meeting – of the "very trivial realism" (*BE* 21) he sees in the practice of most contemporary fiction writers and presents an implicit defense of his own early works. He makes the radical assertion that plots or stories – as in *Die Hornissen* (1966; The Hornets) – are unnecessary: "Above all, it seems to me that the progress of literature consists of the gradual removal of all fictions" (*BE* 24). The rejection of traditional plot and narrative techniques is a stance that Handke later revaluates. The idea of storytelling is reformulated, becoming the narrative ideal of 'script' and 'myth' in his later writings.[14]

Another important essay from the collection is Handke's explanation of his behavior during the 1966 Group 47 meeting, "Zur Tagung der Gruppe 47 in den USA." His often criticized charge of "impotent description" leveled at some of the texts that were read was directed against both their authors' uncritical and naïve use of words and the then popular demand that all creative writing be committed to depicting, in some form, social change.[15] Words, in Handke's estimation, are not objective reality but linguistic representations or signs; they are not windows that look out onto the world (a notion put forth by Jean-Paul Sartre) but are capable of distorting, sometimes for political or ideological reasons, the reality that is described. The medium for Handke is the message. The form of a work of literature is also its content and this is not only an aesthetic issue but also a moral (and political) one: "It occurred to me during this meeting that formal questions are actually moral questions" (*BE* 29). Similar points concerning the nature of writing and social commitment are made in the essay "Die Literatur ist romantisch." He disparages Sartre's idea of socially engaged writing as being foolish and asserts that literary texts by definition never contain objective statements about the world; they are essentially unrealistic and romantic. The early essays are programmatic statements of Handke's poetics at the onset of his career.

---

[14]The rehabilitation of traditional narration, stories with more or less traditional plots, is examined by Coury.

[15]Handke's behavior at the meeting was considered by many to be a ploy to gain media attention. Durzak, for example, considers his actions in retrospect to be an "extremely effective publicity campaign" (*Roman* 315).

*

The Weight of the World, which originally was to be titled
"Phantasy of Purposelessness" (Marquardt 287), is the first of four
journals, which Handke has published thus far. It covers the period
from November 1975 to March 1977 when he was residing, for the
most part, in the environs of Paris.[16] The mid-1970s when he began
his practice of daily journal writing were a time of crisis in his
personal life and, as he attests in *My Year in the No-Man's-Bay*, the
occasion for a profound inner transformation (*MY* 5). Handke's
journal entries are not long or detailed commentaries on daily experience or creative projects as one expects from the more traditional journal or diary of a writer. They are rather extremely brief,
indeed elliptical, poetic, and fragmentary, notations from a variety
of sources. There are numerous comments on seemingly inconsequential events and objects observed in daily life – "Some policemen are blocking the way, but pretending not to know it; they stare
straight ahead, but if anyone approaches, they frighten him away by
tapping their holsters" (*WW* 3) – as well as random thoughts and
philosophical reflections: "To look up at the sky and the drifting
clouds and think: No, I will never commit suicide!" (*WW* 8) and
"Fear of death: you lose all feeling for the things you see, because
your sense of humor is gone" (*WW* 58). There are notes concerning
remembered dreams or dream images: "Dream sounds: 'as if the
house were full of thawing June bugs'" (*WW* 3). There are also his
reading notes, for example, on Kafka (*WW* 64-65), Heidegger (*WW*
131), Hesse (*WW* 99-100), and Novalis (*WW* 138), as well as ideas
for current or future works of fiction: "A beautiful, awkward
woman (a character for a play)" (*WW* 10) and "A woman, strong in
her solitude" (*WW* 11), thoughts that would later be voiced in the

---

[16]*Die Geschichte des Bleistifts* covers 1976 to 1980, *Phantasien der Wiederholung* reports on the years from 1981 to 1982, and *Am Felsfenster morgens*
covers the period from 1982 to 1987. Hage finds *Die Geschichte des Bleistifts*
to be one of the most significant German publications of the 1980s with its
intense focus on the nature of reading and writing (412). Greiner-Kemptner
discusses the first three of Handke's journals and reads them as a postmodern
revitalization of the conventions of the traditional aphoristic form. The entries
strive for a mythic and intersubjective vision of (Homerian) totality of the
"individual and cosmos" (48).

novel *Die linkshändige Frau* (1976; *The Left-Handed Woman*, 1978). The actual notebook entries were revised and edited for publication. These diaries offer some understanding of the author's thought processes, especially as they apply to fictional works written during the same time as the individual journal and to the processes of creative writing in general.[17] Other important themes in the notes are anxiety and panic states, feelings of unreality, and observations on being alone versus being with others.

The critical commentary on Handke's first journal has been varied. It has been categorized, both negatively and positively, as an example of the German new subjective literature of the 1970s and, as such, a clear rejection of the socially committed literature of the 1960s. The journal constitutes an extended exploration, at times rather private and intimate, of the author's unique poetic sensibility: in the best sense of this word, his vigorous inner life and his dynamic experience of the world around him. Bartmann indicates that the word "feeling" occurs some 143 times in the notations ("Gewicht" 36) and terms this first journal "a seismography of feelings in moments" ("Gewicht" 38). Mommsen regards *The Weight of the World* as having great personal importance for the writer in that it chronicles his existential crises and obsessions while at the same time it gives him the means by which he might overcome them through his note-taking (244). König sees it as a deliberate violation of the diary tradition in its abandonment of all context and continuity. Hammer examines the work as a radical alteration of the (traditional) relationship between reader and author, an experiment in hermeneutics, which prompts a revision of the role of reading/writing and the literary text in a postmodern context.

Marschall looks at Handke's first journal as having thematic parallels to Rainer Maria Rilke's Parisian diary novel *Die Aufzeichnungen des Malte Laurids Brigge* (1910; *The Notebooks of Malte Laurids Brigge*, 1972) and to his poetry (especially the "thing poems" of 1907). Both writers suffer from an irresolvable existential estrangement between self and world (Marschall 91) and they

---

[17]*Die Geschichte des Bleistifts*, for example, was composed when Handke was writing his *Slow Homecoming* tetralogy and *The Left-Handed Woman. Am Felsfenster morgens* was written during the creation of several fiction works: *Der Chinese des Schmerzes* (1983; *Across*, 1986), *Repetition, The Afternoon of a Writer* and *Die Abwesenheit* (1987; *Absence*, 1990).

seek the same aesthetic goal: the phenomenological realization of the true essence of things (Marschall 97). Jurgensen looks at *Weight* as a chronicle of observations made by a consciousness that seeks to formalize itself in language in order to transcend its existential anxiety and alienation from others (179). Bartmann also considers Handke's exploration of everyday reality (in an open-ended form that seeks a 'mythic' inclusiveness of Being) in the first journal (*Suche* 110-20). Wesche discusses the paradoxical relationship between fragment and totality in the journals: Handke's fragmentary notes both actively resist and strive for a vision of totality (Wesche 333). Each of these short observations on things and events is an example of the *nunc stans*, the "moment of eternity" in which the world and the human being become one (Wesche 332). The individual entries in the journals are, in essence, metonymic, that is, each note stands by itself as an independent entity and is simultaneously emblematic of the consciousness (and the "weight" of the reality/world) that generated it. Finally, Marquardt (287) sees the journal as striving for a simultaneity of "language and perception, literature and life" in the activity of spontaneous notebook writing.

Handke's preface to the original German edition of *The Weight of the World* gives the reader some insight into what kind of radical literary experiment he is attempting with his journals, an experiment that focuses the attention of both writer and reader on the nature of perception and its formulation in language.[18] Handke calls this first journal "a sort of novel or epic of everyday occurrences" (Schlueter 171). His original intention in keeping these notes was to use them as the basis for some specific literary work, a story or a play. In other words, they were noted down in order to fit into a project or context, a "system," the writer already had in mind: "Daily percep-

---

[18] A brief note at the beginning of the English translation indicates that Handke and his translator, Ralph Manheim, agreed to delete about ten pages from the original German edition; these included passages that were political commentary, expressions that were untranslatable from the German language, and sections Handke simply wanted to cut. Most regrettably, the important preface comments were thus not included in the English translation, presumably at Handke's insistence. He apparently wanted the reader to confront the text without the framework of his explanatory comments. They do help, however, to explain the overall project of the journals. Page numbers that refer to Handke's preface are thus from the original German edition.

tions were translated in my head into the system for which they were supposed to be used, indeed, the perceptions themselves as they randomly occurred were already organized for a possible project." Handke soon realized that he was paying attention to only those thoughts and events that suited his plans and everything else became insignificant and thus forgettable: "But precisely through this state of heightened attentiveness, into which I had thought myself, I became especially aware of the daily forgetting" (*GW* 5).

The idea that any observations noted for some kind of literary project are somehow false or missing something is repeated in *Am Felsfenster morgens* when he suggests that "'*not* observing, *not* staring, *not* looking closely'" serves as the basic guideline for his notations (*FM* 9). He deliberately notes those events and details that are without a context and as such are meaningless. The notion of a "system" or "context" (here for a planned literary project) mentioned by Handke might best be understood with a reference to the oft-cited notion of the paradigm shift used by the post-Kantian history of science philosopher Thomas Kuhn.[19] The creative attitude that results from Handke's unique approach in these journals incorporates his stance of slowness, a practiced concentration on and attentiveness to the flow of daily events, a deliberate "non-forgetting" of the objects and events that pass through consciousness as being insignificant or meaningless experience.[20] The authorial consciousness reflected in each of the journals is highly observant of

---

[19]The paradigm for Kuhn is a grid or complex of relations, events, and objects that are defined as being meaningful according to a set of *a priori* definitions of what constitutes meaning within the scientific community. All things that take place outside the established paradigm of significance are thus designated as meaningless. Handke's insight into this loss of experience constitutes what Kuhn describes as a shift or alteration in the dominant paradigm, a breakthrough into a new dimension of perception. The concept of system or paradigm is fundamental to epistemological thought and can be found in many other philosophical and religious contexts. Handke is engaged in his journal writing in a kind of phenomenological bracketing of the perceptual schemata imposed by his own consciousness.

[20]The conception of perceptual schemata as paradigms or systems is echoed in *A Moment of True Feeling* where Keuschnig speaks of finding a new system in which he can live. Handke's concern here with non-forgetting can also be viewed in terms of its Heideggerian echoes of truth as *aletheia* (the non-forgetting of Being).

both itself and its surroundings, well-read, and intensely focused on, if not obsessed with, literature and the linguistic formulation of thoughts and feelings.[21] Aesthetic production is here the result of patient observation of self and world: "Form: a product of (long) experience" (*WW* 223). Many of the entries express an implicit sense of religious wonder in the myriad manifestations of human existence.

Handke's plan for the notebooks thus changed and they became a vehicle for noting perceptions that were seemingly unrelated to any literary project, a means to remember his experience as it was without the filter of a preconception. Freed from the idea of traditional literary forms and having created what he feels is a new genre of writing, he embraced a new, almost meditative, discipline. Language becomes for him once again vital and authentic in what he comes to experience as virtually epiphanic "moments of linguistic liveliness":

> I trained myself to react immediately with language to everything that I encountered and noticed how in the very moment of the experience, language also became animated for an instant and became communicable; a moment later it would have already become the helpless "You know what I mean" language of the communication age, heard everyday and would have communicated nothing because of its mundane familiarity. For a single moment, the words which passed through me day and night became objectified. Whatever I experienced appeared in this "moment of language" to be universal, freed from all subjectivity. (*GW* 6)

By reacting to experiences with language and without reflection, he strives for a writing style that projects innocence and authenticity. The individual moments eventually turned into a continuous practice and the resulting text is not any kind of narrative but rather what he calls a "documentary report of language reflexes" (*GW* 6).

---

[21]Bartmann ("Gewicht" 37) makes the interesting comment that the journal entries resemble the observations made by the angel figures in Wim Wenders' movie *Der Himmel über Berlin* (1987; *Wings of Desire*) for which Handke wrote a major part of the screenplay. The angels, Damiel and Cassiel, write in notebooks they carry with them. They often express their sense of wonder and sorrow over the vicissitudes of human existence. Several of the lines in the initial monologue of Marion, the trapeze artist, are almost direct quotations from *The Weight of the World* (see Barry, "Weight" 54-55).

At the end of the preface, Handke again links his journal project to the problem of forgetting: "The problem of the present journal is only that it can have no end and so it must break off. But a declared ending would again be an all too passive acceptance of forgetting that is, in any case, eternal" (*GW* 7). This method of responding immediately to perceptions with a linguistic formulation is followed through all of Handke's four journals. In the preface to *Am Felsfenster morgens*, he again refers to this technique of language reflexes:

> If I were to pinpoint the uniqueness of this whole project, it would perhaps be as follows: maxims and reflections? No, rather they are reflexes; reflexes, involuntary, yet at the same time, deliberate; reflexes, which come from a deliberateness, from a fundamental deliberateness, and which, in their progression, soar outward, indeed intend to soar outward, beyond mere reflex as far as one's breath reaches. (*FM* 7)

Despite the often inscrutable and private nature of the entries in these journals, Handke nonetheless claims their universality, that they are a literary document that can be accessed if not by all then by, as the dedication to *The Weight of the World* reads, "To whom it may concern."[22] In a letter to the editors of the first journal, Handke claims the work is a kind of cut-and-paste text from which anyone can assemble or construct the arc of their own life story (cf. Bartmann, *Suche* 113). In this sense, the journals share in the spirit of the early fiction as both deconstructions of a genre (village tale, murder mystery, diary) and in their fragmentary nature, as the elements from which the reader must assemble a plot (childhood trauma, violence, the diarist), a story that ultimately becomes the imaginative reconstruction of the consciousness of the author behind the narrative. Handke again claims here a certain universality for his journal and for his own observations. He notes in *The Weight of the World* that his own feelings of alienation are paradoxically "the source of my feelings for others, whom I see as equally isolated, and that in turn brings me close to them" (*WW* 35).[23]

---

[22]In *Am Felsfenster morgens*, Handke asserts that the dedication from *The Weight of the World* applies to all his journals (*FM* 6).

[23]In another notation, he claims that narcissism (actually here he means self-knowledge) "prepares and equips one for long, steady, penetrating contemplation of others" (*WW* 178).

Some journal entries are often so intuitive and of such a private nature that they seem unintelligible to the reader, appearing like mere lists of the random objects and trivial events that the writer observes. Focused on things which have, for him at least, a degree of metaphoric, that is, metonymic significance,[24] these entries constitute a plethora of "epiphanies of things" (Bartmann, "Gewicht" 38). In *The Weight of the World*, for example, the journalist makes the following enigmatic observations on the seemingly inconsequential in his immediate presence: "The young leaves; the sun shines through them, and now and then the shadows of other leaves move over them" (*WW* 23); or: "A man bends over a child as though wanting to give it mouth-to-mouth resuscitation" (*WW* 33); and "The rustling of paper beside a sick man" (*WW* 55). His focus in the journals remains solely on the perception and formulation of what he finds in his environment, eschewing the imposition of any externally derived interpretive schema on objects and events. The meaning of entities he encounters must evolve from the things themselves: "'perception is attention' (Novalis): an attention that emanates from the perceptible object; my wish to go out into the street as a wish to experiment ('Don't look for anything behind phenomena; they themselves are the doctrine' – Goethe)" (*WW* 224).

In his practice of a meditative slowness, Handke seeks to describe the world in its objective essense: a doctrine of the linguistic

---

[24]The poetic valorization of insignificant objects has occurred throughout Handke's writings and has been associated with states of anxiety and disorientation. The characters of Joseph Bloch and Gregor Keuschnig also experience trivial random objects as metaphors (or metonymies) that signal hidden meanings during the course of their breakdowns. Bartmann notes that the detailed descriptions of trivial objects in Handke's early narrative texts, *Die Hornissen* for example, parallel what is later found in the journals ("Gewicht" 38). Pakendorf (79) makes the claim that Handke's texts are dominated by the metonymic mode of writing associated with Roman Jakobson's ideas on forms of aphasia and language, specifically on contiguity disorder, a breakdown of the ability to combine and order elements on the level of syntax. This syntagmatic disintegration results in fragmentation, loss of coherence, and a collapse of meaning (79). The sense of fear and crisis that dominates so many of Handke's characters indicates for Pakendorf that these language problems are "manifestations of a truly existential problem" (80), for which the solution lies in a "moment of epiphany when the here and now is transcended and the self loses its clear definition in the harmony of a mystical union" (82).

formulation and the aesthetic transformation of things in the *nunc stans*, a moment of eternity. Handke asserts that his deliberate observation of things and their expression in language has become his aesthetic practice: "... for me that has been a kind of recurrent idea. The more I immerse myself in an object, the more it approaches a written sign" (*Zw* 231) This program of form and object shapes much of Handke's later writing. He elaborates the doctrine in discussing Cézanne in *The Lesson of Mont Sainte-Victoire,* and he gives it succinct expression in a 1991 piece on his favorite words: "'Get away from language – stay with the things, and their appearance!'" (*LS* 14).[25] The entries in all of the journals again express a restrained and spiritual sense of awe at the simplicity of the world and all that is the human experience of it. Handke's writing posits an identity of the inner world of words and the outer world of things and this clearly projects "a religious function" (Thornton 115). The word here becomes an expression of the divine *logos.* Handke makes this religious meaning of his writing clear when he speaks of his own spiritual experience: "And [the mystical experience of a threshold] was also the recognition that these two things should be brought together: this world of writing and the world of things that a person can touch" (*Zw*183).

The Afternoon of a Writer bears, in the German edition, the subtitle "narrative" or "tale," although this addition does not appear in the English translation. It is more of a thinly veiled autobiographical third person essay in the manner of *Versuch über die Jukebox* (1990; *Essay on the Jukebox*, 1994) and is to be understood in the sense Handke intends when he refers to *The Weight of the World* as being a novel. The use of the indefinite article in the title would indicate that Handke again claims a certain universality for his text. *The Afternoon of a Writer* suggests, like the journals, that

---

[25]In this same piece, Handke mentions that he likes the word "equanimity" which he had come across while reading the religious anthropologist Mircea Eliade (15). This word gives insight into Handke's idea of slowness and his stance towards his writing in his later texts: to describe the world in a language that stems from the practiced and deliberate objectivity of an unmoved and unattached view. This is a traditional posture of Buddhist meditation – an attitude of mindfulness and equanimity – that results in the Zen *haiku* poem, as Wesche insightfully noted (331). See the essay by Suzuki for a discussion of the Zen and the Japanese *haiku*.

"language and the self are still the two dominant themes in his writing" (Pakendorf 77). The figure of the writer in this text also carries a notebook (*AW* 65) and illustrates the daily practice of observing and noting for the author of the journals. The activity of notation serves for him a spiritual and existential purpose that re-establishes on a daily basis his sense of connection to the world: "Every word, not spoken but written, that led to others, filled his lungs with air and renewed his ties with the world. A successful notation of this kind began the day for him; after that, or at least so he thought, nothing could happen to him until the following morning" (*AW* 3). The syntactic style of these notations is paratactic; the linking of words one after another creates a cohesion that implies a spiritual message. The writer, as he sits in a bar during his solitary wanderings on the edges of the city, imagines "a slow procession of images" (*AW* 62) which closely resemble the listings of random objects in many of the journal entries:

> ... from the stone stairway flanked by fern fronds, all unrolled except for one with the coiled shape of a crosier, to the high plateau with the cloud shadows, where the buzzing of the bees in a tree suggested the unisonal humming of a human chorus, from there to a road where a cyclist, blinded by the fly in his eye, braked abruptly.... (*AW* 63)

Again in *The Afternoon of a Writer*, the author figure writes of his habit of observing and making notes as a kind of meditation: "... where could he still his hunger and thirst and become integrated with the procession of passersby by merely meditating, observing, recording his observations?" (*AW* 46-47). The practice of observing and noting the trivial and fragmentary becomes for the author, on his afternoon walk, an imaginative mode of experiencing a mystical totality in which he is connected to everything, a spiritual system of connections, as it were:

> Did such imaginings in processions of forms take him out of the present reality? Or did it, on the contrary, disentangle and clarify the present, form connections between isolated particulars, and set his imprint on them all, the dripping beer tap and the steadily flowing water faucet behind the bar, the unknown figures in the room and the silhouettes outside? Yes, when he gave himself over to these fantasies, the things and the people present appeared to him all at once with no need to be counted, and like the leaves in the summer tree joined to form a large number. (*AW* 63-64)

This program of observing and noting unimportant objects and random events in *The Weight of the World* and the other journals is also explained in *The Lesson of Mont Sainte-Victoire.*

In this latter novel, the narrator laments the dearth of real objects in the plastic and packaged landscapes of modern urban life after he views the paintings of Cézanne: "What thing today is *food for the eyes*? That is why I search so needily for intact nature" (*LSV* 180). He then commits himself to observing everyday objects in a search for a sense of authentic connection to reality: "Consequently, in my need for continuity, I willfully immerse myself in everyday, man-made things" (*LSV* 180). He goes on to list a number of his observations, which read very much like many of the entries in his journals. For example, he writes: "Didn't I just see a beech copse reflected in the gray-blue of the asphalt? Doesn't the roar of the evening plane occasionally make a day start over? Isn't the tin star on the child's sweater a time-honored tradition?" (*LSV* 180). Handke associates this practice of observation and notation with an aesthetic and spiritual sensibility like that of Cézanne: as "a transformation and sheltering of things endangered" (*LSV* 181) that reestablishes in art a sense of totality or harmony between the individual and a reality beset by the deformations of the language of modern media and popular culture.

The transformation he sees in Cézanne's brushstrokes is a process that moves from the observation of the object to the visual image to its formulation in poetic language: "They were *things*, they were *images*, they were *script*; they were brushstrokes – and all these were in harmony" (*LSV* 178). Handke purposefully uses the antiquated and religiously-tinged word "script" in order to emphasize its difference from the estranged language of the media, the "'You know what I mean' language of the communication age" (*GW* 6). The transformation of things into poetic images overcomes his alienation and brings him closer to nature: "Thing-image-script in one: that is the miracle – and yet it does not fully communicate my feeling of nearness" (*LSV* 178).

The seemingly inconsequential objects and events come to serve the writer in *The Afternoon of a Writer* as the "script" of poetic metaphors, specifically again as metonymies, which intimate in his mind a higher order of meaning. As the writer sits in the bar, he imagines, with a bit of obviously self-deprecating humor, that its patrons have all thought, at some time in their lives, of writing an autobiography ("of at least a thousand pages"): "But if asked about the content, they would refer as a rule to some trifling incident, to something they had seen in a window, a hut burning in the night, rivers of mud in the roadway after a rainfall, but often with deep feeling, as though these trifles stood for a whole long life" (*AW* 61). These images of minor objects and events stand as symbolic representations of a greater spiritual meaning, a universal mythic significance.

Handke's writing seeks to capture the "true being of things" (Pfaff and vom Hofe 64; cf. Bartmann, *Suche* 53-54). Many of the journal entries in *The Weight of the World* seek to express these "mythic moments" and thereby resemble the Japanese *haiku* form of poetry which capitalizes on the poetic expression of the small and inconsequential object and event as a metonymic experience of a spiritual realization, a Buddhist insight into the objective nature of existence (Wesche 331).[26] In *Die Geschichte des Bleistifts*, the journalist observes that an "epic of haikus" (*GB* 52) appears to him as the highest ideal for his writing. Handke speaks of his earlier fiction as being non-traditional, more lyrical-epic poems of "everyday occurrences" (Schlueter 171) than novels in the customary sense. He speaks in a manner that applies not only to his journals but also to his concept of writing:

> These narratives and novels have no story. They are only daily occurrences brought into a new order. What is "story" or "fiction" is really always only the point of intersection between individual daily events. This is what produces the impression of fiction. And because of this I believe they are not traditional, but

---

[26]In Buddhist thought, the perception of reality as it truly is (beyond the interpretive schema imposed by the dualisms of consciousness) is called enlightenment and involves the realization of *tathata,* which in Sanskrit means 'this,' 'that' or 'such.' The Japanese Zen *haiku* form seeks to capture the experience of the insight into the true 'suchness' of reality. Wesche's point here is not to argue by any means that Handke is a Buddhist but that his journal writing seems to move towards this spiritual sensibility. The concept of perceiving reality in its true 'suchness' is not so far removed from the Heideggerian notion of the non-forgetting of Being, a context in which he has been discussed.

that the most unarranged daily occurrences are only brought into
a new order, where they suddenly look like fiction. I never want
to do anything else. (Schlueter 172)

The journals can thus be read as a lyrical narrative of these mythic
moments that intimate the overcoming of the existential estrangement of consciousness. They represent an intuitive spiritual unity of
the inner world of self and the outer world of objective reality in
which both are preserved and not forgotten. At another point, Handke describes such an experience of mystical oneness when he faces
a tree: "the face of the tree and my face become one: totally tree,
totally I" (*GB* 18). Facing the nondescript tree, Handke achieves a
moment of totality, a temporary liberation from and transcendence
of the isolated and shamed self that has propelled his writing from
the beginning of his career.[27]

---

[27]This experience with the tree is foreshadowed in *Der kurze Brief zum langen
Abschied* (1972; *Short Letter, Long Farewell*, 1974) where the narrator experiences a mystical moment when he sees a cypress tree waving in the breeze in
unison with his breathing (*SL* 78-79). It is also echoed in the breathing of the
narrator as he experiences the colors and forms of the landscape at the conclusion of *The Lesson of Mont Sainte-Victoire* (*LSV* 210-11).

Works Cited

Alcorn, Marshall W. *Narcissism and the Literary Libido. Rhetoric, Text, and Subjectivity.* New York: New York UP, 1994.

Barry, Thomas F. "'Sehnsucht nach einem Bezugssystem': The Existential Aestheticism of Peter Handke's Recent Fiction." *Neophilologus* 68 (1984) 259-70.

—. "The Weight of Angels: Peter Handke and *Der Himmel über Berlin.*" *Modern Austrian Literature* 23.3-4 (1990) 53-64.

Barthes, Roland *Mythologies.* Trans. Annette Lavers. New York: Farrar, Straus and Giroux, 1972.

Bartmann, Christoph. "'Das Gewicht der Welt' – revisited." *Peter Handke. Text und Kritik* 24. Ed. Heinz Ludwig Arnold. 5th ed. Munich: edition text + kritik, 1989. 34-41.

—. *Suche nach Zusammenhang. Handkes Werk als Prozeß.* Vienna: Braumüller, 1984.

Cooper, David E. *Existentialism.* Oxford: Basil Blackwell, 1990.

Coury, David. *The Return of Storytelling in Contemporary German Literature and Film – Peter Handke and Wim Wenders.* Lewiston, NY: Edwin Mellen Press, 2004.

DeMeritt, Linda C. *New Subjectivity and Prose Forms of Alienation: Peter Handke and Botho Strauss.* New York, Bern: Peter Lang, 1987.

Durzak, Manfred. "Die Exegese des Autors. Aus einem Gespräch mit Handke." *Peter Handke und die deutsche Gegenwartsliteratur. Narziß auf Abwegen.* Stuttgart: Kohlhammer, 1982. 49-52.

—. *Der deutsche Roman der Gegenwart.* Stuttgart: Kohlhammer, 1971.

Greiner-Kemptner, Ulrike. *Subjekt und Fragment: Textpraxis in der (Post-) Moderne.* Stuttgart: Heinz, 1990.

Hage, Volker. "Warum nicht wie Balzac? Peter Handkes *Die Geschichte des Bleistifts* und *Phantasien der Wiederholung.*" *The German Quarterly* 63 (1990) 412-20.

Hammer, Stephanie. "Spiel und Spiegel: Autor und Leserin. Peter Handkes *Gewicht der Welt.*" *Österreichische Tagebuchschriftsteller.* Ed. Donald Daviau. Vienna: Schaumberger, 1994. 151-69.

Handke, Peter. "Zur Tagung der Gruppe 47 in den USA." *Ich bin ein Bewohner des Elfenbeinturms*. Frankfurt am Main: Suhrkamp, 1972. 29-34.

Jurgensen, Manfred. "Peter Handke's 'Journal' *Das Gewicht der Welt* (1975-1977)." *Handke. Ansätze – Analysen – Anmerkungen*. Ed. Manfred Jurgensen. Queensland Studies in German Language and Literature 7. Bern: Francke, 1979. 173-90.

Klein, Anne. "Buddhism." *How Different Religions View Death and the Afterlife*. Ed. Christopher Jay Johnson and Marsha G. McGee. Philadelphia: Charles Press, 1998. 47-63.

König, Fritz. "The West German and the American Editions of Peter Handke's *Das Gewicht der Welt*." *German Studies Review* 11 (1988) 255-66.

Kolleritsch, Alfred. "Die Welt, die sich öffnet. Einige Bemerkungen zu Handke und Heidegger." *Peter Handke. Die Arbeit am Glück*. Ed. Gerhard Melzer und Jale Tükel. Königstein/Ts: Athenäum, 1985. 111-25.

Kuhn, Thomas. *The Structure of Scientific Revolutions*. Chicago: U of Chicago P, 1970.

Linstead, Michael. *Outer World and Inner World. Socialisation and Emancipation in the Works of Peter Handke, 1964-1981*. Frankfurt am Main: Peter Lang, 1988.

Marcuse, Herbert. *Eros and Civilization. A Philosophical Inquiry into Freud*. New York: Vintage Books, 1962.

Marquardt, Eva. "Moderne österreichische Prosa am Beispiel Peter Handkes und Thomas Bernhards." *Die literarische Moderne in Europa. Band 3: Aspekte der Moderne in der Literatur bis zur Gegenwart*. Ed. Hans Joachim Piechotta, Ralph-Rainer Wuthenow, and Sabine Rothemann. Opladen: Westdeutscher Verlag, 1994. 281-300.

Marschall, Christine. *Zum Problem der Wirklichkeit im Werk Peter Handkes. Untersuchungen mit Blick auf Rainer Maria Rilke*. Bern: Haupt, 1995.

Michaelis, Rolf. "Die Katze vor dem Spiegel oder: Peter Handkes Traum von der 'anderen Zeit.'" *Deutsche Akademie für Sprache und Dichtung. Jahrbuch 1973*. Heidelberg: Schneider, 1974. 55-64.

Mixner, Manfred. "Die alte Masse – Handkes Genauigkeit im Erzählen." *Aporie und Euphorie der Sprache. Studien zu Georg*

Trakl und Peter Handke. Ed. Heidy M. Müller and Jaak De Vos. Leuven: Uitgeveru Peters, 1989. 149-61.

Mommsen, Katharina. "Peter Handke: *Das Gewicht der Welt –* Tagebuch als literarische Form." *Peter Handke*. Ed. Raimund Fellinger. Frankfurt am Main: Suhrkamp, 1985. 242-51.

Nietzsche, Friedrich. "On Truth and Lie in an Extra-Moral Sense." *The Portable Nietzsche*. Trans. Walter Kaufmann. New York: Viking Press, 1954. 42-47.

Pakendorf, Gunther. "Writing about Writing: Peter Handke, *Nachmittag eines Schriftstellers.*" *Modern Austrian Literature* 23.3-4 (1990) 77-86.

Perram, Gavin. *Peter Handke. The Dynamics of the Poetics and the Early Narrative Prose*. Frankfurt am Main: Peter Lang, 1992.

Peter Handke. Die Langsamkeit der Welt. Ed. Gerhard Fuchs and Gerhard Melzer. Graz: Droschl, 1993.

Pfaff, Peter, and Gerhard vom Hofe. *Das Elend des Polyphem. Zum Thema der Subjektivität bei Thomas Bernhard, Peter Handke, Wolfgang Koeppen und Botho Strauß*. Königstein/Ts.: Athenäum, 1980.

Schlueter, June. *The Plays and Novels of Peter Handke*. Pittsburgh, PA: U of Pittsburgh P, 1981. Contains "An Interview With Peter Handke." 163-77.

Springer, Michael. "Im Internat." *Über Peter Handke*. Ed. Michael Scharang. Frankfurt am Main: Suhrkamp, 1972. 185-94.

Strasser, Peter. *Der Freudenstoff. Zu Handke eine Philosophie*. Salzburg: Residenz, 1990.

Suzuki, Daisetz T. "Zen and Haiku." *Zen and Japanese Culture*. Tokyo: Tuttle, 1988. 215-67.

Thornton, Thomas K. *Die Thematik von Selbstauslöschung und Selbstbewahrung in den Werken von Peter Handke*. Frankfurt am Main: Peter Lang, 1983.

Wagner, Karl. "Peter Handkes Rückzug in den geschichtslosen Augenblick." *Literatur und Kritik* 134 (May 1979) 227-40.

Wesche, Ulrich. "Fragment und Totalität bei Peter Handke." *German Quarterly* 62 (1989) 329-34.

Language, Life, and Art:
Handke and/on Nietzsche

Andrea Gogröf-Voorhees

IF THE IMPORTANCE of a writer were measured according to the quantity and variety of comparative studies of him and other prominent writers of the past and present, Peter Handke would be very important indeed. Only in the past ten years, scholars have linked Handke to modern classics such as Wittgenstein, Kafka, Benjamin, Beckett, Heidegger, Celan, and Hofmannsthal, to name only the most illustrious ones (Riedel 139-40). Another author Handke has been brought in connection with is Friedrich Nietzsche, whose personality and work offer Handke the particularly fruitful example and challenge of a fellow player whose existence was also entirely involved in the game of life as literature.

So far, the connection between Nietzsche and Handke has been the object of two specific studies. Michael Vollmer establishes the "affinity of thought" between the two writers from the perspective of the inexhaustible relationship between language and individuality. He draws parallels between Handke and Nietzsche's insistence on the importance of preserving one's individuality, and discusses their respective development of a theory of language that questions language as a fundamental and reliable means to represent the subject and truth. Peter Pütz, on the other hand, situates their relationship within the context of aesthetic modernity as a marker of crisis characterized by "an increased shifting from the center to the peripheries, from the substance to the relations, and in the tension between the intended and at the same time unconsoled destruction of meaning" ("Handke" 72). For Pütz, the connection between Nietzsche and Handke resides in their recognition of the fundamental questionability of modernity and a radical refusal to approach their art systematically.

Pütz perceives in Nietzsche's writing (and by extension in Handke's) a sound of mourning of the loss that always already accompanies the experience of a breach of tradition. Both authors, Pütz argues, share a reflective state that cannot reconcile itself with the traditional moderns who pitched the new against the old (e.g. Storm and Stress, German Early Romanticism, French Symbolism). Nor can their work be reduced to serve the cause of a postmodern deconstructionist activity that Pütz characterizes as either "a simple network of differences and contradictions" or a "liberating play of all possibilities" (74). Rather, in response to the crisis of modernity, Pütz sees in Nietzsche's and Handke's works a dramatization of a sense of loss counteracted and challenged by a relentless practice of self-overcoming that distinguishes itself through a will for cohesion in the knowledge and experience of the fragmentary, of antagonisms and rifts, a glimmer of which can only be gained through a certain dynamism and openness of spirit.

In general agreement with the main arguments of Vollmer and Pütz, the present essay argues, however, that Handke's and Nietzsche's writing is characterized precisely by a will to avoid theory and classification and to affirm and to translate for the reader the immediacy of living as experienced during the process of writing. What connects Handke and Nietzsche is their temperament as resisters and provocateurs, their understanding of writing as an aesthetic and sensual self-expression that seeks coherence in the knowledge of the essentially fragmentary nature of the world, and their solitary commitment to writing lived in movement. The aim of this study, then, is not to show Nietzsche's influence on Handke but to highlight specific temperamental, intellectual, and aesthetic affinities that emerge from Handke's seminal conversation with Herbert Gamper, *Aber ich lebe nur von den Zwischenräumen* (1987; I For One Sustain Myself Exclusively Through the Gaps), other interviews and many of his fictional works.

To both Handke and Nietzsche it matters greatly that the reader be affected by their writing. To sting the reader into indignation, enthusiasm, or best, creative activity is one of Handke's and Nietzsche's greatest concerns and achievements. One might call them modern radicals, radical moderns or representatives of a "radicalized modernity" (Pütz, "Handke" 68), but essentially both make tremendous efforts to elude definitive labeling. At best they may be considered moderns, romantics and at the same time their opposite, with a strong existentialist bent in both cases. They are moderns because they are relentlessly and affirmatively searching for and testing new modes of perception and writing, and because their greatest concern is to revive language from the ground up. They are romantics because they are self-reflecting narcissists; they proceed from experience, never hesitating to share extreme mood swings with the rest of the world, and because they are interested in the in-between twilight zones of perception where the brevity and intensity of the moment melts with a feeling of eternity. They are the opposite, too, classics and anti-romantics. They share a longing for the perfect form and affirm the tradition of antiquity and, of course, Goethe. Their self-critical lucidity and lack of bad faith makes them cool investigators of their own paradoxical positions as artists. Their sense of humor is formidable to those who recognize it.

In the Gamper interview, Handke delivers a short synopsis of how he became a reader of Nietzsche.[1] To make a long story short, Handke went through various stages of reception ranging from a feeling of revulsion to recognition (in the sense of sympathy and respect). In his high school, a former Nazi teacher made the students read Nietzsche's *Zarathustra*: "My thinking was as follows: here someone wants to be a poet and he's lacking control, he's also lacking the eyes for objects, for things, the ability to describe things, the echoes of things" (*Zw* 169). Handke's negative attitude toward Nietzsche did not change dramatically with a later reading of the philosopher's books. Stimulated by his translator Georges-Arthur Goldschmidt, who, as a German-Jewish escapee had found in Nietzsche a helpful companion, Handke took up Nietzsche again as of 1977. Careful to avoid *Zarathustra*, he read the earlier texts such as *The Birth of Tragedy, Human, All Too Human*, and *The Gay Science*. Here too he felt repulsed, but this time more by Nietzsche's attitude than by his language. This is significant, because it was through Nietzsche's language that Handke was seduced into a "stubborn continuation of reading" and that his position toward Nietzsche slowly changed. A certain "luminosity" emitted by his texts captured Handke and made him realize that what had disturbed him earlier – Nietzsche's self-righteous pose – revealed itself as a rather particular kind of self-affirmation resulting from a solitary and desperate struggle familiar to Handke himself (*Zw* 170).

---

[1]Four years earlier, Handke already lets us know: "... little by little I can say that I am a Nietzsche-reader" (*PhW* 8).

Secondary literature abounds and still grows on Handke's many 'attitudes' and his public persona since his entrance in 1966 into the literary establishment through his wave-making attack on this establishment at the meeting of Group 47 in Princeton. Critics do not tire to trace Handke's subsequent booming literary success to this one particular event, whereby Handke, in the role of the "refractory rebel," captured the throne as the great innovator of German literature.[2] Indeed, Handke's works of the 1970s appeared in ultra-rapid succession, became immediate classics, and made Handke into such a phenomenon that relatively quickly camps formed for or against the infant prodigy.[3] Of note here is that the opposition's criticism focuses more on Handke's attitude than on his texts. One discerns what Nietzsche would call a certain resentment when one reads the following: "The fact that he makes himself more important by denigrating others ... is not very original – Cassius Clay did the same thing too. What's more surprising is that he, unlike Clay, doesn't even have to box, to make his self-praise believable. He has found himself a public and critics who cheer him.... Much more interesting than his works are the echoes they find ..." (Werth 331).

What displeases here is that, to all appearance, Handke does not need to fight his way through the literary business world like others, but that "as a self-complacent apostle of a publishing empire, by Suhrkamp's grace" he enjoys the advantage of publishing anything that flows from his pen (Blasberg 186). The Handke controversy ignited once more, if less heatedly, in the 1980s when a rift of highly problematical proportions was found, namely a caesura between those successful works that were experimental and attacking systems of any kind and those that were new and disturbingly different. This shift is largely regarded as a turn-around in Handke's writing.[4] While the first books were acclaimed as innovative and useful for academic debate and literature courses as critical models of various literary genres (drama: *Kaspar*, 1968; trans. 1969; *Der Ritt über den Bodensee*, 1970; *The Ride across Lake Constance*, 1976; detective novel: *Der kurze Brief zum langen Abschied*, 1972;

---

[2]See the article by Blasberg.
[3]For an overview of Handke criticism see the article by Bernard-Eymard.
[4]For a discussion of this issue see Konzett (82-86). The author rightfully questions the existence of a moment of change and argues that Handke's work is marked by continuity.

*Short Letter, Long Farewell,*1978; *Die Angst des Tormanns beim Elfmeter,* 1970; *The Goalie's Anxiety at the Penalty Kick,* 1972; educational novel: *Falsche Bewegung,* 1975; False Move; biography: *Wunschloses Unglück,* 1972; *A Sorrow Beyond Dreams,* 1976), the new works were received as obstinate and uncritically formulated mythographies of an aesthete wallowing in the vagaries of his aesthetic perception (Blasberg 186).[5]

In short, a lot of critics felt that Handke had lost his edge and was now in danger of losing touch with the readership that had so enthusiastically followed him for ten years.[6] Starting with *Langsame Heimkehr* (1979; *The Long Way Around,* 1985) and at the latest with *Kindergeschichte* (1981; *Child Story,* 1985), the public was first taken aback, uncomfortably startled, then impatient and finally simply disappointed. The readers' endurance was put to the test by long and detailed descriptions of landscapes, endless essays on moods, sensations, a particularly meticulous search for "beauty," a "yearning for the epic," poses and especially a "preacher and prophet tone" that irritatingly disrupts the "joyful, distanced coolness of storytelling" for which Handke is known, admired and read (Gabriel 107).

Interestingly enough, however, interviews of Handke are always eagerly awaited and immediately critically reviewed by friends and foes alike, because there the author puts himself on stage, seemingly quite comfortable in the same role of agent provocateur that made him famous in the first place. Indeed, interviews with Handke are

---

[5]The notion of a ceasura is indeed questionable, if only because Handke's works since the eighties continue to challenge and revive the very notion of literary genres. For instance, *Die Wiederholung* (1987; *Repetition,* 1988): educational and detective novel; *Nachmittag eines Schriftstellers* (1987; *The Afternoon of a Writer,* 1991): autobiographical short story à la Fitzgerald; *Das Spiel vom Fragen oder die Reise zum sonoren Land* (1989; *Voyage to the Sonorous Land, or The Art of Asking*): theatre of the absurd; *Die Abwesenheit* (1987; *Absence,* 1990) and *Mein Jahr in der Niemandsbucht* (1994; *My Year in the No-Man's-Bay,* 1998): fairy tale; the three try-outs (1989-1991, trans. 1994): essay; *Der Bildverlust oder Durch die Sierra de Gredos* (2002; The Loss of Images, or Across the Sierra de Gredos): picaresque novel inspired by Cervantes' *Don Quixote* (1615).
[6]The latest and most heated controversy about Handke was ignited by Handke's position and texts dealing with the wars in Bosnia (see Schneider and Ziolkowski).

events, and they seem to make up for what is perceived as lack of bite, excitement and irony in his more recent texts. When André Müller taunts Handke with a commentary about the fact that he always writes hymns to beauty and goodness, the author replies: "You are a nincompoop! I don't mind in the least being accused of writing hymns to beauty, because these are all real, philosophical and super-sexy!" (Müller 77-78). When the interviewer tells him that he all too often appears in the role of prophet, he gets the following answer: "No! I don't know anybody alive who writes as pure a literature as I do. All others just spread opinions. Nothing of what I write points in the least toward my wanting to raise myself up to something. The one achievement in my life of which I am proud is to have avoided a fixed worldview. My books constitute for me the purest reading pleasure. When I read them, my chest expands and I think, this is really well written, he is good, he has done very well!" (Müller 78).

These passages are significant especially because Handke had noted and deplored Nietzsche's "self-intoxication" and "virtual self-deification" (*Zw* 171) in *Ecce Homo* and now displays a similar tendency himself. Irony and seriousness become hard to distinguish here, because, like Nietzsche, Handke certainly has literary ambition, yet he is also, like Nietzsche, ready to expose himself entirely to the ridicule, scorn or contempt of the public. The Nietzschean role of the jester is certainly not foreign to Handke. The reader/discussion partner is challenged to cope with and take a position in regard to the ambiguity of Handke's attitude. Is he joking or has he lost all perspective? Or is this kind of attitude a form of self-defense and self-assertion that intends to preclude any definitive judgment on the part of the audience? In any case, Handke's inflated self-congratulations are indeed reminiscent of Nietzsche's in *Ecce Homo*: one thinks in particular of the hyperbolic chapter titles ("Why I am so wise," "Why I am so clever," and "Why I write such good books") that, while displaying Nietzsche's ongoing altercation with the Socratic myth, nevertheless also reveal a desire for self-affirmation despite opposing forces within and without. Another such instance occurs when Nietzsche pronounces himself master in the arts of "reversal of perspectives," and when he confesses to suffering "unbearable fits of sobbing" while reading his *Zarathustra* (Nietzsche, *Ecce Homo* 223, 246). Even though he concedes the same honor to Heinrich Heine, Nietzsche doesn't hesitate to prophesy for himself: "One day it will be said that Heine and I have been by far the foremost artists of the German language – at an incalculable distance from everything mere Germans have done with it" (*Ecce Homo* 245).

It is noteworthy that Handke does not attribute Nietzsche's demeanor in *Ecce Homo* to his advancing illness but explains it as a result of not being listened to, of finding himself not understood, a situation Handke is familiar with himself in the eighties, at the time of his so-called turn. With time, Handke tells us, he is coming to realize that Nietzsche's self-assertion stems from a will to a general affirmation of life that seeks to win out over the threat of defeat that is always already felt by the serious artist.[7] This is why Handke feels more sympathetic toward Nietzsche now, in particular on account of occasional passages in his work "that were apotheoses, really, of a human being desperate and continuing the fight, and yet seeking sense and, precisely with the help of language, also making one" (*Zw* 170). He detects in Nietzsche a "desperately positive thinking," an impulse to an ongoing self-overcoming and transformation through language that he shares with the philosopher. This is why Handke excuses Nietzsche's tendency to exaggerate with a word from Flaubert which animates his own writing as well, namely that in order to be able to write at all, one must exaggerate harmoniously (*Zw* 170).

Irritating pedantries, which Handke at first takes for a lack of artistry, yield to a more positive overall picture of Nietzsche. This tendency to prefer the sweeping overview of an issue or a rather rough and outlined portrait of fellow contemporaries over details that risk breaking the rhythm and unity of the movement in writing, is another quality Handke shares with Nietzsche, and many – mostly French – neo-Romantics, Flaubert, Baudelaire and Valéry among others. After listing some of Nietzsche's main characteristics, such as childlike demeanor, opposition to everything systematic, his fragmentary, jerky way of writing – qualities that describe Handke as well – he alleges not to remember the details of Nietzsche's texts. This is not that important for him, and he asserts: "I don't mind

---

[7]See the discussion on the fear of loss of language dramatized in *The Long Way Around* (*Zw* 179-83).

being someone who forgets a lot, yet retains the shape, contour and attitude of a writer" (*Zw* 172). The exploration of and search for original form and style are main concerns in both Handke's and Nietzsche's understanding of the creative process, and this process demands a continual overcoming of the self that, embedded in a maze of signs and language, needs to assert itself for and against this web again and again, always anew.

Both writers are committed to their respective present time, a position, however, that requires vigilance, mobility, and agility if one has the high claim, as both have, to create timeless works that have a productive impact on their contemporary audience. Nietzsche's demand of himself "to overcome his time within himself," to become "timeless," and his hope "to work against the time and thereby have an effect upon it, hopefully for the benefit of a future time" (*Observations* 87) anticipate Handke's own insistent wish to write "with his time and not only against it" (*Zw* 123). Nietzsche admits that his writings speak only of his efforts at self-overcoming (*Human* 209), and Handke reflects this position when he affirms that the work of writing is not only a dialogue with one's historical epoch but always also a transgression of it (*Zw* 125). The process of resistance is, according to Handke, the work of recurrent self-overcoming. Looking back, Handke remembers the exuberant and youthful joy he felt after completing his first book, *Die Hornissen* (1966; The Hornets).

For ten years, he continues, he felt receptive to the stimuli of an outside world that resonated within the author (for example, the pleasure of listening to the hit parade, The Beatles, going to the movies, or just 'dig' advertising), and thus he produced his speak-ins ("Offending the Audience," "Self-Accusation," "Prophecy" and *Kaspar*) in the rebellious spirit of the times (*Zw* 124-25). However, to remain authentic, to be vigilant and retain a sense of reality, to be able to continue writing, it is vital to move on, to step out, to resist the times, to resist one's sense of comfort within these times, within the movie theaters and on the streets. Like Nietzsche before, Handke insists on the necessity for a writer to know what he needs to practice his craft.[8] He has to exercise a kind of hygiene, self-

---

[8]Consider Nietzsche's break with Wagner and Handke's break from the demands of the public in the late seventies.

discipline and a ruthless self-analysis that demands a high degree of energy and courage to confront periods of absolute solitude (cf. *Ecce Homo* 223-24). Furthermore, what is needed to not merely survive but even enjoy this particular state is what Nietzsche calls fundamental health, or what we may call a healthy form of narcissism, a quality that both writers share in equal amounts.

Handke discovers in Nietzsche not a "precursor" but a fellow "hand-to-hand fighter" who "also stood at the brink of the times ... when the stakes were high and when he [Nietzsche] saw that there were quite a few things to be kept up and preserved" (*Zw* 171). Although Handke does not explicitly specify what was to be preserved, we may assume from the following that he speaks about Nietzsche's "dramatic sense for preservation" (*Zw* 171) in terms of the philosopher's efforts of re-transmission and re-actualization of the old and great tradition. Nietzsche the philologist, Hellenist, disciple of Dionysus as well as Apollo, and reader of Goethe, elicits respect from Handke, whose work also tackles the challenges of the classical tradition to make them productive for his own literary enterprises.[9] Obviously, tradition is neither the object of blind reverence nor a substitute for one's own lack of ideas. For Handke, as for Nietzsche, the ongoing dialogue with the representatives of the classical tradition functions as a means to fortify oneself and as a stimulus for one's own work: "Well, the best that all those great classical artists have achieved, and are still in the process of achieving, is to lend strength to the nature or the being or the position of the one who sets out to work now" (*Zw* 195).

This attitude holds for Nietzsche as well when he states that there is only one way of honoring the classics, "namely by continuing to seek in their spirit and with their courage, without ever tiring" (*Observations* 13). These reflections on the significance of the classical tradition and its representatives for a revaluation of today's aesthetic standards and as a source of strength raise the topic of philology that Handke broaches, especially in regard to the number of "things to marvel about" (*Zw* 172) in Nietzsche's texts – things that provide joy in a slow reading, which is also a studying. Handke fully agrees with Nietzsche when he considers philology as one of

---

[9]For a concise and fruitful overview on Goethe's presence in Handke's work see the article by Pizer.

the most meaningful sciences: "This slower, thoughtful and carefully measured reading that one practices, that is also one of my
ideals" (*Zw* 239). The act of preservation is also one of affirmation.
It is not only connected to the idea of tradition but, more important,
it expresses and helps to maintain a fundamental attitude toward the
world, life, nature, humanity, and oneself as human being and artist.
The idea that one produces something valuable out of negation is to
miss the profession of writer, Handke says. It is a failure that Nietzsche eschewed, because he was "an incredibly amicable human
being and therefore a great writer" (*Zw* 171).

And he continues in this vein: "Well, out of distaste for existence – and that always plays a role – or let's say out of negation of
existence, well, I couldn't draw any ardor" (*Zw* 223). Handke thinks
it decadent, unprofessional and sloppy if a writer bases his aesthetic
principles only on his personal sufferings, or on a systematic negation that ruins human existence and reduces us to a mere accident of
creation. All the greater is Nietzsche's merit, because he worked
under "much greater difficulties than we do because of his physical
condition" (*Zw* 171). Handke does not deny, however, that occasionally he could not help himself storming away against the
world.[10] Indeed, one thinks of an unforgettable scene in *Child Story*,
Handke's account of single fatherhood in Paris with a small daughter. Having taken advantage of an invitation to stay with friends
until finding a place to live, the struggling young father realizes he
has made the mistake of putting himself and his daughter at the
mercy of these childless "benefactors." With stunning psychological
insight that must be characterized as Nietzschean, the father analyzes the underlying reasons for the growing animosity of the host
couple towards his innocent child who becomes the victim of "their
merciless eyes in frozen faces." He gives vent to his hatred for these
"little prophets," his friends first, and then people in general, who,
childless by conviction, reveal themselves as "monsters" and "scum
of modern times" by daring to criticize and to interfere in the father-
daughter relationship and professing superior knowledge in the
department of child rearing (*CS* 232). Yet, to content oneself with

---

[10]In the interview with André Müller, Handke justifies his occasional fits of anger, especially against contemporary critics, by citing the fact that "Nietzsche
too stormed quite nicely against David Strauss or Richard Wagner" (78; emph.
add.).

throwing "glances of misery and wretchedness" at the world is not Handke's objective, nor was it Nietzsche's: "This sentence of Nietzsche's, that a mature and strong human being overlooks, has the strength to do so, the foul, the ugly, the inferior, that's the word that has always counted for me, too" (*Zw* 121).

What seems to be important for Handke here especially, is to hold on to a certain openness of mind and senses, to detect possibilities where there do not seem any more left, that is, to locate, traverse and decipher in-between spaces, such as thresholds, wastelands, construction sites, city outskirts, margins, and the like. What is at stake is to stay vigilant and mobile. This is why Handke perceives it as the sharpest criticism if not insult when a reader remarks that from his work emanates "the calmness of someone having reached his final destination" (*PhW* 16).

This means that a radical affirmation of existence and our linguistic expression thereof needs to be under check at all times so as not to fall into either uncritical self-complacency or premature conciliatory resignation. When writing, it is crucial to maintain a position of openness, to avoid the closing of one's mind: "It truly all depends on the back and forth, it all comes down to staying open, to pursue the outline, a vague draft in one's mind that should never be vague in its form of course.... I am not willing to decide: negation or affirmation, neither nor; well, it's an ongoing process, and I think that it should end in affirmation, but this is a much more difficult task to achieve with language than negating" (*Zw* 223). This statement, which concerns the chief problem of the very possibility of writing as an honest formulation of one's own existence, explains Handke's understanding of the artist as language artist, as stylist, and above all form-seeker. Handke joins Nietzsche when he affirms: "In any case, what I write is only my existence put into form" (*Zw* 247). Nietzsche translated into language "an exemplary human existence," and through his writings Handke is able to comprehend "how someone refuses to be a systematizer, to interpret the world according to a system" (*Zw* 172). Nietzsche had said this clearly before: "I mistrust all systematizers and avoid them. The will to a system is a lack of integrity" (*Twilight* 25).

The gesture of negation, the destruction of a system through language, is always potentially in danger of becoming systematic itself. This is a problem Handke has fought so shrewdly and skillfully in the beginning of his career that it constitutes the basis of his literary success and his relevance as a writer for us.[11] Anti-systematic writing expresses itself stylistically in Nietzsche and in Handke's exploration of the fragmentary in his journals (*Das Gewicht der Welt*, 1977; *The Weight of the World*; 1984; *Phantasien der Wiederholung*, 1983; Phantasies of Repetition; *Die Geschichte des Bleistifts*, 1985; The Pencil's Story; *Am Felsfenster morgens*, 1998; Mornings at the Natural Arch). This opposition against systems, models and worn-out structures, however, can only become fruitful – and that is the goal – if the artist as gambler risks it all. His commitment is absolute. He will play seriously and put it all on the table because it is in his nature and his existence depends on it. Handke's metaphor of the artist as melancholy gambler whose fate it is to "engage in a game whose price he doesn't know"(*Zw* 47) corresponds to his claim never to write anything premeditated and never to aim at retelling something exactly as it was previously experienced. Despite his melancholy, the gambler-artist continues to get involved in a writing adventure that is also felt as a physical experience of writing: "To only retell something that is behind me, that I could never do. I mean I actually cannot retell at all. To tell you something that I have experienced is extremely difficult for me, and I do not feel any erotic arousal with that. So, I would say only in the foretelling of something that I am on the point to experience, that's when I get hot" (*Zw* 27-28).[12]

In a certain way, Handke's metaphor of the gambler is reminiscent of Nietzsche's image of the uninhibited Heraklitean child-artist described in "Philosophy In the Tragic Age of the Greeks," who is urged by an "ever-awakening drive to play" to engage in an ongoing activity of construction and destruction, and this in childish innocence, yet not without a definite feeling for form. And Nietzsche continues: "As soon as [the child-artist] builds, connects, adjoins and forms, he does so according to inner principles and logic" (*Werke* 1: 830). This is how Handke perceives the role of imagination, of creative activity: "I think for me, at least that's what I believe to have understood about myself, imagination is a cleansing of

---

[11]Pütz (*Handke* 25-30) offers one of the most insightful discussions of Handke's a-systematic stance to this day.
[12]Handke continues: "I am unable to write down a word that has not pulsed through my entire body" (*Zw* 33).

the site: so that I recognize and connect details and things that are unmistakably there, that's my creative activity.... My efforts, my drudgery and joy tend to nothing more than to bespeak through language, through a most clear and pure language, what I simultaneously see and experience" (*Zw* 30-31).

From these assertions follows a common concern for harmony and coherence, a form of romantic yearning for infinite possibilities and artistic combinations, yet without blind nostalgia or claims to transcendental truths (cf. Bartmann). For Nietzsche and Handke, as well as for other Romantics and Symbolists such as Baudelaire, Huysmans and Mallarmé, language/art is the means to a momentary breakthrough, a glimpse of what is, yet cannot remain, nor should remain because its value lies precisely in its unfathomableness. What comes to mind also in this context is Stendhal's famous definition of beauty as "the promise for happiness" (154), wherein he caught the essential motivation for every artist to keep playing, to keep writing, to keep living: the pleasure of anticipation. On the other hand, and this aspect regards Handke and Nietzsche in particular, there is the pleasure of capturing the essence of the moment, be it a glance, an image, or a thought. One thinks of the mystical dimension of Nietzsche's notion of "High Noon," the hour of Pan, the moment of epiphany (and judgment) when a flash of truth is revealed in all its greatness, and vanishes, not without leaving its unforgettable trace (*Zarathustra* 79, 191, 198, 275-78; *Ecce Homo* 291).

In Handke's 1975 bestseller *Die Stunde der wahren Empfindung* (*A Moment of True Feeling*, 1977), both anticipation and promise are essential moments: Gregor Keuschnig, the newly single father and protagonist who undergoes a rather hectic metamorphosis from creature of habit to discoverer of new horizons, sitting on a street bench in Paris, has an existential moment. The three objects that have been lying in front of him in the sand – a chestnut leaf, a piece of a pocket mirror, and a child's barrette – become suddenly, under his gaze, "miraculous objects" (*M* 63). As he looks at them for a long time, they join together and "with them all other things came together" (*M* 64). They "tell" him that all is not yet discovered in this world, there are still mysteries for all of us to dis- and uncover. The transformation of the ordinary into the magic, of the insignificant into the mystical, in brief, a momentary insight gained through a random and explosively intense coming together of unrelated objects, lifts Keuschnig out of the narrow confines of his personal world back into it again, refreshed: "I have a future! he thought triumphantly.... He felt all-powerful again, but no more powerful than anyone else" (*M* 64-65).

What is important here, too, is to reach the feeling of being oneself while actively belonging to the larger community of fellow humans, a trait that is also Nietzsche's. Yet this sensation melts into air before it can ossify, as Marx characterizes the modern condition, because systems, habits, laziness, cowardice, fear, indifference and daily grind threaten the precious balance we seek and sometimes glimpse, as Keuschnig does. At the end, after Keuschnig has undergone so many extreme mood swings of perception – from utter estrangement from the world and panic to a blissful state of belonging and serenity –, we understand that a final resolution for his existential dilemma is not an option. Like the romantic hero, Keuschnig does not aspire to, nor will he ever arrive at a final destination, but in all probability will repeat these motions *ad infinitum*, sometimes tired of but never quitting the game.

Indeed, almost twenty years later we meet Gregor Keuschnig again. Like his author, he has moved from Paris to Chaville, a socially mixed suburb west of Paris, and he tells us the story of his second metamorphosis that presents itself as the last chance before running amok. Handke's decision to end these two particular stories (and others too) on a note of promise translates his unquenchable curiosity to know what comes next:

> Although he saw the same things as before, and from the same angle, they had become alien and therefore bearable. Walking with a firm step, he stretched. An unfamiliar perfume came to him through the dusk, but now it did not, as so often in the past, remind him of stifling, hopeless embraces – he no longer remembered, but only anticipated. Passing a shopping arcade, he thought: It could happen here; the unique never related event could happen here!" (*M* 130).

It might, it might not, yet what counts is to stay agile, to look for it, to provoke it whenever possible and to be ready to catch it when it shines through. This is Gregor's case in *My Year in the No-Man's-Bay*, when he not only relates his own metamorphosis from isolated cynic to sympathetic friend and fellow human in the microcosm of Chaville that becomes the macrocosm of narration, but extends his own to those around him, for instance to the recurring "petty prophet," the proprietor and cook of the Auberge aux Echelles with whom Gregor entertains a Socratic relationship: "I have noticed several times already that precisely the cursors, complainers, and cynics are, as soon as they forget themselves and fall to telling stories, the most profound, warm and all-inclusive storytellers; I have never felt more tranquil inside than when I have been listening to such a Thersites, metamorphosed into an epic narrator" (*MY* 464).

Yet, the "petty prophet," turning thus into a mixture of the Nietzschean madman and Zarathustra at the end does not tell a traditional epic but alternates his story between big questions, subtle insights and prophecies that are concerned with the present and the future of a world that has to be rediscovered on every walk again:

> Why did I not remain where I was from my earliest days, in the desert? The larger the desert around me, the richer the well spring of fairy tales within me ... during this century, another has passed, is still with us, will continue to make itself felt, for instance in the airy dustiness of the suburbs, here and elsewhere. To move things into their place will also be the New World.... A savior of mankind would be the great forgetter.... Why is there no peace? God does not see me because I do not let myself be seen by him. Hair-root wind, from-the-ground wind, Habakkuk wind: it is still there, it still exists. The omega, the last letter of the ancient alphabet, has the form of a jump rope. (*MY* 466)

As one can see, the resistance to a system is the opposite of systematic negation. It is the rejection of predetermined and fixed relations, the search for and affirmation of new, surprising and fresh relations and harmonies discovered through language.

To return to the issue of the fragmentary, it seems, after these previous developments, that the fragmentary stands in opposition to the very notion of coherence. According to Handke, in matters of art one cannot remain on the level of the fragmentary because that would mean a surrender to an ever-threatening impotence, a proof of not being able to "knit together" disparate elements into a coherent world. To remain at the level of the fragmentary would be a defeat, because art is above all "beautiful appearance," that is, art is embodied in an appearance of unity that Nietzsche detected in Greek Attic Tragedy and that Handke seeks to suggest through the art of storytelling. Handke believes that the fragmentary does correspond to the "historical and art-historical reality" of today, yet that is precisely the reason for him not to reflect this reality "realistically" (*Zw* 175).

Just when he has planned (a bad sign, according to Handke) to leave one of his new project in the stage of fragmentary "attempts at telling" and descriptions, a "craving for cohesion" calls and demands from the writer not to surrender to what he perceives as a relative comfort with the fragmentary mode, but to rise to the challenge and engage in the dangerous yet more rewarding work of "text weaving" ("Verknüpfung"; *Zw* 175). The search for cohesion, for the "beautiful appearance" (of unity), and for form is dramatized in Nietzsche and Handke as an always newly engaged battle, between the awareness of the basic incompleteness of individual existence and the stubborn will to achieve a tenable wholeness with the knowledge that this wholeness is, of course, achieved through a lie. Even if Handke does not admit that his idea for Sorger's "Gospel of Falsification" in *The Long Way Around* is based on Nietzsche's "Artist's metaphysics" (*Zw* 173), it is still possible to point to the connection that resides in their shared recognition of the necessity of art as artificial construct (form) and the result of a struggle to bridge the gap between our knowledge/experience of chaos and our need for beauty, order, and justice.[13]

When Handke insists that he can't accept any other position than that of resistance (*Zw* 223), he occupies a position that argues against any entrenched and prescriptive kind of thought and writing that always threatens the individual's vital and creative impulse. Most importantly, this position also supports his project of a revaluation of the role of the writer and that of literature (and art) in general. This is why Handke sees the crossing of the limits of convention and expectation that mark his work as a whole, as a necessity: "I am well aware that in my last works I have dared to cross certain frontiers, or better, that I had to do this…. [I am aware] that literature in the course of time has given up many [valuable] positions and given itself over either to a kind of obscurantism or plays the barrel organ of religion, and I knew that the issue is to

---

[13]Vollmer (102-18) examines in detail Handke's and Nietzsche's understanding and use of the term "justice."

reclaim many positions that once were [rightfully so] the basic force of literature" (*Zw* 106).

One of the motive powers of literature to be revitalized for instance is the appeal to the reader, a "justified project" (*SH* 175), according to Handke, that is not voiced through claims of authority, determination, song of praise or complaints, but through a fundamental "putting into question" and a "factual questioning":

> What is important to me is to find the right question…. So that out of a problem that has preoccupied us since time immemorial – and this is perhaps also part of the writing process – arises all of a sudden the right question. This question can be very lengthy and wearisome, tedious even, but this is precisely the mark of a dramatic question and a question that dramatizes itself. Yet, as soon as I have found the question as well as the moment to ask it, I begin to think that my work has meaning also for others, not only for reading fellow-authors, but also for all readers. I would like to reaffirm and insist on the fact that it is important to me to awaken the writer in the reader. This doesn't mean he needs then literally to sit down and write something, but he should feel like the creative being that he actually is. (*Zw* 107)

Literature's deep-reaching, suggestive and stimulating power leads to self-expression through the right questions. And Handke adds: "Every art should liberate the ones who study it, and not make them into its follower" (*Zw* 247). Art is not a religion. It is an activity whose function is to emancipate, liberate and compel: it should lead everyone who practices or enjoys it to their own formulation of questions that become in the best of cases, works of art themselves.

The proximity to Nietzsche here is undeniable. His entire work reads essentially as a web of dramatic questioning and also as a question that dramatizes itself. To not only pose the right question, but also to want to hear the right question would be in Nietzsche's sense a welcome transgression of limits and would constitute progress. Yet this is not often the case, as Nietzsche observes: "Limits of our hearing. – One hears only those questions for which one is able to find answers" (*Gay Science* 206). For Nietzsche, the modern spirit is lacking will and courage, if not curiosity, to venture out into unfamiliar territory. What we miss out on, then, is the chance to discover the unfamiliar, strange and disturbing and to grow from that experience. If one wants to be Nietzsche's reader, therefore, it is recommended to pursue, investigate and develop Nietzsche's questions that distinguish themselves above all through their richness in ambiguity, allusion, and polyvalence. Handke reads Nietzsche this way, and he wants to represent the same riddle-richness to his own readers.[14]

For Nietzsche, questioning is a matter of "intellectual conscience" and therefore key to a full existence. Unfortunately, in the modern world, "the desire for certainty" which is the "higher being's inmost craving and deepest distress," has completely slackened. Nietzsche's critique of the lack of intellectual conscience addresses the issue of a generalized modern *laisser faire* based on a mixture of misguided, comfortable self-satisfaction and lukewarm, cowardly indifference:

> Indeed, it has often seemed to me as if anyone calling for an intellectual conscience were as lonely in the most densely populated cities as if he were in a desert. Everybody looks at you with staring eyes and goes right on handling his scales, calling this good and that evil. Nobody even blushes when you intimate that their weights are underweight; nor do people feel outraged; they merely laugh at your doubts. I mean: the great majority of people does not consider it contemptible to believe this or that and to live accordingly, without first having given themselves an account of the final and most certain reasons pro and con, and without even troubling themselves about such reasons afterwards.... But to stand in the midst of this *rerum concordia discors* [discordant concord of things] and this whole marvelous uncertainty and rich ambiguity of existence without questioning, without trembling with the craving and the rapture of such questioning, without at least hating the person who questions, perhaps even finding him faintly amusing – that is what I feel to be contemptible, and this is the feeling for which I look first in everybody. Some folly keeps persuading me that every human being has this feeling, simply because he is human. This is my type of injustice. (*Gay Science* 76)

Nietzsche's injustice, then, is to assume that others are as passionate, curious, courageous and upright as he is. Finding, however, that this is not so, that a true dialogue between his solitary self and the many others cannot be, his only hope remains to continue questioning the imaginary other, who, more often than not, ends up

---

[14]On the importance of questions and questioning in Handke's *Das Spiel vom Fragen*, see Strasser (72-90).

being himself.[15] Yet, we must wonder why no other philosopher before and since Nietzsche engages and captures the reader's attention as intensely and lastingly as Nietzsche does. Indeed, his writing conveys an almost physical presence of the author, who continuously provokes questions and teases the reader, and who, as a matter of experience, speaks directly to the reader. And not from above or afar, but rather at level, in a familiar and confidential manner, like in an interview or an address to a small, intimate circle of fellow beings.[16]

What Nietzsche seeks to achieve, and successfully so, is to hammer windows into walls through which gleam new vistas with angles to explore in the world, and to rattle his readers out of indifference and contaminate them with the passion of inquiry and an urgency to live life every moment to the fullest. Handke has this same impetus, yet he seems more affected by the recognition of being a late-comer than Nietzsche, who turned this fateful fact around and pronounced himself the first in a long lineage of future-oriented free-thinkers. For instance, in *The Gay Science*, Nietzsche makes us fellow bystanders of the crowd that surrounds the mad-man who lights a lantern in broad daylight to seek the God we have murdered. As readers, we are equally challenged by the avalanche of questions the madman hurls at us. Indeed, those with an intellectual conscience will end up having to revaluate their position within an absurd and godless world and ask themselves these same questions: "How shall we comfort ourselves, the murderers of all murderers? What water is there for us to clean ourselves? What festivals of atonement, what sacred games shall we have to invent?" (*Gay Science* 181).

It is difficult to believe that Handke did not have Nietzsche in mind when he, in turn, communicates his most profound existential

---

[15]For Handke, the maturity of an artist is judged according to his ability to accept and survive the essential gap that separates him from the people. The artist either comes to terms with his unavoidable fate of isolation, or "he will go mad, like Nietzsche, who was one of the biggest fools ["Kindskopf"] and a most amiable human being who certainly was only looking to be understood by some other Arian being" (*Zw* 92). Handke's condescending stab at the end is symptomatic of his need to establish distance between him and the philosopher.

[16]I would argue that Nietzsche's appeal to the reader today resides largely in the strategy of his texts to shift roles between interviewer and interviewee.

dilemma in *The Afternoon of a Writer*. Just as Nietzsche's madman
stuns the crowd into bewildered silence, provoking them and us to
rethink the fundamental meaning and possible directions of existence, a down-and-out drunk in a gin mill, where the writer takes a
break, destabilizes the writer to a degree that he loses the connection to his work and is forced to revaluate from ground up his "business" as being and writer in the world:

> Was there any such business in this century? Was there anyone,
> for example, whose deeds and sufferings cried out not only to be
> recorded, catalogued, and publicized in history books but also to
> be handed down in the form of an epic or perhaps only of a little
> song? To what god was it still possible to intone a hymn of
> praise? (And who could still summon up the strength to lament
> the absence of a god?) Where was the long-reigning sovereign
> whose rule demanded to be celebrated by something more than
> gun salutes? Where was his successor, whose accession de-
> served to be greeted by something more than flashbulbs? Where
> were the Olympic victors whose homecoming warranted some-
> thing more than cheers, flag waving, and a flourish of drums?
> What mass murderers of this century, instead of rising from the
> pit with each new justification, might be sent back to their hell
> forever with a single tercet? And how, on the other hand, since
> the end of the world is no mere fancy but a distinct possibility at
> any moment, can one just praise the beloved objects of this
> planet with a stanza or a paragraph about a tree, a countryside, a
> season? Where, today, was one to look for the "aspect of eterni-
> ty"? And in view of all this, who could claim to be an artist and
> to have made a place for himself in the world? (*AW* 67-68).

The figures of the madman and the drunk (dark, Dionysian *alter
egos* of the writers) function ironically as catalysts for a sober investigation into the very possibility of meaningful existence and creation in a godless, cynical world, fueled and undermined by biting
irony at best, cool indifference at worst. For both, either solution –
artificial paradise or leap into nothingness and silence – is ruled out.
The golden age – as is one of the main points in Handke's
Untertagblues, ein Stationendrama (2003; Underground Blues, a
Station Drama) – is gone and probably never existed except through
the writer's lens and pen. And that is where the writer, according to
Nietzsche and Handke, takes his place, comes back into the picture.
In his commitment to isolation and gaining distance from the self
and world, that always seem to be his lot, the artist is free. He gets

up, summons his forces, and goes, searches, digs, selects and rejects in a spirit of firmness and openness:

> He who has attained to only some degree of freedom of mind cannot feel other than the wanderer on the earth – though not as a traveler to a final destination: for this destination does not exist. But he will watch and observe and keep his eyes open to see what is really going on in the world; for this reason he may not let his heart adhere too firmly to any individual thing; within him too there must be something wandering that takes pleasure in change and transience. (*Human* 203)

For Handke, as well as for Nietzsche – whom Handke likes to consider more of a writer than a philosopher – language is central as a means to give form to our experience with ourselves and the world at large: "If I have learned anything at all," says Handke, "I have learned that I have to be careful of my creative impulse, of this difficulty, which perhaps everyone has, of this good, of this new-world-creating impulse, where everything, so to speak, can become language and where one thinks one can bring the world to shine with language, and not to betray it as it almost always happens with language" (Schlueter 176).

Nietzsche and Handke share a fundamental passion and caution with language. One thinks of Handke's earlier plays like *Kaspar* and *The Ride Across Lake Constance*, and young Nietzsche's much quoted text "On Truth and Lie in an Extra-Moral Sense." For both writers, language is ambivalent, constructive and destructive, creating meaning and identity as well as distorting them. Obviously, for the writer it is and remains the only medium for expression of his search for form, the only means to suggest the relationship between the subject and the object, between the self and the world. The will and desire alone to express such a relationship in the first place, to assert one's place within the world through writing, as Nietzsche and Handke both affirm, presupposes also the courage and readiness to explore and question this relation – and therefore the self – always anew. As Nietzsche said, if one thing is needful, it is to "give style to one's character," that is to give form to one's chaos (*Gay Science* 232). As with Nietzsche before him, writing for Handke is the creative activity analogous to life itself. As he affirms in *Die Geschichte des Bleistifts*, "I am now convinced that I was right in my dream to see writing as my form of life" (*GB* 122).

The difficulty consists, however, in committing oneself to the struggle of finding a form of writing, a form of life that is one's own, original form following the laws and rules of one's particular style and taste. This is hard work for Nietzsche, who does not tire of challenging what he perceives as the modern lack of willpower to self-expression and self-fashioning. According to Nietzsche, it is of prime importance to resist modern mediocrity by making deliberate choices, by recognizing and then also admitting one's own weaknesses and strengths, arranging them into an artistic whole, not only for the sake of oneself, but also for respect of others. The art of form-searching, as Handke names it, was already essential for Nietzsche, for whom it was an art that is "practiced by those who survey all the strength and weaknesses of their nature and then fit them into an artistic plan until every one of them appears as art and reason and even weaknesses delight the eye" (*Gay Science* 232). This demands of the artist conceptual integrity, vision and a constant vigilance in matters of choice:

> Here a large mass of second nature has been added; there a piece of original nature has been removed – both times through long practice and daily work at it. Here the ugly that could not be removed is concealed; there it has been reinterpreted and made sublime. Much that is vague and resisted shaping has been saved and exploited for distant views; it is meant to beckon toward the far and immeasurable. In the end ... it becomes evident how the constraint of a single taste governed and formed everything large and small. Whether this taste was good or bad is less important ... if only it was a single taste! (*Gay Science* 232)

What counts in this process is the relentless, committed and stubborn passion of imposing one's own order, one's own form on formlessness. Handke also insists that his concern always is that "there, from this formless maelstrom of the world, emerges a little shape, any little shape" (*Zw* 27). Although Handke's plight sounds more modest than Nietzsche's it is no less ambitious. To incite readers to start giving form to their own chaos, to become productive and desirous to create new worlds yet that capture and justify real life is a goal Handke pursues as relentlessly as Nietzsche:

> Oh, I do have my claims: that what I do should offer an alternate world ["Gegenwelt"] that really exists and is not invented, oh yes I have that claim, that the people who pick this up, become enthusiastic at being able finally to cross over into their world,

our world. I mean otherwise I wouldn't write at all, I'm not interested in producing light literature or some kind of reading fodder; I have my claim to draw from what I conceive as the gift of life and then to build an imperative, compelling model that holds as law. (*Zw* 119-20).

This "alternate world" Handke is building for himself and offers to the reader to consider, and especially to work with, is not an anti-world, a basic negation of all that surrounds us, threatens, disgusts or simply displeases us. But to prepare the terrain for new modes of perception, to retrieve and highlight that which is overlooked and yet deserves attention because it enriches one's life in the world, that is Handke's subject matter. He recognizes a similar concern in Nietzsche: "I don't see him as a nay-sayer, but as a dramatic preserver of something that was always already there, and then of course, I see him as a very fruitful destroyer of that which doesn't deserve to be preserved. This dialectic, these two things, they make up Mr. Nietzsche" (*Zw* 171).

This statement, which may be understood as unintended self-characterization brings us back to the fragile balance that artists like Nietzsche, Handke and other originals seek between an aesthetic negation and affirmation of life. Their claim for and pursuit of beauty, the unfamiliar in the familiar, the original, the fresh and undiscovered, as well as their taste for preservation, their desire for and efforts to follow back, retrieve, and revive the valuable traces and signs of earlier times, places and people for the benefit of the present are fueled by an unusual degree of affirmative energy that passes over to the reader. The value of art lies for both in its capacity to represent life justly, and that demands of the artist what Handke calls the "power of metamorphosis," a quality that is unquestionably Nietzschean (*Zw* 163). This power (and it is the power of writing, of giving form/style) is driven by a positive instinct to look for concrete and spiritual frontier territories that still offer room for the imagination to function freely, that is, uncontaminated by the safety of the cowardly and dead-end commonplace. Nietzsche knew, and Handke learned quickly, that a traditional critique of culture (which any true artwork always already is) – be it from the vantage point of pure negation or pure affirmation – would only perpetuate and contribute to that which precisely does not deserve to be preserved: the banality of mainstream concern and discourse that ultimately leads to indifference and alienation from the self and world.

Therefore, what Handke shares with Nietzsche is a commitment to the discovery and exploration of limits and borderline situations, thresholds and in-between spaces that are, while offering themselves to the writer's and thinker's search, however, not without danger. To see oneself as dynamite (*Ecce Homo* 326) or as a "borderline character" (*Zw* 164) is to leave the comfort zone of established norms and models of thought and play with the possibility of irretrievable loss of self and defeat as artist. Nietzsche lost his first round temporarily to madness, death and defamation. He made sure, however, that the player's spirit and game keep alive in his works, that his riddles still puzzle, his questions still sting, his rhythm still pulses, his laughter still rings – often discomfortingly so. Contrary to what some critics may say, Handke's game is not over by a long shot. Undeterred by the outer world's noise, the writer forges ahead, in the spirit of a modern day Don Quixote (cf. *B*), an old friend of Nietzsche's too.

Works Cited

Bartmann, Christoph. *Suche nach Zusammenhang. Handkes Werk als Prozeß*. Vienna: Braumüller, 1984.

Bernard-Eymard, Isabelle. "Peter Handke et ses critiques. Vicissitudes et résistances d'un auteur à la mode." *Partir, Revenir. En Route avec Peter Handke*. Ed. Laurent Cassagnau, Jacques Le Rider, Erika Tunner. Asnières: Publications de L'Institut d'Allemand, 1992. 189-95.

Blasberg, Cornelia. "Peter Handke und die ewige Wiederkehr des Neuen." *Literaturwissenschaftliches Jahrbuch* 38 (1997) 185-204.

Firda, Richard Arthur. *Peter Handke*. New York: Twayne, 1993.

Gabriel, Norbert. "Neoklassizismus oder Postmoderne? Überlegungen zu Form und Stil von Peter Handkes Werk seit *der Langsamen Heimkehr*." *Modern Austrian Literature* 24. 3-4 (1991) 99-109.

Klinkowitz, Jerome, and James Knowlton. *Peter Handke and the Postmodern Transformation: The Goalie's Journey Home.* Columbia, MS: U of Missouri P, 1983.

Konzett, Matthias. *The Rhetoric of National Dissent in Thomas Bernhard, Peter Handke, and Elfriede Jelinek.* Rochester, NY: Camden House, 2000.

Müller, André. "Wer einmal versagt im Schreiben, hat für immer versagt." Interview with Peter Handke. *Die Zeit* 3. Mar. 1989: 77-78.

Nietzsche, Friedrich. *Basic Writings of Nietzsche.* Trans. Walter Kaufmann. New York: The Modern Library, 1969. (Contains *The Birth of Tragedy, Selected Aphorisms, Beyond Good and Evil, On the Genealogy of Morals, The Case of Wagner, Ecce Homo.*)

–. *Ecce Homo.* Trans. Walter Kaufmann. New York: Random House, 1969.

–. *The Gay Science.* Trans. Walter Kaufmann. New York: Random House, 1974.

–. "On Truth and Lie in an Extra-Moral Sense." *The Portable Nietzsche.* Trans. Walter Kaufmann. New York: Viking Press, 1954. 42-47.

–. *Sämtliche Werke. Kritische Studienausgabe.* 15 vols. Ed. Giorgio Colli and Mazzino Montinari. Berlin: de Gruyter, 1988.

–. *Thus Spoke Zarathustra.* Trans. Walter Kaufmann. New York: Viking Press, 1966.

–. *Twilight of the Idols.* Trans. R. J. Hollingdale. London: Penguin, 1975.

–. *Unfashionable Observations.* Trans. Richard T. Gray. Stanford: Stanford UP, 1995.

Pizer, John. "Goethe's Presence in Handke's *Langsame Heimkehr* Tetralogy." *Michigan Germanic Studies* 17.2 (1991) 128-45.

Pütz, Peter. "Handke und Nietzsche: 'Kein Marterbild mehr malen.'" *Peter Handke. Die Langsamkeit der Welt.* Ed. Gerhard Fuchs and Gerhard Melzer. Graz: Droschl, 1993. 63-81.

–. *Peter Handke.* Frankfurt am Main: Suhrkamp, 1982.

Riedel, Nicolai. "Peter Handke: Werk und Literaturwissenschaftliche Diskussion. Eine Auswahlbibliographie 1989-1998." *Text und Kritik* 24/24a. Ed. Heinz Ludwig Arnold. 6th ed. Munich: edition text + kritik, 1999. 124-38.

Schlueter, June. "An Interview With Peter Handke." *The Plays and Novels of Peter Handke*. Pittsburgh: U of Pittsburgh P, 1981. 163-77.

Schneider, Peter. "The Writer Takes a Hike." *The New Republic* 3 Mar. 1997: 34-39.

Stendhal, Marie Henri Beyle. *Racine and Shakespeare*. Trans. Guy Daniels. New York: The Crowell-Collier Press, 1962.

Strasser, Peter. *Der Freudenstoff: Zu Handke eine Philosophie.* Salzburg: Residenz, 1990.

Vollmer, Michael. *Das gerechte Spiel: Sprache und Individualität bei Friedrich Nietzsche und Peter Handke.* Würzburg: Königshausen & Neumann, 1995.

Werth, Wolfgang. "Handke von Handke." *Über Peter Handke*. Ed. Michael Scharang. Frankfurt am Main: Suhrkamp, 1979. 331-39.

Ziolkowski, Theodore. Rev. of *Sommerlicher Nachtrag zu einer winterlichen Reise*. By Peter Handke. *World Literature Today* 71.3 (Summer 1997) 584-85.

Land and Landscape in Handke's Texts

Mireille Tabah[*]

PETER HANDKE HAS DEFINED himself as a writer for whom place is essential: "Yes, I am and have always been a writer of places. For me, places are the spaces, the demarcations which generate any experience to begin with. My starting point is never a story or an event, an incident, but always a place" (*Zw* 19). Indeed, since *Der kurze Brief zum langen Abschied* (1972; *Short Letter, Long Farewell*, 1974) and, more clearly still, ever since the *Langsame Heimkehr* tetralogy (1979-81; *Slow Homecoming*, 1985), the quest for the evocation of a space – or, more precisely, of a landscape[1] in which the hero may feel in perfect harmony with himself and with the universe – has constituted the driving force of Handke's narratives. Frequently it is the account of a real or imaginary journey[2] where the decisive moments are the protagonist's communion with an ideal site through what might be called a landscape epiphany.[3] As

---

[*]Translated by Frank Pilipp, assisted by John Adams and Franca Bellarsi. This essay is a continuation of the author's article of 1994 and examines Handke's stance toward contemporary history and his paradoxical concept of utopia within the context of postmodernism in his works published since *Mein Jahr in der Niemandsbucht* (1994; *My Year in the No-Man's-Bay*, 1998).
[1]The term 'landscape' is used here in its broadest sense of a location which presents characteristic features, referring to both urban and natural landscapes.
[2]*Die Abwesenheit* (1987; *Absence*, 1990) narrates the journey of four characters traveling through spaces in which the familiar merges with the imaginary, thereby lending itself to multiple transformations – hence the subtitle *A Fairy Tale*. In the novel entitled *In einer dunklen Nacht ging ich aus meinem stillen Haus* (1997; *On a Dark Night I Left My Silent House*, 2000), the Taxham pharmacist crosses Europe by car. In the process, he traverses a European continent whose boundaries have become blurred and in which Spanish and Yugoslavian landscapes blend into each other to generate an imaginary space and time.
[3]The term epiphany refers to a fortuitous moment of intensified perception of the world and of the self. Introduced by James Joyce in *Stephen Hero* (1904-1906), the term was used in German for the first time by Adorno within the framework of the aesthetic theories which were being developed in Germany at the time (see Adorno 125, 159, 384, 443). Karl Heinz Bohrer placed it at the

indefatigable travelers fleeing the horrors of history and the alienation of the individual in contemporary society, Handke's heroes
traverse lands and landscapes always with the same goal: to find the
place which will enable them to experience that sensation of plenitude produced by the feeling of being a unified subject in symbiosis
with a world of coherence. This is, according to Handke, the only
'true sensation' in a universe in which the omnipresence of violence
and war, the objectification of the individual through technocracy
and through the oppressive force of reigning ideologies have alienated the majority of human beings from their own desires and
rendered them indifferent not only to unhappiness, but, far worse, to
their very yearning for happiness.[4] Places and landscapes are for the
author the primary factor and the privileged theater of the epiphanic
sensation of plenitude and harmony, as Handke describes it in his
correspondence with Herbert Gamper, and thus the primary framework of the existential experience of a nearly forgotten bliss,
"where one ... experiences oneself more intensely" (*Zw* 138):

> ... where I experience myself in these moments of realization
> most strongly as the one who I really am. This occurs above all
> in the presence of nature, to which one has somewhat striven to
> come closer ..., and actually, that is the law that one projects
> this plenitude – because it is really a kind of plenitude – ..., this
> plenitude of being which one experiences in such moments
> before nature, as the law of action and, in a more elaborate
> sense, of writing. (*Zw* 113)

To rediscover the idea of and thus the desire for happiness – in the
primary intrinsic meaning of this feeling so difficult to define

---

center of his aesthetic theory (originally in *Ästhetik* 354 et passim). As regards
Handke's work, the term has been applied mainly in a negative sense, namely
as a refusal of history in favor of moments of communion between the self and
the world; see, for example, Durzak (155-56), Bartmann (193-94), and
Zschachlitz (145-46). Contrary to these critics, an earlier essay by this author
("Structure") highlights the utopian potential inherent in Handke's conception
of epiphany.

[4]This consideration derives from the double meaning of the 1972 narrative
Wunschloses Unglück (*A Sorrow Beyond Dreams*, 1975) in which Handke
shows that it was the repression of desire by history and society what led his
mother to suicide. *Wings of Desire*, the English title of Wim Wenders's film
Der Himmel über Berlin (1988), whose dialogues were written by Handke, adequately conveys this theme which is both central to the film and to Handke's
overall work.

through language –, to become one with oneself and the world, and to mediate this desire through writing, are the foundations upon which Handke's entire work has developed since 1972.[5] Furthermore, the author affirms in his last journal, *Am Felsfenster morgens* (2000; Mornings at the Natural Arch): "Without place, no happiness" (*FM* 151).

Beyond its subjectively existential and identity-forming function, the landscape epiphany mediates a lesson of history to the one who experiences it. Places and landscapes are for Handke carriers of a "message"[6] of universal love and peace, in that the desire for happiness activates the vision of "another" form of history – Handke speaks of a "world structure" (*Zw* 55) – radically different from the age-old one founded upon violence and alienation. He conceives of lands and landscapes as the "space for possibilities," a "space of projection, in which the possible emerges in outline" (*Zw* 115). The insinuation of this future potential ultimately encapsulates the utopia of a world of peace and harmony.

The at once identity-defining and utopian purpose fulfilled by the evocation of landscapes nevertheless raises a number of issues that have divided Handke's critics into fervent admirers and fierce adversaries. Analyzing the structure and function of places and landscapes in Handke's texts delineates this problem, which centers around the principal notions of utopia and of myth[7] and leads to the question of whether Handke's work falls within the scope of modern or of postmodern literature.[8] It is a matter of determining to what extent the utopian potential of epiphany-inducing places and landscapes which Handke unflaggingly describes is thwarted by a contradictory purpose: the mythicization of reality and history.[9] A closer examination of Handke's landscapes should shed light on the way in which the author and his protagonists connect and interact

---

[5]The quest for happiness in Handke's work is the theme of the volume edited by Melzer and Tükel.

[6]Handke talks of "messages of places" in *Versuch über die Jukebox* (1991; *Essay on the Jukebox*, 1994 [*J* 111]).

[7]This problem is at the center of the conversation between Handke and Gamper (see *Zw*). Among the more recent studies, see also Gottwald and Kniesche.

[8]See among others Konzett and Kniesche.

[9]Handke's mythicization of reality is viewed by critics sometimes in positive (e.g. Gottwald) but more often in negative terms (e.g. Bartmann; esp. Renner).

with reality. It should also help to determine whether, ultimately, the "message of places" reveals itself to be the utopian message promised by the author, or, contrarily, whether it amounts to an ideological message: a message where the description of locations in which nature occupies a primordial place is meant to suggest the natural essence of reality, and thus declare it a universal and absolute principle.

The answer to this question, then, should determine more clearly the extent to which Handke's work, since *Short Letter, Long Farewell*, has unfolded in the wake of modernity or postmodernity. Whereas postmodernity renounces the dream of a world destroyed by modern civilization, in which the individual would have lived in harmony with himself and with the universe, and sees in such a conception an ideology that rejects the plurality of opinions and the right to be different, modernity clings to this dream with a sense of nostalgia. In this vein, Kniesche, with reference to Lyotard, adequately summarizes the "melancholy" which characterizes modernity "as the pathological inability to forget an imaginary symbiosis between self and world, a symbiosis which has been lost" (318). Yet, despite the postmodern aversion to every form of ideology, it is precisely through their evocation of landscapes that Handke's stories seem to reflect this modern nostalgia for an imaginary world of harmony and of coherence. That they themselves are not exempt from a totalitarian and reactionary ideology is shown by the melancholy idealization of the war-devastated landscapes of the former Yugoslavia.

One thing, however, is certain: Austria and, to an even greater extent, Germany do not form part of those spaces which, conducive to the experience of epiphany, awaken in Handke and in his protagonists the desire for happiness and for peace. These are nations too heavily burdened with historical traumas. For the author and his heroes, Germany represents first and foremost the country of Nazi savagery, which caused an atrocious war. The thundering noise of the bombardments in the closing days of the war still resonates in the ears of the heroes of *Die Hornissen* (1966; The Hornets) or of *Short Letter, Long Farewell*. And it is above all everyday violence which the narrator of *Die Lehre der Sainte-Victoire* (1980; *The Lesson of Mont Sainte-Victoire*, 1985) perceives in the present-day "increasingly evil and sclerotic Federal Republic" where he attempts in vain to find a new country (*LSV* 184). Austria appears to Handke as the ally of the aggressor and as a country dominated today by that reactionary petite bourgeoisie which carried Kurt Waldheim to power and has become a master in the art of repressing its National Socialist past.[10] In *Versuch über die Müdigkeit* (1991; *Essay on Tiredness*, 1994), Handke lashes out against the Austrian people in vengeful tirades reminiscent of the fierce vehemence of Thomas Bernhard. He goes so far as to call his compatriots a "swarming mob of habitual criminals and their accomplices" and "untiring mass murderers of both sexes" and concludes that "the Austrians ... are the first hopelessly corrupt, totally incorrigible people in history, forever incapable of repentance or conversion" (*J* 17, 18). Handke's diary *Am Felsfenster morgens* abounds with negative reflections on his native country and concludes with the observation that the attempt to return to Austria at the end of the seventies has ended in failure: "As far as my own country, Austria, is concerned, I believe to have failed" (*FM* 435). "No, Austria is not my country" (*FM* 456).

Nonetheless, Handke claims to love his country: "Because it is here in Austria, in our, yes our country, that our eyes are open to the woods and water and that our ears are pricked up for the sound of the wind and the snowfall ..." (*LS* 72). It is thus through the mediation of nature that Handke is able to reappropriate Austria as a country for himself. From his window, from the height of the Mönchsberg cliff in Salzburg, the author contemplates an immutable nature which brings him a feeling of peaceful happiness (*FM* 462-63). Thus fortified, he ventures forth into the suburbs of the city, those anonymous transitional spaces where nature merges with civilization, where history leaves no traces. These locations, found in *Der Chinese des Schmerzes* (1983; *Across*, 1986), *Nachmittag eines Schriftstellers* (1986; *The Afternoon of a Writer*, 1989), and, a decade later, in the novel *On a Dark Night I Left My Silent House*, are nevertheless neither unique to Salzburg nor specifically Austrian. The village of Taxham, in the vicinity of Salzburg, as described in *On a Dark Night* offers, for example, a striking resemblance to Chaville, the Parisian suburb in *My Year in the No-Man's-Bay*. Both

---

[10]See "Eine andere Rede über Österreich" (A Different Speech About Austria) in *Langsam im Schatten* (*LS* 64-73).

represent impersonal constructions. Taxham is actually referred to as a "no-man's-land" (*DN* 9) situated on the threshold of a big city sealed off at one end by a dense web of railroad tracks and at the other by woods. Both are "bays" or "enclaves" (*DN* 6) in the midst of modern civilization, in which outcasts – such as immigrants, the unemployed, and the elderly – have found refuge from society. The Austrian natural world which the author discovers from the heights of the Mönchsberg, and which each morning reinvigorates him[11] and induces him to write, also recalls many aspects of the landscapes of America, Spain, or Yugoslavia described in *Slow Homecoming*, *Essay on Tiredness*, or *Repetition*: the wind-swept "virgin forest" that Handke glimpses from his window, the snowflakes which flutter over it well into March (*FM* 460, 462), the vast Salzach plain; all these do not form, in his eyes, a site characteristic of the environs of Salzburg, but an atemporal and universal landscape "in which all forms ranging from the city to the countryside yielded a greater one. Was it China, South America, Alaska?" (*FM* 415).

Traveling through Spain, the narrator of *Essay on the Jukebox* the *alter ego* of the author, likewise notices that "Almost every strange place ... had revealed itself to him ... as part of the world" (*J* 62). Unable to identify with the Austrian people and their history, Handke has evidently found in the Salzburg landscape a set of geographical features which make it an ideal place. It is represent-ative of all those vital spaces on the surface of the earth which have the power to confer upon him the all-important feeling of belonging in the world. But if it is through the landscape that the author reappropriates his homeland, Austria represents no more of a father-land than all those other countries graced with those "magical" (*LSV* 147) places in which Handke and his protagonists experience the 'true sensation' of being in harmony with themselves and the universe. This 'magic' is the only provision that makes a place "a small piece of homeland": "one experiences a reintegration of the fatherland or one feels reintegrated by it" (*Zw* 32).

Every landscape representation proceeds from an array of char-acteristic elements, some more important than others. From the recurring motifs, structures, and signs emerges a limited range of

---

[11]Cf: "And: Place and Vitality; *Locality* and Vitality" (*FM* 133).

significant landscapes privileged by the author, regardless of their geographical or national affiliation. They can be grouped into two types: the natural and the urban or semi-urban landscape. If human traces are present in the natural landscape, they tend to become one with the original elements of nature: earth, light, water, and air. They are usually wide-open, nearly empty spaces, delineated by the curve of the horizon. Some are altogether deprived of vegetation, such as the polar landscape described at the outset of *The Long Way Around* or the stone desert of *Absence*, while others are sparse in flora – Handke compares them frequently to steppes or to savannahs – like the Yugoslavian Karst in *Repetition* or the Spanish steppe in *On a Dark Night*. Handke often situates these spaces on raised ground, like the Yugoslavian Karst, the "Philosopher's Plateau" (*LSV* 160 et passim) in *The Lesson of Mont Sainte-Victoire*, the "Grand Ballon" mountain overlooking the Rhine in *Kindergeschichte* (1981; *Child Story*, 1985), or the high Castilian plateau in *Essay on the Jukebox*. Stillness reigns in these vast spaces bathed in luminous colors, which set off every element in all its natural purity.

It is well known that Handke is partly color-blind and mainly perceives impressions of light that are relatively intense. The absence of green hues and of any type of lush vegetation in general is striking. The intense blue of the sky, the red of the berries of a mulberry tree in the glistening sun as for example in *The Lesson of Mont Sainte-Victoire* remain equally rare in the author's landscapes which are dominated by white and yellow tones. In *Across*, Loser is fascinated by the gleam of white, which for him is the carnal color radiant with the force of life (*Ac* 96). While the limestone of both the Karst and of the Sainte-Victoire range are white, the white matter *par excellence* for Handke's protagonists is snow. It is synonymous with joy and rejuvenation (*DN* 54) and covers innumerable landscapes painted by the author: Alaska in *The Long Way Around,* the suburbs of Salzburg in winter in *Across* or *Afternoon of a Writer*, Castile in winter in *Jukebox*, the Drina Valley bordering Serbia and Bosnia (*JR* 54), and, by way of an apotheosis, the village of Taxham on the last page of *On a Dark Night*. Another color of light is yellow, which in its warmest tones illuminates the landscapes. The yellow sun beams forth in the blue sky over the polar snows, on the "Grand Ballon" mountain or over the Sainte-Victoire massif.

Nevertheless, large white-gray clouds often subdue the glare, as in the paintings of the great seventeenth-century Dutch masters, whose works inspire Handke (*LSV* 187, 201). It is also a softer light which shines on a landscape at sunrise or at twilight, for example at the time of the "event in space" in *Long Way Around* (*LWA* 15), during the epiphany of the mulberry (*LSV* 175), and in the description of the woods of Morzg in the last chapter of *Sainte-Victoire* or in the "mystical moment" on the bank of the Seine in *Child Story* (*CS* 228). In those spaces of silence and light, peaceful waters often flow, generally meandering rivers, like those of Alaska, the Seine and the Rhine, or the rivers of Serbia in *Eine winterliche Reise* (1996; *A Journey to the Rivers: Justice for Serbia*, 1997). Yet it can also be just a simple canal as in *Across*. Finally, over the high plateaus, across the steppes and savannahs, or over the streams of flowing waters, it is a lively wind which sharpens the senses, allowing one to distinguish in the apparent disorder of nature each thing and each form, both as a whole and in its complementarity, from all other elements of the landscape.

These natural landscapes, frequently vast, open and greatly elevated spaces, allow a synthetic view of the environment and thereby reveal its deep geological structure. The protagonist perceives there, in a veritable cosmic vision, what he senses to be the original order and cohesion of the universe (*LWA* 4 *et passim*). In these vast landscapes which Sorger refers to as "primeval" (*LWA* 27), where nature still reigns unspoiled, the protagonist is "initiated" through wind, light, earth, and water into "the law of the world" (*R* 201), which is for Handke none other than the eternal "*prevail*[ing]" (*Ac* 137) of the essential elements of nature. This "law" which directs nature and the world is not a succession of natural catastrophes which have transformed the surface of the earth, as borne out by the absence of chaotic and jagged landscapes:

> Destructive as they may have been (and still were) in the objective world, the forces that went to make up this landscape, in becoming present to him ... were transformed by their own laws into a benign inner force, which calmed him and gave him strength. ... his consciousness of standing on a flat beach ... gave him the feeling that the planet earth was a civilized, homelike, intelligible place.... (*LWA* 5)

Handke's "law of the world" is analogous to the "gentle law" articulated by Stifter in the celebrated prologue to the collection

Bunte Steine (1853; *Many-colored Stones*, 1968), referred to in
Sainte-Victoire (*LSV* 176): a sweet and regular succession of
peaceful and immutable phenomena, which brings humankind a
sense of permanence and stability: "The world was solid, sustaining
soil" (*LSV* 148-49). This fundamental aspect of nature as envisaged
by Handke manifests itself, on the one hand, in the coherence of the
landscape structure and, on the other, in the plethora of symbols expressing security, unity, and balance. These landscapes constitute
configurations in which diverse elements dissolve into tranquil
harmony. Inspired by pictorial methods of composition, the author
spaces out the landscape distinguishing between foreground, center,
and background (cf. *Zw* 57; *LSV* 161; *LWA* 33). The sky is vast as in
the paintings of Jakob van Ruisdael (*LSV* 200-01), but in the foreground, a flock of birds, a pathway, houses, or a tree make the area
of the center ground appear less empty.

Like Cézanne, Handke evidences a predilection for terraced
inclines which form a natural and well-ordered picture.[12] He prefers
the curves of vales and hills to the rigor of straight lines. The
prototypes of these spaces – "broad horizons with a gentle, even
hilliness" (*JR* 38) – are the Slovenian and Serbian landscapes,
which for Handke represent the very image of the sweetness of
paradise, and he cannot forgive history for having destroyed them,
as he testifies in his essay *Abschied des Träumers vom neunten
Land* (1991; The Dreamer's Farewell to the Ninth Land). It is
equally significant that the curve, the "Line of Beauty and Grace,"
dominates the landscape of the hills of the Seine in *Essay On the
Successful Day* (*J* 121), where an epiphany experience gives the
narrator an idea what should epitomize a successful day: a
succession of similar instants of pure joy in the serene contemplation of the tranquil harmony of a scenery. The numerous concave
shapes (vaults, arcades, and cupolas) which occupy the places
described by Handke and which have not escaped the attention of
critics (e.g. Bartmann 161, 230) likewise represent many signs of
balance, stability, and security. The sheltering crown of umbrella
pines, which lends its title – "The Great Arch" – to the first part of
The Lesson of Mont Sainte-Victoire, conjure up the image of the

---

[12]Examples are the Sainte-Victoire range, the Grand Ballon mountain, the
slopes from Mönchsberg to Salzburg, or those of Jesenice in Slovenia.

world as an unshakable foundation where anguish no longer has a
place (*LSV* 147). In *The Long Way Around* the sky vaults forth to
enclose all humanity under the shelter of its cupola (*LWA* 15, 87),
and even the oval of beech leaves in the woods of Morzg exudes an
"eternal peace" (*LSV* 209).

The tendency towards reconciliation signified by the "gentle
law" governing a quiet and harmonious nature manifests itself just
as much in the descriptions of urban and semi-urban landscapes as
in the natural ones. Generally it is nature in its rawest state that
frightens Handke's protagonist. Absolutely bare stretches of land
awaken in him the fear of a void which seems to "devour" him (*LSV*
180). In the long run, the solitude and silence indispensable to
triggering the experience of epiphany threaten to cut him off from
himself and from the world: "You are in danger of ending up
beyond the confines of the world," realizes the pharmacist of
Taxham and decides to bring an end to his quest across the steppe
(*DN* 159). The natural landscape thus always tends to become
inhabited. It is situated at the edge of civilization, in the proximity
of its villages or suburbs, and bears the traces of man: a roadway
which unfolds at length, a train or passing bus, an airplane flying
across the sky. Conversely, nature invades urban civilization, conferring an atmosphere of peaceful serenity upon anonymous and
oppressive metropolitan centers, which, in Handke's earliest works,
were still symbols of modern alienation.[13] Already in *Short Letter,
Long Farewell*, the narrator paints a synthetic portrait of New York
resulting in an orderly and serene impression which he compares to
the "gentle panorama of nature" (*SL* 47). In *The Long Way Around*,
the wind, the snow, the sun, and the birds pervade New York, which
for Sorger becomes transformed into "a living and powerful natural
organism" (*LWA* 116). In *The Lesson of Mont Sainte-Victoire*,
Berlin, at first envisioned as the symbol of a universe of blind
violence, metamorphoses into a haven of serenity once the narrator
discovers the coherence of its geology (*LSV* 186-88). And
ultimately, it comes as no surprise that the parks – Marigny Square

---

[13]One thinks of Vienna in *Die Angst des Tormanns beim Elfmeter* (1970; *The
Goalie's Anxiety at the Penalty Kick*, 1972) of Paris and Berlin in the essay
"Die offenen Geheimnisse der Technokratie" (The Open Secrets of Technocra-
cy; *Wü* 31-38).

in Paris, Central Park in New York[14] –, enclaves of nature and calm
in the very midst of the urban hell, are precisely those places where
an epiphanic experience reveals the cohesion which unites all things
in sweet harmony.

Serene nature continually cuts into the chaos of modern civilization in order to 'naturalize' and harmonize it. Hence it is understandable why Handke feels a particular affinity for those transitional spaces between nature and the big city that the suburbs represent
– suburbs like Kronberg near Frankfurt in *Die linkshändige Frau*
(1976; *The Left-Handed Woman*, 1978); Kronberg and Clamart near
Paris in *Child Story*; Chaville, a Paris suburb verging on the forest
of Meudon, in *My Year in the No-Man's-Bay*; the outskirts of
Salzburg in *Across*, *The Afternoon of a Writer*, and *On a Dark Night
I Left My Silent House*. Particularly in his last two extended narratives, the city outskirts are impersonal spaces with deserted streets,
where people still quietly slip into cafés or into the typical, anonymous supermarket, where, side by side, individuals nonetheless
manage to preserve their respective autonomy. Situated on the outskirts of forests and dotted with gardens, these enclaves, moreover,
remain linked to the big city and to the world at large through the
proximity of roads, railroads, and airports. They represent, *par excellence*, the "thresholds" so dear to the author (*Zw* 113, 183),
because they constitute points of transition between nature and
civilization, between the isolated individual and the human community. It is at such points that Handke and his protagonists have
the secure feeling of belonging to humanity, while at the same time
being able to protect the space of freedom indispensable to the
contemplation of the "sweet law" which controls the eternal phenomena of nature and the immutable, simple, and tranquil motions of
everyday life (*MY* 164-65).

Whether natural, urban, or semi-urban, Handke's landscapes
constitute a collection of signs representative of an authentic form
of writing which transmits to those who "read" them the "message"

---

[14]It is in Marigny Square – at twilight of course – that the protagonist of *Die
Stunde der wahren Empfindung* (1975; *A Moment of True Feeling*, 1977) ex-
periences the epiphany of the "three miraculous objects" (*MTF* 63-64). In *The
Long Way Around*, Sorger experiences a similar epiphany in a coffee shop on
the verge of Central Park, which, however, extends to the whole of humanity
(*LWA* 113-16). This event is referred to again in *Essay on Tiredness* (*J* 28-29).

(*J* 111) inscribed in the depicted location. It is in this way that the narrator of *Repetition* conceives of the importance of every landscape: "... I had taken in the details of the valley, but now I saw them as letters, as a series of signs ... combining to form a coherent script" (*R* 82). Ever since *Short Letter*, but even more so since the publication of the *Slow Homecoming* tetralogy, the "message" conveyed by the places which the author describes is a constant. On the one hand, all these spaces evoke order, coherence, harmony, balance, stability, permanence, serenity, in that the landscape "gives body to a vision of peace" (*LSV* 144). On the other hand, this notion of peace is depicted as a natural "law," both universal and eternal, insofar as it is inscribed in unspoiled nature or in the places where civilization still carries its imprint: "I now interpreted this land before my eyes, ... this describable earth, as 'the world'" (*R* 82-83). This idea of harmony represents the true essence of the world.

The peaceful and harmonious essence of the universe reveals itself to the protagonist once the landscape in view generates its own epiphany before his eyes. In those magical instants in which the protagonist feels in perfect symbiosis with the landscape, he is intuitively overcome by the inherent coherence of the world as a primary truth that has been forgotten in the chaos of modern civilization: "For I knew that unity is possible. ... without intermediate links" (*LSV* 190; cf. *LWA* 75). The certainty that the universe forms a tranquil and coherent whole is not just a simple subjective conviction for Handke. On the contrary, it can be felt by any individual with an attentive and perceptive gaze devoid of any ideological bias. According to Handke, the spiritual union produced by the contemplation of landscapes awakens in every human being an irresistible feeling of solidarity with and love for all humanity. Already in *A Moment of True Feeling*, an epiphany of three everyday objects brought about the same sensation: "At the encouraging sight of those three miraculous objects in the sand, [Keuschnig] felt a helpless affection for everyone, but he had no desire to be cured of it, because it now seemed perfectly sensible" (*MTF* 64).

The narrator of *Sainte-Victoire* experiences a similar emotional response of universal brotherhood during the epiphany provoked by a mulberry bush in the mountains of the Provence:

> In addition to innocently uniting the fragments of my own life
> with the mulberry spots on the dust, the moment of fantasy ...
> revealed to me anew my kinship with other, unknown lives, thus
> acting as an unspecified love and striving to communicate itself
> in a form conducive to fidelity, namely, as a justified project
> aimed at the cohesion of my never-to-be-defined nation as our
> common form of existence.... (*LSV* 175)

The universality of the epiphanic experience thus engenders in the
protagonist a sense of belonging, of being part of a human community united by the revelation of the harmonious essence of the
universe that every place not totally corrupted by modern civilization can commune with each individual.

The soothing contemplation of the wholeness of a landscape can
thus abolish the absurd rifts that cause violence and war. The
driving force of history will then no longer be cruelty and barbarism; instead, the fundamental idea of peace, if rediscovered through
the epiphanic experience generated by landscapes, will reconcile all
humanity in a shared feeling of solidarity and altruism. Such is the
true "message of places" (*J* 111) that he movingly opposes to a
history of conquests, wars, oppression, and violence, which humanity has known. The epiphany provoked by a landscape untouched by
the cruelty of history allows Handke's characters to envisage a
totally different form of history, which the narrator of *Sainte-
Victoire* calls "an existence in peace" (*LSV* 147), and which Sorger,
in *The Long Way Around*, refers to as a "promising history, in which
nothing violent or abrupt ever happened" (*LWA* 33). This vision
becomes manifest before Sorger's eyes in the immense vale of a
polar river that appears to him as "a human valley in a possible
eternal peace" (*LWA* 34). Thus, the landscape ultimately becomes
the manifestation of a historical utopia: "I have learned," affirms
Sorger,

> that history is not a mere sequence of evils ... but has also, from
> time immemorial, been a peace-fostering *form* that can be
> perpetuated by anyone (including me).... Thus the night of this
> century, during which I searched my face obsessively for the
> features of a despot or a conqueror, has ended for me. My
> history (our history, friends) shall become bright, just as this
> moment has been bright.... (*LWA* 114-15)

Handke has repeatedly and unequivocally emphasized the utopian potential that he sees embedded in the aura of landscapes. The

fundamental idea of calm fulfillment that the narrative is to confer upon the reader only has meaning insofar as it embodies a vision of the future: "This idea ... cast its beam exclusively forward, on the future. If it can be told, then only in the future form, a future story ..." (*J* 129-30). As Cézanne in his paintings, Handke conceives of his narratives not as affirmative descriptions of happiness and serenity regained, but rather as "proposals" (*LSV* 180) envisioning existence and the world from a different perspective, a more content and harmonious one than that which society and history have effectively imposed upon the individual: "Narrating always implies the projection of a humane world, well, for me at least" (*Zw* 167). Handke defines the ideal narrative as "a world, a history of mankind, that tells itself as it should be. Utopian? The other day I read here on a poster: 'La utopia no existe ...'" (*J* 31-32).

The contradiction here is only an apparent one. The non-place – or non-*topos* – is a fiction, precisely because there exist those places conveying the "message" that the history of humanity can be transformed into one of tranquility and harmony. The structure of the landscape is the materialized anticipatory vision – "a primal form" (*R* 210) – of this other "structure" of the story of the world (*Zw* 55) that the narrator of *Repetition* in turn discovers in the Yugoslavian Karst: "Nowhere, up until now, have I found a country which with all its divers [sic] components ... struck me, like the Karst, as a possible model for the future" (*R* 210). In general, landscapes are visions of "possibility" for Handke.

Hence, the ideal narrative amounts to an "epic" journey in which the description of places spared by the violence of history is to evoke the possibility to realize, at least in part, the harmonious essence of the universe. Whether they be natural landscapes sheltered from civilization or transitory spaces, enclaves of nature verging on urban areas, these "oases of emptiness" (*Ab* 43) devoid of any historical imprint are for Handke the only places that can still convey the perception of a fundamental harmony and the utopian vision of a human race reconciled in universal love. In *Absence*, the old man thus reflects the author's credo: "I believe in those places without fame or name, best characterized perhaps by the fact that *nothing* is there, while all around there is *something*. I believe in the power of those places because nothing happens there *anymore* and nothing has happened there *yet*" (*Ab* 43).

This "not yet," which Handke emphasizes, is the promise of a future happiness which would consist of rediscovering (*Ac* 36) or remembering (*R* 73) a happiness which no longer exists, but which landscapes that have not yet been disfigured by history allow us to imagine: "There exists a strange feeling like ... watermarks of something that once was, which can be imagined, precisely because of the emptiness, the no-longer-at-hand quality, as if the return of that something – admittedly in a different form – was inevitable" (*Zw* 152-53).

One understands at once that the primary mission of the writer is to safeguard these places and to bestow their "lesson" on the "people" who make up humanity, before such locations become totally annihilated in the tempests of history. For Handke, this is precisely what Cézanne had achieved in painting: to "realize" a landscape by highlighting its structure and substance, that is, to render visible to our weary eyes the tranquil harmony of essentials and to convey to us their "lesson" of before it became too late, "as though these things were the last of their kind" (*LSV* 179): "His reality became the form he achieved, the form that does not lament transience or the vicissitudes of history, but transmits an existence in peace" (*LSV* 147).

It is always this objective that Handke pursues in the narrative of his travels in Slovenia and Serbia between 1991 and 1996 – narratives correctly regarded as controversial. The politically unacceptable stance of siding with the Serbian aggressor was intended, paradoxically, as a message of peace. The provocation of these texts lies precisely in the fundamental significance Handke accords to the "lessons of history" that can be conveyed by those rare landscapes of the former Yugoslavia that war has not totally destroyed. Admittedly, he recognizes that the miraculously preserved beauty of these places is secondary to the omnipresence of horror; nevertheless, it matters to him more than ever to safeguard their message of peace in a universe ravaged by barbarism, before such spots are forever erased: "sheltering of things endangered" (*LSV* 181), the "re-remembering" of a vanished tranquility thanks to the description of landscapes at the margins of history – this was exactly the "lesson" of *Sainte-Victoire*, of *Repetition* and *Absence*:

> To record the evil facts, that's good. But something else is ·
> needed for a peace, something not less important than the facts.

So now it's time for the poetic? Or say, rather than "the poetic," that which binds, encompasses – the impulse to a common remembering, as the possibility for reconciliation of individuals, for the second, the common childhood. ... that second, common childhood will arise exactly through the detour of recording certain trivialities.... (*JR* 82)

Journey to the Rivers demonstrates better than any other text that the utopian message associated with places in Handke's writing goes back to the romantic project of the dialectical return to a happy "childhood" for humanity which can only be accomplished by a radical withdrawal from history: "pull[ing] out of this history that repeats every century, out of this disastrous chain, pull[ing] out into another story" (*JR* 80) are two complementary movements. Handke's overtly reactionary position on what he conceived of as a utopia of places does not constitute a utopian vision of history, but a myth that may degenerate into revisionist aberrations.

The mythicization of reality occurs at three levels. First of all, it transpires at the level of ideology or the 'holistic' fantasy inherent in the myth conveyed by the landscapes, in other words, the plunge into the universal. Secondly, it can be detected at the level of semiotics in Handke's nature images of the vision of a universe of peace and harmony, insofar as this vision is presented through the description of landscapes seemingly originating in the intrinsic quality of the universe. And finally, one can see this mythicization at work in Handke's absolute de-historicizing of reality, which can ultimately amount to its negation altogether.

Nevertheless, Handke affirms that he simply confines himself to realizing a landscape *à la* Cézanne. He insists that he strives to remain faithful to places in his accounts of them, that he limits himself to 'cleansing' them of certain accidental or minor details in order to protect their essential properties and their immanent structure:

Should you approach or experience the places which I have tried to describe, I think that you would find that imagination goes hand in hand with faithfulness...; what represents at the same time my efforts, my difficulties, and my joy is nothing else but the attempt to match through language, through a language as clear and pure as possible, that which I see and simultaneously experience. (*Zw* 31)

Yet it is precisely to the exclusion of everything else that Handke describes those places which correspond to his yearning for a pre-established harmony, as the sentence from Grillparzer's *Der arme Spielmann* (1847; *The Poor Fiddler*, 1967) illustrates, which Handke has chosen as his motto: "I trembled with a longing for unity" (*LSV* 190). Handke proceeds selectively; he depicts only those ideal places that fulfill his yearning for serenity and permanence, and creates the aesthetic illusion of a singularly peaceful and harmonious world. This principle which takes a part for the whole clearly reveals itself through the spatial metaphors compounded with the term "world," metaphors which abound in Handke's descriptions of landscapes: *Weltkreis, Weltstadt, Weltreich, Welt-Räume.* During the shooting of the film version of *The Left-Handed Woman* in 1977, the author had already declared: "I want what I create to embrace the whole world and to include all of humanity. It has to be mythical. Mythical!" (Schober 182).

Handke goes even further when he transcends the imagination of a coherent universe by setting up a philosophy of the world and of history, or, in other words, by constructing an ideological concept and positing it as universal and eternal. It is no longer a matter here of realizing what Jean-Paul Sartre (12-13) or Roland Barthes (220) call the immanent "poetry" of place or its natural significance, its intrinsic substance or "essence." The description of landscapes is above all a pretext or alibi which allows the author to bestow ideology to the appearance of objective reality. Barthes' semiological approach to myth perfectly illustrates the process of mythicizing in which Handke engages: the natural meaning immanent in the landscape described, i.e. the signifier of the mythical sign, is clearly distorted by the ideological concept which it is intended to signify, though distorted in a way that makes this concept seem natural by virtue of the primary meaning of the sign. And what could be more 'naturalizing' than the description of nature itself:

> Here we touch upon the very foundation of myths: they transform history into nature.... Everything occurs as if the image naturally brought forth the concept, as if the signified was founded upon the signifier.... Myth does not negate the objects ..., it simply purifies them, absolves them, merges them with nature and eternity, gives them a clarity which does not derive from explanation, but from reported observation.... Things seem to signify in and by themselves. (Barthes 215-16, 219-20)

Myth, according to Barthes, is "depoliticized speech." It is "constituted when objects lose their historical quality.... The function of myth is to evacuate reality (230). There is no better way to define the radical dehistoricizing and depoliticizing which Handke openly professes: "The mountain blue is – the brown of the pistol holster is not.... Ignore the hiccup of the dying.... Yes, stay forever away from impotent-brutal power, power strutting about as power. The good power is that of overlooking" (*WV* 100, 101, 103). Such is the message uttered by Nova at the close of *Über die Dörfer* (1981; *Walk About the Villages*, 1996). No sooner is history introduced into the recollection of places than it becomes eliminated by the imagination in order to restore the site to its original purity. In *My Year in the No-Man's-Bay*, for instance, the camp at Dachau gets buried under the snow (*MY* 212); the Mont Valérien, west of Paris, metamorphoses into a volcano whose lava sweeps away the Gestapo execution grounds at its summit and the memorial which had been erected there (*MY* 348-49); and Germany emerges purified from her traumatic past at the end of a fictitious civil war which functions as an agent of catharsis (*MY* 408). "History's glorious forgetfulness" (*J* 164) surreptitiously manifests itself in the revolting abbreviation of Srebrenica as "S." (*SN* 65, 66, 81), the letter which also designates the author's companion in *Journey to the Rivers* (*JR* 7) and Salzburg in *Am Felsfenster morgens* (*FM* 24). The devastated and pillaged Bosnian houses are raised to the order of 'essential' objects of which the remains exemplify "the house itself, the house 'house,' the essence of the house" (*SN 30*), which no form of destruction can annihilate. In these extreme examples, the utopia of a world of peace which Handke detects in the landscapes does not only reduce itself to the premodern myth of an essentially coherent universe: such instances demonstrate that, since the second half of the twentieth century, this myth can only be propagated as a bulwark against the barbarism of history at the price of revisionism.

In the final analysis, Handke's utopian message of places is but a nostalgia for a paradise lost, which characterizes modernity and which postmodernity has definitively renounced (Kniesche 317-18). The author's desperate attempt to salvage and restore, through writing, a presupposed universal and atemporal coherence, of which nature would be the ultimate witness, is, from a postmodern perspective, indicative of a totalizing ideological discourse with the goal of purporting an imaginary solution to real social and historical conflicts. This is the very preserve of every mythological account and just as much, so it appears, the objective of the travel narratives centering on the quest for ideal landscapes which Handke offers his readership.

However, in the accounts of this quest for harmony, the idealization of places is thwarted by an opposing tendency, which fundamentally puts into question their message of peace. Indeed, despite the author's frantic efforts to affirm the reality of his fantasies and to withdraw from history, the latter constantly and brutally re-emerges in his texts and invalidates any claim to universality (Gabriel 93-103; Ruckaberle 66-72; Zschachlitz 430-31). Thus, in *Child Story*, the father inadvertently finds himself confronted with the German past when his child is threatened with death by a Jew. In *Across*, Loser surrenders to a murderous act of folly by killing a neo-Nazi who paints swastikas on the ramparts of the Mönchsberg. Elsewhere, war and violence suddenly burst upon idyllic nature. For example, the landscape which allowed the four travelers in *Absence* to imagine for an instant that they were in "a region offering an escape from history, yet at the same time a new country where something might be begun" (*Ab* 99), metamorphoses into a hostile terrain advanced upon by tanks and heavily armed soldiers (*Ab* 101). In *On a Dark Night*, commandos of young killers invade the peaceful village where the pharmacist has taken refuge (*DN* 128-29), and at the end of the narrative, the steppe has become the theater of innumerable "current wars" (*DN* 181). The latent aggressiveness of Handke's protagonists corresponds to a collective violence and bursts forth in sudden attacks against their nearest of kin. In *Child Story*, the father beats his child, and hatred remains the single bond that connects the narrator of *No-Man's-Bay* and the pharmacist in *On a Dark Night* with their respective sons. Similarly, hatred characterizes male/female relationships, condemned from the outset to end in jealousy, violence, and, in the best of circumstances, in separation.[15] "Violence and Inanity – are they not ultimately one

---

[15]For example, Keuschnig's altercation with his wife and his terrifying sexual encounter with his girlfriend in *No-Man's-Bay*, or, in *On a Dark Night*, the silent hatred in which the pharmacist and his wife live separately under the same roof, and the violent pursuit of the protagonist by the mountain woman. Already in *Short Letter, Long Farewell*, Judith follows her husband to the United States and attempts to murder him, while in *Left-Handed Woman*, the

and the same thing,?" wonders Handke, quoting Max Horkheimer in the epigraph to *A Moment of True Feeling*. Nevertheless, the reality of violence imposes itself against the desire for peace of the author and his characters.

Since *Absence*, Handke has relativized the myth of universal reconciliation in an increasingly evident manner through the very form of the narratives in which he presents his landscapes. As in *No Man's-Bay*, the narrator becomes fragmented into several characters of contradictory opinions, whose quest for a New World perpetually remains suspended. The seemingly most peremptory affirmations are put in doubt by the questioning principle thematized in the play *Das Spiel vom Fragen* (1989; *The Art of Asking*, 1996) and expressed in Handke's texts by the numerous question marks at the end of the sentences or paragraphs most heavily laden with meaning. The fairytale ending, as that of *Short Letter*, underlines the unreal and compensatory character of the idyllic perspective positing a peaceful world. Taken in its primary meaning of a try-out (*Versuch*), the essay – an open form *par excellence* – by definition opposes any reduction of the plurality of experiences to a unique concept, and therefore emphasizes the fleeting nature of happiness. If the possibility of the latter is intuited in the course of the epiphany generated by a place, its actualization is constantly deferred: "'Have you ever experienced a successful day? With which for once a successful moment, a successful life, perhaps even a successful eternity might coincide?' 'Not yet. Obviously!'" (*J* 166). The very idea of a lasting and shareable happiness which Handke's protagonist derives from the transient sensation of harmony with a particular place, turns out to be nothing but a "dream" (*J* 166), a dream that remains unrealized and, no doubt, unrealizable.

The myth of universal harmony is thus constantly brought back to what it truly is: the illusory and irresolute attempt to cope with the inability to attain peace and serenity beyond the individual and ephemeral experience of a landscape epiphany. On the one hand, the landscapes in Handke's work effectively mythologize reality and history, insofar as these landscapes pass off what is a mere figment of the imagination or an ideological concept as the natural meaning

---

title character abruptly starts to strangle her son in a moment when he tenderly leans on her.

of the world; and insofar as the realization of this myth is presented as a genuine possibility, as a hope for the future of humanity, in other words, as a utopia. Yet, on the other hand, it has become apparent that Handke deconstructs the double myth which he constructs as he reintroduces in the places described the brutal reality of history from which he so desperately strives to withdraw (cf. Zschachlitz) and returns these myths to the realm of imagination.

His texts are thus constituted by a movement and countermovement of ideological (re)construction and deconstruction, whereby they meet the pluralism claimed by postmodernity. The message of these texts is ultimately embedded in their very contradiction. Although Handke's descriptions of places mythicize the real, his texts nevertheless also reveal the illusory nature of the happiness and harmony which characterize his landscapes, and suggest no more than an imaginary resolution of the real conflicts facing the individual and humanity. As a result, the landscape no longer expresses the myth of accomplished fulfillment, but becomes the sign of an unfulfilled desire for peace and happiness and thus of a lack – Handke speaks of a "void" or an "absence" – which the contemplation and literary representation of landscapes are meant to fill, even though there is no hope of ever attaining that promise.

"Why is there no peace? Why is there no peace?" (*MY* 466), Keuschnig desperately asks at the end of his year in the "no-man's-bay." At the close of *The Long Way Around*, contemplating Manhattan under snowfall at dusk, Sorger feels with an overwhelming intensity the desire to be part of the "peaceful beauty of this present and in the dark paradise of this evening" (*LWA* 135). However, this almost erotic impulse is swiftly followed by harsh disillusionment:

> Cleansed of all self-interest till nothing remained but presence of mind, desirous only of completing the world ("I want you and I want to be part of you!") – he was struck by the consciousness of an incurable deficiency.... He no longer wished himself in any other epoch – but that part of the world which, even with the purest, most fervent passion, he attained and staked out was still *far too little*. (*LWA* 135-36)

While the panicked anxiety which this instant of lucidity provokes in Sorger subsides and hope revives, doubt persists and desire remains unquenched: "You no longer knew who you were. Where was your dream of greatness? You were no one" (*LWA* 136).

At the end of every book, what is left to make the lack of fulfillment bearable is the unattainable promise of a yearned-for happiness, a yearning which nevertheless keeps one alive, as in *Essay on the Successful Day*: "Phrases and more phrases in the void, to no good purpose, addressed to a third incomprehensible something, though the two of us are not lost" (*J* 166-67). Thus, myth is reborn as utopia: a minimum of uncertain hope – without question the only one still granted by history to postmodern man.

Works Cited

Adorno, Theodor W. *Ästhetische Theorie*. Frankfurt am Main: Suhrkamp, 1970.

Barthes, Roland. *Mythologies*. Paris: Seuil, 1957.

Bartmann, Christoph. *Suche nach Zusammenhang. Handkes Werk als Prozeß*. Vienna: Braumüller, 1984.

Bohrer, Karl Heinz. *Die Ästhetik des Schreckens*. Munich: Hanser, 1978.

Durzak, Manfred. *Peter Handke und die deutsche Gegenwartsliteratur: Narziss auf Abwegen*. Stuttgart: Kohlhammer, 1982.

Gabriel, Norbert. "Handkes 'doppelte Optik.'" *Text und Kritik* 24. Ed. Heinz Ludwig Arnold. 5th ed. Munich: edition text + kritik, 1989. 93-103.

Gottwald, Herwig. "Verzauberung und Entzauberung der Welt. Zu Peter Handkes mythisierendem Schreiben." *Mythos und Mythisches in der Gegenwartsliteratur*. Stuttgart: Heinz, 1996. 34-86.

Kniesche, Thomas W. "Utopie und Schreiben zu Zeiten der Postmoderne: Peter Handkes 'Versuche.'" *Zeitgenössische Utopieentwürfe in Literatur und Gesellschaft. Zur Kontroverse seit den achtziger Jahren*. Ed. Rolf Jucker. Amsterdam: Rodopi, 1997. 313-36.

Konzett, Matthias. "Cultural Amnesia and the Narration of the Everyday: Peter Handke's Post-Ideological Aesthetics." *The Rhetoric of National Dissent in Thomas Bernhard, Peter Handke, and Elfriede Jelinek*. Columbia, SC: Camden House, 2000. 57-94.

Melzer, Gerhard, and Jale Tükel (eds.). *Peter Handke: Die Arbeit am Glück*. Königstein/T.: Athenäum, 1985.

Parry, Christoph. "Peter Handkes Schriftlandschaften." *Text und Kritik* 24. Ed. Heinz Ludwig Arnold. 6th ed. Munich: edition text + kritik, 1999. 59-67.

—. "Der Prophet der Randbezirke." *Text und Kritik* 24. Ed. Heinz Ludwig Arnold. 5th ed. Munich: edition text + kritik, 1989. 51-61.

Renner, Rolf Günter. *Peter Handke.* Stuttgart: Metzler, 1985.

Ruckaberle, Axel. "Aggression und Gewalt. Schwellenerfahrungen im Erzählwerk Peter Handkes." *Text und Kritik* 24. Ed. Heinz Ludwig Arnold. 5th ed. Munich: edition text + kritik, 1989. 66-71.

Sartre, Jean-Paul. *Qu'est-ce que la littérature?* Paris: Gallimard, 1947.

Schaad, Isolde. "Ein Fleck, der nicht ausgeht. Über das Frauenbild bei Peter Handke." *Text und Kritik* 24. Ed. Heinz Ludwig Arnold. 6th ed. Munich: edition text + kritik, 1999. 100-09.

Schober, Siegfried. "Es soll mythisch sein, mythisch!" Interview with Peter Handke. *Der Spiegel* 2 May 1977: 182.

Tabah, Mireille. "Le paysage dans l'œuvre de Peter Handke, reflet de la vision du monde de l'auteur." *Recherches Germaniques* 24 (1994) 104-27.

—. "Structure et fonction de l'‘épiphanie' dans l'œuvre de Peter Handke à partir de *La courte lettre pour un long adieu* et *L'heure de la sensation vraie.*" *Etudes Germaniques* 47.2 (1993) 147-66.

Zschachlitz, Ralph. *"Epiphanie" ou "illumination profane"? L'œuvre de Peter Handke et la théorique esthétique de Walter Benjamin.* Bern: Peter Lang, 2000.

Handke's Yugoslavia Work

Scott Abbott

In his 1991 plea for Slovenia to remain part of the Federal Republic of Yugoslavia, Peter Handke noted that he

> was born in a village in Carinthia. At that time, in the Second World War, the majority, no, the whole of the people was Austrian-Slovenian and communicated in the appropriate dialect. In her youth, my mother saw herself as being from that people, influenced above all by her oldest brother who was studying fruit-growing on the other side of the border in Yugoslavian-Slovenian Maribor ... but my father was a German soldier, and German became my language.... (*AT* 7-9)

Die Hornissen (1966; The Hornets), Handke's first novel, was written by a very young man on the Yugoslav island of Krk. Twenty years later, a young Austrian wanders through Slovenia in search of his lost brother in the novel *Die Wiederholung* (1986; *Repetition*, 1988). In the following decade, Handke's short prose pieces compiled in *Noch einmal für Thukydides* (1995; *Once Again For Thucydides*, 1998) include several set in what was then already becoming the *former* Yugoslavia. A section of one of these stories, "The Tale of Hats in Skopje," can perhaps best serve as an introduction to an essay about Handke's insistent and consistent argument for a Yugoslav state shared by diverse peoples, a state free of the destructive influence of American, French, German and Vatican powerbrokers, free of war between Serbian and Croatian and Bosnian Muslim nationalists, a state fostered by complex and searching and self-questioning rhetoric – an impossible and beautiful state (of mind?):

> A possible brief epic: the different hats passing by in large cities. For example, in Skopje in Yugoslavian Macedonia on the tenth of December, 1987.... And then a kepi embroidered with a white oriental pattern passed under the dripping snow, followed by a blond girl in a thick, bright ski hat (with a tassel on top), and right after her came a man wearing glasses and a beret with a dark blue stem. A soldier's beret followed, then police hats in pairs with visors.... Then another [man] went by with a rose pattern on his hat, while bareheaded passersby also appeared

occasionally, with their own hair as headwear…. A young man with a scarf over his ears and around his neck. A boy with skier's earmuffs, the brand: TRICOT. And so forth. A beautiful procession, so on and so forth. (*Th* 25-28)

That "beautiful procession" of "so on and so forth," as it continues in *Abschied des Träumers vom neunten Land. Eine Wirklichkeit die vergangen ist: Erinnerung an Slowenien* (1991; The Dreamer's Farewell to the Ninth Land. A Reality That Has Passed: Memories of Slovenia), and in the 1990s with two essays, *Eine winterliche Reise zu den Flüssen Donau, Save, Morawa, und Drina oder Gerechtigkeit für Serbien* (1996; *A Journey to the Rivers: Justice for Serbia*, 1997) and *Sommerlicher Nachtrag zu einer winterlichen Reise* (1996; A Summer's Postscript to a Winter's Journey), a play, *Die Fahrt im Einbaum oder Das Spiel zum Film vom Krieg* (1999; Voyage by Dugout, or The Play of the Film of the War), and finally further reflections published as *Unter Tränen fragend* (2000; Questioning While Weeping), will guide the course of this essay.

*

Abschied des Träumers vom neunten Land

14 May, 1989. I sit on a balcony of the Gostilna Rozić, a pension in Bohinj, Slovenia, and watch the white-tailed swallows wheel around me. We are surrounded by mountains, but thick clouds and intermittent rain veil them completely this morning.

In Repetition, *Filip Kobal rides a train through a tunnel between Villach, Austria and Jesenića, Yugoslavia, out of the political and cultural terrors of Europe into the fabled "Ninth Land" of Slovenia. We couldn't exactly duplicate Kobal's fictional trip in our rented Opel Kadett, but we counted it close enough to drive through a parallel tunnel.*

Somehow we missed the tunnel and found ourselves driving along a lake shore. We turned back, then back again, sure of where we were because of correspondences between countryside and map, then suddenly, inexplicably lost. The tunnel was carefully marked on the map, as was the Autobahn leading to it; and the name "Karawanken Tunnel" stood in tiny red letters next to the marks that meant "mountains." We could see the actual mountains. We could see the lake. We could drive through the streets of neighboring St. Jakob. But the map's promised 7.6-kilometer tunnel ("toll required") was simply not there.

Finally Žarko asked an Austrian policeman for directions to the Karawanken Tunnel. The officer smiled so broadly that his

*thin moustache quivered. No such place, he said, not until the
Yugoslavs finish their half. The map had brought us, anticipating the 1991 completion of the tunnel, to a place that did not yet
exist. Thus was our desire to enter Yugoslavia deferred.* (Abbott
and Radaković 24)[1]

*

In response to the Slovenian declaration of independence (the first
of Yugoslavia's republics to do so), anticipating the subsequent disintegration of Yugoslavia, Handke published what would later become *Abschied des Träumers vom Neunten Land* as an essay in the
Süddeutsche Zeitung the last weekend of July, 1991.[2] In this essay,
he argues against Slovenian independence with ideas about the Slo-
vene people (*Volk*) that outraged many Slovenians.[3] Handke had
earlier raised the question of belonging to a *Volk* in his tetralogy
*Langsame Heimkehr (*1979; *Slow Homecoming,* 1985). The narrator
of the third volume, *Kindergeschichte (*1981; *Child Story,* 1985),
choosing to raise a daughter in Paris, away from the German-speaking people that a few years earlier had made the word *Volk* as problematic as the word *Führer,* enrolls his daughter in a Jewish school.
The Jews, he writes, are the only *Volk* to which he has ever wanted
to belong. They qualify, the narrator explains, because they have
remained a *Volk* without a national center.[4] A similar dual quality –
of being a *Volk* yet having no nation – has made Slovenia a place
like none other in the world. There is no country where as a
foreigner Handke has felt so at home as in Slovenia.

Handke's first explanation for this is an odd one in a political
discussion. In Slovenia, he writes, things like a bridge or an orchard
used to seem more real than elsewhere. What these Slovenian things
had in common, he argues, is a "certain hearty insignificance" (*AT*

---

[1]The narrative passages that introduce each of the following sections are from
an unpublished sequel to *Ponavljanje* that chronicles Abbott's and Radaković's
journey along the Drina River with Peter Handke, whose writing on Yugoslavia
they have both translated.
[2]Aside from some minor changes that were made for this version, this section
was published previously as "Modeling a Dialectic: Peter Handke's *A Journey
to the Rivers or Justice for Serbia,*" *After Postmodernism: Austrian Literature
and Film in Transition,* ed. Willy Riemer (Riverside, CA: Ariadne, 2000) 340-
52.
[3]Also republished in *Langsam im Schatten* (1992; Slowly in the Shadow [*LS*
182-97]).
[4]See also Abbott ("Material Idea").

13). As to what created this "hearty insignificance" that made things more present than usual, Handke suggests that it was the appearance of standing outside history. Because Slovenia was part of the larger nation of Yugoslavia, as Slovenia it was absent from history. But because it was Slovenia, because Croatia was Croatia, and the same for Montenegro and Serbia and the other states making up Yugoslavia, the country as a whole had a balanced unity productively different from the destructive nationalism Handke saw in his own nation of Austria. In response to earlier discussions by Václav Havel, Milan Kundera, and others about a 'central Europe' in which the Czech Republic, Slovenia, Croatia, Italy, and similar countries would join in some sort of 'natural' loose grouping that would split Yugoslavia into southern Balkan and northern European nations (*AT* 28), Handke worries in this essay that that would drag Slovenia into history and put the quiet, unseemly things and people of the country into a political context that dissolves productive presence into absence and jolts productive absence into destructive presence. To put it in another way, language enables us to see things we might not otherwise see. It can open or expand our horizons. A second language continues that opening. But as a language names and defines it also sets limits and closes off possibilities, becoming what Nietzsche called the 'prison house of language.' Nationalism of the kind Handke decries here is fostered by language that tends toward an exclusive, limiting worldview in which the things and people in that nation grow more alike and less different and the things outside national boundaries grow more different and less alike. In the process, the other is sacrificed for the same. Even material things like church towers become nationalized, and the Catholic towers of Slovenia no longer share a landscape with southern minarets.

Handke understands the political reality of Serbian domination of this historically disparate set of countries, and still he argues against dissolving the federation. With all its problems, the multi-ethnic state has produced people who know how to live as foreigners in their own country. Handke could give many examples – the blind Slovenian photographer Evgan Bavcar or the Croatian painter Julija Knifer whose "meanders" wander over gallery and museum walls in Paris and Cologne; but a Serb, someone from the dominant group, is his best example. And that, he contends as this essay continues, is "my dear comrade and translator Žarko Radaković."

Intellectuals like Radaković, Handke writes, are indistinguishable from intellectuals in international cities like Paris or New York, cities whose diversity allows foreigners to feel at home and natives to be foreigners (*AT* 26). If he should mention a hike he took, Radaković "will immediately serve up his new greater and lesser Serbian theory 'On Hiking along Rivers' and will soon prepare an international anthology – contributions from George Steiner, Jean Baudrillard, Reinhold Messner" (*AT* 28). Greater *and* lesser Serbia – the ironic phrase models that "beautiful procession," that ability to move back and forth in an ongoing dialectic, a dialectic most possible, most probable, Handke argues in this essay about the looming disintegration of Yugoslavia, in a multiethnic state.

According to Julia Kristeva, we will never be able to live at peace with the strangers around us if we are unable to recognize and tolerate the otherness in ourselves. In Kristeva's world it is Freud who awakens us to ourselves as strangers. For Handke it used to be Slovenia as a Yugoslavian state that encouraged foreigners to live as natives and natives as foreigners. After Slovenia's independence, that political space disappears. Handke told André Müller that the only thing he had actually achieved in his life that has made him proud is "to have avoided a worldview" ("Schreiben" 78). And speaking with Žarko Radaković, he described his writing as an attempt "to make the world appear in its richness and in its peace…. Nothing else."[5] This attempt to describe (and thus create) a rich and peaceful world, to find adequate, alternative, and peaceable ways to represent a country distorted by the rhetoric of statesmen and journalists, is a constant in the texts that follow *Abschied des Träumers*.[6]

*

A Journey to the Rivers: Justice for Serbia

Translating Peter Handke's Eine Reise zu den Flüssen Donau, Save, Morawa und Drina oder Gerechtigkeit für Serbien *into English, I called Žarko to ask about the phrase: "Do we need a new Gavrilo Princip?" What kind of principle is this? I asked. Is it a term from business management? Gavrilo Princip, Žarko explained with a chuckle, was the young assassin of Archduke Franz Ferdinand in Sarajevo.*

---

[5]From a recorded conversation between Peter Handke and Žarko Radaković in Salzburg, 27 Feb. 1985.
[6]See also Fabjan Hafner's insightful article about Slovenia in Handke's work.

Later, traveling with Žarko in his country, I struggled with a broader question: How to tell a new story about the old land of the southern Slavs (Yugo = south). After all, what do I know? A foreigner, in the country for a few days. A self-styled translator with no command of this language.

*

The foreword to the American edition of *Journey to the Rivers* provides a glimpse into the colorful history of the essay's reception:

> This text, appearing on two weekends at the onset of 1996 in the *Süddeutsche Zeitung*, caused some commotion in the European press.
>
> Immediately after publication of the first part, I was designated a terrorist in the *Corriere della Sera*, and *Libération* revealed that I was, first of all, amused that there were so few victims in the Slovenian war of 1991, and that I was exhibiting, second, "doubtful taste" in discussing the various ways of presenting this or that victim of the Yugoslavian wars in the western media. In *Le Monde* I was then called a "pro-Serbian advocate," and in the *Journal du Dimanche* there was talk of "pro-Serbian agitation." And so it continued until *El País* even read into my text a sanction of the Srebrenica massacre.
>
> Now the text is translated, and I trust that you will read it as it is; I need not defend or take back a single word. I wrote about my journey through the country of Serbia exactly as I have always written my books, my literature: a slow, inquiring narration; every paragraph dealing with and narrating a problem, of representation, of form, of grammar – of aesthetic veracity; that has always been the case in what I have written, from the beginning to the final period. Dear reader: that, and that alone, I offer here for your perusal. (*JR* vii-viii)

At issue are the effects of rhetoric: Handke's own, that of the journalists he attacks, and that of his critics. Handke claims his work is a self-reflexive, "slow, inquiring narration" in the service of peace and accuses specific journalists and newspapers of demagogy. His critics argue that his self-deluded inattention to the war promotes nationalism. The following observations trace a pattern in the text that reveals it as a model of dialectical rhetoric, of narrative or non-systematic philosophy, of that 'beautiful so on and so forth' in the service of peace.

The essay, whose double title – *A Journey to the Rivers: Justice for Serbia* – indicates that this will be a travel narrative and a political essay in one, is divided into four parts with the simple titles: "Before the Trip," "Part One of the Trip," "Part Two of the Trip," and "Epilogue." "Before the Trip" and "Epilogue" contain most of the controversial accusations about the European press and its coverage of the wars in Yugoslavia, while the middle two sections contain most of the actual travel narrative. In "Before the Trip," written, like the rest of the essay, after the trip, Handke describes his preparations. He contacted the two Serbs who would accompany him. He saw, just before leaving, Emir Kusturica's new film *Underground*, and found it an engaging combination of dreaming and actual history. He was surprised, then, to see the film reviewed by Alain Finkielkraut in *Le Monde* as pro-Serbian and terroristic. From what he sees as Finkielkraut's misreading (which foreshadows how Handke's essay will be read on its part), he turns to press reports of the wars in Yugoslavia. He cites European and especially German-Austrian complicity in the disintegration of Yugoslavia – a favoring of, acceptance of, and support of the breakaway republics of Slovenia and Croatia that, in his estimation, led to the war, or better said, made it likely. The political actions, Handke argues, have their basis in a bias against Serbia that European culture has promulgated for decades (he mentions, for example, the post-empire Austrian rhyme "Serbien muss sterbien" – Serbia must die) and that newspapers like *Le Monde* and the *Frankfurter Allgemeine Zeitung* have played up. After questioning the reported facts, he ends the opening section by asking: "Who will someday write this history differently, and even if only the nuances – which could do much to liberate the peoples from their mutual inflexible images?" (*JR* 26).

The essay's second section begins with the trip to Belgrade. Žarko Radaković and Zlatko Bocokić meet Handke there. They walk through the city, visit a market in Zemun, drive to see Bocokić's parents, drive to a monastery with the writer Milorad Pavić and meet that night with the writer Dragan Velikić. The travel narrative continues in the third section with a description of a drive to the town of Bajina Bašta on the Drina River. There they hear about the war, they are snowed in, they cross a bridge briefly to the other side, they listen to heroic tales sung by a Serbian folk singer, and they finally leave Serbia by way of Novi Sad. Before the section ends, Handke remembers a trip to Slovenia just a month earlier which confirmed his fears that the new state had lost the multicultural openness it once had as part of Yugoslavia. Finally in the epilog, Handke recounts a morning in Bajina Bašta when he walked alone to the bus station and then to the Drina River. While standing on the shore he asked questions about what really happened at Srebrenica and returned to his attack on the media in general and on the *Frankfurter Allgemeine Zeitung* specifically. The epilogue ends with a suicide note left by an ex-partisan who shot himself in despair as his country began its civil war.

Although this summary is generally accurate, it is simply inadequate. Like the readings by Handke's critics, it leaves out the multiple and conflicting voices the essay manages to incorporate. For a more careful reader, Handke's essay asserts in the context of self-doubt, recognizes its own contingency in the face of justice, finds justice in contingency and multiplicity, and models honesty in complexity of style while attacking the dishonesty of simplistic journalism.

Handke has long been interested in the possibilities of dialectical thinking. In his interview with Herbert Gamper, for example, he returned several times to the subject of Nietzsche and the dialectic: "I see [Nietzsche] not as a negator, but as a dramatic custodian of something that was always there, and yet naturally also as a very fruitful destroyer of that which did not deserve to be conserved. This dialectical relationship, these two things, make Nietzsche who he is" (*Zw* 171).[7] This and other statements about the purposefully paradoxical philosopher who argued for contingency *and* a will to power make explicit Handke's sense of dialectic as an interplay between despair and hope, conservation and destruction, furthered by an anti-systematic, fragmentary, and positive creation of meaning through language: "The law of art: glorification, but dialectical glorification (it is not the Golden Age, but rather the Dialectical Age)" (*GB* 344).

---

[7] Cf. also: "One can see in [Nietzsche] a model human existence: one who does not in any sense want to establish systems, who does not want to interpret the world according to a system. The fragmentary, halting style of writing and the few wonderfully painful poems ... allow the reading of his works to be a joyful slow studying" (*Zw* 172). On Handke and Nietzsche, see the book by Vollmer as well as the chapter by Andrea Gogröf-Voorhees in this book.

A recent attempt by an American philosopher to read Nietzsche as thinking after, even if still in the language of metaphysics, provides a helpful context for reading Handke as dialectician in *A Journey to the Rivers.* In *The Question of Ethics: Nietzsche, Foucault, Heidegger,* Charles Scott looks at what he calls Nietzsche's self-overcoming, an open process occasioned by questions about the values that structure his own discourse as well as the discourses of traditional morals: "In the discussion of the play of will to power and eternal return in Nietzsche's writing – a play of metaphysical assertion, antimetaphysical assertion, and nonmetaphysical recoil in the process – we discern not only the conflicting directions that are methodically maintained, but also a middle-voiced recoiling function." The middle voice, thinkable neither in the active nor the passive voices, is where self-overcoming in metaphysics takes place: "It is the voice of differing, moving of itself, without the thought of transcendence" (Scott 32). Scott's argument may be seen as an example of what Handke may mean when he speaks of dialectical thinking. It is thought within polarities (for example, the metaphysical and antimetaphysical assertions Scott mentions) that nevertheless recoils at its own dualistic structure. It is a momentary break in the structure that allows difference and motion and play to reveal metaphysical thought's repression of the always present play of conflicting forces. It is self-overcoming thought that calls into question the presumptive authority of its organizing ideas to make room not for its own truth but for other truths (Scott 30).

Handke's essays on Yugoslavia are generically related to his essays on tiredness, on the jukebox, and on the successful day.[8] With these works, Handke practices a literary form with a long history, a form whose peculiarities have been well described by Theodor Adorno in "The Essay as Form." In the context of his ongoing attack on the dogmatic identity thinking of post-Enlightenment scientific thought, Adorno formulates ideas that also appear pertinent to the form of Handke's work. That the essay, as a form, "rebels against the doctrine, deeply rooted since Plato, that what is transient and ephemeral is unworthy of philosophy" (Adorno 10);

---

[8]These essays appeared separately under the titles *Versuch über die Müdigkeit* (1989; *Essay on Tiredness,* 1994), *Versuch über die Jukebox* (1990; *Essay on the Jukebox,* 1994), and *Versuch über den geglückten Tag* (1991; *Essay on the Successful Day,* 1994).

that the "customary objection that the essay is fragmentary and contingent itself postulates that totality is given, and with it the identity of subject and object"; that the essay's "weakness bears witness to the very nonidentity it had to express" (Adorno 11); that "[t]his kind of learning remains vulnerable to error, as does the essay as form; it has to pay for its affinity with open intellectual experience with a lack of security that the norm of established thought fears like death" (Adorno 13); and that "[t]he daring, anticipatory, and not fully redeemed aspect of every essayistic detail attracts other such details as its negation; the untruth in which the essay knowingly entangles itself is the element in which its truth resides" (Adorno 19). These fragments of Adorno's essay read like descriptions of the formal experiments of Handke's essays. One need not, however, rely exclusively on Adorno or Scott for the theoretical underpinnings, for Handke's essays are themselves self-reflexive commentaries on the essay.[9] In the *Essay on the Successful Day*, for example, the narrator's interlocutor insists on a direct, certain description of a successful day (in contrast to the indirect and halting nature of the essay up to that point):

> But with all your digressions, complications, and tergiversations, your way of breaking off every time you gain a bit of momentum, what becomes of your Line of Beauty and Grace, which, as you've hinted, stands for a successful day and, as you went on to assure us, would introduce your essay on the subject. When will you abandon your irresolute peripheral zigzags, your timorous attempt to define a concept that seems to be growing emptier than ever, and at last, with the help of coherent sentences, make the light, sharp incision that will carry us through the present muddle in medias res, in the hope that this obscure 'successful day' of yours may take on clarity and universal form. (*J* 126)

In response, the narrator suggests a double form that includes the form the interlocutor has rejected: "Isn't it typical of people like us that this sort of song keeps breaking off, lapsing into stuttering, babbling, and silence, starting up again, going off on a sidetrack – yet in the end, as throughout, aiming at unity and wholeness?" (*J* 127) It is exactly this double form, this ongoing dialectic that aims

---

[9]On this point, see the article by David N. Coury in this book.

at wholeness through fragments, that Handke's detractors, along with most of his defenders, have missed.

While *A Journey to the Rivers* ends with a suicide note, the first part of the final paragraph provides crucial context. During the trip through Serbia, Handke writes, he noted only two things in his notebook: "'*Jebi ga*!' – Fuck him! the common curse" (*JR* 83) and the section of the suicide's farewell letter. These are the poles between which the entire essay moves: obscene aggression and fatal resignation. There are moments of both along the way, especially in the first and last sections of the essay; but for the most part, especially in the travel narrative, Handke describes what he calls, citing Hermann Lenz and Edmund Husserl, "third things," things colored by the bipolar aggressions and despairs of war, but also somehow independent from them, third things not unrelated to the "middle-voiced recoiling functions" Scott sees in Nietzsche's thought.[10]

Because he fears he will be misread, Handke raises red flags for readers used to undialectical dualisms, for readers with appetites for shocking images rather than for quiet and peripheral "third things": "And whoever is thinking now: Aha, pro-Serbian! or Aha, Yugophile! ... need read no further" (*JR* 2-3). "And whoever understands that not as retching, but as indifference, likewise need read no further" (*JR* 17). Handke requires similar discipline of himself in his writing. Early in the essay, for example, a critical voice breaks in to ask: "What, are you trying to help minimize the Serbian crimes in Bosnia, in the Krajina, in Slavonia, by means of a media critique that sidesteps the basic facts?" Handke, the narrator Handke, answers: "'Steady. Patience. Justice.' The problem – only mine? – is more complicated, complicated by several levels or stages of reality; and I am aiming, in my desire to clarify it, at something

---

[10]Cf. the following quote from Handke's play *Voyage to the Sonorous Land, or The Art of Asking*: "Our play of questions as I envisioned it, joyous as the new morning, dew lining our questioning brows – will it turn into another tragedy against my will? Is there no third way? Didn't I often manage to escape precisely because I tried only when I thought it was hopeless anyway? But isn't death the Third Way in fairy tales?... Unlike the Cheyennes' heroic return to their homelands, will our trek to the sonorous land be remembered some day as one of the most senseless journeys in history?... What faith – in anything that makes no sense, in senseless enterprises" (*V* 70-71).

thoroughly real through which something like a meaningful whole can be surmised in all the mixed-up kinds of reality" (*JR* 12). Near the essay's end, S., Handke's wife, asks: "'You aren't going to question the massacre at Srebrenica too, are you?'"; to which he answers: "'No,' ... 'But I want to ask how such a massacre is to be explained, carried out, it seems, under the eyes of the world ...'" (*JR* 73). "Note well," he writes, "[t]his is absolutely not a case of 'I accuse.' I feel compelled only to justice. Or perhaps even only to questioning?, to raising doubts" (*JR* 76).

In the face of this self-critique, what does it mean when critics claim that Handke is denying the massacre at Srebrenica?[11] It may mean that they are reading unfairly, taking statements out of their dialectic context. Alternately, perhaps, they mistrust his complicated sense for justice, they suppose his questions and denials are simply camouflage for an unbridled polemic, they feel that while claiming the opposite, Handke's images are as inflexible as their own, that his history is as rigid as theirs. It is possible, of course, that they are right. But when compared with the one-sided rhetoric of his critics, Handke's text appears like a model of dialectic reasoning. Of many possible examples one will have to suffice. Note here the almost excruciating care Handke takes to demonstrate his command of multiple sides of the issue, as well as his moral commitment to a justice that embraces them all:

> Later, from the spring of 1992 on, when the first photographs, soon photo sequences or serial photos, were shown from the Bosnian war, there was a part of myself (repeatedly standing for "my whole") which felt that the armed Bosnian Serbs, whether the army or individual killers, especially those on the hills and mountains around Sarajevo, were "enemies of humanity," to slightly vary Hans Magnus Enzensberger's phrase in reference to the Iraqi dictator Saddam Hussein....
>
> And in spite of that, almost coincidentally with the impotent impulses to violence of someone visually involved from afar, another part of me (which in fact never stood for my whole) did not want to trust this war and this war reporting. Didn't want to? No, couldn't. Because the roles of attacker and attacked, of the

---

[11]See, for example, Tilman Zülch's foreword to *Die Angst des Dichters vor der Wirklichkeit*, which ends by identifying Handke with the "long tradition of denial of genocide in the Europe of the twentieth century" (22).

pure victims and the naked scoundrels, were all too rapidly determined and set down for the so-called world public. (*JR* 17-18)

Of the two parts of himself, only the one shocked at Serb aggressions stands for all of him. There is no question, then, of absolving the Serbs of responsibility for their violence. And still, justice in this situation is broader than that initial and final response. It requires that other questions be asked as well.

What could be more reasonable? And what could be more conducive to peace? Why can't journalists covering the wars in Yugoslavia, Handke asks, read and tell a more complicated story? "And with this kind of maturity, I thought – as the son of a German – pull out of this history that repeats every century, out of this disastrous chain, pull out into another story" (*JR* 80). Let others write the factual story of these wars, Handke writes: "Nothing against those – more than uncovering – *dis*covering reporters on the scene (or better yet: involved in the scene and with the people there), praise for these other researchers in the field!" (*JR* 74), for: "To record the evil facts, that's good" (*JR* 82). He, however, the son of a German and thus heir to a propensity for Wagnerian totality, wants to write another story, an additional story.

The conjunction "and" that connects the paragraphs on the two parts of himself cited above and its proliferation in initial position in sentences and paragraphs as the essay comes to a close, work formally to create the continuing motion of a dialectic. While this is not a new device for Handke,[12] it is a crucial move in this essay that

---

[12]Handke employs it with similar intent in *Mein Jahr in der Niemandsbucht* (1994; *My Year in the No-Man's-Bay*, 1998), and *Repetition* ends with the admonition to the storyteller: "... take a deep breath, and start all over again with your all-appeasing 'And then ...'" (*R* 246). Toward the end of *My Year in the No-Man's-Bay*, the use of "and" is intensified, repeated not only at paragraph inceptions but increasingly throughout paragraphs. For example, "And what happened then?" (*MY* 443) becomes a refrain as the book nears its end. Both the question and its introductory conjunction connect the new sentence or paragraph to what has been before, making sure that it doesn't stay at that, that something new follows and the narrative proceeds. The conjunction "and," even as it introduces the second, oppositional half of a polarity, becomes, in its repetition, the third. Not a final third, not the last word but the new attempt, the new world, the transformation the book thematizes. The "and" ensures that the new is not radically new and simultaneously denies a radical

risks the untruths of obscene defiance and suicidal despair, that asserts that the "transient and ephemeral" (Adorno 10) are worthy of description during a war, that relies on density of texture in place of infallible argument for its truths. The "untruths" in which the essay knowingly entangles itself, turning on the axis of the coordinating conjunction, are more truthful finally than the non-dialectical assertions with which politicians and journalists and pundits assail Serbs and the writer who asks the questions justice requires.[13]

Finally, the essay's final questions and assertions. Is this the writing of a benighted advocate of a nationalistic *Blut und Boden* ideology or of an essayist whose courageous play of ideas lays him open to error and to truth as well:

> But isn't it, finally, irresponsible, I thought there at the Drina and continue to think it here, to offer the small sufferings in Serbia – the bit of freezing there, the bit of loneliness, the trivialities like snow flakes, caps, cream cheese – while over the border a great suffering prevails, that of Sarajevo, of Tuzla, of Srebrenica, of Bihać, compared to which the Serbian boo-boos are nothing? Yes, with each sentence I too have asked myself

---

return to an origin. Instead, it questions the unitary origin through the multiplicity of another possibility and reinforces unity through an initial example. "And" is the arbiter both of the same and of the other. In ancient Greek, most sentences begin with connective particles. One of the most common, *kai*, usually translated as "and," flavors as well as connects with meanings of "and," "even," "also." One of the characters of *My Year in the No-Man's-Bay*, a priest, is said to desire a new translation of the New Testament, "as literal as possible, from the Greek" (*MY* 281), and with its preponderance of sentences begun by conjunctions, Handke's book approaches this Greek ideal. Several pages before the end there is an instructive section in which a narrative is reduced to its barest form, to the conjunctions. "From the two histories at odds, a third will emerge. And how will it go? For instance: When I was still slow. Or.... Or.... Or.... And.... But...." (*MY* 466).

[13]Cf. this statement from the interview with Wolfgang Ritschl: "It is always nice to reveal everything about oneself. Everyone likes a writer who doesn't present himself to the world completely armored and self-righteous, rather exposes himself as well. In my Yugoslavia essay, too, I expose myself with my romaniticizing of Yugoslavia. I expose myself in order to speak the truth, in order to be assailable. Truths reach others through assailability. I make a fool of myself, yet speak a few truths. That's much better than if one only speaks truths" (55).

whether such a writing isn't obscene, ought even to be tabooed, forbidden – which made the writing journey adventurous in a different way, dangerous, often very depressing (believe me), and I learned what "between Scylla and Charybdis" means. Didn't the one who described the small deprivations (gaps between teeth) help to water down, to suppress, to conceal the great ones?

Finally, I thought each time: But that's not the point. My work is of a different sort. To record the evil facts, that's good. But something else is needed for a peace, something not less important than the facts.

So, now it's time for the poetic? Yes, if it is understood as exactly the opposite of the nebulous. Or say, rather than "the poetic," that which binds, that encompasses – the impulse to a common remembering, as the possibility for reconciliation of individuals, for the second, the common childhood. (*JR* 81-82)

The common is seen here in the context of the uncommon; the binding, encompassing dialectical poetic in the context of undermining nationalisms and war. That 'beautiful so on and so forth.'

*

Sommerlicher Nachtrag zu einer winterlichen Reise
29 May 1998, Višegrad, Republika Srpska
Was denkt in dir? Peter asks.
What? I ask, unable to hear him over the noise of Milka and her band.
What is thinking in you?
Sorrow, I answer.
For two months in 1992 there was intense fighting here. Marauding Muslims. Marauding Serbs. And now the town is devoid of Muslims. Since we crossed the border into the Republika Srpska, I have been imagining Muslims and Serbs lying in bed those 60 nights. Worrying, as they lay there, about possible futures. About a sudden end to possible futures.
Tonight we sit at a long linen-covered table in the dining room of a large resort hotel tucked back into the forested hills above the town. Guests of the Mayor of Višegrad.
Of the 20,000 inhabitants of Višegrad, he says, 2500 are refugees. Yes, there is high unemployment. The town's factories have shut down. There are, of course, no tourists. The hotel is a cavernous home to men convalescing from the war.
A young man limps into the dining room with two women, one his girlfriend perhaps, or sister, the other old enough to be his mother. They take a table. They talk. They drink a bottle of wine. They don't speak. The young man twirls his box of cigarettes between the table and his finger.

Milka, backed by an accordion, a keyboard, and drums (was there a drummer?), is a sultry lounge singer with a Serbian repertoire, traditional sad love songs sung in a middle-eastern quaver.

The town, the mayor explains, was 2/3 Muslim before the war. In 1992 the Muslims chased the Serbs out of the city. The Serbs retook the city through the grace of the Muslim Murad Šabanović, who captured the hydroelectric dam above the city and threatened to blow it up. The Muslim population fled the threat of flooding. The Yugoslav army arrived and dislodged the crazy terrorist. And the Serbs moved back in.

A small man with a dark beard pushes past a concerned waiter to crutch his way toward our table. He breaks into the conversation and with a sweaty palm shakes each of our hands. He pulls two photographs out of a coat pocket.

The waiter signals to Milka. She skips toward our table, cordless microphone in hand, armed with a vigorous Serbian song.

The small man holds out two worn photos. The first is a glossy celebrity shot of Radovan Karadžić. The second is a snapshot of a soldier. My brother, he says, killed in the war. My brother, killed in the war. My brother.

At pointblank range, Milka belts out "O Višegrad!" The convalescing soldier puts away his photos and retreats slowly on his crutches. Milka hits three quick high notes, kicks up a shapely heel, and dances away.

*

In *Sommerlicher Nachtrag zu einer winterlichen Reise*, the third of this series of essays about Yugoslavia's disintegration, or rather, in response to that tragic process, Handke revisits many of the people and places of his winter's *Journey to the Rivers*, retelling, refiguring, and revising his initial account, as he "began to reconsider [his] published sentences" (*SN* 20). He travels finally into the Republika Srpska, to Višegrad and Srebrenica, and ends his account with questions: "And this is supposed to be a contemporary story? Who will read it these days – a story without villains who are enemies of humanity, without a stereotypical enemy?" (*SN* 91). As examples, then, from a story without such enemies, a story rather of images that are the antithesis of such stereotypes, *Bilder* for an age that has lost, given up, sold, or propagandized its images (see, of course, Handke's recent novel *Der Bildverlust oder Durch die Sierra de Gredos*, 2002; The Loss of Images, or Across the Sierra de Gredos), consider a cluster of observations in *Sommerlicher Nachtrag* from one of the most notorious sites of the civil war.

In the silver-mining city of Srebrenica, that mountain-valley site of atrocity and revenge, Handke, traveling with Bocokić, Radaković and a librarian from Bajina Bašta, finds stark scenes he, as narrator, populates with wishful and then self-negating hallucinations. Earlier, in Višegrad, the narrator's fantasy had been of a woman wearing a scarf and a man in a fez who were welcomed into the crowd at a real soccer match, characters whose head-coverings are reminiscent of the passersby in Skopje (*SN* 59). Now, while describing a ruined mosque below a mostly intact orthodox church ("and far below it the remains of the mosque, part of a cupola, still recognizable even though, like all the other parts of the building, it had collapsed, the last fragment of form in the otherwise totally formless debris all around"), the narrator thinks it is time for the late-afternoon call to prayer and then hears, from the wreckage, along with the sound of the mountain stream that once flowed here, just such a call. That thought, of course, that fantasized sound, cannot stand in the face of present reality: "No, and twice no, neither the call nor the stream – had it once flowed here? – still existed.... Nothing but the ravine-filling cracking of plastic tarpaulins" (*SN* 68-69).

Later he will suggest a world map with Srebrenica as its center, but for now this narrator, so often accused of ignoring the realities of a vicious war, begins a new series of "ands," beautiful only by virtue of the fact that they continue a narrative that could end suddenly in despair: "And thrust my hand deep into the stinging nettles near the church, into the just blossoming and thus most sharply stinging ones, and then again" (*SN* 69). And then a real, if fleeting, image of hope, conjoined to the self-destructive anger by another "and": "And on one steep slope, up in the clear-cut, a couple of people hoeing in such narrow, often single-rowed beds, that even all together they didn't add up to anything close to a garden ..." (*SN* 69). Thinking back on Srebrenica three paragraphs before the story ends, the narrator takes a page from Patricia Nelson Limerick's *The Legacy of Conquest* where she notes that "[i]n thinking about American Indian history, it has become essential to follow the policy of cautious street crossers: Remember to look both ways" (18). What if, the narrator asks, we think of the Serbs and Muslims in Srebrenica as Indians and settlers, "but don't the evil

Indians in the westerns also appear up on the rocky cliffs, attacking
and massacring the peaceful American wagon trains – and aren't the
Indians fighting for their freedom? And 'very last question': Will
someone, sometime, soon, who?, also discover the Serbs of Bosnia
as such Indians?" (*SN* 91-92). The Serbs/Indians did indeed massacre peaceful settlers (residents and refugees) in Srebrenica, *and*
they also had been provoked. Can't we look both ways? Handke
asks once again: Can't our sentences be complicated by the conjunction "and"?

*

Unter Tränen fragend
30 May 1998, Višegrad
    *We drive to a construction site on a hill overlooking the Drina
and its Turkish bridge. Three stories high, typical orange-brick
construction. A hundred people, perhaps, work at the site. A line
of women and men unload a truck, passing orange tiles from
hand to hand in a long chain. On the high roof men are
interlocking the tiles in undulating rows. On the highest ridge
are nailed a small evergreen tree, a ragged red, blue, and white
Serbian flag, and an improvised rack from which hang three
bottles of brandy and three new plastic-wrapped shirts.*
    *These are refugees from Sarajevo, the Mayor says. They have
formed an organization and with a government grant of land,
tools, and materials are building 158 apartments here. He
introduces us to the president of the refugee group, a thin man,
maybe 70 years old, bright-eyed and erect, who speaks an eager
English as he shows us around.*
    *Mr. Handke, he says, you are a writer. And I too am a writer.
I write children's books. We are colleagues. You are big and I
am small. But we are colleagues.*
    *Peter introduces Žarko and me as his translators. The
president has eyes only for Peter.*
    *We meet the young architect. She and her husband, she says,
have moved into an abandoned Muslim house. Through third
parties they are trying to exchange their house in Sarajevo for
the one in Višegrad.*
    *TV cameras arrive and Peter joins the chain to pass a few roof
tiles for Serbian television. Then it's time for lunch. We share
cold cuts and tomatoes and plum brandy at a long table.*
    *This is the Austrian writer Peter Handke, the President
announces. He has come to visit our building. We will now hear
words of wisdom from this great man. Mr. Handke, would you
please honor us with words to remember on this proud
occasion?*

Peter stands and raises his cup of brandy. He looks at the President. He looks at the refugees along both sides of the table. He turns back to the President. He speaks words to remember: Jebi ga. Fuck it. The surprised refugees raise a boisterous cheer. Peter grins and raises his cup again.

*

The fourth of Handke's essays on the language of this war, *Unter Tränen fragend* (the first half published in the *Süddeutsche Zeitung* on 5/6 June 1999) continues the Quixotic attempt to present simple images in complex sentences from a country Handke believes has been deformed, misrepresented, and caricatured by the world press and by Western press agents.[14] Like the earlier books, *Unter Tränen fragend* attempts to present images – "(images still exist, then? the loss of images is not yet absolute?)" (*UT* 151) – from a Yugoslavia besieged "not only with cluster bombs and rockets but above all with 'context' and 'idea'" (*UT* 157-58). The first trip, while bombs are falling, is a quick one from Hungary to Belgrade and back, while the second one, also during the NATO bombardment, takes the author, Zlatko Bocokić, and Thomas Deichmann through Slovenia, Croatia, and Bosnia into Serbia, where they visit bombed factories and bridges and buildings, accompanied by a government spokesman.

The book's title is drawn from an incident near the end of the second trip. An oncologist from a nearby hospital, a woman who has often traveled in the United States, joins the three travelers at their table and asks, with tears in her eyes, why her country is being bombed: "Are we really that guilty?" (*UT* 154). In a book about what Handke calls "verbal and iconic pornography" (*UT* 155), about the loss of language – "'The first victim of war is truth'? No, it is language" (*UT* 23) – the oncologist's calling into question *and* weeping, critique *and* sorrow, are gestures indicating her ability to experience conflicting impulses. But the real question, given the history of the reception of Peter Handke's Yugoslavia work, given the author's public persona, remains the question of a difficult dialectic upheld against a relentless political and cultural entropy. How will the author of the controversial *Journey to the Rivers*, the

---

[14]Parts of this and the following section appeared previously as "Peter Handke and the Former Yugoslavia: The Rhetoric of War and Peace," *World Literature Today* 75.1 (Winter 2001) 78-81.

famous writer greeted by Serbian television cameras when he arrives at the bombed Kragujevac auto assembly plant, the honored guest hosted by Yugoslavia's minister of culture, preserve his beloved dialectic in what now-predictable critics will call a piece of propaganda?

To loosen up his argument, Handke's narrator employs the self-critical voice present, in one way or another, in each of his Yugoslavia texts. In *Unter Tränen fragend*, a voice posts warnings after especially passionate passages: "Warning: Antirational Mysticism!" (*UT* 30); "Warning: One-Sidedness!" (*UT* 39); "Warning: Anti-American!" (*UT* 44); "Warning: Paranoia!" (*UT* 48); "Warning: Bellicosity and Anti-Civilization Affect!" (*UT* 60). The text thus parodies its critics and gently questions its own images. Further, to avoid static images, the narrator presents double or triple, progressing or moving images. He describes sympathetically, for example, both the Croatian Catholic Bishop of Banja Luka, at risk now in a largely Serbian town, *and* a Serbian Partisan, aged and poor, whose World-War-II comrades suffered under Croatian Catholic oppression. The narration moves from image to image to image by employing the familiar "and" – an "and" that connects and continues and complicates, an "and" that appears in the title of Tolstoy's *War and Peace* owned by the old Partisan and also in the Holy Trinity the author evokes during a mass: "yes, it is true, the personage of God acts as 'Father,' as 'Son,' and as 'Spirit'" (*UT* 108). Hearing NATO bombers overhead one night while staying in the mountains, the narrator laments the loss of such conjunction: "In another time, this moment would have been a deeply peaceful 'And' of trinity: the rush of mountain streams, and the nightingales, and high above the nightly jetliners with passengers underway from Frankfurt, perhaps ..." (*UT* 125). Now, however, the machines of war break the peaceful pattern.

Once invoked, the "and" initiates a cascade of sentences as the narrative struggles to find images adequate to the damage done by the NATO bombers to the destroyed automobile assembly plant in Kragujevac: "And again, in Kragujevac.... And oddly.... And in the center.... And ... those '124 badly injured workers'" (*UT* 117-19). Carefully, self-reflexively, the narrator expresses concern about himself as a constructed image, as a political tool for the Serbs: "... unexpected flashbulbs, video cameras: suddenly we are, unsuspecting till that moment, a *delegacija*. But why not, *zašto da ne*? (one of the most common enduring Yugoslavian phrases, along with 'nema problema'): don't wince, even as a 'delegation' observe as accurately as possible, remember, witness!" (*UT* 116-17). Then, as he sees the damage to the factory, especially to its tools, the narrator returns to thoughts he had in the Slovenia essay about things and reality and being – things were more real, "the things ... were ready-to-hand" [*gingen einem zur Hand*] (*AT* 13):

> Strange too how the destruction of the *tools*, the workbenches, the hammers, the pliers, the vices, the measuring devices, the nails and screws (even the smallest items flattened and twisted) affected me more than that of the massive machines. It was as if, with these tools – wasn't "tool" once an indication of becoming human? – the violent powers from above had destroyed labor, that is, all collaboration and being (existing) for the entire region for a long time to come. (*UT* 117)

In similar terms, Heidegger writes in *Being and Time* about how the world reveals itself through a broken tool:

> The modes of conspicuousness, obtrusiveness, and obstinacy all have the function of bringing to the fore the characteristic of presence-at-hand in what is ready-to-hand.... But when an assignment has been disturbed – when something is unusable for some purpose – then the assignment becomes explicit. Even now, of course, it has not become explicit as an ontological structure; but it has become explicit ontically for the circumspection which comes up against the damaging of the tool. When an assignment to some particular "towards-this" has been thus circumspectively aroused, we catch sight of the "towards-this" itself, and along with it everything connected with the work – the whole 'workshop' – as that wherein concern always dwells. The context of equipment is lit up, not as something never seen before, but as a totality constantly sighted beforehand in circumspection. With this totality, however, the world announces itself. (Heidegger 104-05)

As Handke fights for phenomenological accuracy in his prose, he finds a kind of Heideggerian revelation of being (existing) in broken tools. That NATO bombs have caused the destruction would be beyond Heidegger's concern. The loss of collaboration and being is at the heart of Handke's.

NATO's bombs have destroyed the tools of humanity, and by implication, the verbal bombs Handke has cited from *Le Monde* and the *New York Review of Books* have flattened and twisted the language of peace, asserting with clenched fists rather than questioning while weeping. Once again, Handke ventures here into the narrative landscape of war and peace, acutely aware of his precarious position as possible propagandist, as producer of images that will tend to war or peace. *Unter Tränen fragend* is the kind of self-reflective assertion Adorno and Horkheimer, drawing on Hegel, called "determinate negativity" (24), and as such, it would seem, the sentences of the essay can be trusted.

*

Die Fahrt im Einbaum oder das Spiel zum Film vom Krieg
1:30 a.m., 1 June 1998
I'm sitting in my room in the Hotel Višegrad, looking out onto the Drina and the Turkish bridge, still lit by floodlamps. The bridge's eleven arches are reflected in the silky black river.

From the terrace below there is an occasional burst of laughter from Peter, Zlatko, Thomas, and Žarko, who are still talking with the two women from the Organization for Security and Cooperation in Europe, the younger one from Spain, the older from France. We argued for hours about the role of organizations like theirs in Yugoslavia.

How long have you been in Yugoslavia? Peter asked the French woman. For a year-and-a-half, she answered. Do you speak Serbo-Croatian? Peter asked. No, she answered. I've been too busy to learn. The first town I was in was under attack for nine months. I worked through an interpreter.

You are here to tell the people how to run their country and you don't understand their language! Peter exclaimed. You can't bother to learn their language?

Who are you? the woman asked. What are you doing here? What gives you the moral right to judge what I'm doing?

Go home, Peter said.

Fuck you, the woman said.

Go home.

Fuck you.

The night air had chilled, and the French woman was shivering. Peter took his coat from the back of his chair and draped it around her shoulders. There, he said, that will help.

Fuck you, she said, and pulled the coat around herself.

*

Die Fahrt im Einbaum features a casting call by two filmmakers, an American (essentially John Ford) and a Spaniard (Luis Buñuel, in effect), who want to make a film of the war in Yugoslavia approximately a decade after it has occurred. The directors discuss narrative strategy, listen to the war stories of a local historian, an ex-journalist, three Internationals, and others, and finally decide not to make the film. The final conversation between the filmmakers turns to the need for good translators: "During mutual insanity and hatred," the John Ford character argues, "one side often laughs deep within itself. But the laughter never breaks the surface. Let's have translators, for both sides – maybe exactly the same laughter exists inside the other." The Buñuel character agrees that "[s]uch a translator would be the antithesis of the Inquisition" (*FE* 122), and then comments on the kind of (hi)story being constructed by the international "community": "And this latter-day apocryphal horde, our patron, needs a single guilty person for this story and has itself taken the role of the hero" (*FE* 123).

History, the telling of history, flawed and sensationalist accounts of this Yugoslavian history – one of the characters unfurls Mark Danner's series of articles in the *New York Review*, dissected in the play as simplistic and bombastic (*FE* 84) – is the center around which Handke's violent and sweet and troubling fantasy of a play circles. June 9, 1999, the day of the play's premiere, was also the day NATO representatives announced that their seventy-eight-day bombing of Yugoslavia would cease. Claus Peymann directed the play, his last production at the Burgtheater after thirteen high-profile years. In early March, in protest of ecclesiastical and government support for NATO intervention in the war, Handke had renounced his membership in the Catholic Church and had returned the ten thousand Marks awarded him in 1973 for Germany's Büchner Prize. There had been rumors that Handke would withdraw his play in protest of the bombing and there were rumors that protestors would disturb the premiere. The play opened as scheduled, to a packed house, to a largely appreciative audience.

Although Peter Handke can be blunt, as he was in a nationally televised discussion after one of his readings of *A Journey to the Rivers* when he chose a rather vulgar expletive to label an obtuse critic, the virulence of the attacks on him for his writing about Yugoslavia is still puzzling. Not until the war in Yugoslavia and Handke's written pleas for a more complex, more self-ironic, more peaceful rhetoric did he become, in the European press, a "pro-Serbian advocate" (*JR* vii), a pariah like the pariah people. If one were to ask Handke if he is indeed a lover of Serbs, he would likely point out that the question is racist and then answer affirmatively. The question that ought to be raised, however, is whether Handke is a nationalist – the kind of nationalist who would vilify Croats, Slovenians, Bosnians, or Kosovars, who would stir up hatred, welcome war, and condone genocide. Here, the record is clear, for Handke has spent a lifetime attacking the kinds of ideological absolutisms that produce nationalism, hate, and war.

It is a relief, Handke writes in *Phantasien der Wiederholung* (1983; Phantasies of Repetition), to be released from such domination: "We, after the world wars: the wonderful knowledge that we are not masters ('You are the caretaker of a meager garden,' Virgil)" (*PhW* 26). Handke finds it morally liberating to be rid of words like "masters"; but beyond that he wants to construct new metaphors, fruitful ways of thinking – and thus, perhaps, the Virgil quotation that defines us as humble gardeners. Repeatedly Handke has attempted to unmask truth as what Nietzsche called a "mobile army of metaphors" (Nietzsche 46), for awareness of truth as arbitrary construction undermines the rulers whose truth claims are enforced by violence: "Thus the night of this century, during which I searched my face obsessively for the features of a despot or a conqueror, has ended for me" (*LWA* 115).

Die Fahrt im Einbaum works on the same levels as the previous works, attacking "truth" as assumed by various accounts (including film, newspapers, histories, and the play itself) and creating the kinds of self-conscious myths or fairy tales Handke feels we need to order our productively multivalent societies. The planned film will draw dialectically on John (Ford) O'Hara's penchant for legends, stories and little historical lies and on Luis (Buñuel) Machado's bull-tickling craziness. And once again, language is the cause and possible cure for what ails the former Yugoslavia:

GREEK. Is there such a thing? Rotten language for a good cause? The end of aesthetics? The end of a sense for truth and beauty. The end of a care for form.

THE THREE. (*Laughing*) Of a care for form?

GREEK. Of a care for form. Of a care for form. The world has never had a chance against you sonorous babblers. You throw your weight around because you recognize the authority of no court. You are the final judges and at the same time the criminals. That no one can depend on you – okay, that's your ideal, taken from one of your ancestors – but that nothing can be expected from you, nothing at all, absolutely nothing: Shame on you! We are saturated with hate, increasing hatred of the familiar and the unfamiliar. Because our hatred of the familiar has no outlet, it must turn against the unfamiliar. And more and more is made unfamiliar and unrecognizable by daily announcements and by a surfeit of information. And so hatred of the unfamiliar eats at our bowels.

FIRST INTERNATIONAL. (*As if understanding*) You won't change that. That's the way it is. That's the state of affairs. That's the world. That's the marketplace. That's the price.

SECOND and THIRD. (*Sing*) That's the price. We are the market place. We are the world. We are in power. We write the history.

FIRST. And history now requires guilt, evildoers, retribution, mercilessness.

GREEK. Says who?

FIRST. We do.

GREEK. And whose guilt is beyond mercy? (*FE* 86-87)

At the end of the play, after the appearance of a dugout that may be read as a mobile, dialectical site for a multifarious *Volk* – "The Balkans! Other countries have a castle or a temple as a holy site. Our sacred site is the dugout" (*FE* 115-16) – O'Hara and Machado decide not to make their film. O'Hara refuses on the grounds that a tragic film makes no sense. Machado says he won't make the film because his films have always been about society, and "[s]ociety no longer exists.... it's a single commercial and moral horde.... People have forgotten what it means to stand up for oneself while allowing the other a place to stand" (*FE* 123-24).

Not allowing the other a place to stand is the mark of a violent nationalism. In Handke's play, however, even the most despicable characters, the aggressive mountain-bike riding Internationals, those shrill and certain European-Americans who have come to judge and punish Yugoslavia, are given succor by the Greek they have attacked so viciously: "To the SECOND INTERNATIONAL: Are you cold? You're shivering! (*He puts his coat around her shoulders*)" (*FE* 99). As he has since his earliest texts, Handke here stands up for the Serbs while allowing Croats, Bosnian Muslims, Kosovar Albanians, and even the obnoxious Internationals a place to stand.

A final incident, extraneous to the play, will further illustrate Handke's unrelentingly dialectical thinking, the two-edged gesture none of his critics to date have been able or willing to reproduce.

When Günter Grass, with whom Handke has repeatedly crossed pens, spoke out publicly in favor of NATO intervention in Yugoslavia (the same intervention that led to Handke's leaving the Catholic Church and returning his literary prize), Serbs in Belgrade announced that that they would collect Grass's books and send them back to the German Nobel Prize winner. Handke urged them to forego this action, to keep reading Grass's self-critical, dialectical literary works while opposing his political statement. – The action of a nationalist?

*

Postscript

6 June 1999, Vienna

In the city center, I stumble onto a Sunday-evening demonstration against NATO and for Yugoslavia. "NATO – fascistik, NATO – fascistik!" the crowd of maybe 2000 chants.

Back in my room, unable to sleep, I turn back to my translation of Peter's new play. I wish Žarko were here to compare notes. How did he translate "Fertigsatzpisse"? Pissing your finished, your modular sentences? Sententious piss?

At 10:30 I watch a report on Peter done for Austrian TV (ÖRF2). Peter's crime, the reporter and his commentators agree, is that he is a "Serbenfreund," a friend of the Serbs. Not good to be a friend of the enemy. Peter should have known better, it's an old story: Jap lover, Kraut lover, Jew lover, Nigger lover, Serb lover.

I turn off the sententious piss and return to Peter's play.

9 June 1999, before midnight, Žarko's birthday, Vienna

I ought to go to bed, but I'm still reeling from the events of the day. Several hours ago NATO and the Yugoslav Parliament came to some kind of agreement ending the bombing after 78 days.

And, I'm just back from the world premiere of Peter's "The Play of the Film of the War," directed by Claus Peymann. I've seldom been this moved, this challenged, by a work of art.

The really bad guys of the play, three "Internationals" who know all the answers, who dictate all the terms, who can think only in absolutes, appear on the stage as follows: "Three mountainbike riders, preceded by the sound of squealing brakes, burst through the swinging door, covered with mud clear up to their helmets. They race through the hall, between tables and chairs, perilously close to the people sitting there." American and European moralists, functionaries with no hint of self-irony or humor, absolutists who run the world because of their economic power – these sorry excuses for human beings were depicted this evening as mountainbike riders.

"Žarko," I said, "Don't you ever tell Peter I ride a mountain-bike."

"No, my friend," he whispered, "I'd never do that."

The play drew on several incidents from our trip, including when Peter put his coat around the shoulders of the OSCE woman in Višegrad. After the play, flushed with enthusiasm and insight, I told Peter how well he had integrated a real event into an imaginative play. "Brilliant to put her and her friends on mountainbikes!"

"Doctor Scott," he chided, "Doctor Scott. Always on duty."

Works Cited

Abbott, Scott. "'The Material Idea of a *Volk*': Peter Handke's Dialectical Search for a National Identity." *Amsterdamer Beiträge zur neueren Germanistik* 38/39 (1995): 479-94.

Abbott, Scott, and Žarko Radaković. *Ponavljanje putovanja u predele romana* [Repetitions: Travels in a Novel(ist)'s Landscape]. Belgrade: Vreme Knjige, 1994.

Adorno, Theodor. "The Essay as Form." *Notes to Literature: Volume One.* Trans. Shierry Weber Nicholsen. New York: Columbia UP, 1991. 3-23.

Hafner, Fabjan. "Expeditionen ins Neunte Land: Slowenien und die Slowenen im Werk Peter Handkes." *Peter Handke: Die Langsamkeit der Welt.* Ed. Gerhard Fuchs and Gerhard Melzer. Graz: Droschl, 1993. 215-27.

Heidegger, Martin. *Being and Time.* Trans. John Macquarrie and Edward Robinson. New York: Harper and Row, 1962.

Horkheimer, Max, and Theodor W. Adorno. *Dialectic of Enlightenment.* Trans. John Cumming. New York: Continuum, 1994.

Kristeva, Julia. *Strangers to Ourselves.* New York: Columbia UP, 1994

Limerick, Patricia Nelson. *The Legacy of Conquest.* New York: W.W. Norton, 1988.

Müller, André. "Wer einmal versagt im Schreiben, hat für immer versagt." Interview with Peter Handke. *Die Zeit* 3 Mar. 1989: 77-79.

Nietzsche, Friedrich. "On Truth and Lie in an Extra-Moral Sense."
The Portable Nietzsche. Ed. Walter Kaufmann. New York:
Viking Press, 1954. 42-47.

Ritschl, Wolfgang. "'Nein, Serben und Kroaten hassen sich nicht!'
Interview über den Krieg in Jugoslawien, die Lächerlichkeit des
Poeten und seine Hilflosigkeit." Interview with Peter Handke.
Die Weltwoche (Zurich) 5 Nov. 1992: 55.

Scott, Charles. *The Question of Ethics: Nietzsche, Foucault, Heidegger.* Bloomington: Indiana UP, 1990.

Vollmer, Michael, *Das gerechte Spiel: Sprache und Individualität
bei Friedrich Nietzsche und Peter Handke.* Würzburg: Königshausen & Neumann, 1995.

Zülch, Tilman. *Die Angst des Dichters vor der Wirklichkeit: 16
Antworten auf Peter Handkes Winterreise nach Serbien.*
Göttingen: Steidl, 1996.

The Works of Peter Handke

Aber ich lebe nur von den Zwischenräumen. Ein Gespräch, geführt von Herbert Gamper. Zurich: Ammann, 1987.

Abschied des Träumers vom neunten Land. Eine Wirklichkeit, die vergangen ist: Erinnerungen an Slowenien. Frankfurt am Main: Suhrkamp, 1991.

Die Abwesenheit: Ein Märchen. Frankfurt am Main: Suhrkamp, 1987.

Die Abwesenheit: Eine Skizze, ein Film, ein Gespräch. Dürnau: Edition 350, 1996.

Als das Wünschen noch geholfen hat. Frankfurt am Main: Suhrkamp, 1974.

Am Felsfenster morgens (und andere Ortszeiten 1982-1987). Salzburg: Residenz, 1998.

Die Angst des Tormanns beim Elfmeter. Frankfurt am Main: Suhrkamp, 1970.

Begrüßung des Aufsichtsrats. Frankfurt am Main: Suhrkamp, 1967.

Der Bildverlust oder Durch die Sierra de Gredos. Frankfurt am Main: Suhrkamp, 2002.

Der Chinese des Schmerzes. Frankfurt am Main: Suhrkamp, 1983.

Chronik der laufenden Ereignisse. Frankfurt am Main: Suhrkamp, 1971.

Deutsche Gedichte. Frankfurt am Main: Euphorion, 1969.

Don Juan. Frankfurt am Main: Suhrkamp, 2004.

Eine winterliche Reise zu den Flüssen Donau, Save, Morawa und Drina oder Gerechtigkeit für Serbien. Frankfurt am Main: Suhrkamp, 1996.

Das Ende des Flanierens. Frankfurt am Main: Suhrkamp, 1980.

Die Fahrt im Einbaum oder Das Stück zum Film vom Krieg. Frankfurt am Main: Suhrkamp, 1999.

Falsche Bewegung. Frankfurt am Main: Suhrkamp, 1975.

Gedicht an die Dauer. Frankfurt am Main: Suhrkamp, 1986.

Die Geschichte des Bleistifts. Salzburg: Residenz, 1982.

Das Gewicht der Welt. Ein Journal (November 1975 – März 1977). Frankfurt am Main: Suhrkamp, 1977.

Der Hausierer. Frankfurt am Main: Suhrkamp, 1967.

Die Hornissen. Frankfurt am Main: Suhrkamp, 1966.

Ich bin ein Bewohner des Elfenbeinturms. Frankfurt am Main: Suhrkamp, 1972.

In einer dunklen Nacht ging ich aus meinem stillen Haus. Frankfurt am Main: Suhrkamp, 1997.

Die Innenwelt der Außenwelt der Innenwelt. Frankfurt am Main: Suhrkamp, 1969.

Kaspar. Frankfurt am Main: Suhrkamp, 1967.

Kindergeschichte. Frankfurt am Main: Suhrkamp, 1981.

Der kurze Brief zum langen Abschied. Frankfurt am Main: Suhrkamp, 1972.

Langsam im Schatten. Gesammelte Verzettelungen 1980-1992. Frankfurt am Main: Suhrkamp, 1992.

Langsame Heimkehr. Frankfurt am Main: Suhrkamp, 1979.

Die Lehre der Sainte-Victoire. Frankfurt am Main: Suhrkamp, 1980.

Lucie im Wald mit den Dingsda. Frankfurt am Main: Suhrkamp, 1999.

Mein Jahr in der Niemandsbucht: Ein Märchen aus den neuen Zeiten. Frankfurt am Main: Suhrkamp, 1994.

Mündliches und Schriftliches. Zu Büchern, Bildern und Filmen. Frankfurt am Main: Suhrkamp, 2002.

Nachmittag eines Schriftstellers. Frankfurt am Main: Suhrkamp, 1987.

Noch einmal für Thukydides. Salzburg: Residenz, 1995.

Phantasien der Wiederholung. Frankfurt am Main: Suhrkamp, 1983.

Prosa Gedichte Theaterstücke Hörspiel Aufsätze. Frankfurt am Main: Suhrkamp, 1969.

Publikumsbeschimpfung und andere Sprechstücke. Frankfurt am Main: Suhrkamp, 1966.

Der Ritt über den Bodensee. Frankfurt am Main: Suhrkamp, 1971.

Rund um das Große Tribunal. Frankfurt am Main: Suhrkamp, 2003.

Sommerlicher Nachtrag zu einer winterlichen Reise. Frankfurt am Main: Suhrkamp, 1996.

Das Spiel vom Fragen oder die Reise zum sonoren Land. Frankfurt am Main: Suhrkamp, 1989.

Stücke 1. Frankfurt am Main: Suhrkamp, 1972. (Contains *Publikumsbeschimpfung, Weissagung, Selbstbezichtigung, Hilferufe, Kaspar.*)

Stücke 2. Frankfurt am Main: Suhrkamp, 1973. (Contains *Das Mündel will Vormund sein, Quodlibet, Der Ritt über den Bodensee, Der Ritt über den Bodensee.*)

Die Stunde da wir nichts voneinander wußten. Ein Schauspiel. Frankfurt am Main: Suhrkamp, 1992.

Die Stunde der wahren Empfindung. Frankfurt am Main: Suhrkamp, 1975.

Die Theaterstücke. Frankfurt am Main: Suhrkamp, 1992. (Contains *Publikumsbeschimpfung, Weissagung, Selbstbezichtigung, Hilferufe, Kaspar, Das Mündel will Vormund sein, Quodlibet, Der Ritt über den Bodensee, Die Unvernünftigen sterben aus, Über die Dörfer, Das Spiel vom Fragen oder Die Reise zum sonoren Land, Die Stunde da wir nichts voneinander wußten.*)

Über Musik. Salzburg: Droschl, 2003.

Unter Tränen fragend: Nachträgliche Aufzeichnungen von zwei Jugoslawien-Durchquerungen im Krieg, März und April 1999. Frankfurt am Main: Suhrkamp, 2000.

Untertagblues. Ein Stationendrama. Frankfurt am Main: Suhrkamp, 2003.

Die Unvernünftigen sterben aus. Frankfurt am Main: Suhrkamp, 1973.

Versuch über den geglückten Tag. Frankfurt am Main: Suhrkamp, 1991.

Versuch über die Jukebox. Frankfurt am Main: Suhrkamp, 1990.

Versuch über die Müdigkeit. Frankfurt am Main: Suhrkamp, 1989.

Warum eine Küche? Salzburg: Edition Korrespondenzen, 2003.

Die Wiederholung. Frankfurt am Main: Suhrkamp, 1986.

Wind und Meer. Vier Hörspiele. Frankfurt am Main: Suhrkamp, 1970.

Wunschloses Unglück. Frankfurt am Main: Suhrkamp, 1972.

Zurüstungen für die Unsterblichkeit. Ein Königsdrama. Frankfurt am Main, Suhrkamp, 1997.

Handke as Coauthor:

Handke, Peter, and Klaus Amann. *Wut und Geheimnis. Peter Handkes Poetik der Begriffsstutzigkeit: zwei Reden zur Verleihung des Ehrendoktorates der Universität Klagenfurt am 8. November 2002 an Peter Handke.* Klagenfurt: Wieser, 2002.

Handke, Peter, and Adolf Haslinger. *Einige Anmerkungen zum Da- und Dort-Sein.* Salzburg: Jung und Jung, 2004.

Handke, Peter, and Didi Petrikat. *Wiener Läden.* Munich: Hanser, 1974.

Handke, Peter, and Lisl Ponger. *Ein Wortland. Eine Reise durch Kärnten, Slowenien, Friaul, Istrien und Dalmatien.* Klagenfurt: Wieser, 1998.

Handke, Peter, and Heinz Schafroth. *Die Tage gingen wirklich ins Land: Ein Lesebuch.* Ditzingen: Reclam, 1995.

Handke, Peter, and Wim Wenders. *Der Himmel über Berlin. Ein Filmbuch.* Frankfurt am Main: Suhrkamp, 1987.

Handke's Works in English Translation

A Journey to the Rivers: Justice for Serbia. Trans. Scott Abbott. New York: Viking, 1997.

A Moment of True Feeling. Trans. Ralph Manheim. New York: Farrar, Straus and Giroux, 1977.

A Sorrow Beyond Dreams. Trans. Ralph Mannheim. New York: Farrar, Straus and Giroux, 1975.

Absence. Trans. Ralph Manheim. New York: Farrar, Straus and Giroux, 1990.

Across. Trans. Ralph Manheim. New York: Farrar, Straus and Giroux, 1986.

The Afternoon of a Writer. Trans. Ralph Manheim. New York: Farrar, Straus and Giroux, 1989.

Child Story. Trans. Ralph Manheim. *Slow Homecoming.* New York: Farrar, Straus and Giroux, 1985. 213-79.

The Goalie's Anxiety at the Penalty Kick. Trans. Michael Roloff. New York: Farrar, Straus and Giroux, 1972.

The Innerworld of the Outerworld of the Innerworld. Trans. Michael Roloff. New York: Seasbury Press, 1974

The Jukebox and Other Essays on Storytelling. Trans. Ralph Manheim and Krishna Winston. New York: Farrar, Straus and Giroux, 1994.

Kaspar and Other Plays. Trans. Michael Roloff. New York: Farrar, Straus and Giroux, 1969. (Contains *Offending the Audience, Self-Accusation, Kaspar.*)

The Left-Handed Woman. Trans. Ralph Manheim. New York: Farrar, Straus and Giroux, 1978.

The Lesson of Mont Sainte-Victoire. Trans. Ralph Manheim. *Slow Homecoming.* New York: Farrar, Straus and Giroux, 1985. 139-211.

The Long Way Around. Trans. Ralph Manheim. *Slow Homecoming.* New York: Farrar, Straus, and Giroux, 1985. 3-137.

My Year in the No-Man's-Bay. Trans. Krishna Winston. New York: Farrar, Straus and Giroux, 1998.

Nonsense and Happiness. Trans. Michael Roloff. New York: Urizen Books, 1976.

On a Dark Night I Left My Silent House. Trans. Krishna Winston. New York: Farrar, Straus and Giroux, 2000.

Once Again for Thucydides. Trans. Tess Lewis. New York: New Directions, 1998.

Plays 1. Offending the Audience, Self-Accusation, Kaspar, My Foot My Tutor, The Ride Across Lake Constance, They Are Dying Out. Trans. Michael Roloff (in collaboration with Karl Weber). London: Methuen, 1997.

Repetition. Trans. Ralph Manheim. New York: Farrar, Straus and Giroux, 1988.

The Ride Across Lake Constance. Trans. Michael Roloff. London: Methuen, 1973.

The Ride Across Lake Constance and Other Plays. Trans. Michael Roloff (in collaboration with Karl Weber). New York: Farrar, Straus and Giroux, 1976. (Contains *Prophecy, Calling for Help, My Foot My Tutor, Quodlibet, The Ride Across Lake Constance, They Are Dying Out.*)

Short Letter, Long Farewell. Trans. Ralph Mannheim. New York: Farrar, Straus and Giroux, 1974.

Slow Homecoming. Trans. Ralph Manheim. New York: Farrar, Straus and Giroux, 1985. (Contains *The Long Way Around, The Lesson of Mont Sainte-Victoire, Child Story.*)

They Are Dying Out. Trans. Michael Roloff (in collaboration with Karl Weber). London: Methuen, 1975.

Three by Peter Handke. Trans. Michael Roloff and Ralph Manheim. New York: Avon Books, 1977. (Contains *The Goalie's Anxiety at the Penalty Kick, Short Letter, Long Farewell,* and *A Sorrow Beyond Dreams.*)

Two Novels by Peter Handke. Trans. Ralph Manheim. New York: Avon Books, 1979. (Contains *A Moment of True Feeling* and *The Left-Handed Woman*.)

Voyage to the Sonorous Land, or The Art of Asking and the Hour We Knew Nothing of Each Other. Trans. Gitta Honneger. New Haven: Yale UP, 1996.

Walk About the Villages. Trans. Michael Roloff. Riverside, CA: Ariadne Press, 1996.

The Weight of the World. Trans. Ralph Manheim. New York: Farrar, Straus and Giroux, 1984.

Handke's Films

Die Abwesenheit. Gemini Films, Road Movies, Marea Films, 1992.
Chronik der laufenden Ereignisse. WDR, 1971.
Die linkshändige Frau. Road Movies, 1977.
Das Mal des Todes. ORF, 1985.

Notes on Contributors

SCOTT ABBOTT is Professor of Philosophy and Humanities at Utah Valley State College and the author of *Fictions of Freemasonry: Freemasonry and the German Novel* (1991). He translated Peter Handke's *A Journey to the Rivers or Justice for Serbia* (1997); and with Žarko Radaković, Handke's Serbo-Croatian translator, he published a travel narrative called *Repetitions* (1994).

THOMAS F. BARRY received his doctorate from the University of Virginia. He is currently Associate Professor of English and Comparative Literature at Himeji Dokkyo University in Japan, a school which had its origins as a private German club during the Meiji period of Japanese history. He has published on Handke, Schiller, and Walker Percy, among others.

David N. Coury is Associate Professor of German and Humanistic Studies at the University of Wisconsin-Green Bay. He is the author of *The Return of Storytelling in Contemporary German Literature and Film – Peter Handke and Wim Wenders* (2004), and has published articles on Paul Celan, Heinrich Böll, Wim Wenders and on various topics regarding German cinema. His research interests include contemporary German-language literature and film, as well as the role of the writer-intellectual in public discourse.

JOHN E. DAVIDSON is Associate Professor and Director of Graduate Studies in German at Ohio State University, where he teaches film, literature, and cultural theory. He has published articles on the representation of the radical Right, Nazi cinema, ecological issues in film, and German post-wall cinema. He is the author of *Deterritorializing the New German Cinema* (1999) and co-editor of *German Cinema of the 1950s*, which is forthcoming.

ANDREA GOGRÖF-VOORHEES is Associate Professor in the Department of Liberal Studies at Western Washington University. She is the author of *Defining Modernism: Baudelaire and Nietzsche on*

Romanticism, Decadence, Modernity, and Richard Wagner. Her research interests are 19th and 20th century French and German literature and philosophy, with special emphasis on the development of Romanticism and its continuous and varying manifestations in contemporary literature and culture.

ROBERT HALSALL is a Lecturer in the Department of Communication and Languages at Robert Gordon University in Aberdeen, Scotland. He has published several articles on Austrian authors, including Peter Handke, Gerhard Roth and Christoph Ransmayr. He is the author of *The Problem of Autonomy in the Works of Hermann Broch* (2000).

FRANK PILIPP is Professor of German at the Georgia Institute of Technology. He is the author of *The Novels of Martin Walser: A Critical Introduction* (1991) and *Ingeborg Bachmanns DAS DREISSIGSTE JAHR: Kritischer Kommentar und Deutung* (2001). He has edited essay collections on Martin Walser (1994) and *The Legacy of Kafka in Contemporary Austrian Literature* (1997), and has published numerous articles on contemporary German and Austrian writers, as well as on film.

MARIA LUISA ROLI studied German and Romance Languages at the University and is Associate Professor of modern German literature at the State University of Milan. Her publications include articles on German South-Tirolean literature, the literature of the *Biedermeier*, turn-of-the-century and postwar prose. She has edited an Italian version of Stifter's *Schriften zur Literatur und Kunst* (2004) and is currently at work on a monograph on the same author.

MIREILLE TABAH received her doctorate from the Free University of Brussels where she teaches German language and literature. Her research focuses on contemporary Austrian literature, gender studies and women's literature. She is the author of *Vermittlung und Unmittelbarkeit. Die Eigenart von Peter Handkes fiktionalem Frühwerk* (1990) and articles on Ilse Aichinger, Ingeborg Bachmann, Jurek Becker, Thomas Bernhard, Max Frisch, Handke, Peter Weiss, and Christa Wolf among others.

KARL WAGNER is Professor of German Literature at the University of Zurich. He is the author of *Herr und Knecht: Robert Walsers Roman 'Der Gehülfe'* (1980) and the editor of *Autobiographien in der österreichischen Literatur: Von Franz Grillparzer bis Thomas Bernhard* (1998) and of a reader on *Moderne Erzähltheorie* (2002). He has also published a number of articles on Austrian and English authors, among others on George Eliot, Adalbert Stifter, Peter Rosegger, Erich Fried, and Handke.

FRITZ WEFELMEYER is Reader in German and Comparative Literature at the University of Sunderland in Great Britain. His main research interests are in Romantic and twentieth-century literature, film and theatre. He has published on a number of authors and directors, including Goethe, Fontane, Fassbinder, Handke, Wenders, Strauss, and also on cultural theory and the plastic arts. He is the editor of a forthcoming volume on Martin Walser.

CHRISTIANE WELLER received her doctorate from Monash University in Melbourne, Australia, where she is Lecturer in German Studies. Her research interests include colonial literature, *fin-de-siècle* writing and psychoanalytic theory. She is the co-editor of *Die Lektüre der Welt. Zur Theorie, Geschichte und Soziologie kultureller Praxis. Festschrift für Walter Veit* (2004).

Index